Gary O'Toole has studied ;
specialising in Jyotiṣa (Vedic astroiogy). rus uist uvun,
Cosmic Bodies, explored the relationship between
Āyurveda and Jyotiṣa. He writes a blog and produces a
magazine, podcast, and online learning at
patreon.com/timelineastrology.

His astrology readings impart an empowered view of the
timeline of your life. For more information, or to book a
reading or event, contact Gary:
info@timelineastrology.com

DAŚĀ VIDYĀ

Timelines of Indian Astrology

GARY O'TOOLE

For Pearl,
For lighting my lamp

Oṃ Gaṃ Gaṇapataye Namaḥ

CONTENTS

LIST OF TABLES

LIST OF CHARTS

LIST OF DAŚĀS

ACKNOWLEDGEMENTS

First, I must thank my astrology teacher Pearl Finn. I have fond memories of spending hours disappearing down many a rabbit hole with her over the years. Other teachers and mentors to thank are Freedom Cole, Visti Larsen, Sanjay Rath, Barry Rosen, and Komilla Sutton.

The calculations used for this book are taken from *Bṛhat Parāśara Horāśāstra*, a compendium on Indian astrology by Sage Parāśara. Vaidyanatha Dikshita's *Jātaka Pārijāta* was used as a supplementary text. There are numerous other Indian and Western astrology books that have informed my writing in one way or another over the years, too many to list here, as there are astrologers whom I've had the good fortune of interacting with. Thank you all for your enthusiasm and support.

Thank you to all my clients and patrons for inspiring me to write every day. Many of these interactions have inspired many of the words in this book. Patrons' comments on early drafts and ideas helped me gauge how some of the material was landing.

Thank you to Rikki Blythe, Douglas Gould, Jacob Singh, and Kartik Srinivasan, for feedback on the first draft.

A special thank you to Samir Mahmood for his wonderful cover painting and illustrations, and for the emotional support throughout the writing process. Thank you to my family for their support and encouragement over the years. I feel very fortunate to have been able to dedicate my life to this study.

Lastly, I would like to thank the Heinrich Böll Association for the use of their cottage on Achill Island, where I wrote the bulk of the manuscript in June 2021. There was something special about its writing room that allowed me to channel the *Jyotir Vidyā*, this 'science of light'.

INTRODUCTION

There are a multitude of astrological indications that could explain who you are. This is wide open for interpretation. Yet you cannot deny what is happening in your life. The astrology of who you are is not as relevant, or as precise, as the astrology of what is unfolding.

Cycles of time have always fascinated me. When I first had my Vedic birth chart calculated, it was the planetary cycles, or *daśās*, that grabbed my attention. I realised my life had a timeline and how dynamic it was. I no longer felt stuck. Whatever you are experiencing right now, however stuck you may feel, take a moment to realise you are on a planet that is spinning at about 1,000 miles per hour at the equator. Nothing is as static or stuck as you imagine it to be.

And it's all happening perfectly. It may not always feel wonderful but it's all meant to be in the grand scheme of things. Everything. Every moment of your life is in alignment with the stars. From the time of your birth, right up to the moment of you reading this. Even if you cannot quite get on board with this idea, you couldn't argue with the planets' positions, could you? So, why argue with the way things are right now? To think that something in your life should be another way would be like trying to move planets around in space. And yet, by coming to this realisation, it gives you more freedom to be who you are. Astrology is a tool to accept yourself and how your life is unfolding. It helps you align with the person you were always meant to be.

Everything you experience can be viewed as a pattern. Astrology gives language and stories to these patterns. And all patterns change with time. We can see your daśās, explored in PART 1, in every thought, mood, feeling, action, and reaction mapped out at the time of your birth. The Sanskrit word *daśā* means 'circumstance'. Daśās and transits reflect the circumstances of your life, an ever-expanding learning curve as viewed in the Golden Ratio, a pattern that can be seen in daśās, too. This, and other patterns, are explored in PART 2.

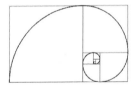

We live in a spiral galaxy, after all. Your life is an expanding pattern, perfectly timed with astrology, mapped out in the configuration of planets at the time of your birth. You expand exactly as you should, in your own unique way. There are times you may feel you are growing and other times when you seem to take a downward curve, returning you to familiar themes you may wish to avoid. This may feel restrictive, but when viewed from afar, it is growth all the same. This awareness is available to you through the gift of daśās, an intricate part of a Vedic tradition that originated on the Indian subcontinent.

The configuration of planets at the time of your birth may show the potential, but it is your daśās that show how your birth chart comes to life. And while you experience daśās in your own unique way, there are themes we can all relate to. How else do novelists, movie makers, and storytellers tap into something profoundly personal while producing something for mass audiences? We all share a common thread. This book is about that thread.

The primary daśā I have focused on is based on the position of the Moon when you were born. The Moon represents your emotional and instinctual reactions. This has a stronger charge. The Moon reflects your likes and dislikes. How you feel about what is happening is more important than what is actually happening.

The lunar mansions are explored in the PART 2, including each sign's myths and symbols, an integral part of your personal story. While you may not always be able to change the way you feel with words alone, you can always change the way you tell your story.

PART 3 looks at timelines we all experience based on solar and lunar phases, while also dividing daśās into different portions. This part also explores planets' transits, as general trends and triggers for events in your life.

While there is much to glean from daśās and transits, there are always caveats to consider. You must make these stories relevant to you. You can be respectful to a Vedic tradition without reinforcing a pattern that is not relevant or true for you now. I trust you can place my interpretations in the context of your own life experience. All daśās are potentials that lay dormant until you are ready to experience them. When you live long enough, you see these patterns repeat within various circumstances. By viewing them over time, you can begin to change your perspective and preconceived ideas, engaging with your astrology in more creative ways. With a cosmic view, you can change how you see your life. And this may be all that's needed to change its trajectory.

YOUR HOROSCOPE & DAŚĀS

You will get more out of this book if you have your sidereal horoscope and daśās calculated for you. You may seek an online resource to provide the information. If this is what you choose, please make sure you use more than one resource to source and verify the correct data. If there are any discrepancies, you can source your correct data from a reputable astrologer. Search the term 'Vimshottari Dasha' online and source your timeline using your exact time, date, and place of birth. The more exact your time of birth, the more exact your daśās.

You can download the *Timeline Astrology App*, which will calculate your daśās. I have listed other options under RESOURCES at the end of this book.

TROPICAL & SIDEREAL CALCULATIONS

I refer to sidereal calculations throughout the book, which you can adjust from your tropical placements. The current difference between tropical and sidereal calculations is between 22 and 24 degrees according to most astrologers. I use 24 degrees, placing the star Spica at 0 degrees of sidereal Libra to calculate the beginning of sidereal Aries. The difference may have been 23 degrees when you were born.

The vernal equinox around March 20th is when the Sun is seen to pass through the first degree of tropical Aries. The 24-degree difference means the Sun is at 6 degrees of sidereal Pisces on that date. This is because of the 30-degree Sun sign divisions. The view of the zodiac is actually moving because of a tilt of the Earth on its axis. When the Earth returns to the same position each year, there is a difference in the fixed stars (sidereal) beyond the zodiac. This is referred to as the 'Precession of the Equinoxes'. Both tropical and sidereal calculations were at the same position in 285 A.D. but have been moving apart at a rate of about 1 degree every 72 years.

If your tropical rising sign is Aries, or you have planets in tropical Aries, they most likely move back to sidereal Pisces, unless the rising degree or planet had reached the very end of tropical Aries. You can simply subtract 24 degrees from your tropical placements to calculate your sidereal chart.

Everything has a place and a purpose, you told us.
A viper must be true to his creed.
The fang needs sharpening, the lethal venom a victim,
Come my beloved, lie with me today and always.
No telling if poison and ambrosia are the same,
Unless you savour them both.

From *Cuckold* by Kiran Nagarkar

PART 1: DAŚĀS

There are 9 planetary daśās based on the 9 traditional 'planets' of Indian astrology. These 9 are called *grahas*, a Sanskrit word to mean 'grip', 'grab', and 'grasp'. This reflects each planet's ability to influence your life, to impel you to act based on the configurations in your birth chart. The 9 grahas include the two luminaries: the Sun and Moon, the five visible planets: Mercury, Venus, Mars, Jupiter, and Saturn, and the lunar nodes: Rāhu and Ketu. The lunar nodes are the two points which mark the crossing of the paths of the Earth around the Sun and the Moon's journey north and south of the ecliptic. The northern or ascending node is called Rāhu, while the southern node or descending node is called Ketu.

Each of the 9 'graspers' have their own nature and impulse, and each lines up in a particular order in the planetary daśās to express an order for the human potential for growth. They also have a unique expression for you, depending on their position at the time of your birth. During their daśās, they express their desire through you, whether you are conscious of this desire or not.

Unlike the natural stages of life as we all age, you experience different planetary daśās at different times. These are the 9 characters in the story of your life. Each holds certain imprints for your lifetime, as seen in story of your birth chart. This shows the seeds you have sown and what you must reap at different times. The daśās show the timing of events when viewed alongside the transits of these planets.

Planetary daśās bring to life your desire for an experience. Your desires are the planets' desires, which look for expression through each daśā. We can observe this in the planets' aspects, an astrological phenomenon of *dṛṣṭi* or 'sight'. More on this later. Planetary daśās show what you are ready to experience on some level. Yet we must take these in context, observing each planet's position in your birth chart, along with their transits. Also, the signs show whether something is available in your environment, as seen in sign-based daśās and transits to the signs.

You experience planetary daśās in your own unique way, while we all experience transits at the same time. A transit may merely hint at something, a desire for an experience without any particular event. If it's not in your birth chart to begin with, a daśā or transit will not make it happen, even if a daśā brings a wish for that thing.

The three parts to examine to see if any event is to happen in your life are: the patterns in your birth chart, your daśās (planetary and sign-based), and the transits. I explore some of the patterns in the birth chart in Part 2 and transits in Part 3. Daśās are the primary timing tool and building blocks of prediction in Indian astrological analysis.

VIMŚOTTARĪ DAŚĀ

The most commonly used daśā in use today is called *vimśottarī*, which means '120'. We calculate a *mahādaśā* or 'major daśā' from the Moon's position in your birth chart, dividing an ideal life span of 120 years between each of the 9 grahas:

Ketu (7 years)
Venus (20 years)
Sun (6 years)
Moon (10 years)
Mars (7 years)
Rāhu (18 years)
Jupiter (16 years)
Saturn (19 years)
Mercury (17 years)

The Moon's position in one of the 27 lunar mansions dictates where in the daśā sequence you began at birth. Though the 9 planets express themselves uniquely for you based on your birth chart, they line up in the planetary daśās in the same sequence for everyone. Each daśā lasts the same length of time for everyone, although we each begin at a different point based on the position of the Moon at birth.

The Moon represents your individuated sense of self. This colours your perceptions of the world. The Moon is always changing shape, reflecting your ever-changing mind and emotions. Your feelings give you your minute-by-minute experience. This shows how you feel your life is going; navigating you towards what feels good and away from what feels bad. Thus, planetary daśās, based on the Moon's position, are of the utmost importance when analysing your birth chart.

Major daśās are divided into sub-daśās, or *Bhuktis*. *Bhuki* is a Sanskrit word, which means 'to enjoy, 'to eat'. Planetary daśās show the conditions of your life circumstances, the ripening of your karmas; when these are ready to be consumed and digested. The sub-daśās show if you are enjoying the fruits of your major daśās, in periods as long as three years, or for just a few months. We calculate your first major and sub-daśās, and thus, each subsequent daśā, based on how far into the lunar mansion the Moon had transited. This is an important consideration. How you began your life – the daśās that were active at the time – says a lot about your life experience. This is much like how the chart you were born with shows what it is you experience, although the planets have moved on since then.

In the beginning, you may not see these patterns, although you may know other people's. Eventually, you can equate your needs and wishes, your triumphs and downfalls, with an order that fits into the ebbs and flow of a life experience. You can then join the dots and find a correlation with others' lives and bigger life lessons.

The order of the planetary daśās shows a common thread we all experience throughout our lives. Venus follows Ketu, followed by the Sun, and so on. After a period of Ketu, often a confusing time, there comes a time for more comfort in a Venus daśā. Once you have tasted all those pleasures in a Venus daśā there comes a time when you seek something more. A connection to something higher within you, and in a higher position in the world around you, is reflected in the following Sun daśā. Once you know yourself, you are now ready to connect with others, as seen in a period of the Moon. Once you address the needs of others in a Moon daśā, there comes a time for your own needs to be met. This occurs more so in a Mars daśā. After having experienced a more a need to strengthen your will in a Mars daśā, there is a need to push things further in a Rāhu daśā, a period that can push your boundaries beyond what you thought possible. After an often chaotic expression of pushing things too far with Rāhu, Jupiter brings order and clarity. This leads to more growth and opportunity. Yet you cannot expand forever, and thus, Saturn arrives to slow you down and reign you back in. Once you have felt restriction for any length of time, even if it were beneficial to focus your attention, there comes a time when you're likely to feel more engaged in a Mercury period. You can integrate all you have learned from the big lessons of Saturn and apply them in a practical way with Mercury. By the end of Mercury daśā, Ketu brings you back to the beginning, to start over from scratch once more. After a period of working things out practically in a Mercury daśā, Ketu reminds you there is something beyond. On and on it goes, year after year, day after day, minute by minute. Places and faces may change, but you have a sense of these same life patterns repeating. Although the sequence and themes of each are the same, you experience each depending on the position of these planets in your birth chart.

There are many things to consider how you experience each daśā, which we will explore later. This includes whether the planet is seen as malevolent or benevolent, what is termed 'cruel' or 'kind'. According to Parāśara, the *krūra* or 'cruel' planets are Saturn, Mars, Rāhu, Ketu, Sun, and 'dark Moon' (waning phase or New Moon), and the *saumya* or 'kind' planets are Jupiter, Venus, Mercury, and 'bright Moon' (waxing phase or Full Moon).

PLANETS' STRENGTHS

To first consider the impact of any daśā, it helps to know if a planet is 'strong' or 'weak' in your birth chart. Planets are either moving towards, or away from, their place of exaltation or debilitation, much like the waxing and waning cycles of the Moon. Table 1.1 shows these degrees and strengths as a percentage.

Table 1.1

Planet	Exaltation 100%	Debilitation 0%	Root Strength 75%	Own Sign 50%
Sun	Aries 10°	Libra 10°	Leo 0-20°	Leo
Moon	Taurus 3°	Scorpio 3°	Taurus 3-30°	Cancer
Mars	Capricorn 28°	Cancer 28°	Aries 0-12°	Aries, Scorpio
Mercury	Virgo 15°	Pisces 15°	Virgo 15-20°	Gemini, Virgo
Jupiter	Cancer 5°	Capricorn 5°	Sagittarius 0-10°	Sagittarius, Pisces
Venus	Pisces 27°	Virgo 27°	Libra 0-15°	Taurus, Libra
Saturn	Libra 20°	Aries 20°	Aquarius 0-20°	Capricorn, Aquarius

A planet's 'root strength' refers to an effective range where it functions well. You may notice that all planets have this range within a sign they rule (see Table 1.2 for sign rulers), apart from the Moon, though some Indian astrology consider the Moon as co-ruler of Taurus alongside Venus because of its strength in the sign. Each of the 5 visible planets rule two signs, while the Sun and Moon rule one.

Table 1.2

Sign	Ruler(s)
Aries	Mars
Taurus	Venus
Gemini	Mercury
Cancer	Moon
Leo	Sun
Virgo	Mercury
Libra	Venus
Scorpio	Mars & Ketu
Sagittarius	Jupiter
Capricorn	Saturn
Aquarius	Saturn & Rāhu
Pisces	Jupiter

Planets function well in their own signs. It's as if they were at home. This is often a better situation than even exaltation. Exalted planets often experience diminished results due to other indications. They may also reflect a lot of idealism. The bar may be so high that life doesn't always rise to their expectations. Likewise, debilitated planets are more often than not mitigated due to other factors. Most often, a debilitated planet is assisted by other planets. Venus can help the Sun out of debilitation as it rules the sign it is debilitated in (Libra). Saturn, which exalts in Libra, can also help, as can Mars, which rules where the Sun exalts in Aries. If any of these planets are at an angle from your rising sign or Moon, or if they 'look at' or aspect the Sun, this mitigates the weakness of the Sun.

If you are feeling under-confident (Sun debilitated), one thing that helps is relating to others (Libra). Other things, such as fashion (Venus) help. Dressing well can do wonders for one's self-esteem. Another way is to work hard towards a goal. You may experience a hard-won confidence over time (Saturn). Mars can help by being more proactive and productive. When you take something on and win, you naturally feel more confident.

Mars can lessen the Moon's debilitation in Scorpio, as it rules the sign. Venus also helps, as it rules the opposite sign, Taurus, where the Moon is exalted. Facing down your demons and ridding yourself of any perceived weaknesses is one way of helping your mind cope with challenges, as can surrounding yourself with good company and nourishment with healthy foods. These are the themes of Taurus and Venus.

The Moon can mitigate Mars' debilitation in Cancer, as it rules the sign. Saturn, which rules Capricorn, where Mars is exalted, can also help, as can Jupiter, which is exalted in Cancer. Taking care of yourself is one way to mitigate any feelings of lack; either lack of vigour or a lack of willpower. The Moon can help calm the frustrations of Mars in Cancer by taking some much-needed time for self-care, addressing how you are feeling. Saturn can help Mars out by focusing your energy. Saturn offers Mars containment, a focus for disciplined action. Jupiter can help by connecting to something more meaningful, beyond your personal drives and motivations. Realising you are part of a bigger picture, you may find support from your family and community.

Venus and Jupiter can help to mitigate Mercury's debilitation. Venus, which is exalted in Mercury's sign of debilitation, Pisces, can help by allowing things to be as they are without having to work it all out. Jupiter can help by seeing the connection to one and everything, knowing deep down what is right without having to over-analyse.

Saturn can mitigate Jupiter's debilitation in Capricorn, as it rules the sign. Mars, which exalts in Capricorn, can help, as can the Moon, which rules the opposite sign: Cancer, where Jupiter is exalted. Saturn can help by developing a firm commitment to what is right, even if there are doubts. Doubts may indeed be as necessary in building a strong faith (Jupiter). Mars can help by being more courageous and action-orientated. You may build faith through more positive and focused actions. The Moon can help by feeling connected to your family and community, which may assuage any sense of doubt.

The Sun can mitigate Saturn's debilitation in Aries, as the Sun is exalted in the sign. Mars can also help, as it rules Aries. Venus can help, too, as it rules the opposite sign, Libra, where Saturn is exalted. The Sun can help by building confidence in your abilities. This may be about getting clear about where your weaknesses lie; where you need to draw some healthy boundaries. Mars can help in this endeavour also, as you take more positive actions and learn from your mistakes. Venus can help Saturn by relating to others who can teach you much of your own shortcomings. You realise your challenges are everyone's challenges.

Rāhu's and Ketu's strengths are a debated topic, as is always the case with the lunar nodes. Many astrologers disagree about their exaltation and debilitation. Some consider Rāhu exalted in Taurus and Ketu in Scorpio, while others consider Gemini and Sagittarius. There are sound arguments for each. Some astrologer consider Ketu as co-ruler of Scorpio alongside Mars, with Rāhu as co-ruler of Aquarius alongside Saturn. Wherever they are placed, they often express their strengths and weaknesses in more extremes. If these 'shadow planets' are strong, they have more strength to create more shadows. When weak, they are likely to create even more confusion about the issues. We must not consider the lunar nodes' weakness or strength in isolation. The planet ruling the sign they are in has a big role to play, as does any planet conjoined or aspecting/influencing.

KETU DAŚĀ – 7 YEARS

Keywords: spirituality, and spirits, mindfulness, or mindlessness, irrationality, impulsivity, unusual experiences, foreigners, foreign cultures, outsiders, outcasts, fringe groups, renunciation, and liberation.

Your experience of Ketu, the southern eclipse point, depends on the planet that rules the sign it is in. Ketu can show you being more spiritually orientated or feeling challenged through some sense of loss. You may wish to challenge the status quo and society. Either way, Ketu can show an impulsiveness and reactivity, feeling ungrounded and lost in the world in some way. Yet Ketu represents the centre around which everything is expanding and contracting, the witness to that which is moving around a central still point. It can be a profound experience or very confusing. It all depends on your birth chart.

Ketu points you back to your beginnings from a spiritual perspective, the spirit from which you came, your cosmic roots. But it's also like a black hole, pulling you back for annihilation and reassimilation. It is the void, but also the awareness; the experiencer, not the experience itself.

There are differing opinions among astrologers as to the strength of Ketu in the signs. Many Indian astrologers consider Ketu to be exalted in Scorpio, which it is also said to rule, and is debilitated in Taurus. It may be more suited to the 12th house of liberation. It's least conducive to the 2nd and 4th houses. These represent the needs of family, resources, and stability. Ketu's nature is to remove material comforts in favour of a spiritual focus. It is especially challenging in the 4th house of home and contentment. It may show someone feeling ungrounded without a stable home environment or emotional security.

Like a black hole, Ketu daśā can be a perplexing time. As an eclipse, it both obscures and enlightens. It obscures that which is not your true nature, and, in doing so, highlights something beyond any form you have identified with thus far.

Eclipses obscure our view of the Sun or Moon; hence Ketu's tendency to confuse. It is the sense of shock and awe when there is loss. It's the sense of bewilderment when you lose someone close or a role you once played. But it also shows you we are all connected to one another through the shared experience of loss. It is a reminder you are spirit in a 'bodysuit', a body you must drop one day, as you re-emerge into the wholeness of who you truly are.

You are likely to experience some sense of confusion as to your role during Ketu daśā. Its impulse is to destroy all that is not you is necessary from a spiritual point of view. Many experiences in Ketu daśā may be challenging in some form or other. Ketu is the awareness that you are 'no-thing' and nobody, and yet paradoxically, you realise you are everything and everybody. It removes the blocks to this essential awareness.

The void at the centre of your being is a sense of the 'You' that is and always will be. It does not have a name, a title, or any adjectives that do it any justice. Everyone's experience of this void is very different. It can be a liberating experience for some and a scary place for others. It all depends on the details of Ketu in your chart, the planets that it associates with.

You can always engage with Ketu in more positive ways, whatever it is doing in your chart. You can acquaint yourself with your spiritual nature. There may be shocks, some loss, someone or something to grieve. But you can soon see the rhyme and reason, as the realisation of your true nature emerges.

It helps not to identify with wanting some material success when entering a daśā of Ketu. If you do, the losses that are inevitable are harder to bear. Once you relinquish desire for anything, even spiritual awakening, you actually get it all. When you want for nothing, you get everything!

If you only think of 'being somebody', as opposed to simply being, you are likely to run into problems. The opposite node of the Moon, Rāhu, represents the need to achieve something worldly. Rāhu's impulse is to identify with something smaller than the vastness of You. Ketu connects you to everything, not the separate you. You are everything and 'no-thing'. In fact, the more of 'a nobody' you can be during a Ketu daśā, the better off you will be.

Once you have tasted the void, the essential nature of your formless being, you have tapped into something that will never leave you. Everything begins to take on an extra dimension. Your experiences actually become fuller, richer. The craving for something, to be someone, fades, leaving you with a profound sense of stillness and completeness.

VENUS DAŚĀ – 20 YEARS

Keywords: marriage, partners, sexuality, sensuality, pleasures, enjoyments, diplomacy, tact, decorum and good manners, compromise, attractiveness, receptivity, fashion, arts, culture, and refinement.

After a period of uncertainty during the previous Ketu daśā, Venus is like a soft landing after being in free fall. Venus daśā cushions the fall, bringing some kind of comfort and pleasurable experiences. How you go about getting them, depends on Venus' position in your birth chart. Venus represents desire and sensual pleasure, bringing about the need for some sensual fulfilment. And while there are many desires during a Venus daśā, there is also the possibility of compromise. Actually, you may have to compromise to get what you want!

Venus rules the sign Taurus, the most sensual sign of the zodiac. Taurus represents the face, where most of our senses are, while it also rules Libra, the sign of relationships. Thus, there is a lot of sensual desire to negotiate in Venus daśā. We all want the basics of food, shelter, comfort, and support, represented by Taurus.

Once we meet these basic needs, we can focus on others (Libra).

A strong Venus may show you enjoying the finer things in life. It may show you appreciating life's simple pleasures. You may enjoy good relations. A weak Venus may show a lack of appreciation, either for others or from others. A weak Venus may represent feeling less attractive or loved, and thus, you may overcompensate through sexuality and pleasure-seeking.

Venus exalts at 27° Pisces and is debilitated at 27° Virgo. Its root strength is between 0° and 15° of Libra. It rules both Taurus and Libra. It is strongest in the 4th house and least conducive to the 6th house, which has to do with work, not pleasure.

There is always something to enjoy in Venus daśā. If not, you may wish for it, but find it lacks something. Venus in Virgo, for example, may show someone focused on getting the setting just so. In doing so, they may not be happy with any imperfections. Life is messy and imperfect, as are relationships. This may be an issue for someone with Venus placed in such an exacting sign.

If you can look beyond the superficial to see that pattern of perfection beneath, you are more likely to be happy with your lot in Venus daśā. It represents the underlying patterns in nature that seem more beautiful to the eyes of someone in Venus daśā. Venus daśā is a time to find happiness, to look for things to enjoy, including relationships.

After Ketu's period of forced changes in perception, Venus daśā is usually a richer experience. It usually brings at least some pleasures to appreciate.

SUN DAŚĀ – 6 YEARS

Keywords: soul, self, ego, power, father, authority, fame, governments, profession, resources, rhythm, heart, music, dance, health, vitality, luminosity, knowledge, and nonduality.

After the pleasurable experiences of Venus, Sun daśā is about connecting to your 'higher self', your essential being. This may mean you consider your needs more than others. Yet the more connected you are to your higher self, the more you feel connected to everyone. The Sun represents the non-dual state, 'The One'.

The Sun represents your father, or anyone who is in charge of you. When strong, you feel guided, not only by those around you, but by a strong sense of self within. A strong Sun is reflected in a confident, creative, self-assured individual, with a healthy sense of self-esteem. It reflects someone with a generous spirit and natural leadership capabilities. A weak Sun may show someone who lacks confidence but who may overcompensate by being proud, egotistical, and self-centred.

If the Sun were weak in your horoscope, you may find you have to work at developing a healthy sense of self-esteem. Relationships with those in charge of you may bring challenges. Your relationship with your father, or those in charge of you, may prove difficult in your Sun daśā.

The Sun exalts at 10° Aries and is debilitated at 10° Libra. It has its root strength between 0° and 20° Leo, a sign it rules, and is strong throughout the sign. The Sun is strongest in the most prominent 10th house, the highest position of the chart. The 12th house of loss is the least suited to the Sun, as it can show a loss of confidence and self-esteem, or someone not being seen. You may not wish to be seen with the Sun in the 12th house, of course.

With a strong Sun, there is a natural sense of confidence that rises to the surface, whatever the circumstances. You may face challenges as life throws its curve balls, but you can pick yourself up and dust yourself off. You return to a sense of strength when these transitory challenges pass. The challenge is that you may not be humble when life demands it. When things don't always work out the way you want, you may feel you have further to fall. Remaining humble, even while being confident, is the best of both worlds.

With a weak Sun, you may find it more challenging to pick yourself up and may need a little more support in doing so. Playing the victim may help you gain a sense of self. You may not rise to the great heights a strong Sun individual can reach. You may knock yourself down before reaching any height, blaming others for your apparent lack. Although you can be humble, there is a fine line between humility and low self-esteem. Anyone with a weak Sun is familiar with walking that line.

No matter how strong or weak the Sun may be in your birth chart, you can find a connection to your higher self. This connection is a greater source of power than your individual self can muster, anyway. The Sun shines on all and sundry. It does not pick and choose. We must all find our spark in our own unique way. Some find it with ease, some through struggle.

This sense of a higher self leads to confidence, no matter what you may achieve in a worldly sense. A weak Sun can show someone finds a life of service and humility is an easier route than more obvious expressions of confidence. The Sun is weak in Libra, which is all about serving others' needs, but also about finding yourself in the other. The Sun exalts in Aries, which is all about the self.

A guaranteed route to a healthy sense of self is a spiritual practice. This negates any sense of being less than, or greater than, others, while honouring something greater within. We are a spark of 'The One'. When you come to that realisation, you can be both confident and humble at the same time.

MOON DAŚĀ – 10 YEARS

Keywords: mind, emotions, feelings, instincts, mother, home, well-being, likes and dislikes, attachments, fickleness, changeability, reactivity, and duality.

Once you have accessed a sense of self in Sun daśā, you yearn to connect with others and nurture your heart and relationships in Moon daśā. The Moon builds on connections you made to yourself in the previous Sun daśā. Once you truly know yourself, you can connect with others more.

This may come as a need to look after yourself and family, or community, or even the whole of humanity, depending on the Moon's expression in your horoscope. The Moon's impulse is about finding harmony, like the Sun, tuning you into higher perspectives, beyond selfish needs and desires. The Moon's position in your birth chart shows many more needs as well.

The Moon represents your likes and dislikes, as well as safety and attachment issues. The Moon daśā has the potential to be more balanced in that respect. When you can meet your own, and others' needs, you feel more supported. By having a community or family to count on in times of need, you feel more secure. First, you must learn to look after yourself, and then you can look after others.

The Moon is the archetypal mother, as well as your actual mother or caregiver. It shows how and where you seek comfort and reassurance. A weak Moon can be a challenge to your mental and emotional well-being, yet still causes you to focus on these in Moon daśā.

A strong Moon may show a stable and content individual, a sense of calm and well-being. It may show someone with a caring nature and natural nurturing instincts. A weak Moon may show someone who lacks a sense of mental stability, and who overcompensates through behaviours that give them some semblance of peace.

The Moon exalts at 3° Taurus and is debilitated at 3° Scorpio. It has root strength between 3° and 20° Taurus, a sign it also rules. It is thus strong throughout the sign. The Moon is strongest in the more private 4th house and least conducive to the 8th house of uncertainty and change. This may show a lack of peace when dwelling on the uncertainties of life.

When there are no planets on either side of the Moon, this may mean feeling isolated. This does not support the impulse of the Moon; that of connection. When the Moon is aspected by Saturn, or you were born during an eclipse, this can show challenges to feeling supported and cared for. Likewise, when the Moon is in Scorpio, its sign of debilitation, there can be a challenge to one's peace of mind, and yet a powerful urge to find it all the same.

During Moon daśā, the need for comfort becomes prominent. Yet the Moon is fickle, like your mind and emotions; what comforts you is an ever-changing phenomenon. One day you feel like this, another, you feel like that. Moon daśā represents a need to observe the forever changing nature of your mind and emotions. The Moon rejects any sense of discomfort. If you deem things unsuitable, you may make a lot of changes. Yet it may be a challenge to stay with a plan, as your feelings change constantly.

It's helpful to go with the flow of these feelings and emotions, to allow anything that needs expression to come up for assimilation. You can observe the ebb and flow daily, as the Moon changes signs, or as a general theme based on its position in your horoscope.

MARS DAŚĀ – 7 YEARS

Keywords: strength (mental and physical), courage, bravery, will power, energy, vitality, youthfulness, impulsiveness, aggressiveness, competitiveness, motivation, challenge, forcefulness, mental acuity, brothers, action, and adventure.

Mars daśā is all about developing a strong will and courage to face your weaknesses. It is usually the most rewarding daśā for finding strength to face life's challenges, but it may also challenge you to step outside your comfort zone. Mars is about defending yourself and your personal needs.

It represents your willingness to do what it takes to destroy anything that stands in your way of getting what you want. At its worst, it can create needless destruction. When weak, there may be a lack of drive and direction, a certain timidity, an inability to state what you want.

In Mars' daśā, you will fight some battle or other, whether this is external or internal. Of course, it's always both. You will grow stronger throughout this period, although it may initially be more of a challenge than you think you can handle. Sometimes, a weak individual may become stronger through a sense of lack they are overcompensating for. If you were born with a weak limb, chances are you would work hard at improving the function of that limb. You may do this to where it becomes stronger than it would have been otherwise. This applies to weak-willed individuals. These people may become so focused on improving their lives, rallying everything they have to improve the situation. Any sense of strength is coming from a sense of lack.

Mars represents the needs of the ego. The ego needs a role. All too often, that can be a tyrant or a martyr, both of which are extreme expressions of Mars. Those with a weak Mars may play the martyr, but they may also play the tyrant if they overcome a sense of weakness to the point of tyranny. Mars represents certain individuals in your life, so a challenged Mars may show up in that person as a challenging relationship. This relationship is an opportunity for you to find strength, even if they appear to be obstructing your will.

A strong Mars may show a powerful individual, with a need to assert his or her will to attain desired results. It may show someone who can achieve a great deal, being able to process experiences quickly. It may show someone with a strong nerve and ability to take on a great deal. A weak Mars may show someone who lacks all the above, a timid person who may overcompensate and lash out, or who may lack any drive or motivation.

Mars exalts at 28° Capricorn and is debilitated at 28° Cancer. It is especially strong in Aries and Scorpio, especially between 0° and 13° Aries. Mars is strongest in the 10th house of career and ambition. It is least conducive to the 4th and 7th houses. The 7th house is especially challenging as it can show a lack of marital harmony when someone perceives others as a threat or competition.

There are usually some mitigating factors which determine how well you overcome the weakness of Mars. The position of other planets can take planets out of weakness.

Whether Mars is weak or strong, it can create problems in some sphere of life. This is the case for all the planets in the horoscope, of course, but the cruel planets, Mars and Saturn, can create more problems. These planets challenge you to improve yourself. Mars' challenge may mean doing something that doesn't always feel comfortable.

RĀHU DAŚĀ – 18 YEARS

Keywords: inventiveness, ingenuity, unusual experiences, ambitions, chaos, disorder, impulsivity, irrationality, compulsiveness, originality, insightfulness, foreigners and foreign cultures, outsiders, and imposters.

Rāhu can be a tumultuous daśā. It can either be an exciting time or completely chaotic, depending. Actually, it's usually both. One thing you can do is to get organised beforehand, so you can manage it better throughout. If you can do that while enjoying the new avenues opening up ahead, you can remain more balanced.

After Mars instilled a sense of strength, often after being challenged in some way, there comes a time when you wish to shake things up, to challenge your boundaries further. Rāhu is your shadow, however, and you may not be conscious of this need. Your shadow holds your primal fears and subconscious desires. Often, its impulses are hidden from you. You may question why something is happening at all. You may say, "I would never do that", when referring to someone else's seemingly inappropriate actions. As Jeanette 'Kishori' McKenzie has relayed to me of her epic poem, *The Song of Rāhu*,[1] Rāhu is a "call to the

---

[1] *The Song of Rāhu* is an epic poem by Jeanette 'Kishori' McKenzie, available for pre-order (2022) from kishori.net.

radical withdrawal of projection." Rāhu daśā is a time to realise that the other person reflects your own unintegrated parts.

Rāhu's strength depends on the strength of the planet in which sign it is in. A strong Rāhu may show someone who is inventive, insightful, and progressive in their thinking. A weak Rāhu may show someone compulsive and irrational, deluded, and reckless.

There are differing opinions as to the positions of strength by sign or house by astrologers. Many Indian astrologers consider Rāhu to be exalted in Taurus and debilitated in Scorpio. Rāhu may be strong in the 3rd, 6th, 10th, and 11th houses, as these areas of life require ambition. It is said to be least conducive to the 9th house of tradition, as Rāhu wishes to change the status quo.

Your sense of self can get exaggerated beyond recognition in Rāhu daśā. That self is the same self that was developed in the Sun daśā, which was then nurtured in a Moon daśā and fortified in Mars daśā. That self can get distorted in Rāhu daśā. Rāhu is a shadow (the northern eclipse point) that is cast over the Sun or Moon, obscuring your true nature and higher self, expressed in an exaggerated sense of self. It highlights the ego. You may seek recognition at any cost. Many times, the cost is very high, but you may not be conscious of it front the start. What you wish to be recognised for depends on its position in your birth chart. Even if placed in a challenging position, promoting something you would not consciously choose, you may find it rearing its head all the same. This is your shadow making itself known in some form.

Rāhu daśā brings to life the need to be seen as a unique individual. It shows an insatiable appetite for experience. It may even show a need for spiritual enlightenment, if highlighting such. Either way, the desire itself can squeeze the life out of the very thing you want, the grasping for something actually limiting that very thing. Your obsessions can lead to a sense of lack. It's a period you may wish to 'be somebody', which is the biggest problem from a spiritual perspective. Rāhu is opposite the most spiritualising force: Ketu (the south eclipse point). To be somebody, an individual, means being disconnected from everybody else. Thus, this can be a very isolating period, despite your successes.

Ketu can balance Rāhu, so you can find more stillness, at your core, beyond anything you may achieve in a worldly sense. You can express this by being more body conscious, sensing what is happening in the moment. Rāhu never dwells in the moment, preferring instead to take you into the future and your desire to have something you think you need.

While Rāhu may bring you your greatest successes, you may tell of your lack of satisfaction. Rāhu is not about what you get, but about the need you have. It's a bottomless pit of ambition. No matter how much you get, it is only a temporary relief from wanting. You are likely to replace whatever you achieve with a bigger ambition. Rāhu daśā is a negotiation between all you can get, while realising that no matter what you get, it cannot please you deep down.

Rāhu daśā is a period when you may be so out of touch with the reality of who you are that life itself may feel like a beast to be tamed. Rāhu is depicted in myth as a head of a serpent, a gapping mouth hungry for more and more. But it also represents the calling forth of *kuṇḍalinī śakti*, the energy coiled at the base of your spine, lying asleep, yearning to be awake. When released, you may need to manage its energy. Even if you do not have a 'kuṇḍalinī awakening', Rāhu represents all kinds of manipulations, for good or ill.

You can always play more consciously with these manipulations, so they do not have as tight a hold on you. But you may not wish to control it completely, as that may wreak havoc in its own way. You need to at least organise the energy through some sort of discipline, otherwise you will probably experience Rāhu as chaotic.

Rāhu's expression, as with Ketu, cannot function without a body to express itself through. It needs a host. You are the host during Rāhu daśā. Best to keep your new guest happy and acknowledged so it doesn't run amok.

If you know you are entering Rāhu daśā, you can make the most of it. You can achieve all you can, while acknowledging desire itself as unquenchable. That way, you don't beat yourself up for not achieving all you think you should. By reminding yourself how far you have come, as opposed to how far you wish to go, you can mitigate much of the dissatisfaction. Rāhu keeps taking you into a future where you have all your wishes fulfilled. It leaves you wanting. Yet it opens something else within you, beyond all your ambitions.

JUPITER DAŚĀ – 16 YEARS

Keywords: teachers, guides, mentors, advisors, counsellors, priests, lawyers, clarity, order, wealth, abundance, prosperity, purpose, meaning, good luck, blessings, expansion, children, husband or partner, studies, travel, hope, optimism, faith, religion, and philosophy.

After attempting to satiate your desires in a Rāhu period, the problems of not getting your fill teaches you it's never going to be enough. This is when the wisdom of Jupiter wakes up in you, when sanity prevails. I have often heard from clients expressing their relief upon entering Jupiter daśā, where they can finally be still. Although the transition is not always that simple, there is usually a sense of their life settling down. In doing so, there comes the most important thing Jupiter offers; growth.

Jupiter is a blessing, and there are usually many things to be grateful for. These are not necessarily the things you think you want, as expressed by Rāhu, but they are certainly the things you need to grow. Rāhu may have taken you in all kinds of unusual directions, places which may seem against the natural order of things. In Jupiter's daśā, you can see the benefits of having done so for a time. You realise that the seemingly unnatural direction was perfectly natural in the greater scheme of things. You become more philosophical, more hopeful.

Jupiter and Rāhu are each other's opposite. Rāhu is chaotic and uncertain; Jupiter is coherent and clear. Jupiter represents tradition, teachings, and natural laws - the natural order of things. When you follow a well-worn path during Jupiter daśā, there is clarity about how to get where you want to go. Raising a family is one example of the expansion that is possible in Jupiter daśā, as is studying. Any studies would need to be of a higher nature to suit the Jupiter impulse, either higher education, such as a PhD, or spiritual studies. Travelling (another Jupiter signification) expands your awareness, broadening your mind. Jupiter can also broaden the waistline if it influences the 1st house in your horoscope, so something to be mindful of!

Usually, there are many things to be grateful for in Jupiter daśā. Jupiter is the largest planet, bringing growth to the areas of life it influences, even if there is not an obvious outer expansion. There is usually a sense of depth and meaning in your life. This is especially welcome after a period of confusion in Rāhu daśā.

A strong Jupiter may show someone who has a strong faith, hope, and optimism. It can show someone who feels blessed in life. There may be a sense of profound meaning and purposefulness. Yet a weak Jupiter may show someone who lacks faith. It may show someone who doubts everyone and everything, someone who is unclear about what they are doing in life.

Jupiter exalts at 5° Cancer and is debilitated at 5° Capricorn. It is strong in Sagittarius and Pisces, two signs it rules, especially between 0° and 8° degrees of Sagittarius, its root strength. It is strong and protective in the 1st house, while it is least conducive to the 3rd and 7th houses, which are more about enjoyment than meaning and purpose. The 3rd house is especially challenging for Jupiter, as it may show a loss of meaning in favour of frivolous fun.

When Jupiter is debilitated in Capricorn, it may show lack, but there is always a way to expand in a systematic way, even if it's not so clear from the outset. There is always some way to find something auspicious with Jupiter. Its purpose is to expand your consciousness positively, although sometime it may challenge you to see the purpose.

Jupiter represents righteousness. It upholds natural laws and ways of living. Although challenged when weak, Jupiter will bring some sense of order always. Jupiter is the glue that binds everything, holding communities, families and partners together. Usually, this shows relationship bonds because of having children. Jupiter and children represent your hope for the future and future generations.

Jupiter represents your inner guidance and knowing, your intuition. This is something you develop in its daśā. You may meet a guide to help you in this endeavour, or you may find your own way. Some may need more guides to help, while others have a strong sense of knowing that they need only look within.

SATURN DAŚĀ – 19 YEARS

Keywords: maturation, (physical, mental and emotional), disease, longevity and death, hard work, service, focus, commitment, consistency, detachment, isolation, doubts, fears, anxiety, responsibility, objectivity, realism, practicality, actualisation, and surrender.

It's all too easy to default to a negative narrative with Saturn. Delays, obstruction, and limitations are what it can bring. But how you react is another matter. Old age and death are Saturn significations. He is the 'Lord of Time'. But death only happens once, so clearly Saturn daśā is more about endings than anything else. This can bring up fear, of course; fear of losing something or someone. Fear of death may be the ultimate fear, but Saturn's fears may point to a deeper awareness of what is coming your way. We all know we are going to die, so that should not come as a surprise. We all know what lies ahead on some level.

There may be fear of some outcome that eventually comes to pass. Some may say, "Well, you made it happen." I prefer to think that we know of its existence from the 'start'. From subtle experiences that filter down to the mind, it leads to its manifestation. This is our awareness of the imprint we came in with and the debt we must repay to Saturn. We may experience this as a feeling of anxiety and would prefer to avoid thinking about it until there is no choice left. Usually, at that point, the problem has become a bigger one than would have been if we were to deal with it sooner. But here's the thing: Saturn has something it wants to express, as a part of us that is more detached. It is our soul that decides what to experience when reincarnating, although the mind and body may be unwilling or unable to deal with it. It may be more helpful to think of fear as the soul's desire and the mind's resistance. Pain, another Saturn signification, is a sensation accompanied by the need to withdraw, a common impulse in Saturn daśā. Detachment is a possible expression; rather, a necessity, within Saturn daśā.

A strong Saturn can show a stoic individual who achieves a great deal with a great deal of hard work. It can show someone who is more able to bear pain, whether physical or emotional. A weak Saturn may show someone who may find it hard to work consistently towards a goal, and thus laments failings. Yet it may also show someone who overcompensates and does not know when to quit.

Saturn exalts at 20° Libra and is debilitated at 20° Aries. It is strong in Capricorn and Aquarius, two signs it rules, especially between 0° and 20° Aquarius, its root strength. Personal responsibility and service to others are easier to attain in the 7th house, while it is least conducive to the 1st house, which may show a lack of vitality and confidence. This may also lead to someone working hard on themselves, a signification of the 1st house, especially if placed in a powerful position by sign, but it can often show someone beating themselves up.

In Saturn daśā, you must consider your age, of course. Saturn shows the passing of time. If you are younger, you may have more energy to cope with the challenges, although you may lack the responsible approach Saturn requires. If you are older, you may find it easier to accept the limitations. But you may not have the energy to deal with any challenges. Losses throughout your life may have taken their toll, mentally, emotionally, and physically. Anyone may struggle with accepting the course of events, clinging to how things have been up to that point.

Whether weak or strong in your birth chart, Saturn produces some challenging effects. You must deal with these. You must acknowledge some loss or delay. If you can let go, you can move on feeling lighter and freer once the daśā has passed. Those with a strong Saturn may have a more stoic nature. They may have more of an ability to do some mental and emotional accounting during its daśā. Those with a more challenged Saturn may struggle with accepting the losses, or, at the very least, the delays.

Having a strong or weak Saturn is not an escape from responsibility. The difference being that a strong Saturn may help with being more responsible. A strong Saturn helps you to react appropriately. Saturn teaches you to stay present. Yet it may also take you out of the moment, too, bringing worry about your future, feeling depressed about what you lost in the past. This teaches you a valuable lesson in restraint. Saturn daśā is a time to reign in your wandering mind through some sort of focus. Whether you are meditating or working on a task, Saturn is about bringing you into the moment.

When Saturn is weak, there may be a general sense of antagonism, a questioning of everything. There can be a certain mistrust that needs mitigation. The illumination of the Sun, the rhythm of life, can build confidence in what you are doing, while Mars' courage can help you face any struggle. Venus helps by realising that we are in this together and that you can help others out who are in need and help yourself.

Charity work is one of the easiest and quickest ways to mitigate the challenges of Saturn. By helping others, you taking the focus off yourself and placing it on others who need your help at this time.

MERCURY DAŚĀ – 17 YEARS

Keywords: Intellect, analysis, rationality, discrimination, communication, language, speech, learning, teaching, facts, debate, conversation, interaction, mental acuity, adaptability, nervousness, excitement, stimulation, playfulness, wit, humour, fun, and games.

After a period of hard work and limitation during Saturn daśā, Mercury daśā helps with integrating the experiences. Mercury assists with practical matters. You can only work so hard, remove so much, before you learn to work smarter. In Mercury daśā, you learn that you can have more fun, too. There comes a time when you wish to try something new. Mercury daśā brings a sense that you can rebuild after being emptied of all you thought you knew. After the humbling, maybe even humiliating experiences of Saturn daśā, Mercury daśā is a return to a child-like innocence. You are likely to feel more open to learning something new.

Mercury builds your life from the foundation up. Practical concerns are paramount. This can bring with it many choices and distractions, too. The placement and strength of Mercury will show how well you can manage the new options. When strong, Mercury gives you the ability to discriminate between what you should do and what is a needless distraction. If Mercury were weak, you may experience confusion, especially if there are too many choices. But at least there are more possibilities than Saturn presented. A strong Mercury may show someone who can discriminate fact from fiction. It may show someone who is mentally adaptive and capable of expressing their thoughts and opinions concisely and clearly. A weak Mercury may show someone who lacks proper discrimination. It may show someone who thinks more creatively but may become overwhelmed, unable to think rationally.

Mercury exalts at 15° Virgo and is debilitated at 15° Pisces. It rules Gemini and Virgo, and is especially strong between 0° and 15° Virgo, its root strength. It is stronger in the 1st house, and weaker in the 7th. The 4th and 7th houses prove especially challenging for Mercury, as peace of mind (4th) and relationships (7th) don't benefit from Mercury's wandering nature.

In Mercury daśā, you experience the fastest moving planet (apart from the Moon), after a daśā of the slowest, i.e., Saturn. This is like going from 1st gear in your car to 5th. It's the change of pace that needs to be managed now. You may experience a more frenetic energy.

Mercury is the 'messenger of the gods', as it travels between the Sun and Earth. This movement back and forth relays the soul's messages. This highlights the planet's ability to convey deep spiritual truths in very practical terms. But it could convey too many choices that confound. Add a pretty regular Mercury retrograde phase, and you have the potential for being stimulated much of the time.

Life can get overly bogged down in practicalities during Mercury daśā, where you may forget about your spiritual nature. If you overdo it mentally, you never settle. Mercury can lead to nervousness if you pile choice upon choice into an already exhausted mind, unable to cope with the added stimuli.

Most will welcome the added stimuli in Mercury daśā, of course. After a slower period when Saturn had diminished choices, it's nice to have more. As long as there is an awareness of having too much on your mind, you can channel the energy into practical pursuits.

The following daśā of Ketu returns you to your spiritual roots and the beginning of the planetary daśās, asking you to start again from scratch.

SUB-DAŚĀS

Each of the 9 major daśās has within them 9 sub-daśās, which have within them 9, and so on – right down to the minute. Each sub-period is the same proportional length of time. Sub-daśās influence many levels of your being. Some astrologers use up to three levels, while some only use two: the major daśā and sub-daśā or bhukti. This is usually enough to find out what is happening for an individual over the course of a few years. We examine the relationship between major and sub-periods to see the impact. The combination of any two planets' daśās represents a fructification of certain indications. This is based on each planet's nature and rulership, as well as their relationship with each other.

The major daśā has a tremendous influence because of its predominance over a decade or two. The longest is that of Venus, which lasts 20 years, the shortest that of the Sun, only 6 years. The major daśā is like a constant background hum, whether you are attuned to the frequency or not. This shows the theme of your life over many years. Sometimes, you are in tune with the major daśā, especially when you first begin the major daśā. That is because the first sub- daśā within a major daśā is of the same planet. If you begin a major daśā of Jupiter, which last 16 years, Jupiter will be active on all 6 levels for a short time. It will be active on the first two levels for 3 years, i.e., Jupiter-Jupiter. The shorter sub-daśās are a way of fine-tuning birth times. The 6 levels bring the longer daśās of decades into years, months, weeks, days, hours, and even minutes.

The 1st level influences you circumstantially, which reflects a developmental need for your soul, which may or may not be consciously wanted. The 2nd level influences you for up to 3 years and 4 months at most (Venus-Venus daśā). This level has a stronger impact on how you feel. This sub-daśā shows how you are feeling about longer daśās and your life circumstances. How you feel about your life is more important than what is happening, so the second level of the daśās is perhaps the most important consideration. The 3rd level shows your reaction to all the above, and how you apply your intelligence in response to these influences. This shows the decisions you make based on how you feel about your life circumstances.

The 4th, 5th, and 6th levels bring things down to the wire, and actual experiences, minute-by-minute, day-by-day. These need an exact time of birth, as well as ongoing and careful consideration. Most astrologers use only 3 levels within the context of an astrological consultation.

To calculate the length of each sub-daśā, we multiply the length of the major daśā by the number of years of the major daśā of the sub-daśā planet. The first 2 digits of this 3-digit number (if only 2 digits place a 0 before it) represents the length of time in months. The last digit represents the length in days. We calculate this by taking the last digit and multiplying it by 3 to show the number of days. We can thus divide the major planetary daśās into sub-daśās, taking each month as a 30-day period.

Ketu Sub-Daśās – 7 Years in Total

1) Ketu-Ketu (4 months, 27 days)
2) Ketu-Venus (1 year, 2 months)
3) Ketu-Sun (4 months, 6 days)
4) Ketu-Moon (7 months)
5) Ketu-Mars (4 months, 27 days)
6) Ketu-Rāhu (1 year, 18 days)
7) Ketu-Jupiter (11 months, 6 days)
8) Ketu-Saturn (1 year, 1 month, 9 days)
9) Ketu-Mercury (11 months, 27 days)

Venus Sub-Daśās – 20 Years in Total

1) Venus-Venus (3 years, 4 months)
2) Venus-Sun (1 year)
3) Venus-Moon (1 year, 8 months)
4) Venus-Mars (1 year, 2 months)
5) Venus-Rāhu (3 years)
6) Venus-Jupiter (2 years, 8 months)
7) Venus-Saturn (3 years, 2 months)
8) Venus-Mercury (2 years, 10 months)
9) Venus-Ketu (1 year, 2 months)

Sun Sub-Daśās – 6 years in Total

1) Sun-Sun (3 months, 18 days)
2) Sun-Moon (6 months)
3) Sun-Mars (4 months, 6 days)
4) Sun-Rāhu (10 months, 24 days)

5) Sun-Jupiter (9 months, 18 days)

6) Sun-Saturn (11 months, 12 days)

7) Sun-Mercury (10 months, 6 days)

8) Sun-Ketu (4 months, 6 days)

9) Sun-Venus (1 year)

Moon Sub-Daśās – 10 Years in Total

1) Moon-Moon (10 months)

2) Moon-Mars (7 months)

3) Moon-Rāhu (1 year, 6 months)

4) Moon-Jupiter (1 year, 4 months)

5) Moon-Saturn (1 year, 7 months)

6) Moon-Mercury (1 year, 5 months)

7) Moon-Ketu (7 months)

8) Moon-Venus (1 year, 8 months)

9) Moon-Sun (6 months)

Mars Sub-Daśās – 7 Years in Total

1) Mars-Mars (4 months, 27 days)

2) Mars-Rāhu (1 year, 18 days)

3) Mars-Jupiter (11 months, 6 days)

4) Mars-Saturn (1 year, 1 month, 9 days)

5) Mars-Mercury (11 months, 27 days)

6) Mars-Ketu (4 months, 27 days)

7) Mars-Venus (1 year, 2 months)

8) Mars-Sun (4 months, 6 days)

9) Mars-Moon (7 months)

Rāhu Sub-Daśās – 18 Years in Total

1) Rāhu-Rāhu (2 years, 8 months, 12 days)

2) Rāhu-Jupiter (2 years, 4 months, 24 days)

3) Rāhu-Saturn (2 years, 10 months, 6 days)

4) Rāhu-Mercury (2 years, 6 months, 18 days)

5) Rāhu-Ketu (1 year, 18 days)

6) Rāhu-Venus (3 years)

7) Rāhu-Sun (10 months, 24 days)

8) Rāhu-Moon (1 year, 6 months)

9) Rāhu-Mars (1 years, 18 days)

Jupiter Sub-Daśās – 16 years in Total

1) Jupiter-Jupiter (2 years, 1 month, 18 days)

2) Jupiter-Saturn (2 years, 6 months, 12 days)

3) Jupiter-Mercury (2 years, 3 months, 6 days)

4) Jupiter-Ketu (11 months, 6 days)

5) Jupiter-Venus (2 years, 8 months)

6) Jupiter-Sun (9 months, 18 days)

7) Jupiter-Moon (1 year, 4 months)

8) Jupiter-Mars (11 months, 6 days)

9) Jupiter-Rāhu (2 years, 4 months, 24 days)

Saturn Sub-Daśās – 19 Years in Total

1) Saturn-Saturn (3 years, 3 days)

2) Saturn-Mercury (2 years, 8 months, 9 days)

3) Saturn-Ketu (1 year, 1 month, 9 days)

4) Saturn-Venus (3 years, 2 months)

5) Saturn-Sun (11 months, 12 days)

6) Saturn-Moon (1 year, 7 months)

7) Saturn-Mars (1 years, 1 month, 9 days)

8) Saturn-Rāhu (2 years, 10 months, 6 days)

9) Saturn-Jupiter (2 years, 6 months, 12 days)

Mercury Sub-Daśās – 17 Years in Total
1) Mercury-Mercury (2 years, 4 months, 27 days)
2) Mercury-Ketu (11 months, 27 days)
3) Mercury-Venus (2 years, 10 months)
4) Mercury-Sun (10 months, 6 days)
5) Mercury-Moon (1 year, 5 months)
6) Mercury-Mars (11 months, 27 days)
7) Mercury-Rāhu (2 years, 6 months, 18 days)
8) Mercury-Jupiter (2 years, 3 months, 6 days)
9) Mercury-Saturn (2 years, 8 months, 9 days)

We can further divide sub-daśās into sub-sub-daśās, reflecting the more immediate changes in the progression of your birth chart. We do this by multiplying the length of each major daśā for each planet and then divide this by 40 (1/3 of the 120 ideal life span). For example, Ketu-Ketu-Venus is calculated as 24.5 days (7 x 7 x 20 ÷ 40 = 24.5). See APPENDIX for lengths of each sub-sub-daśā.

PLANETS' RELATIONSHIPS

Before delving into each sub-daśā, we can first observe if the major and sub-daśā planets are friendly to each other or not. The planetary relationships in Table 1.3 shows the Sun as friendly to the Moon, Mars, and Jupiter. It is neutral towards Mercury and sees Saturn and Venus as enemies. The Moon is friendly towards the Sun and Mercury. It is neutral towards Mars, Jupiter, Venus, and Saturn. The Moon sees no planet as an enemy. All other planetary relationship are highlighted in Table 1.3. These relationships are important in terms of the sign a planet is placed in and when these planets are placed together. The relationship they form between each other also makes a difference.

I have excluded Rāhu and Ketu from the list, as they have complicated relationships with all planets. Some astrologers consider Rāhu to be like Saturn and Ketu to be like Mars. Thus, their relationships may be similar. Rāhu and Ketu are not embodied; instead, they are shadows cast over the Sun or Moon. They obscure the Sun, Moon, and planets. Although Jupiter can tame Rāhu's distortions, Rāhu can disturb Jupiter's clarity. Ketu's ability to remove blocks can sometimes remove too many, leaving you feeling uprooted. Jupiter may calm the impulsivity of Ketu, while the Sun can bring more clarity if there is confusion. Any involvement of Rāhu or Ketu can lead to a sense of confusion.

Table 1.3

Planet	Friendly to	Neutral to	Inimical to
Sun	Moon, Mars, Jupiter	Mercury	Venus, Saturn
Moon	Sun, Mercury	Mars, Jupiter, Venus, Saturn	None
Mars	Sun, Moon, Jupiter	Venus, Saturn	Mercury
Mercury	Sun, Venus	Mars, Jupiter, Saturn	Moon
Jupiter	Sun, Moon, Mars	Saturn	Mercury, Venus
Venus	Mercury, Saturn	Mars, Jupiter	Sun, Moon
Saturn	Mercury, Venus	Jupiter	Sun, Moon, Mars

Each sub-daśās is like a conjunction between the two planets involved. If you were in Rāhu-Mars daśā, for example, it's much like experiencing a Rāhu-Mars conjunction. Rāhu and Mars are not an easy pair, although their sub-daśā may be easier for you because of their position relative to each other. Jupiter-Moon daśā may be easy for most, but that would also depend on other indications in your birth chart.

Taking the Rāhu-Mars daśā as an example, Rāhu exaggerates Mars' energy and free expression. It may initially exaggerate it but can then create a very up and down experience because of excesses. Your energy may be all over the place. It is as if Rāhu has one last gasp at the end of its daśā, and Mars, which is the previous major daśā, has one last gasp, too. That is a lot of gasping! Rāhu's obsessions and compulsions can take one last hold during Rāhu-Mars daśā. This is so you can rid yourself of all it promised but failed to deliver. And because Rāhu promises a lot, there is a lot to rid yourself of.

Combinations such as the Jupiter-Moon daśā may be easier to deal with, a combination that can feel very comforting and supported. If Jupiter and the Moon are also in a supportive position from each other, this can be all the sweeter.

One way to find out what general theme each sub-daśā will bring into your life is to count from the major daśā to the sub-daśā and the same again. Counting from one to the other, and the same again, you arrive at a third sign/house. Observing the placement of the planets from each other, you can get a good idea of how well they will get on with each other. Planets are friendly or not, while their placement from each other will show the result. No matter how friendly two planets are to one another, if those same planets are in a more confrontational relationship, it will bring more challenges. It may be that these challenges are easy to negotiate. It is like two friends having an argument, as opposed to two enemies. One is going to be more helpful than the other.

Table 1.4

PISCES	ARIES	TAURUS	GEMINI
AQUARIUS			CANCER
CAPRICORN			LEO
SAGITTARIUS	SCORPIO	LIBRA	VIRGO

The South Indian-style chart layout in Table 1.4 highlights the four corners of the chart, the signs Gemini, Virgo, Sagittarius, and Pisces. These signs are opposite each other. Aries and Libra are opposite; Taurus and Scorpio are opposite; Cancer and Capricorn are opposite; and Leo and Aquarius are opposite.

If planets are opposite one another, i.e., in a 1/7 relationship, it can bring a relationship in their daśā. Yet it may also show just that: an opposition. It may also bring some issues that is unavoidable. The 7th house shows something that is in direct sight from both planet's perspectives. Oppositions can be enjoyable, especially if you meet a partner. Yet two friendly planets forming an opposition are very different to two inimical planets having to deal with one another.

When planets line up in signs that are adjacent to one another, this requires a certain give (12ᵗʰ house) and take (2ⁿᵈ house). Yet this alignment may show one not seeing the other. If Mars were in Taurus and Venus were in Gemini, they would form a 2/12 relationship (counting inclusively from Mars to Venus is a 2-count, while counting from Venus to Mars is a 12-count). This may mean one person or area of life feels like it is losing out for the other to feel supported.

When two planets are in a 3/11 relationship, this is more helpful, but may require a little effort on your part. The 3ʳᵈ house is the house of efforts, while the 11ᵗʰ is the house of gains. Even planets that are usually inimical will cooperate with one another in this case. If planets are in a 4/10 relationship, there may be a sense of contrast that you may feel as conflicted or tense. You may get what you want, but there may be some conflict involved in getting it. If planets are in a 5/9 relationship, this is helpful, as they are in the same element. This is when planets who might otherwise be unfriendly are on the same page. If both planets are also usually friendly, this is the best situation. Yet this does not mean this is always the best thing, as and when something you would prefer not to happen, happens with ease.

If planets are in a 6/8 relationship, this may be the most challenging. An example of this would be one planet in Taurus and another in Sagittarius. Two planets who may be friendly to one another are now behaving as enemies. If two planets that are already enemies are in this alignment, it can create a lot of conflict. There is at least a certain amount of antagonism possible with this combination. Challenges are not always a bad thing, of course, as and when you improve your life because of it. You may not like it, but you end up in a better position.

KETU SUB-DAŚĀS

The 1st sub-daśā within any major daśā is the same planet. So, the first sub-daśā in the major Ketu daśā is Ketu, i.e., Ketu-Ketu. Although Ketu is the tail end of the serpent in Vedic myth and can show a complex end to its major daśā, there is uncertainty that is likely right from the start. Ketu removes your ignorance of your true nature – that which is beyond this world. It is likely that you will experience at least a loss of certainty during the first sub-daśā in a worldly sense. This depends on what Ketu represents in your chart. Ketu rules the sign Scorpio, while its placement by sign has a say, as well as its dispositor, i.e., the planet that rules the sign Ketu is in. More on sign rulership later.

There may be losses you are grateful for, yet it may not be obvious why you experience losses. You may not be conscious of wishing to renounce from this deeper part of you. Thus, it can be quite a perplexing time. Ketu will remove any ignorance of your true nature and core being. There may be things you have to say goodbye to in Ketu-Ketu daśā. This can lead to much vulnerability, as if your life were in free fall. It is a time to lean into the uncertainty a little more.

The 2nd sub-daśā within Ketu daśā is that of Venus, i.e., Ketu-Venus. Venus can provide the soft landing in a sub-daśā that brings more comforts within an overall period of uncertainty. The second sub-daśā of any major daśā is that of the major daśā that is to follow in years to come. Ketu-

Venus points to the change from Ketu's major daśā to that of Venus in later years. This will give you clues about what lies ahead, as if offering you a preview of where your life is going. This helps you deal with what you may have lost. A Venus sub-daśā is a time to enjoy the simple pleasures in life. There is a sense of appreciation for the finer things. Yet Ketu's impulse invokes a need to get rid of excesses, to simplify your life, and enjoy simple pleasures.

The 3rd sub-daśā in Ketu daśā is that of the Sun, i.e., Ketu-Sun. The Sun follows Venus in the sequence, reminding you of your sense of self and purpose. This gives you something beyond life's simple pleasures and enjoyable pursuits. The Sun is your essence, your soul. If you do not connect to your purpose, a Ketu-Sun daśā may lead to some kind of existential crisis. Thankfully, Sun daśās are the shortest, so Ketu-Sun daśā passes by quickly. This reorientates you to a higher perspective. By struggling with an existential dilemma, you find your true self, beyond your identity in any worldly sense. Ketu-Sun reminds you of this even more so. Your true self is a non-self. The presence within is unaffected by what is happening. As Ketu is the centre around which everything is spinning, a Ketu-Sun daśā can be an intense reorientation. Your witnessing presence shines like a Sun blazing awareness at your core.

The 4th sub-daśā in Ketu daśā is that of the Moon, i.e., Ketu-Moon. This daśā brings a need to connect with others, after a period of questioning who you are. But

Ketu-Moon can offer its own questioning. You may deal with some mental blocks. It can be a very rewarding period of connecting with something deeper within. This may mean renouncing others, as Ketu's influence can obscure those who you would have sought for comfort in the past. Ketu can take away comforts, perhaps by removing people you no longer feel reflect a deeper awareness and core being. Remaining centred may be a challenge while there are emotional changes afoot. You must orientate yourself to something beyond, while nurturing yourself and your relationships.

The 5th sub-daśā in Ketu daśā is Mars, i.e., Ketu-Mars. Following an emotional Ketu-Moon period, a Mars sub-daśā can be more proactive. After dwelling on how you feel in Ketu-Moon daśā, Mars shows more likelihood of decisive actions. Yet, despite the need to act, nothing you do is completely clear in a Ketu major daśā. This may frustrate at this point. You may try to act at this stage but find that you are in the dark about what is the right action take. There is a need to accept not everything is in your control. Losing control during any Mars daśā is not acceptable, but you must relinquish some control because of Ketu.

Many astrologers liken Ketu to Mars, because it is fiery, and they are both said to rule the sign Scorpio in Indian astrology. This brings hidden dynamics, which, if you could make yourself more aware of, could be an effective period in making some changes. There is something subversive about Ketu, while Mars pushes things out into the open. You are developing more strength in the face of uncertainty, if nothing else. You are developing inner and outer strength. Yet this could lead to extremes in your behaviour, especially if Ketu and Mars are in a challenging configuration in your birth chart. Although an unconscious need, you may project it onto someone or something else you label a problem. Ketu-Mars is about you getting over something, some problem you would do better without.

The 6th sub-daśā in Ketu daśā is Rāhu, i.e., Ketu-Rāhu. This is when the kārmik issues of the lunar nodes are in full effect. While Ketu is about renunciation, Rāhu is all about your wants and desires. This sub-daśā is an ambitious, even obsessive, period. This could lead to attempting to fill the void of recent losses with something, anything, to gain a footing in the world again. Yet nothing and no one can fill that void. But it doesn't mean you won't try! A Ketu-Rāhu period is a time that you may feel torn between two apparently disparate parts of you; the renunciate and high achiever. You must acknowledge this inner conflict. If not, you are likely to project it into the world with a sense of bewilderment. Being still in your ever-present being, you can hold space for all that is happening. All that you wish to make happen, from a still place within yourself, can come to you. In that case, you can remain at peace while still being able to experience a hunger for more. It may sound paradoxical, but that is indeed what this period may feel like.

The 7th sub-daśā in Ketu daśā is Jupiter, i.e., Ketu-Jupiter. Jupiter brings more awareness and cohesion after a period of conflicted impulses in Ketu-Rāhu daśā. Jupiter brings about a change of direction, even a change in what you believe is possible. This changes the course of your life in very meaningful ways. Jupiter adds depth to the experience of Ketu, especially if loss and uncertainty have left you feeling hollow and ungrounded. Jupiter is an antidote to the loss, allowing you to integrate the changes that have occurred. On the other side, this could offer more mind-bending alternatives that leave you lacking clarity about what is true and what is not. It all depends on their relationship in your birth chart. Ketu-Jupiter changes what is meaningful to you.

The 8th sub-daśā in Ketu daśā is Saturn, i.e., Ketu-Saturn. This daśā can be more challenging, depending on how willing you are to let go of certain things. Both planets wish you to let go of something, but they get you to do so in very different ways. Ketu is the renunciate part of you, while Saturn is the responsible part of you. Saturn wishes to experience something here and now, so you can pay back your debts. Ketu brings things up from the past, but you may wish to run away from it. One part of you may want to run for the hills, while another part asks you to deal with your responsibilities. It can, at the very least, create a conflict between what you must do and what you must give up. You may not know which is which. While both challenge you to go beyond the temporal, Saturn keeps you grounded in reality, although it may be a reality you wish to avoid.

The 9th and final sub-daśā in Ketu daśā is Mercury, i.e., Ketu-Mercury. The Mercury sub-daśā brings you to the end of the Ketu major daśā, which can be a confusing time. You may experience losses at the tail end of Ketu, but you are looking to build a more practical base in your life now. Mercury points you to the previous major daśā, to integrate the past in a practical way, while Ketu shows a time that is full of uncertainty and doubt. These two impulses vie for space in your consciousness and may lead to a state of confusion about how to progress. While Mercury asks you to get on with it, Ketu can be impulsive and reckless. The tail end of the serpent in Vedic myth loosens its grips. The things you were once tethered to may come undone. As the uncertainty of life drains away, it can take other things with it. You should take this step with great care, as you build on a spiritual orientation and foundation for your life. The spiritual is probably the most practical approach at this point. You can finally let go of all the uncertainty.

This period is an integration of all these seemingly disparate parts, a part of the course for Mercury, the planet of communication, as you integrate your soul's desire. The Mercury sub-daśā is a transition to something else, beyond the major daśā of Ketu. Whatever it brings is temporary. It is but a steppingstone to something else in the Venus major daśā that is about to begin in your life.

It's Mercury's job to prepare you mentally and emotionally for a major change. It is a period to let go of all your doubts, those confusing times and all those losses, so you can assimilate what you need to progress. A client once reported to me that moving from Ketu to Venus was as if landing on a soft cushion (Venus), after a period of being in free fall (Ketu). It's Mercury's task to prepare you for the landing, to deal with the practicalities of arriving back down to earth.

VENUS SUB-DAŚĀS

The 1st sub-daśā in the major Venus daśā is that of Venus itself, i.e. Venus-Venus. This is a time to rejoice after the uncertainty and losses of the previous Ketu daśā. It brings comforts and enjoyments in some form. At the very least, Venus brings a desire for pleasures which may have taken a back seat in the previous daśā. There is a sense of coming to your senses in the longest major daśā, spanning 20 years. Venus is a benevolent planet and most likely experienced in some beneficial way. Not that it is without its own challenges. You may wish for some pleasure, such as a partner, but not find one from the outset. Still, searching for love and things to enjoy is better than the existential crisis of Ketu!

The 2nd sub-daśā in Venus daśā is that of the Sun, i.e., Venus-Sun. This gives you a hint of what is coming further down the line when you enter the Sun's major daśā in 20 years. More immediately, the Sun shows a need to seek something beyond sensual indulgence. This period is about something higher, and deeper, within. This deeper connection usually leads to a firmer sense of self in the outer world as well. If you have a strong Sun, the Sun's sub-daśā is a time for building more confidence in your abilities. Yet the Sun's sub-daśā is but a few months while Venus is the predominant impulse for many years. The Sun may instil a sense of confidence and self-assurance, yet you may experience a certain conflict; between the desires of the flesh (Venus) and the needs of the soul (Sun). This is usually not such a conflict, as Venus is one planet that can take the Sun out of debilitation in Libra. Forming relationships and enjoying yourself are certainly ways to build more confidence in this sub-daśā.

The 3rd sub-daśā in Venus daśā is that of the Moon, i.e., Venus-Moon. After a period of getting to know yourself and what you want (Venus-Sun), there comes a time to connect with others, within your community and/or family. The more you know yourself, the more you can connect with others, of course. The less authentic you are with yourself, the less you are with others. Venus and the Moon are both kind, benevolent planets, unless the Moon is waning or dark (New Moon), or afflicted by Saturn, Mars, or the eclipses (lunar nodes). This means that the impulse during this sub-daśā is to enjoy life, to connect to what makes you happy. Conflicts may arise between sense pleasure and a deeper connection, as Venus is about a need to feel appreciated, while the Moon represents an unconditional love. The 4ᵗʰ sub-daśā in Venus daśā is that of Mars, i.e., Venus-Mars. After a period of focusing on others' needs, there comes a time for you to focus on your own. Mars represents your personal power, the courage to do what you want. This may involve neglecting others, as you build the strength needed to do what is necessary. Venus-Mars daśā can be a very passionate period, mixing up the two 'gender' planets. Whatever you want for yourself requires a little compromise. Otherwise, you may not get what you want. Venus and Mars create a need to balance the push-pull dynamics of these planets. Venus attracts things to you, while Mars may push your own agenda, creating problems with others if you overdo it.

The 5ᵗʰ sub-daśā in Venus daśā is that of Rāhu, i.e., Venus-Rāhu. All that power and drive, the will to succeed, in the previous Mars daśā can go to your head in Rāhu daśā. If not tamed and expressed appropriately, this can create many distortions. This period could send you off in search of more and more pleasure. This can create a lot of sensual indulgence, but it may leave you feeling as if you are lacking. The more you indulge, the more you need, creating further desires and excessive longing. This can lead to feelings of dissatisfaction, no matter how much you get, creating problems in relationships, especially if you feel your partner is not giving you what you want. It may be a more intense period of searching for a partner, or partners, if you are single. Although Venus can tame the wild ride that is Rāhu, offering more compromise and negotiation, it can still leave you hungry for more.

The 6th sub-daśā in Venus daśā is that of Jupiter, i.e., Venus-Jupiter. Jupiter brings more sanity into proceedings and a much needed settling down after the indulgences of Venus-Rāhu. Sensual indulgence leads way to more meaningful pursuits. Venus is all about enjoying yourself, while Jupiter is more about purpose and meaning. You may ask yourself if your pleasure-seeking is meaningful, or if there is something more to life. This may mean having more meaningful relationships, of course. You may deepen your bonds with others. But as is the nature of the biggest planet Jupiter, it may also increase these pleasures, leading to too much of a good thing. Venus and Jupiter are the two most benevolent planets in Indian astrological analysis, and thus, this period can be very enjoyable indeed. Jupiter is the planet of expansion, which can literally be the case if you overindulge with food and drink. Jupiter offers expansion in every which way. It may be by getting married, and/or having children, or through study and travel, developing a broader perspective on life. As the saying goes, 'travel broadens the mind', and this period can certainly broaden your horizons.

The 7th sub-daśā in Venus daśā is that of Saturn, i.e., Venus-Saturn. After the indulgence and blessings of the previous period, a Saturn daśā brings you back down to earth; sometimes, with a bang! Jupiter expands your life, giving you different ideas and ideal situations to think about. Saturn is about putting these ideas to the test, focusing on what is possible. This can be like a rude awakening, a reality check, as Saturn puts the brakes on. Saturn asks you to restrain yourself, even within the major daśā of Venus. This can bring the much-needed balance between pleasures and doing the work you need to do. Saturn brings responsibility in some form. This may conflict with the Venus impulse to enjoy yourself. Saturn may also provide the containment for such pleasures, and more appreciation for the simple pleasures. Yet Saturn is more likely to ask you to cut back and be grateful for what you already have.

It may be a time you mourn the loss of what you once had and wish to have it back. Saturn limits your experience, but as long as you limit yourself, it can be a very productive time. Venus-Saturn daśā is a time to work hard and play hard. It just may be a time to leave the party a little earlier than usual. This way, you do not experience the negative effects of Saturn. Saturn reminds you of your indulgences through some problem that you need to address. There is no getting away from what you must do in a Saturn daśā, despite the pleasures of Venus. If you've pushed the boat out too far up to this point, Saturn asks you to rein it in.

The 8th sub-daśā in Venus daśā is that of Mercury, i.e., Venus-Mercury. Like Venus, a Mercury period is excitable, offering many options and things that excite. This period is usually at the very least a little busy. Mercury brings more options than the previous Saturn daśā. Venus-Mercury can be very stimulating indeed. If you are not looking for love (Venus), you are looking for money (Mercury). And if you're not looking for either, you are looking for something to enjoy. Too much indulgence, whether sensual or intellectual, can actually dull the mind. This may lead to an imbalance between agitated states of desire and dull states of exhaustion. Too much socialising and parties can leave you feeling worse for wear. This is usually a practical period, with Mercury showing a need to build your life from the ground up again. This is especially important if you felt knocked off course in the previous Saturn daśā. It is not enough to enjoy life; you must make a living. You will most likely deal with these concerns in Venus-Mercury sub-daśā.

The 9th and final sub-daśā in Venus daśā is that of Ketu, i.e., Venus-Ketu. Ketu finishes the 20 year long daśā of Venus, bringing back themes of the previous major daśā of Ketu. You may experience something from the past you thought you had left behind. This is a transition period into the next major daśā of the Sun in a year, so try not to get too bogged down in what you must let go of at this stage. This can be a pause and a need for reflection as you undo old kārmik knots before moving on. The final year of Venus major daśā can be an uncertain time. It may bring up past issues, even losses. It is a major transition period in your life that requires a steady focus on what is not changing, even amid these many changes. If you must say goodbye to something at this stage, realise it is a temporary phase that will lead to a new beginning in the upcoming Sun daśā. Take some time out to connect with your soul essence, beyond all sensual enjoyments, before connecting to your soul's purpose.

SUN SUB-DAŚĀS

The 1st sub-daśā in the major Sun daśā is that of the Sun itself, i.e., Sun-Sun. Sun daśā are the shortest, the major daśā lasting only 6 years, and thus, the Sun-Sun daśā is only a few months. These months are usually a time to come into your own. After many years of focusing on Venus-type pleasures, and others, the Sun is about focusing on your unique gifts and purpose. The Sun connects you to your higher self, a self which fuels a longing for something greater within. You may express this in worldly success, of course. This adds to your sense of confidence. Even if your Sun were weak, there is a need to connect to your true source of power. The Sun is your light, bringing clarity, a sense of direction and confidence. Sun-Sun daśā is about finding your strength and vitality so you are clear about who you are and feel more alive.

The 2nd sub-daśā in Sun daśā is that of the Moon, i.e., Sun-Moon. The Moon points you to the years to come and what you will develop after you have connected to yourself and built your confidence. Once you know yourself, you can connect more to others, be it a family, a community, or any kind of relationship. The Moon daśā is about putting down roots, to connect with those who support you and your vision. The Sun-Moon daśā, a period when both luminaries are active in your life, is a time to feel connected to your higher self and purpose. This includes connecting with others, especially those who support you and your needs. When you feel more supported, you can support others who share your vision.

The 3rd sub-daśā in Sun daśā is that of Mars, i.e., Sun-Mars. Mars brings more selfish needs into sharp focus, along with the Sun's need to connect to something higher. You may express Mars as a more selfish desire. Sun and Mars represent the difference between your higher self and ego. Your higher self does not feel the need to fight anyone. Your ego does. This can bring with it a need to defend yourself. Sun-Mars may create conflict with others. It may also bring a need to rid yourself of something that makes you feel weak. It may be something that does not serve your higher purpose. If you lack either of these perspectives, your higher self, or egoic needs, someone may challenge you to find it.

The 4th sub-daśā in Sun daśā is that of Rāhu, i.e., Sun-Rāhu. This phase can exaggerate your sense of self to the point of distortion. While the Sun represents your true self, Rāhu is your shadow. Rāhu's influence may create such a powerful need for ego gratification and recognition that nothing is enough at this point. This can distort your sense of where you are getting your power from, using manipulations to gain more. But you are unlikely to be aware of the power-plays of this period. You may project these manipulations onto others who you may label as power hungry or obstructing you. These feelings are mere projections of your inner struggle. If you acknowledge this, you may tame the beast that is Rāhu. You may create the environment you need to gain recognition while empowering others. This is a more elevated expression of Sun-Rāhu. If not, you are likely to meet with your shadow in others, in power struggles with people who seems to have power over you.

The 5th sub-daśā in Sun daśā is that of Jupiter, i.e., Sun-Jupiter. Jupiter brings the much-needed clarity after a period of Rāhu has brought some internal struggle. Jupiter can bring a sense of ease. A Sun-Jupiter combination can bring a strong sense of self, too. You may have such high expectations that nothing or no one can meet your expectations, of course. You may feel let down by others who do not see it the way you do. Usually, though, Sun-Jupiter daśā is a glorious period of feeling confident and connected. You are building trust and faith in yourself, instilling a sense of vitality into whatever you are doing.

The 6th sub-daśā in Sun daśā is that of Saturn, i.e., Sun-Saturn. This daśā can pose a problem. How you manage it will depend on many factors in your chart. Saturn is opposite in nature to the Sun. The Sun is your vitality, your trust and confidence. Saturn is your weakness, your lack of confidence, your doubts, and mistrust. This light and dark theme can play out in many ways, of course. It's an inner struggle that can play out in the world around you. The struggle lies between feeling connected and feeling isolated. You may feel 'less than' in Saturn daśā, despite the power of the Sun. It's a period of questioning what you are doing, your direction in life, while you may also work hard, taking on more responsibilities. The work that you do now, the struggle that you may experience, is all part of the greater plan. Doubts are as much part of the plan as anything. Doubts get you to work harder than you would have otherwise. Although the rewards may not seem forthcoming in Saturn daśā, if you keep up the hard work, while letting go of any great expectation, you will fare much better.

The 7th sub-daśā in Sun daśā is that of Mercury, i.e., Sun-Mercury. Mercury brings you back down to earth to deal with your life in more practical ways. After a period of doubt, Mercury is usually a more productive period. It is always a more stimulating time. You may engage more with the world around you. You may have more options available than in the previous daśā of Saturn. Sun-Mercury can bring more clarity and intelligent choices, where the previous Saturn may have lacked any choice at all. Mercury daśā can bring the much needed discrimination, where you know what you need to do, and you feel more confident doing it.

The 8th sub-daśā in Sun daśā is that of Ketu, i.e., Sun-Ketu. No matter how much you learn about yourself in Sun-Mercury daśā, the intellect has its limitations, which may seem more obvious in Sun-Ketu daśā. Ketu brings a need to develop an alternative approach, a deeper sense of guidance, which may be described as a more intuitive sense. While this period may confuse, it also has the power to enlighten and enrich your life. Yet you may need to relinquish something that is not your true calling. Usually, that sense of what your calling is comes through loss of something tangible. By tapping into who you are beyond all forms, be it a status in society, a title, or position, Ketu reminds you that you are so much more.

The 9th and final sub-daśā in Sun daśā is that of Venus, i.e., Sun-Venus. Venus points you back to the previous major daśā and reminds you of past enjoyments. This may bring more comforts and pleasures to enjoy, of course. Yet this is a transition period, one that is preparing your mind for the upcoming major daśā of the Moon, so you can connect to your heart. As you transition from the Sun's major daśā to the Moon, it reminds you of the things that nourish you. While you have developed a stronger sense of self and self-esteem throughout the Sun daśā, it's time to connect to your heart's desire. As you enter the Moon daśā, you realise that in order for you to be happy, you must make others happy, too. A Venus sub-daśā shows the ability to compromise as it prepares your mind to go beyond selfish pursuits. This may come as a relationship that teaches you this important lesson.

MOON SUB-DAŚĀS

The 1st sub-daśā in the major Moon daśā is that of the Moon itself, i.e., Moon-Moon. This begins the 10-year search for comfort in some form, from the circumstances you wish to create, to the people you wish to create it with. This may include your family or community, or it may involve creating your own family or community. The Moon reflects your need for safety and security. The Moon is also the most changeable; reflected in your ever-changing mind and emotions. Likewise, this period in your life can be a changeable one. If well-placed, the Moon can confer all manner of comforts, while a more challenged Moon may show some challenge to these, but a need for them all the same.

The 2nd sub-daśā in Moon daśā is that of Mars, i.e., Moon-Mars. Mars brings more decisiveness into what is otherwise a reflective daśā. This creates more potential for actions and productivity. When combined with the Moon, Mars can show a need to do something, despite any emotional challenges or reactivity. The proactive impulse of Mars can balance out the more emotive and thoughtful Moon, leading to a balance between thoughtfulness and action.

The 3rd sub-daśā in Moon daśā is that of Rāhu, i.e., Moon-Rāhu. Unless you channel Rāhu in more helpful ways, it can distort your mental outlook. Rāhu is best experienced by acknowledging your need for an overhaul, a complete shakeup of the way you think and feel. Rāhu can exaggerate what is already on your mind, which can be good or bad, depending on how you feel. Whatever you would label it, Rāhu is a time when you are ready to try something different, but you may not be conscious of the need and project what you want deep down onto others.

The 4th sub-daśā in Moon daśā is that of Jupiter, i.e., Moon-Jupiter. After the shake-up of Rāhu, Jupiter steadies your mind and emotions, creating more stillness. The Moon-Jupiter combination can be a very beneficial time. It can expand on themes of care in your family and community, adding more of a sense of purposefulness and meaning in all your interactions. This can bring a new outlook, a more hopeful expression and sense of possibility, with new opportunities arising with more ease.

The 5th sub-daśā in Moon daśā is that of Saturn, i.e., Moon-Saturn. Saturn brings the need to focus, restricting you in some way. After a more connected period in the Jupiter sub-daśā, Saturn shows the need to withdraw and focus. Depending on what the focus is, it can either be a productive or very isolating period. It's probably both. Saturn's influence can be a little serious or pessimistic. Saturn requires focus, even a retreat from the world, to deal with any emotional issues that you may have avoided until now. There is no avoiding the issues once Saturn daśā begins. Allow them to come up and release them.

The 6th sub-daśā in Moon daśā is that of Mercury, i.e., Moon-Mercury. Both aspects of the mind are active in Moon-Mercury daśā. The Moon represents your subconscious, while Mercury represents your intellect. Mercury is the least emotional aspect of your being, bringing the much-needed practicality after a period of restraint. Head and heart can mingle in this period, so they can get on the same page and connect to what you truly want.

The 7th sub-daśā in Moon daśā is that of Ketu, i.e., Moon-Ketu. Ketu can bring a need to look deeper within, although you may reject anything that is not connected to your longing for release. Ketu's influence can show impulsive reactions and emotional outbursts. There may be a sense of disillusionment with worldly pursuits. It is important to keep things in perspective. You may experience some loss, which is another way of finding a new perspective, a more spiritual orientation. Any loss in a worldly sense, even if it's just a loss of certainty, leads to gains in a spiritual sense.

The 8th sub-daśā in Moon daśā is that of Venus, i.e., Moon-Venus. Venus brings with it more comforts and things to enjoy. These things are more enjoyable because of any loss experienced in Ketu daśā. The Moon and Venus are both kind in nature and can show a need to enjoy yourself and connect to others. Yet there may be a conflict of interest. On the one hand, the Moon shows an unconditional love, while Venus often comes with conditions, a need to negotiate and come to an agreement.

The 9th and final sub-daśā in Moon daśā is that of the Sun, i.e., Moon-Sun. The Sun period points back to the previous Sun major daśā, highlighting similar themes of connecting to your sense of self and self-esteem. This may mean letting go of connections to others that are not in helping you find it. This is the last phase within the Moon daśā, and one where you may move on from the connections you made in recent years. You may be thinking more about your commitment to your own needs and life's purpose. This eventually brings you to a more selfish period of Mars, where you are challenged to get clear about what you want.

MARS SUB-DAŚĀS

The 1st sub-daśā in the major Mars daśā is that of Mars itself, i.e., Mars-Mars. A double dose of Mars can be a force to be reckoned with, reflecting a need to find healthy outlets for your selfish desires. Raging war on your weaknesses is the major theme, and yet, you may not be aware of this. This may come as a challenge from others or some event. This is showing you where to find the strength within to overcome it. This is an energising and encouraging period. After many years of emotional considerations and hesitations in a Moon daśā, you wish to act. This is certainly a time to be more proactive.

The 2nd sub-daśā in Mars daśā is that of Rāhu, i.e., Mars-Rāhu. Rāhu exaggerates the Mars impulse to act, but in doing so, it can also lead to exhaustion and an inability to do anything. Rāhu distorts the energy of Mars, bringing up subconscious fears about what you are doing. You may question what you are doing at this point. You may project your shadow desires onto others who may seem to do what you would, or could, never do. This is a time to acknowledge your shadow needs and go for something you want deep down without overdoing it. Rāhu is all about desire and greed, while Mars is all about selfish pursuits. This period is about finding a place for impulses you have long since shunned, some of which you may have difficulty admitting to even yourself.

The 3rd sub-daśā in Mars daśā is that of Jupiter, i.e., Mars-Jupiter. Jupiter brings calmness and clarity after the tumultuous Rāhu. This leaves less room for doubting what you are doing, and more positive and affirmative actions on your part. This can be a great time to take on a bigger project and to plan on expanding your life with some strategy. Jupiter goes big, and Mars likes to get there yesterday, so you might bite off more than you can handle. But you may also learn to delegate tasks and manage this exuberant energy.

The 4th sub-daśā in Mars daśā is that of Saturn, i.e., Mars-Saturn. Saturn can restrict your movements, although Mars just wants to jump. Saturn's influence on Mars can be very helpful if you focus on the task at hand, one at a time. If you get too bogged down in what seems to take longer, you may end up frustrated. Work for work's sake. Mars-Saturn is like having one foot on the accelerator (Mars) and one on the brake (Saturn). This could create frustrations, as you may feel you are not getting what you want as fast as you would like. Saturn is teaching you an important lesson in patience. The things you work hardest for are the things worth waiting for.

The 5th sub-daśā in Mars daśā is that of Mercury, i.e., Mars-Mercury. Mercury brings more possibilities. It could also express itself as frustration when there are too many things to choose between. Mercury and Mars need more patience, even while things seem to take off in your life once again. The previous Saturn sub-daśā would have slowed you down, but now you may feel revved up and ready to go. Make sure you are clear about what you are doing, and not taking on too many things that disperse your energy. On the other side, there's no point sitting on the fence about anything right now, even if more choices present themselves. Mars requires action. Mercury requires discrimination. Both need some channel for the stimulating energy.

The 6th sub-daśā in Mars daśā is that of Ketu, i.e., Mars-Ketu. This can be an explosive mix of energies unless you are mindful of the potential hazards of handling explosives! This could lead to impulsive actions which seem to come from nowhere. Yet the triggers may seem obvious to you in hindsight. Ketu brings the past up to deal with, while Mars ploughs ahead regardless. This would be a time to be mindful of overdoing anything, or not doing anything at all. Either approach could lead to problems unless you take a mindful approach. The 7th sub-daśā in Mars daśā is that of Venus, i.e., Mars-Venus. A combination of the 'gender' planets can bring many passions. Mars is about getting what you want, while Venus is about attracting others to help you get it. This can be a real 'go-getter' time in your life, but unless you include others, you may find yourself wanting. This is as much about compromise as it is about taking steps towards your desires. You must give both impulses a voice if you are to please everyone, including yourself, in this period.

The 8th sub-daśā in Mars daśā is that of the Sun, i.e., Mars-Sun. This brings a lot of heat to manage. There's the more toxic heat of Mars and the illumination of the Sun. Mars can be toxic because it represents your selfish desires. It shows a need to protect yourself, at any cost. Sometimes, relationships are the cost. The Sun shows a more inclusive sense of self, a self that is not separate from anyone else. You can give both expressions in this daśā, of course. This is a good time to find strength through some competition or personal advancement, while connecting more deeply with yourself and others.

The 9th and final sub-daśā in Mars daśā is that of the Moon, i.e., Mars-Moon. This can be a confusing transitional phase. The Moon points you back to the past, as the impulse to drive ahead continues in Mars daśā. This is soon to be replaced by a super-charged phase in a major Rāhu daśā. Rāhu is all about creating a different future for yourself, although you may not be conscious of this need. As the youthful energy of Mars gives way to darker tones of Rāhu, your energy can be all over the place. Best to calm yourself during this transitional phase, to prepare for the changes that are to come. You won't recognise your life in a few years, so best make the most of the reminiscing before moving on.

RĀHU SUB-DAŚĀS

The 1st sub-daśā in the major Rāhu daśā is that of Rāhu itself, i.e., Rāhu-Rāhu. This can be quite intense, as Rāhu is the head of the serpent in Vedic myth, so the beginning phase is like your first bite. On some level, you want to have your life turned upside down. While this is likely an unconscious need, it may be best to keep things as calm as possible as the inevitable changes take place. You can channel the creative energy of Rāhu to create the life you want, while letting go of how you think things should pan out. Rāhu guarantees many twists and turns. The previous Mars daśā is many times a more regimented period, whereas Rāhu is anything but. It can actually be quite chaotic unless you are conscious of reining it in and organising your life. This is a time to seal your energy leaks, so you can manage yourself better. It is likely you will feel life is much more unpredictable, and you are going in a completely different direction, bringing with it many things you may not admit to yourself you want.

The 2nd sub-daśā in Rāhu daśā is that of Jupiter, i.e., Rāhu-Jupiter. Jupiter brings the much-needed sense of calm and clarity after an intense first few years of Rāhu. Jupiter is like the antidote to Rāhu's disorder, bringing cohesion and order out of chaos. While Rāhu may still bring chaotic experiences, Jupiter can calm your mind and emotions to help you deal with them with more ease. Jupiter points to where this daśā is taking you in the future, many years from now, as Jupiter's major daśā follows Rāhu, where clarity replaces any sense of uncertainty.

The 3rd sub-daśā in Rāhu daśā is that of Saturn, i.e., Rāhu-Saturn. You may feel conflicted at this point. It depends on how Rāhu and Saturn are placed from each other in your birth chart. Even if they are well-placed, they are like each other's alter egos. Rāhu is all about hunger for experience. Saturn is about making do with what you've already got. These two together can increase a sense of pressure. Saturn shows what you cannot avoid, while Rāhu shows a huge ambition to achieve more. The conflict of wanting more, while working with what you have, can take its toll unless you are conscious of these two. You may find it challenging to stay present with what you need to do, while you are busy making plans to take on the world. Rāhu knows no bounds, making one part of you fearless, whereas Saturn is your fear, what limits you. You must negotiate your ambitions with at least some limitations.

The 4th sub-daśā in Rāhu daśā is that of Mercury, i.e., Rāhu-Mercury. After an ambitious period that may not have offered as many choices, Mercury can bring more options. All that is a relief, but it poses another challenge: being too stimulated by the faster pace of life. Rāhu exaggerates whatever it influences; here, it is likely to be mental stimulation. Mercury alone can bring many options, while Rāhu further exaggerates and distorts these. You may long for the slow pace of the previous Saturn once again. The best use of this is to get busy, while getting plenty of rest to balance the tendency to overstimulate your mind. While Rāhu may not let you rest, it's important you take as much time out as possible, and when time permits, while acknowledging the many choices you do have.

The 5th sub-daśā in Rāhu daśā is that of Ketu, i.e., Rāhu-Ketu. This phase can be complex, but also peaceful. It all depends on where you are in relation to the lessons of Rāhu and Ketu, as both of the lunar nodes are active now. Rāhu points you forward, eager for more, more, more, while Ketu points you back to where you've come from. This requires at least a different perspective than mindlessly ploughing ahead. It may involve you taking a break while you work out some complex issues. For many, this can be like the eye of the storm within the major daśā of Rāhu. It can be like a welcome pause in an otherwise chaotic time in your life. Past issues crop up, while unforeseen circumstances create situations you seem to have less control over. The only control you actually have is how you perceive this phase of your life. The less reactionary you are, the better. Stay open for a new twist while keeping the past and future in perspective. The past influences the future, but the future also influences your past. How you feel will dictate how you see your past, which changes how you view your future.

The 6th sub-daśā in Rāhu daśā is that of Venus, i.e., Rāhu-Venus. After a year of uncertainty and changes that seemed to be outside of your conscious control, Venus can be a time to enjoy life's simple pleasures once again. Yet Rāhu is anything but simple. Rāhu complicates things, exaggerating whatever impulse is present. Here, Rāhu exaggerates the need to find sensual stimulation, which can express itself in many ways. More pleasure, more relationships, can be some ways you enjoy. But whatever you are enjoying, if you do not rein it in somewhat, you will probably find yourself worse for wear. Overindulgence can lead to problems. It's never enough. This can be a dissatisfying period, despite the many things you have to enjoy. As long as you are aware of this possibility, you can mitigate it by reminding yourself of all you have while striving for more. Otherwise, Rāhu-Venus can feel like nobody and nothing can ever be enough.

The 7th sub-daśā in Rāhu daśā is that of the Sun, i.e., Rāhu-Sun. The Sun represents your true self, while Rāhu is your shadow, a distorted sense of self, and need to feel all powerful. This impulse will become even more prominent at this stage. Rāhu eclipses the Sun, so although you want more and more power, more recognition, it's never enough for Rāhu. If the Sun were strong in your birth chart, and in a helpful relationship to Rāhu, you are more likely to achieve a great deal. But whatever you achieve leaves you wanting more. It's not enough to gain recognition; you'll want more. Whatever you get, there is always a price to pay with Rāhu. So, if you were to be acknowledged, you must accept being in the limelight brings with it its own issues, shining the spotlight on something you may prefer to keep hidden.

The 8th sub-daśā in Rāhu daśā is that of the Moon, i.e., Rāhu-Moon. This can be a little complicated, as Rāhu overshadows the mind and emotions. Whatever you have achieved at this stage, the Moon shows a need to feel safe and nourished. Yet Rāhu's impulse is to make you feel like nothing is ever enough. This stage can bring up emotional issues which you must address. Otherwise, anxieties may float around you in a fog. These are usually irrational fears, impulsive reactions to any sense of lack, or desires for things you cannot quite fathom. Recognising these as reactions, as 'unrealities', can help mitigate any faulty thinking, while keeping a balanced lifestyle.

The 9th and final sub-daśā in Rāhu daśā is that of Mars, i.e., Rāhu-Mars. This last phase and year within the 18-year daśā of Rāhu can be quite intense. Mars is already intense, of course. It shows a selfish desire, making you feel like life is a competition. Rāhu further exaggerates and distorts this impulse. This can create a lot of drive, one last big push for something you feel you lack. If only you could get x, y or z, you would be complete. The journey of this last sub-daśā is to realise that nothing and no one on this earth can fill that hole. But it doesn't mean you will not try! In fact, you will try even harder to achieve something at this stage. Yet you may not always be conscious of this need. It may seem like life itself is pushing you into situations, while also bringing up old fights you used to have with yourself or others. This is because Mars was the previous daśā to Rāhu and is once again impressing itself upon you.

Whatever you have achieved at this stage, it's merely a steppingstone to something else at this point. The next stage shall reveal itself in the upcoming major Jupiter daśā in a year's time. Try not to get too fixated on what's happening right now. Work at mitigating the tendency to overdo it, which will only leave you feeling spent. Be mindful of your energy levels, as Rāhu's influence on Mars reveals more extremes. It's been a long and winding road through the 18 years of Rāhu. This one's like the last sprint down the home straight. Dig deep. Look at where you are going in the long run.

JUPITER SUB-DAŚĀS

The 1st sub-daśā in the major Jupiter daśā is that of Jupiter itself, i.e., Jupiter-Jupiter. After many years of confusion about where your life is going, Jupiter brings a sense of clarity. Usually, this is a time to feel purposeful and find more meaningful pursuits. Jupiter is the largest planet in our solar system, which means growth is more possible. Growth requires order and cohesion, which this period offers you. After the chaos and disorder of Rāhu, Jupiter brings opportunities with more ease. If you are of child-rearing age, and you are looking to have children, you may start a family. Jupiter represents growth, including future prospects through progeny and creative pursuits. If children are not on your path, Jupiter will bring growth in other ways. This may be through meaningful work, home life, prosperity, study or travel, or indeed, all the above. The only growth not welcome is when Jupiter represents weight gain; unless this is something you want. Whatever you gain, this is a time to settle down and experience something more meaningful.

The 2nd sub-daśā in Jupiter daśā is that of Saturn, i.e., Jupiter-Saturn. After some years of growth, Saturn can feel restrictive. If you have bitten off more than you can chew, Saturn's period requires you to slow down and digest it all. Saturn is a cleaning up of any excesses brought about in recent years, which can either feel overdue or ill-timed, depending. Saturn often feels ill-timed, anyway. It represents the payback that is due. And although you may know that deep down, you may be unwilling to accept it. That's the first step. Accept whatever is happening right now, while looking at all you have to be grateful for. Saturn is a reminder you cannot expand forever. You must do some trimming, some mental and emotional accountancy. Time to get rid of what is no longer necessary, to declutter your life and take some time out on retreat. It is time for you to figure it all out by yourself. This doesn't have to mean going on a retreat. You can incorporate Saturn into your daily life through some sort of commitment. Daily meditation and due diligence in whatever you are doing is a must in Saturn daśā. You must do this even if whatever you are doing doesn't seem to garner rewards. The work needs to be done. Rewards will come later. The things you achieve in Saturn daśā are so much more rewarding because you have had to wait for them. When they show up, you are even more grateful.

The 3rd sub-daśā in Jupiter daśā is that of Mercury, i.e., Jupiter-Mercury. After hitting a speed bump in Saturn's daśā, Mercury opens up the road ahead with lots of opportunities. This will probably occur in very practical ways. The only conflict may be a need for something more meaningful. Depending on how Jupiter and Mercury relate to one another, your thoughts may require an overhaul. This is a time to integrate many things. Mercury presents many opportunities within a Jupiter daśā. But it may also show lots of distractions for a mind overstimulated with choice. Too much mental stimulation may disturb your peace, your ability to be still. You can channel Mercury's curiosity into more meaningful activities. And you can make the most of the many opportunities while resting in 'beingness'.

The 4th sub-daśā in Jupiter daśā is Ketu, i.e., Jupiter-Ketu. Jupiter can balance the impulsivity of Ketu. Yet Ketu's influence on Jupiter can show changes to what you believe is possible at this stage. Changes are on the cards in a daśā of Ketu. It brings up the past for you to heal the issues now. This could mean you must relinquish some outworn beliefs at this stage. This can be a profound experience. Your changing beliefs can fuel possibilities you failed to recognise before. This gives you another opportunity to make things right and take advantage of what is possible now. While there may be some confusion about what you initially experience, your intuition can guide you, a guidance system you can take with you throughout Jupiter daśā.

The 5th sub-daśā in Jupiter daśā is that of Venus, i.e., Jupiter-Venus. After a somewhat perplexing year of Ketu, Venus combines with Jupiter to bring more enjoyable moments that you will most likely welcome with open arms. Yet Jupiter and Venus have different objectives. Jupiter shows more meaningful pursuits, while Venus shows enjoyments. You can make your enjoyments more meaningful, of course. Having the two most benevolent planets activated can be very enjoyable and rewarding. It all depends on the strengths of each planet in your birth chart, of course. Usually, there is plenty to appreciate. While there may be some conflicts of interest, it is a conflict of interest you are more likely to feel happy about. It is much better to feel conflicted about things that are enjoyable.

The 6ᵗʰ sub-daśā in Jupiter daśā is the Sun, i.e., Jupiter-Sun. Any conflict of interest felt in the previous daśā can dissipate in the Sun daśā. The Sun and Jupiter are usually on the same page, although they may be at odds in your birth chart. They are the two most illustrious, the two giants of the solar system. They bring with them a powerful sense of self, along with a clearer direction – usually, at any rate. It would depend on the position and strength of the Sun and Jupiter in your birth chart. Usually, Jupiter-Sun daśā is a time to find a confidence you never thought you had. The only downside is the obvious pitfall of overdoing it, or over stating what you can do. Otherwise, this period should give you the much-needed boost to your self-esteem and provide you with a clarity of purpose.

The 7ᵗʰ sub-daśā in Jupiter daśā is the Moon, i.e., Jupiter-Moon. After you have built yourself up, it is time to connect to what makes you happy. We all want happiness, of course, and a Jupiter-Moon daśā can grant you that. This combination can bring a sense of peace and contentment. If there are any emotional challenges to deal with, you are more able for them. You feel comforted by the emotional stability and can connect more to others.

The 8th sub-daśā in Jupiter daśā is Mars, i.e., Jupiter-Mars. After feelings take centre stage in Moon daśā, Mars gives you the opportunity to take some decisive steps again. This is when you can act on the opportunities presented. This is a lucky break combination, and you are likely to feel fortunate in whatever you do. As always, the only downside is overdoing it, taking on too much. Make sure you are taking advantage of this lucky time in your life but remind yourself that luck can always run out if you overdo it. Hopefully, you experience this period as a time to take big leaps forward. You may feel challenged, but you are likely to be up for it.

The 9th and final sub-daśā in Jupiter daśā is Rāhu, i.e., Jupiter-Rāhu. This is a complex period. You have achieved so much in recent years, using the many opportunities that have presented themselves. Now you are ready to push your boundaries. Yet you are not likely conscious of this need. It may mean your boundaries, and buttons, are pushed. Rāhu is an unconscious part of you, your shadow, a 'part' of you that will stop at nothing until it gets what it wants, whether you actually need it.

Jupiter and Rāhu combined can be all too much to handle in this period, creating all kinds of extremes in your life. It may all be overwhelming. This sub-daśā is pointing you back to the previous Rāhu daśā; something you thought you were done with. But here it is again, the hungry ghost that is Rāhu rearing its head for one last swipe at success. Whatever success comes with Rāhu has a price. And because you have been there and worn the t-shirt many times before, this may feel like too little too late. Even if you achieve a great deal in this period, it is unlikely to satisfy. You are likely to be aware of the need to settle for what you've got. And that's the tricky part of this period. You still have desires, but you know they don't completely meet your expectations. So you go along with it, waiting for a more peaceful time to enter your life once Saturn begins.

SATURN SUB-DAŚĀS

The 1st sub-daśā in the major Saturn daśā is Saturn itself, i.e., Saturn-Saturn. After the excesses of Jupiter, and more recently of Rāhu, you are glad of the downturn at this stage, most likely. Although you may feel the restriction, you are likely to welcome the peace. This is especially if the previous Jupiter-Rāhu daśā was overwhelming. A double dose of Saturn for a few years will put that right, though it may feel too restrictive for some. You may wish for the opportunities and possibilities of Jupiter while Saturn grinds things to a halt. Saturn is the slowest moving visible planet, which means you must slow down and pay attention. You must be present to experience peace. Saturn doesn't teach you this important life lesson in any straight-forward manner, however. It will probably teach you by not being able to focus. It may teach you this by taking you out of the present moment. You may worry about the future or feel depressed about the past. Saturn can show you doubting what you once took for granted in Jupiter daśā. This requires a mental shift from the more buoyant and optimistic Jupiter to the more real and stoic nature of Saturn. It is time to make reality your friend, to work with what is. As long as you can make that shift in your philosophy, you can make the most of Saturn.

The 2nd sub-daśā in Saturn daśā is Mercury, i.e., Saturn-Mercury. You transition from the slowest moving planet to the fastest in Mercury's sub-daśā. This gear shift points out where your life is heading once the 19-year long daśā of Saturn has ended. For now, Saturn-Mercury can teach you how to use the time productively. It is a more practical time to work hard at some task. The issue with Mercury is having too many things to consider, too many choices to navigate. But this shouldn't be much of an issue in a Saturn daśā. You are likely to feel glad about anything new that comes along at this point and take more practical steps forward. Saturn is always there to remind you to be in the present and not get lost in the many choices. Saturn teaches you to train your mind so you can focus on one task at a time.

The 3rd sub-daśā in Saturn daśā is Ketu, i.e., Saturn-Ketu. This is quite a complex period. Saturn teaches you restraint and responsibility, as Ketu is shows you the past, and a part of you that wants to check out on some level. Ketu may show a need to run for the hills, yet Saturn's impulse doesn't allow you to do so. This could create a conflict within you. Be mindful of the need to let go while doing what you must. And do so for the sake of the work itself, not the rewards. Let go of any expectation. This is not a long period, so you can manage it with more awareness.

The 4th sub-daśā in Saturn daśā is Venus, i.e., Saturn-Venus. Despite Venus bringing some much-needed certainty after a period of Ketu, and more things to enjoy in the 'real' world, it can be a complex time. Venus shows your need to enjoy yourself, but Saturn's impulse of restraint is still humming away in the background. Although both planets can work well together, there may be a conflict between doing what you want and doing what you must. Saturn gives form to Venus' love of beauty, art, and social connection. You may find ways of expressing your chosen art in some new form. You may also find a relationship. As long as you are doing what you love, while doing it as a service to others, you can mitigate any of the potential conflict. I often see this period as a turning point in a person's life. When you ask yourself what or who you love, while working hard at what you must do to make it happen, it is likely you will make big changes, whether in your relationships or the direction your life is taking.

The 5th sub-daśā in Saturn daśā is the Sun, i.e., Saturn-Sun. This triggers your light and darkness; the clarity of the Sun; the doubts of Saturn. This inner conflict can play out in more obvious ways in various relationships. Those who are in charge of you, a boss, or some government officials, for example, may highlight this identity struggle. The Sun is your sense of power and trust in yourself, while Saturn shows you questioning everyone and everything. You trust the Sun will rise every morning. You don't doubt that. But Saturn can doubt everything, especially if Saturn has a powerful influence on your Sun or your Sun were weak. These two planets are opposite in every which way. The Sun exalts where Saturn is debilitated, and vice versa. This means you must negotiate your need to be of service, to surrender your power, while connecting to what makes you feel powerful.

The 6th sub-daśā in Saturn daśā is the Moon, i.e., Saturn-Moon. After the struggle between your strength and weakness, your light and dark, the Moon period can feel a little sombre after the battle. It may feel 'less than'. Indeed, how you feel becomes more important in Sun-Moon daśā. Saturn-Moon combinations require detachment and discipline. You must avoid the tendency for negativity to become habitual.

Saturn and the Moon are opposite, just as the Sun and Saturn are opposite. They rule signs opposite each other in the zodiac, i.e., Leo and Cancer are opposite Capricorn and Aquarius. The Moon is the closest heavenly body to earth, while Saturn is the furthest we can see with the naked eye. This opposition can feel like that: an opposition. It may feel as if you are putting up a wall and detaching yourself from those around you. Or maybe you cannot deal with how you are feeling and take it out on others around you. Either way, this is a time to deal with how you are feeling, not run away from it. By doing so, you can gather in and express what Saturn-Moon combinations are best for: loving detachment. This is a time to slow down and check in with what your heart needs. But it also asks what others in your life need. This is not an overnight sensation. It is a time to ask yourself the question: What would make me happy in the long term?

The 7th sub-daśā in Saturn daśā is Mars, i.e., Saturn-Mars. Their impulses can conflict with each other, depending on how well you manage feeling restricted. While there is the possibility that Mars gives you more energy, it can express itself as frustration. This is especially true if you feel you're not getting what you want as fast as you would like it. This combination is best expressed through focusing your energy and will. Mars and Saturn are not the best of friends, but if you can negotiate with yourself and with others, you can achieve a great deal. Better to find something to work hard on and get on with it during this phase of your life. Otherwise, this combination will work hard on you, making you feel tense and frustrated.

The 8th sub-daśā in Saturn daśā is Rāhu, i.e., Saturn-Rāhu. This can be complex. You have two very ambitious parts of your being. One is greedy for more (Rāhu) and the other is dwelling on what may or may not happen (Saturn).

Both can create anxiety. Note if you are present in your life. You may want something so bad that you may obsess over it (Rāhu), yet you have to learn patience. You may feel conflicted throughout this period. The best way to tackle it is to have some goal you wish to achieve, something that is grand in scale, one you know would take time. Focus on the day-to-day tasks, instead of getting lost in what may or may not happen. That would give you something to focus on for a few years, as opposed to getting out of step with reality. Saturn represents your genuine fears, while Rāhu is unreal. Rāhu represents all your irrational fears and future projections, which only add to your worries. Find some healthy outlets during this period, and ways to care for yourself. Once this penultimate phase within the long Saturn daśā is over, you will open your mind up to new possibilities. You cannot see these right now. Trust that they are waiting for you in the upcoming daśā.

The 9th and final sub-daśā in Saturn daśā is Jupiter, i.e., Saturn-Jupiter. This last phase of Saturn offers more hope and optimism than you've been feeling of late. It is Jupiter's role to prepare your heart and mind for the changes that are upcoming as you enter Mercury's major daśā in a few years. You could not change from Saturn to Mercury, from the slowest to the fastest planet, without going through an interim phase. Jupiter prepares you for this by opening up your mind to new opportunities and possibilities. This process will take a few years, of course, so there is no rush. Best to use this time to open up to the new while healing the losses and hurts of Saturn daśā. As you learn to shift gears, you will see more and more potential for growth in the coming years. Yet these opportunities, whatever they may be, are a stepping-stone to what comes next in Mercury daśā.

Mercury is all about learning something new once you have been emptied of all you thought you knew during Saturn daśā. Jupiter brings expansion to counterbalance the limitations of Saturn.

MERCURY SUB-DAŚĀS

The 1st sub-daśā in the major Mercury daśā is Mercury itself, i.e., Mercury-Mercury. After 19 years of some form of limitations in Saturn daśā, Mercury opens up a path ahead. This gear shift can be exciting and nerve-wracking in equal measures. But you are likely to welcome the new fast pace and new options presenting themselves at every turn. It is also likely that you will, at some point, pine for the slow days of Saturn. This is the tragedy of life, it seems. You don't know what you've got until it's gone. It's important to say your last farewells to Saturn.

I have noted in those having been through 19 years of Saturn that they often have difficulty letting go. Past hurts or challenges can be difficult to drop, even while settling into the new pace in Mercury daśā. While you entered a new chapter in your life, the old story can remain embedded. I have also noted a spring in their step, a newfound youthfulness, no matter their age. This time of your life is more playful and fun, but also more practical, more down-to-earth. This may express itself through retraining or up-skilling, or even going back to school to learn something completely new. I've seen it repeatedly. No matter what age someone is, when they enter Mercury daśā, they are more willing to try something new. This may involve travel, a new business, or job, new studies, or any new ventures. These new possibilities may have presented themselves in the previous Jupiter sub-daśā. Now is the time to hit the ground running.

The 2ⁿᵈ sub-daśā in Mercury daśā is Ketu, i.e., Mercury-Ketu. This period points you to what lies ahead many years from now, when you will enter a major Ketu daśā. This phase requires tapping into something beyond the intellect and intellectual pursuits. The mind can only take you so far before you look for something deeper, within, something beyond. A combination of Mercury and Ketu can confuse, as you deal with practical issues while learning some spiritual lesson. Best to use this time to develop what Vedic astrologer Komilla Sutton refers to as an "intuitive intelligence." Ketu may bring with it losses, or at least a sense of uncertainty around the practical steps you have recently taken. Lean more into the uncertainty, while stilling your mind on a deeper sense of who you are beyond the mind.

The 3ʳᵈ sub-daśā in Mercury daśā is Venus, i.e., Mercury-Venus. Venus comes to the rescue after a period of uncertainty in Ketu sub-daśā, bringing more enjoyable, down-to-earth experiences. Mercury and Venus work well together. If they are also in a helpful relationship in your birth chart, you are likely to experience this as a very enjoyable phase. Again, the downside to Mercury, and now Venus, is too much of a good thing. You may feel overstimulated, as you experience more enjoyable interactions with others. This is a significant period for work and relationships, or whatever sphere of life these planets activate in your chart. Usually, they bring added excitement and many enjoyable moments.

The 4ᵗʰ sub-daśā in Mercury daśā is the Sun, i.e., Mercury-Sun. This combination can be an enlivening, and even enlightening, phase of your life. There is a clarity that is possible now, fuelling a powerful sense of self and clear direction. This represents a strong need to express yourself and your soul's desire. Mercury is the planet of communication. It transits between the Sun and Earth, relaying messages from your soul to your mind. These messages are practical, guiding you along your path while you speak your truth. This brings clarity around your purpose in life, building confidence in your practical abilities.

The 5ᵗʰ sub-daśā in Mercury daśā is the Moon, i.e., Mercury-Moon. Both aspects of the mind are now active in a mentally stimulating period. Your thoughts may feel emotionally charged. It may be a better time to communicate how you feel, although your inability to communicate how you feel may also be relevant. The head and heart get mixed up in a way that needs more coherence. It would be best to balance both aspects of the mind, the rational and irrational; the intellectual and the instinctual. While both can get confused with each other, there is an opportunity to get clear about what it is you think and feel. There is also the possibility of being clear about what you want, and to communicate this to yourself and everyone else.

The 6th sub-daśā in Mercury daśā is Mars, i.e., Mercury-Mars. Mercury and Mars do not make good bedfellows. They are bitter enemies. Interestingly, Mars rules the bitter taste in Indian astrological analysis. This means communications may become at least a little sharp. While Mercury is about keeping it neat, effective, and business-like, Mars is brash and sometimes inappropriate. This is especially true if you are dealing with issues that would anger you. If you don't face these issues, you are likely to meet with problems from others. If you do not express what you want, you may feel irritable. Anger can be such an uncomfortable emotion to deal with, but especially other peoples' anger. But this is what this phase is all about. Find the strength to speak your truth, hurting no one with your words. You do not want to hurt your chances of getting what you want at this stage of your development.

The 7th sub-daśā in Mercury daśā is Rāhu, i.e., Mercury-Rāhu. While Mercury and Rāhu may be seen as friendly to one another, it can pose some issues. After a period of Mars, where you were likely focused on your own needs, Rāhu can take any success you achieved and blow it out of proportion. Rāhu is extreme. It can be extremely good, or extremely bad, depending on what it associates with in your birth chart. When it combines with Mercury, it can be very stimulating – for good or ill. This can mean a lot of mental stimulation, as a lot of choices and new possibilities present themselves. Or it can be an anxious time in your life. Likely, it will alternate between both. The best use of the time is to acknowledge you have something you want and go for it. But be mindful that you may lose perspective while planning. This requires a balanced approach, so as to not overshoot the mark, leaving you mentally exhausted.

The 8ᵗʰ sub-daśā in Mercury daśā is Jupiter, i.e., Mercury-Jupiter. This penultimate phase in Mercury's major daśā can bring with it many opportunities for growth. There are many practical things that you can enjoy. While Mercury and Jupiter are not on the same page, it can be a very rewarding time in your life. Mercury is rational, practical. Jupiter's ideals are sometimes impractical. Your point of view will be important at this stage, as Jupiter would like to communicate something more profound through Mercury, as Mercury communicates what it wants through Jupiter. Looking at what you believe and how these impressions dictate your mental outlook is part of the process. You can expand on what you believe is possible. Explore your grand designs and ideals with more hope and optimism.

The 9th and final sub-daśā in Mercury daśā is Saturn, i.e., Mercury-Saturn. Saturn brings Mercury's major daśā to an end by ending something in your life. By ridding you of any excesses, you can move on feeling lighter and unburdened. You may, however, only focus on what is being lost and not on what is opening up for you. You must relinquish something of what you have built up in your life to some extent. This is an important time of letting go and moving on. Something beyond all the worldly pursuits that have gripped you in recent years is opening up in you. That phase begins once you enter Ketu's major daśā in a few years. For now, Saturn is here to prepare your mind and body for the mental-emotional cleanse.

Mercury and the intellect can only take you so far. There is a deeper truth that the mind cannot grasp; a truth of who you are that your intelligence cannot fathom. It may be best to let go of everything you thought you knew at this stage, so you can leave this phase of your life unencumbered. You will feel much lighter for it. You will be ready to go deeper once this period is over. During the detox, as with any kind of detox, it may create a healing crisis. There may be some discomfort. Saturn may bring up issues from the past around themes of loss. Doubts you thought you were over may rear their heads once again. Stay the course and go within. You will tap into a deeper sense of who you really are when finished here.

CONDITIONAL DAŚĀS

The planetary daśā hitherto referred to is the most popular in use in Indian astrology today. But there are many others, including those that need certain conditions for their use. Table 1.5 includes a short list of some (not all) conditional daśās and the conditions required.

Aṣṭottarī is 108 years, divided up between all planets apart from Ketu. Rāhu must be at an angle or trine for a Night birth during the waxing Moon or for a Day birth during a waning Moon. Rāhu must also aspect the ruler of the ascendant for this to apply. You can use Aṣṭottarī to time foreign travel and other Rāhu-related topics. We can use another conditional daśā when the 10th house ruler is in the 10th house. *Chaturaśīti* is 84 years in total and relates to 10th house matters, i.e., career. We can time events around status and career prospects with these daśās. Yet another is when the ascendant ruler is in the 7th house, or vice versa. *Dvisaptatī Samā* is 72 years in total and relates to the 7th house, i.e., relationships and marriage. This daśā will give the full picture and help us time relationships. And yet another is when the Sun is in the ascendant. *Ṣaṣṭi-hāyanī* is 60 years in total and relates to the Sun's prominent position in the 1st house. This is used to time when someone may reach a high status in the world. I explore some of these conditional daśās in one of the case studies in PART 4.

Table 1.5

Daśās	Duration	Conditions Required
Aṣṭottarī	108 years	Rāhu in 4th, 5th, 7th, 9th or 10th from ruler of ascendant, *and* Night birth during waxing Moon, or Day birth during waning Moon
Chaturaśiti Samā	4 years	10th house ruler placed in 10th house
Dvisaptatī Samā	72 years	Ascendant ruler in 7th house, or 7th house ruler in ascendant
Ṣaṣṭi-hāyanī	60 years	Sun in ascendant

There are other conditional daśās with other conditions necessary to be applicable, including *Ṣodaśottarī, Dvādaśottarī, Paśchottarī, Sātābdikā,* and *Ṣaṭ trimśata.*

Another popular daśā that can be applied to all charts is *Yogini* daśā, where a 36-year daśā is divided between Moon (1 year), Sun (2 years), Jupiter (3 years), Mars (4 years), Mercury (5 years), Saturn (6 years), Venus (7 years), and Rāhu (8 years).

SIGN DAŚĀS

The planets' positions show your desires on some level. Planets' daśās express their desires through you; their placement and sight (aspects) show what you focus on in their daśās. Signs, on the other hand, show your environment; what you have access to, whatever you desire. You may wish to get married, if you experience a daśā of the 7th house ruling planet, but whether you will marry is dependent on meeting someone. A sign that relates to marriage may need to be active for this to happen. Yet it must be seen in your birth chart in the first place. By turning the signs over in various planetary and sign-based daśās, we can see what is being activated in your birth chart at any given time.

In a daśā of the 7th sign, for example, you are likely to experience a relationship. If you are also experiencing a planetary daśā of Venus, and your 7th house ruler, then you desire the same. This guarantees a relationship, as long as there are no indications that conflict with this in your birth chart. Usually, when the stage is set, the time is ripe for a relationship. Once triggered, it is just a matter of time. Your major sign-based daśās show the circumstances. The sub-daśās fine-tune the timing along with transits.

There are many sign daśās used in Indian astrology that show the timing of various circumstances. Some show the timing of 'curses', even death. Most simply look at where the focus is in the chart. Two of the most popular sign-based daśās used today are *Nārāyaṇa* and *Chara*. Both of which show signs, and thus, which houses or areas are being activated in your life. *Āyaṇa* means 'direction' and Nārāyaṇa daśā shows the direction your life is taking. *Chara* means 'movement' and shows the progression through the signs, counting in sequential order, either zodiacally or anti-clockwise, depending on the sign in question. Chara daśā is the sign-based daśā utilised in this book.

Another sign-based daśā is *Kālcakra*, meaning 'wheel of time', which, although given great importance by Parāśara, has many complex calculations, as has Nārāyaṇa. Kālcakra takes the Moon's position to show the sign that is active; jumping around the chart because of several different progressions; dividing signs up with different lengths of time.

Traditional Indian astrology mostly utilises whole sign houses, so you can think of a sign as a house and a house as a sign. If Aries is active in your chart, Aries relates to a certain house and area of your life. This area is active in a daśā of Aries. Any planets placed in Aries are also more active. Planets in signs influence other signs due to sign aspects. Although planetary aspects are active in a planetary daśā, sign aspects are a constant. When both are active in a planetary and sign-based daśā, and both work together to achieve the same thing, the event will more likely come to pass.

Chara daśā shows the sign that is active based on whether the sign is movable, fixed, or dual. These are the three modes or impulses of the signs (more on this later). Moveable signs are Aries, Cancer, Libra, and Capricorn. Fixed signs, Taurus, Leo, Scorpio, and Aquarius, aspect the movable signs. The dual signs: Gemini, Virgo, Sagittarius, and Pisces, reflect the balance between moveable and fixed. The dual signs influence each other. This can be seen in the South Indian chart layout as the four corners in Table 1.6.

Table 1.6

PISCES *Dual*	ARIES *Moveable*	TAURUS *Fixed*	GEMINI *Dual*
AQUARIUS *Fixed*			CANCER *Movable*
CAPRICORN *Movable*			LEO *Fixed*
SAGITTARIUS *Dual*	SCORPIO *Fixed*	LIBRA *Movable*	VIRGO *Dual*

Movable and fixed signs that are adjacent do not aspect each other, i.e., Aries and Taurus, Cancer and Leo, Libra and Scorpio, and Capricorn and Aquarius. These signs have no sight of signs right beside them. Taurus does not aspect Aries, although the other fixed signs Leo, Scorpio, and Aquarius do. Aries does not aspect Taurus, although Cancer, Libra, and Capricorn do. Movable signs keep things moving until there is something to stop them or slow them down. Fixed signs do not move until something gets them going.

While active signs show what is in your environment, you must observe this in relation to your planetary daśās. Both tell the complete story. Transits are the trigger for events within this timeframe. Planetary daśās show your circumstances, too. The major daśā relates to the level of the soul, the Sun, and corresponds to your circumstance and resources. The 2nd level relates to the mind and the Moon; how you are feeling about what is happening; your emotional resources. It shows people you meet. If both daśās, planetary and sign-based, are on the same page, you are more likely to experience something you want. It will more likely come to you, as you want what your environment is offering you. This is the best scenario. Yet this is not always the case. You may experience something you do not want or want something that is not available.

You must view all this in context, of course, considering your age and natural stage of life. More about the natural stages of life in PART 3.

It does not matter if a daśā of the 7th sign is active at the same time the ruler of your 7th house is active if you are too young to get married. Keep every daśā in context.

Sign daśās show how your birth chart is being activated over the years. Various things in your environment present themselves. The Sun may be in the 10th house of career and status in your chart. Although this is a powerful position for gaining power in the world, you may experience a sign daśā of the 7th house of partnership. This would place the Sun in the 4th house from this house's perspective. This would likely show a focus on home, as well as relationships, despite the strength of the Sun in the 10th house of career. The birth chart keeps turning over, showing different possibilities from different perspectives.

The signs of the zodiac colour your experience of a house or area of life. Signs show *how* you experience it. The house positions show *where* you experience it. As my teacher, Pearl Finn, used to say, "We are all the signs." We all experience the signs in different areas of our life. For example, you may experience Aries in the 2nd house, Taurus in the 3rd house, Gemini in the 4th house, and so on. The rising sign or ascending sign (ascendant) on the eastern horizon is your 1st sign, or 1st house. As Indian astrology utilises whole signs most often, whatever part of that sign was rising when you were born, the whole sign is the 1st house. If you were born with Taurus rising, whether it was at the very beginning or very end of the sign, Taurus becomes your 1st house. The sign Gemini becomes your 2nd house, Cancer your 3rd house, and so on. It is the houses that make general sign-based interpretations more relevant to you.

The 1st sign/house is an important consideration, as it places everything else in context. It is an important part of who you are. Whatever the sign in your 1st house, this is how you approach life. This is how you entered the world, as seen as the sign rising on the eastern horizon. This is where the heavens met the earth, encapsulating you in physical form. It is for this reason that the 1st house represents your body, your intelligence and your sense of self, as well as your energy and vitality. It represents how you approach anything, be it a relationship, a job, whatever. The 1st house shows how you apply your intelligence to any area of your life. You do so based on your rising sign, as well as the planet that rules this sign. This planet adds another layer to interpret, based on the sign it is in. You may have Taurus rising, for example, but Venus, the planet which rules Taurus, may be in Gemini.

The houses show where in your life you experience any of the planets and signs. In any planetary daśā, it brings the planet's desires into focus. The sign-based daśās show what is being activated, what you are experiencing in your environment. It is too general to say that Venus will bring enjoyments into your life, although that is usually the case. You need to know where that will occur, with whom, and under what circumstances.

Without houses, we cannot communicate astrology in any relevant way. Unless we know someone's 1st house, interpretations are vague. Many times, they are completely wrong. The houses are the most practical tool for an astrologer, as they show where something is experienced. Each planet takes on a specific role. Without houses, the signs of the zodiac only show general themes, the 'how' of the 'what', 'how', and 'where' of astrology, the planets, signs, and houses.

It is the houses that pin things down in a chart. A planet becomes a certain thing for you. You can only know this when you know your 1st house. Once you know your 1st house, and thus, all other houses, your astrology begins to makes sense. You can see *what* (planet) is happening, *where* (house) it's happening, and *how* (sign).

Each house shows a certain planet and theme. The 1st house represents your vitality and energy. This relates to the Sun. The 12th house represents your need for a retreat from the world, represented by Saturn (see Table 1.7).

Chara daśā is a simple yet effective tool for timing events. It shows the signs that are active at any given time, beginning with your 1st house at birth. The progression for Chara daśā is in order, from one sign to the next, although the sequence of signs may be zodiacally or anti-clockwise, depending on the rising sign. Ketu reverses the direction, whatever the sign, while Saturn sends the count forward.

Table 1.7

House	Indicative of...
1	Sun
2	Jupiter
3	Mars
4	Moon
5	Jupiter
6	Mars
7	Venus
8	Saturn
9	Jupiter
10	Mercury, Sun, Saturn, & Jupiter
11	Jupiter
12	Saturn

We must ascertain which direction to count for each sign. If you were born with Aries rising, for example, count in sequential order from Aries, i.e., Aries, Taurus, Gemini, and so on. Here is the order of the count for each sign using Chara daśā:

- For Aries, Leo, Virgo, Libra, Aquarius, and Pisces, the count is 'zodiacally', i.e., clockwise.
- For Taurus, Gemini, Cancer, Scorpio, Sagittarius, and Capricorn, the count is anti-clockwise.

The duration of each sign's daśā is based on the position of the sign's ruling planet in your birth chart.

To calculate how long you experience a period of any sign, count inclusively from the sign to its ruler, and then subtract 1. This shows how many years the sign is active.

- Count clockwise when calculating the number of years for Aries, Taurus, Gemini, Libra, Scorpio, and Sagittarius.
- Count anti-clockwise for Cancer, Leo, Virgo, Capricorn, Aquarius, and Pisces.

If we take Gemini rising, we need to count from Gemini to Mercury, the sign's ruler, to find out the time the sign will be active. If Mercury were in Virgo, we would count clockwise from Gemini to Virgo. Always count inclusively. This is a 4 count, i.e., Gemini + Cancer + Leo +Virgo. We would then subtract 1 (4 − 1 = 3). Thus, the sign Gemini will be active for the first 3 years. If we take Capricorn rising, we would count anti-clockwise from Capricorn to its ruler, Saturn. If Saturn were in Aries, the count is 10, counting backwards from Capricorn to Aries. We then subtract 1. This would show the sign Capricorn is active for the first 9 years (10 − 1).

Parāśara advises subtracting another 1 when the planet is in debilitation, and to add 1 when the planet is in exaltation. However, not all astrologers do so. One reason for this is if we count from Sagittarius to Jupiter in

Capricorn we get 0. Jupiter is debilitated in Capricorn, which would subtract an extra 1. This would exclude Sagittarius from the daśās altogether. We could argue that a debilitated Jupiter would indeed show exclusion. But whether it bears out in practice is something that requires further study.

There are two signs that have two rulers: Scorpio and Aquarius. Mars and Ketu are said to co-rule Scorpio, while Saturn and Rāhu co-rule Aquarius. When calculating the length of these signs' daśās, we must decide which planet to count to. Take the planet that is with the most planets and count to that one. Take the higher degree planet if both are with the same number of planets. If one of these planets is in the sign, count to the other planet. If both are in the sign, the duration for the sign is a full 12 years. For any planet in its own sign, regardless of that sign, take the daśā to be a full 12 years.

There are sometimes exceptions to these rules, and other things to consider. It is always best to check with a reputable astrologer or astrology resource, and to double check these against another.

Whatever sign and house are active, we can read the chart from this new perspective. This will help us time events based on the house position of the sign. We could look at what is happening in your life and refer to your chart, to see if that is indeed the case.

The signs ruled by the cruel planets, Mars, Saturn, and the lunar nodes, generally bring more challenges, although this is not necessarily a bad thing. These are Aries, Scorpio, Capricorn, and Aquarius. Those ruled by kind planets, Jupiter, Venus, and Mercury, generally show an easier time, although this is not necessarily always good. These are Taurus, Gemini, Cancer, Virgo, Libra, Sagittarius, and Pisces. The results of the Sun's and Moon's signs, Leo and Cancer, depends on the position of the luminaries and their associations.

ARIES DAŚĀ

Aries is the natural 1st sign of the zodiac, which represents you and your personal desires. When triggered in a daśā, it shows your need to take the initiative and to be more proactive. It may challenge you to do so, of course. It's ruled by the cruel Mars. Sometimes, it may lead to impulsive behaviour and problems if you overdo it. But you must do something, as Mars is the planet of action. If Mars were strong in your birth chart, you are likely doing what must be done. If not, you may want to do something but feel discouraged in some way.

Mars represents the courage to overcome challenges. Unless there are contradictory indications, you are likely to rise to the challenge. This would be more pronounced if Mars were prominent in your birth chart. Delays would be very frustrating, as Saturn, the planet that represents restrictions, is debilitated in Aries. This would especially be the case if Saturn were in Aries in your birth chart. Usually, Aries shows plenty of energy to do what the house placement shows. Yet you may not always see it through. Saturn is the planet of commitment, so its placement here may express itself as acting out in some way, especially if you feel hampered in doing what you want, when you want to.

The Sun is exalted in Aries, showing its leadership capabilities. This is all about inspiring yourself and others through confident and self-assertive actions. Whatever area of your life impacted, you are likely doing something, for good or ill. Whatever the planet, it will take on Mars' action-orientated nature. Some planets prefer to it take on, while others may feel pushed.

TAURUS DAŚĀ

Taurus is the natural 2nd sign of the zodiac, which represents possessions and resources; the things that give you a sense of comfort and security. When triggered in a daśā, it is likely to bring some form of stability. This is especially so if Venus, the planet that rules the sign, were well-placed. This may include a relationship or a family/community that provides a sense of support and well-being.

Venus is the planet of love and affection. It represents the finer things in life. Taurus is one of the most practical signs. It can show a practical approach to building something beautiful. It may be through some artistic endeavour, or anything that you enjoy, including relationships. The Moon is exalted in Taurus, bringing steadiness to the mind when you feel protected and cared for. Sensual enjoyments bring you into the present moment, instilling a sense of joy.

No planets are debilitated in Taurus, unless we consider Ketu. If Ketu were here, it may indeed show a loss of comfort and security. Ketu favours a more spiritual orientation. Physical enjoyments can block this. Mars can take you out of your comfort zone if placed here. The kind planets, particularly Venus and the Moon, can bring many enjoyable experiences. Saturn may be useful for building things that give you a sense of security. Rāhu may bring an excessive want that requires more stability. Rāhu is seen as exalted in Taurus but this may be a case of too much of a good thing, along with the fear of losing out. Obsessing about something can lead to problems. Although you may have lots to enjoy, you may not feel it is enough. Whatever planet is in Taurus in your chart, the sign itself usually brings something to appreciate.

GEMINI DAŚĀ

Gemini is the natural 3rd sign of the zodiac, which represents communication and interaction. When triggered in a daśā, there may be many interactions, inquisitiveness, and learning. Mercury, the excitable planet, rules it, and is always looking for more stimulation. Gemini periods are usually more exciting for that reason. But you should be able to deal with added stimulus, especially if Mercury were strong in your chart. If not, you may feel overwhelmed.

The mind can be busy and there may be an interest in some sort of learning in a Gemini period. Yet there is also a need to choose your company carefully. You may need to limit the amount of information you expose yourself to so as not to become mentally overstimulated.

Rāhu is seen as exalted in Gemini, according to some. Yet you may express this strength as information overload and nervous exhaustion. Ketu may be debilitated here, leading to a complete rejection of rational thought. This could hamper your decision-making capabilities unless you have developed a strong intuition. Ketu in Gemini could show a deeper knowing or intelligence, one that is somatic, embodied. Whatever the planet, Gemini offers more excitement and nervous energy, more options to choose between in its daśā.

CANCER DAŚĀ

Cancer is the natural 4th sign of the zodiac, which represents the home and well-being. This brings up issues relating to family, happiness, and your mother, whether she is alive or not. When triggered in a daśā, it brings up themes of finding safety, security, and peace of mind.

The Moon, the fastest-moving heavenly body, rules the sign. This reflects your ever-changing mind and emotions, as seen in the ever-changing phases of the

Moon. You may feel swayed by moment-to-moment considerations more than other daśās. You may deal with sentimental issues around your parents, family, and home life, or any other relationship this sign represents for you. If the Moon were well-placed in your chart, this can be a time of great comfort and connection. Yet the mind and emotions are always in flux, drawing you into the ebb and flow of life and its many changing phases. Once the stormy waters of the mind are calm, it can reflect your true nature in the stillness of your being. This daśā may instil a need to find more peace precisely because of your ever-changing emotional landscape.

Jupiter exalts in Cancer, promoting the well-being of others in your family and community, alongside your own needs. Jupiter enhances the positive qualities of Cancer. It shows those who care and nurture you, too. You may feel more connected to others, and the world at large. Mars, the planet of action, is debilitated here. This can lead to feeling incapable of doing what you know you must. Feelings may override the instinct to just do it. If you feel like it, great, if not, then you may not do what you know you must. Mars here may challenge you to step outside your comfort zone. Otherwise, a Cancer daśā is a time to address how you are feeling, while doing what you can to help your mind.

LEO DAŚĀ

Leo is the natural 5th sign of the zodiac, which represents creativity, children, and fun. When triggered in a daśā, it can show the need to enjoy and express yourself more. It may be a time for self-aggrandisement and promotion. If you have any leadership skills, this may be when they come to the fore. While this could lead to many great strides forward, it may cause problems in your relationships if taken too far. The Sun rules Leo and is somewhat cruel. Yet the malevolence of the Sun is not such a bad thing. This only occurs if you become a tyrant about achieving what you want. Children, no matter how well-behaved at times, can be tyrants, too.

Embodying the Sun in a Leo daśā, you can shine your warmth and generosity on others, especially if the Sun were strong in your birth chart. If not, you may sense a lack of self-esteem and feel challenged by some authority. This is so you can find it in yourself to step up to the mark. It teaches you something important about your abilities.

While there are no planets exalted in Leo, the Sun is powerful in the sign. Saturn is opposite the sign's nature and a challenge to Leo's fun and lightness. Your sense of authority and self-determination may feel hampered if Saturn were here or impacting in some way. One positive way it could express itself is in a commitment to what you hold dear. Yet you may feel challenged to be clear. The balance between the Sun and Saturn is to realise you are but a spark from our great luminary. Whatever the planet, you realise you can shine your light to inspire others, as others reflect back your sparkle.

VIRGO DAŚĀ

Virgo is the natural 6th sign of the zodiac, which represents the elimination of debts and disease. This may express itself as a need to be of service to others. When triggered in a daśā, it can show a need to solve problems and improve your life. Mercury's earthy domain can show skills at practically overcoming any obstacles. Your task is to sort out what doesn't work and drop it for your betterment. Problems begin when you attempt to micro-manage, focusing only on what is wrong. You may not 'see the wood for the trees'.

Mercury represents the analytical mind. A daśā of Virgo may be a time to bring back a sense of order, so you can arrive at the best possible way of doing things. This would especially be the case if Mercury were strong in your birth chart. The perfectionist tendencies of the sign can create problems if you are never happy with anything less than perfect. This could lead to mental exhaustion. You may even do this for others, attempting to fix them.

Mercury rules the sign and is also exalted here, making it the best place for the rational mind and its activities. Venus is less than happy here. You may become unhappy and critical of yours, or others', imperfections. If you mitigate this tendency, you can learn to improve your life while letting go of the impossible task of attaining perfection. You may even enjoy the process of improvement.

LIBRA DAŚĀ

Libra is the natural 7th sign of the zodiac, which represents how you relate to others and find harmony in your life. When triggered in a daśā, it can bring a relationship. At the very least, it brings a need to cooperate. The 7th sign is your doorway into the world; it shows how you engage with others. Libra is all about finding more balance, between your needs and the needs of others. We can see this balance in your body, as represented by your kidneys, for example, an organ represented by Libra.

Venus, the planet of artistic expression, rules the sign. A Libra daśā may show a need to express yourself through some form of art, and a life which is, at the very least, lived in an aesthetically pleasing environment. If Venus were well-placed, you are likely to have much to enjoy. Even if it's not, there is a desire for enjoyment and some way of finding your way to it.

Saturn, the planet of limitation, is exalted here, as Libra is about being of service to others. This may involve disregarding your own needs. If Saturn were in Libra in your birth chart, you may express this through some form of service work, for example. Those who work in the service industry have Libra prominent many times. The Sun is debilitated in Libra, which is often experienced as humility, but could also be felt as feeling less than in some way. Service and compromise are better expressions. Yet it may also express itself as an overcompensation and focus on yourself. The needs of the self must take a back seat during a daśā of Libra to some degree. You may have to move into the passenger seat for a while and let someone else do the driving.

SCORPIO DAŚĀ

Scorpio is the natural 8th sign of the zodiac, which represents sexuality and transformative experiences. When triggered in a daśā, you may look for strength in less obvious places. Scorpio represents things that are hidden, buried within. Its daśā can show a need to find strength, as Mars and Ketu co-rule the sign. This combination intensifies the search for some transformative experiences. Yet it may bring up issues of insecurity as things change around you. Scorpio represents secrets, and, as the saying goes, 'you are only as sick as your secrets'. This shows a need to deal with you're trauma and heal hidden aspects that can often fester if untreated. If Mars and Ketu were well-placed, you may have no problem 'going there', doing the necessary to gain strength. If not, this is likely to challenge you to build inner reserves of strength.

There are no planets exalted in Scorpio, while the Moon is debilitated here. This may leave you open to emotional manipulation, especially if the Moon were here in your birth chart. You can find the strength you need by plummeting down through some stormy emotional waters, to your calm centre. It is through this process that you build emotional stamina. Your outer demeanour may not always express the intensity with which you delve deep, of course. Either way, you can develop the determination you need to see you through any uncertainty.

SAGITTARIUS DAŚĀ

Sagittarius is the natural 9th sign of the zodiac, which represents your beliefs and guiding principles. When triggered in a daśā, you are likely to feel guided by some tradition or other, be it formal education or a spiritual path. This can inspire you to reach higher, in your studies or through ecstatic states. Travel may be another route. If it's a relationship that is activated, it is likely to expand your horizons. Sagittarius broadens the mind, as long as Jupiter, the planet that rules it, is well-placed. If Jupiter were weak, it may challenge you to see the meaning behind what you are doing, even if you achieve a great deal. You may doubt yourself or others. Doubt is an important part of faith, of course. The challenge itself can propel you onward and upward.

This may be a time to connect to a higher source and organising principle in the universe. You may find this through some type of devotional practice. You may devote yourself to a cause or relationship, or whatever makes you feel more inspired.

Some astrologers consider Ketu exalted here. This can show more spiritual inclinations, beyond the traditional forms of organised religion. You may go against the grain on your quest. Rāhu may be debilitated here. This can lead to all kinds of nefarious routes, all of which can take you on some interesting journeys in a Sagittarius daśā.

CAPRICORN DAŚĀ

Capricorn is the natural 10th sign of the zodiac, which represents the work you do - 'for your sins'. It shows your status and reputation, how high you climb the professional ladder. When triggered in a daśā, you may find yourself more focused on work-related issues. You may be more aware of the systems that govern your life, some of which seem to control you; some of which you implement. This control is a safety rail, so you don't go too far off course.

Saturn, the planet of hard work and sacrifice, rules the sign. Mars, the planet of action, is exalted here. Together, Saturn and Mars can show a great deal of ambition and hard work, combined with a service orientated role. Saturn placed here would create an even harder work ethic, or if Saturn were well-placed elsewhere in your chart. Mars would intensify the need to achieve something. Jupiter's placement here, its sign of debilitation, can lead to a lack of ethics and morals in getting ahead. This may be fine for business dealings but may challenge you to see the meaning behind what you are doing. Earning money may feel a little hollow, despite any successes.

Capricorn represents the impulse to put your ideals to the test in a practical way. It shows a need to knuckle down and get on with what needs to be done. Yet any work would ideally have no rewards other than the reward of the work itself. Otherwise, you may find this daśā may challenge you when you don't seem to get where you want to fast enough.

AQUARIUS DAŚĀ

Aquarius is the natural 11th sign of the zodiac, which represents your friendships, networks, and ambitions. When triggered in a daśā, you may be looking at your long-term objectives more. And you may think about these in relation to bigger societal themes.

Saturn and Rāhu rule Aquarius, both of which make you think a lot about your goals. Rāhu can show an unusual approach to whatever you wish to achieve. If Rāhu were in Aquarius in your chart, this would be more pronounced. If Saturn were here, or strong elsewhere, you are more likely to do the necessary.

There are no planets exalted or debilitated in Aquarius. Saturn does its best work in this, its own sign. This can show a stoic nature, an ability to keep your eye on the bigger picture as you work towards your lofty gaols. The sign's impulse is to take a forceful role in developing and involving yourself with groups at large. This could lead to neglecting your own needs, of course, so something to be mindful of. A strong Saturn shows a strong service-orientation and work ethic, while a strong Rāhu can show egotism, but also a more innovative approach to helping others. This could set you off in all kinds of interesting directions during an Aquarius daśā.

PISCES DAŚĀ

Pisces is the natural 12th sign of the zodiac, which represents time spent away in search of liberation. When triggered in a daśā, it may incline you towards spiritual or religious journeys. Or it may incline you towards liberating yourself through other means. Drug and alcohol use could be one way you find freedom. Prayer and selfless service are others.

Jupiter, the planet of expansion and mysticism, rules the sign. This can open your mind to other possibilities and opportunities if Jupiter were well-placed. Venus is exalted in Pisces. This can express itself as an unconditional love for others, for all humanity. Pisces is symbolised by the vast oceans, representing the cosmic oceans of consciousness and a more expansive view. You may take on everyone else's thoughts and feelings in a Pisces period, so there is a need to address your own needs, including more time for self-care. As the last sign of the zodiac, this daśā may show you looking beyond the reaches of your everyday life.

PRIMARY DIRECTIONS

We categorise the houses in 4 primary directions or āyaṇa (see Table 1.8). Nārāyaṇa is one of the sign-based daśās that shows the direction your life is taking. These 4 directions are *dharma*, *artha*, *kāma* and *mokṣa*, simply translated as 'purpose', 'work', 'enjoyment', and 'release'. You express each of these four areas in the different houses of astrology.

Table 1.8

Dharma	1. Self	5. Creativity	9. Blessings
Artha	2. Wealth	6. Work	10. Career
Kāma	3. Initiatives	7. Partners	11. Friends
Mokṣa	4. Home	8. Changes	12. Losses

We can see your sense of purpose from the 1st, 5th, and 9th houses of your birth chart. These show your innate sense of self (1st), your future direction (5th) and the past guiding you (9th). We can see your sense of duty and responsibility from the 2nd, 6th, and 10th houses. These show the resources you have at your disposal (2nd) to work (6th) at reaching a higher status in life (10th). We can see your sense of enjoyment from the 3rd, 7th, and 11th houses. These show your ability to get what you want (3rd), to enjoy the company of others (7th), and create a support network of friends and associates (11th). We can see your sense of surrender and release from the 4th, 8th, and 12th houses. These show your home and peace of mind (4th), unexpected and inevitable changes (8th), and your ability to surrender (12th).

The 1st, 4th, 7th, and 10th houses cover all the directions: dharma (1st), artha (10th), kāma (7th), and mokṣa (4th). The 1st is yourself; the 4th is your home and happiness; the 7th is your relationships; and the 10th is your career and status. These areas of life get a lot of attention. They represent the 'four pillars' of your life.

The 2nd, 5th, 8th, and 11th houses represent your future, while the 3rd, 6th, 9th, and 12th houses represent your past. The 6th, 8th, and 12th houses represent painful areas of life, while the 3rd, 6th, 10th, and 11th houses represent areas you improve with time. The 6th house can be both a painful area and one which can improve with lots of effort.

HOUSE STRENGTHS

When any house is active in a sign-based daśā, it brings all kinds of experiences based on what the house suggests. Whatever it is to bring, the house in question may be helped or hindered because of various indications in your birth chart. Each house prospers when the kind planets, Jupiter, Venus, Mercury, and Moon, occupy or aspect, as long as these are unafflicted by other indications. Houses benefit from being aspected by their own ruler, the ruler of the 10th house from it, or if the ruler itself were in a powerful position.

A house and area of your life may suffer when the ruler is weakly placed or conjunct any of the cruel planets, Saturn, Mars, Rāhu, Ketu, or Sun. The Sun will burn up the significations of the planets, i.e., combustion. A house may also suffer if unaspected by its ruler or any of the kind planets. It may also suffer if linked to the 6th, 8th, or 12th ruler, or if its ruler were conjunct another planet by exact degree. It may suffer if it were in a weak state because of some other negative indications. This may be challenging house placements for planets such as Saturn in the 1st or Sun in the 12th. More on these placements later. There are many indications to calculate house strengths that are not under the scope of this book. Yet these indications will give you an idea of whether a house and area of life is challenged or not.

Even when there is a challenge, it doesn't mean you cannot rise to the challenge. If you have a lot of cruel planets influencing a house, or the planet which rules that house is weak, you may experience some challenges. This is especially likely once the sign-based daśā of that house gets triggered, or the planet that rules it is active in a daśā.

Cruel planets cause some obstruction. Kind planets bring some sort of beneficial effect. The Sun, although somewhat cruel, is well-suited to the 1st house. This house shows energy and vitality. Yet other indications may compromise the strength of the Sun. It is best to have cruel planets in the 3rd and 6th house, and kind planets in all other houses, except the 8th and 12th. Cruel planets do well in the 3rd and 6th, as these areas of life require challenge and effort to succeed. When either of these signs is active with cruel planets, you are likely to succeed through your effort and will. If you have kind planets in these houses, you are less likely to fight for what you want, which means you are less likely to get what you want. Any planet is more helpful in the 9th and 11th houses. Even cruel planets do well here.

The 6th, 8th, and 12th houses from any house show challenges you must overcome. These houses represent enemies (6th), obstacles (8th), and losses (12th). The 6th house is also an area of improvement, the others being the 3rd, 10th, and 11th. So, although the 6th may bring a challenge to deal with, you can improve your life because of it. The 8th and 12th houses represent a need for liberation. This allows you to let go of any or all the pain they sometimes represent.

The 2nd and 7th houses can bring up health issues, too. The 7th house is the 12th house from the 8th, showing the loss (12th) of longevity (8th). The 2nd house is the 12th from the 3rd of vitality. The 3rd is also the 8th from the 8th, representing longevity. The 2nd and 7th are called *māraka* in Indian astrology, meaning 'death'. This does not usually mean your literal death, of course. That only happens once, although you experience these houses many times in different daśās. Instead, there may be a sense of endings or challenges that you must overcome in their daśās.

There may be some blocks felt when cruel planets are in both the 5th and 9th houses, especially in equal numbers. The 5th and 9th represent your future direction and past experiences. Cruel planets here can hinder progress. An equal number of planets may show feeling trapped in seeing things a certain way.

When any sign is active, treat that sign as the 1st house and read the chart from this new perspective. There will always be a mixed bag of results and indications, so do not worry if you see a lot of cruel influences. Yes, there may be challenges in these areas, but you also have the kind planets somewhere to help with other indications. And even the cruel planets can help you out with a more concerted effort on your part.

BĀDHAKA

There are certain areas or houses that cause a hindrance for each sign. These are called *bādhaka*, an area that can show an 'obstacle'. These houses represent certain psychological blocks which can create actual blocks. The bādhaka houses are the 11th house for moveable signs, the 9th house for fixed signs, and the 7th house for dual signs.

For the moveable signs, Aries, Cancer, Libra, and Capricorn, this is Aquarius, Taurus, Leo and Scorpio, respectively. Aquarius is the natural 11th house from the natural first, Aries. Aquarius has this quality of creating blocks, but more so for an Aries ascendant. Fixed signs block the moveable signs, and vice versa. Capricorn blocks Taurus, Aries blocks Leo, Cancer blocks Scorpio, and Libra blocks Aquarius. Although the 9th house is the most fortunate in the chart, the house of good luck, there are more complex dynamics at play here for fixed signs. Fixed signs experience this in relation to the father, or father figures, guides, or teachers.

Movable signs block fixed signs by getting them out of their fixed nature. Often, this comes as a teacher getting them to pay attention or forcing them to change their views. Fixed signs block the moveable signs from continuing to move. The 11th house from the movable signs can show issues around groups, either friends and associates or networks. The 11th house also represents listening, so these signs can have issues with listening to what is being said, or not wishing to hear it. Aquarius blocks Aries; Taurus blocks Cancer; Leo blocks Libra; and Scorpio blocks Capricorn.

The dual signs block each other, the 7th or opposite sign. For Gemini, this is Sagittarius, and vice versa. For Virgo, it's Pisces, and vice versa. Relationships can become a hinderance for these signs and their ideals or ideas about what a relationships should be. They may have a dynamic of student-teacher, as Mercury and Jupiter rule opposite signs. Playful Gemini and exacting Virgo must balance themselves with the philosophical Sagittarius and mystical Pisces, and vice versa.

CHALLENGING HOUSE PLACEMENTS

There are certain houses in which planets do not function according to their needs (see Table 1.9). This concept is explored in *Jātaka Pārijāta*.[2] Saturn is not conducive to the 1st house of health, as Saturn is the planet of restriction. While there are other areas of your life you would prefer to restrict, I'm sure it wouldn't be your health. This not only impacts the individual's health but also the houses Saturn rules in the chart. The house positions of Capricorn and Aquarius are areas they may feel a challenge. Likewise, the Sun is not conducive to the 12th house of loss, as the Sun is all about strength and vitality, confidence, and self-esteem. If you put it in the 12th house, there can be a loss of these things, which challenges a person's sense of self. This will also impact the house position of Leo, the Sun's sign.

Jupiter does not function as well in the 3rd house, as the 3rd is all about fighting for something you want, and Jupiter represents a part of you that doesn't wish to fight. Kind planets don't function as well in the 3rd house for this reason. Jupiter is even more challenged here. It's about religion and belief, purpose, and meaning. The 3rd house is about sexuality and fun. Someone with Jupiter in the 3rd may spend too much time on frivolous fun, yet not find

---

[2] V. Subramanya Sastri, Vaidyanatha Dikshita's Jataka Parijata, vol. III (New Delhi: Ranjan Publications, 2008).

any meaning in it. They may also be timid about getting what they want or feel as if fighting for something lacks purpose.

Table 1.9

Planet	House
Saturn	1
Jupiter	3
Ketu	4
Venus	6
Mercury	7 (4)
Mars	7
Moon	8
Rāhu	9
Sun	12

Mercury in the 7th house of relationships may challenge relationships, where added stimulation, and partners, may upset others. Mercury in the 7th can show too many choices that overstimulate, too many interactions. It may challenge Mercury to be in the 4th house of education, much like trying to get a young child to sit and study.

It challenges Venus to be in the 6th house of work and service, as Venus is about enjoyment and relationships. The 6th is about the drudgery of everyday life. Venus in the 6th may not feel like working for things that should come easy. It can show a lack of appreciation or feeling appreciated. Venus in the 6th may show someone looking for reasons to be happy, which can express itself as finding many reasons not to be. It challenges Mars to be in the 7th house of relationships, as Mars is not a part of your being that likes to compromise. Mars is about getting what you want – when you want it. This can challenge relationships. This placement can spoil relationships, unless mitigated by other factors in the chart.

It challenges the Moon to be in the 8th house of change and uncertainty. The Moon represents a need for safety and stability. There are always inevitable changes the mind must deal with. If one adds to the uncertainty by catastrophic thinking and negative expectations, it only adds to the problem. Rāhu challenges the 9th house, which relates to traditional knowledge and following a well-worn path. Rāhu's nature is absolutely opposite that of the 9th house, preferring instead to shake things up, to find new ways of thinking. This can lead to being led astray, either by others or by your own questioning of traditional beliefs.

While *Jātaka Pārijāta* does not include Ketu in the list, some astrologers are of the opinion that Ketu is least conducive to the 4th house. This may show Ketu challenging home life and the relationship with the mother. This places Rāhu in the opposite 10th house, showing someone seeking to promote themselves in the world, which could lead to neglecting family life.

While any of these planetary placements may challenge the significations of the planet and areas of life, there are usually some mitigating factors. Jupiter's aspect is said to help, as long as it is not itself involved, as is the strength and position of the planet in question. If the planet is strong due to Day or Night birth, it may mitigate the situation. Sun, Venus, and Jupiter are strong for a Day birth, while Moon, Mars, Saturn, and the lunar nodes are strong for Night births. Mercury is said to be strong for both Day and Night births according to Parāśara. This has been translated by some to mean the twilight hours.

DIRECTIONAL STRENGTH

Sun and Mars are conducive to the 10th house, the most prominent house. The 10th is about career and recognition. Both Sun and Mars represent the ego, so they both suit this prominent part of life. Sun represents a more mature expression. A powerful and prominent Sun can show someone gaining recognition with ease. Mars is a more immature expression, a need to prove oneself.

Moon and Venus are conducive to the 4th house, as it relates to home life and home comforts. Both Moon and Venus here can show more of these comforts. The learned planets, Mercury and Jupiter are more conducive to the 1st house of intelligence. They can both express themselves intelligently here. Mercury represents the intellect; Jupiter, an 'inner intelligence'. Saturn is conducive to the 7th, as it represents responsibility in dealing with others. Saturn is the planet of service, of selfless actions. This is more conducive to the 7th house of others, opposite the 1st house of self.

Table 1.10

Planet	Best Placement
Sun, Mars	10th House
Moon, Venus	4th House
Mercury, Jupiter	1st House
Saturn	7th House

MAHĀPURUṢA

Planets are at their best in their own or exalted signs when in an angle; houses 1, 4, 7, or 10. This is a sign of a "great soul", or *Mahāpuruṣa*. This shows someone positively expressing the 5 elements. Each of the 5 elements are represented by one of the 5 visible planets, Saturn, Jupiter, Mars, Venus, and Mercury.

Saturn rules the element of air. It is strongest in its own signs, Capricorn and Aquarius, while exalted in Libra. When in an angle in any of these signs, the air element is strong. The person can express a strong, stoic nature. They are likely more committed, responsible, hard-working, and persevering. This seems to contradict an earlier list that shows Saturn in the 1st as challenging. For the significations of the 1st house, i.e., health, this is true. They don't cancel each other out. Someone with Saturn in the 1st in any of these signs is likely to manage the challenges. The element of air dries things up, represented by the aging process. The passing of time challenges the body. Yet the positive expression of air is an ability to face one's fears and find maturity. Facing one's fear of death means achieving a great deal while alive.

Jupiter rules the element of space. It is strong in its own signs, Sagittarius and Pisces, while exalted in Cancer. This may show an ability to 'hold space' in any of these signs, in an angle. Although Jupiter has directional strength in the 1st, the 7th can show deep connections and care for others, especially if Jupiter were exalted in Cancer. This may express itself in roles such as teaching or community building.

Mars rules the element of fire. It is strong in its own signs, Aries and Scorpio, while exalted in Capricorn. This may show great will power in any of these signs, in an angle. Though fire can be a destructive element, they may channel it constructively. The 7th is Mars' least conducive house position in another way. This may show up as a personal power that can challenge their personal relationships. Yet the person may have great courage to face life's challenges and may use this to protect others as well.

Venus rules the element of water. It is strong in its own signs, Taurus and Libra, while exalted in Pisces. This can show a great capacity to enjoy life's pleasures when in these signs, in an angle. It may show more of these things are available to enjoy. The water element's strength can show a sense of support, either through relationships or in life in general. The person may easily find people and things to support their sense that all is well.

Mercury rules the element of earth. It is strong in its own signs, Gemini and Virgo, while exalted in Virgo. The strength of the earth element can show a lot of practical application. This may be through great learning and business acumen, when in any of these signs, in an angle. It may show someone who can create a business, for example, or one who is proficient in anything they do.

DAŚĀS OF HOUSES

1ˢᵀ HOUSE – DHARMA

Keywords: head (brain), body, appearance, temperament, constitution, strength, and confidence.

The 1ˢᵗ house represents you in the broadest sense, but also in a more accurate way, as it shows your body. The sign rising on the eastern horizon encapsulated you in physical form, where the heavens met the earth. The word, *lagna*, meaning 'marriage', is used to describe your rising or ascending sign in Vedic astrology. If you were to take any one sign to show who you are, it would be the 1ˢᵗ. Yet you can look at this from any perspective, from the physical (ascendant), from the Moon (mental-emotional), or Sun (soul), whatever you wish to observe.

The 1ˢᵗ house is indicative of the Sun and Aries. This represents your sense of self, your energy levels, and your confidence. It gives you a sense of direction. It shows your outlook on life and strength of your chart. The strength of your ruling planet, the planet that rules this sign, is paramount. Any planets placed in your 1ˢᵗ house will colour your chart in a more obvious way.

If you have a strong 1ˢᵗ house and ruling planet, you can overcome any other adversity in the chart. If you have a weak 1ˢᵗ house, or 1ˢᵗ house ruler, even the smallest challenge can bring you down. This is something to consider when you look at the daśā of the 1st house, a daśā that begins your life. You began with your body. How you begin has a lot to say about how you continue through your life. But this could either catapult you to greater things or weigh you down, depending. Your body is more intelligent than you may realise. It reacts to situations as they arise, without having to think about it. We see how you use your body and intelligence in your 1st daśā.

Everything you approach in life, whether a relationship or the work you do, is with this in mind. This is how you operate in the world. This is how you apply your intelligence in any situation. The position of your ruling planet, by sign and house position, shows how you react to situations as they arise (rising sign). It shows what you spend your energy on, where your focus lies.

A major daśā of the 1st house may come around again later in life. This is a time for a recalibration of yourself, including your body and intelligence. This may be a period you recall your youth and relive your early years in your latter stage of life. 1st house sub-daśās come around often, recalibrating you all along your path.

2ND HOUSE – ARTHA

Keywords: family, food, finances, face (the 4 'f's), throat, speech, vision (literal vision and an inner vision), values, self-worth, and early childhood.

The 2nd house is that of resources; the things in life which sustain you. Your values sustain you as much as the food you eat sustains your body or the wealth you accumulate. The 2nd house represents your early childhood. This instilled in you a set of beliefs and values that continue to sustain you throughout life. You may rebel against these, but they set the stage for your growth all the same. The values your family instilled set you on a journey to figure out what you value as an individual. The 2nd house represents what is important to you. It is also about being part of a family or community – a community that has its own set of values. It shows whether you felt valued as part of the group and, thus, how you value yourself. The 2nd house is indicative of Jupiter and Taurus. These represent wealth and plenty. This may include food and finances, as well as things you value beyond tangible things.

We are all born into a family and community. Whether they clothed and fed you properly can be seen from your 2nd house. You develop an appreciation for the finer things in life at this stage, and a healthy sense of self-worth. Any block to this, any planets showing obstacles here, will show up in a lack of worth. This will probably show up in less accumulated wealth, or an overcompensation and obsession with money. The more you value yourself, the more money you can earn. But also, the more you value yourself, the less important material wealth is beyond the basics.

The 2nd house represents food. If you value yourself, you will eat foods that nourish you. If there are blocks to this, you can see problems with food and sustenance. Your parents may have taught you to value monetary wealth growing up, while each family has their own set of values. How you speak your truth, about what you value, says a lot about who you are. Speech and vision are other important indications of the 2nd house.

All these issues will be more prominent when you experience a 2nd house daśā or sub-daśā. Depending on the order you experience the signs, a major daśā of the 2nd may come very early in your life, or much later. Either way, self-worth and what you value are paramount. If this is experienced later on, it may be a period of recounting all your family taught you early on. You may look at the things that sustained you throughout life, looking beyond the tangible things you have accumulated to more profound beliefs and values at a more advanced age.

3RD HOUSE – KĀMA

Keywords: siblings, neighbours, courage, desire, communication, short journeys, neck, shoulders, arms, and hands.

The 3rd house represents your self-interests, as well as your interactions with others. This can show you fighting over resources with others, including your siblings, another signification of the 3rd. Whatever you have accumulated in the 2nd house, you fight for it in the 3rd. That's my stuff! Siblings (or neighbours) teach you how to fight for your share early on. Sometimes, siblings play nice, but other times there is a fight for survival. The 3rd house represents the armour you put on, so it is not your true self, in a way. It is a mask you wear, a shell you don so you can brave the world. Whenever you engage with others or state your case and fight for what is yours, you are engaging with the 3rd house.

The 3rd house is indicative of Mars and Gemini. This shows your ability to stand up for yourself, to fight your corner and communicate with confidence. You learn this valuable lesson by engaging with your siblings and neighbours when you are young. You learn this lesson at other times, especially once a daśā or sub-daśā of the 3rd house is active.

The 3rd house represents your ego, a selfish area of the chart. But we all need a healthy ego to function in the world, to get what we want. If you recall how you fought and played with your siblings and neighbours, this will tell you a lot about how you go for what you want. The 3rd house represents all kinds of communication, including listening. The 2nd house shows speech, while the 3rd house is all kinds of communication. This includes writing and emailing.

The sign Gemini and the 3rd house represent your sexual desires. We can include the arts here as well. Desires keep you moving about, which is another manifestation of the 3rd house, i.e., short journeys. The 3rd house is all that coming and going you do in your day-to-day life. It represents the mind chatter constantly going on in your head. The 3rd house represents choices because of the constant interaction with the world around you. It represents your neck, arms, and hands. This gives you the ability to turn your head from side to side to look for more choices, while your hands are for grabbing what you want.

When you communicate with others, you may defend or offend others based on your set of values (2nd house). The 3rd house is as a minor malefic house, so it can sometimes create problems with others. This can show challenges in relationships in its daśā, as it is more about what *you* want. How all these dynamics played out in childhood says a lot about how you experience a daśā of the 3rd house later in life.

All of this would depend on what is going on in your 3rd house. You may 'play dirty' to get what you want. This would depend on whether the 3rd house has cruel or kind planets in it or influencing. Cruel planets are well-placed in this house; kind planets can show a timid individual who rolls over at the first sign of a fight.

Either way, the 3rd house challenges you to get clear about what you want and how to ask for it. You will probably get better at this as you get older.

4ᵀᴴ HOUSE – MOKṢA

Keywords: home, comforts, vehicles, mother, security, education, happiness, the heart, and lungs.

The 4th house represents your happiness and security, the things in life which give you a sense of peace of mind and safety. After having fought for what you want in the 3rd house, you develop a sense of safety and belonging. You nest in your home and with your comforts surrounding you, the things in life which reflect your core being, your deepest heart. If the journey has gone well so far, you have a deep sense of belonging.

The 4th house is indicative of the Moon and the sign Cancer. These show the need for comforts, happiness, and a safe home environment. The 4th house is your bedrock, your base, the lowest house underneath you in the zodiac when you were born. You can see this in your mother, embracing you, the care from which you can grow and develop. Of course, it is not everyone who has a cheerful story to tell about their relationship with their mother. The story of an unhappy childhood and home environment is common, found in the 4th house. Other things that are your bedrock include formal education. If there are any impediments to the 4th house, this may represent blocks to your studies.

Look at the 4th house ruling planet and its placement to see the dynamics. This shows how secure you felt at home, as well as how you go about finding happiness later in life. Wherever the planet ruling this house, it will show how you go about finding happiness, and what makes you happy.

The 4th house shows your private life, where you can be yourself, regardless of the bricks and mortar house, although this is also relevant. Your 4th house ruler may be in the 10th house of work, so you may find happiness at work. If you feel safe, you are more able to venture out, to leave your mark in the world. The saying, 'a tree can only grow as tall as its roots are deep', reflects this sentiment. This includes a good education to help you can reach great heights in your chosen profession.

When the home environment is not a happy one, you may attempt to make a success of your profession. You may also plant new roots and develop a firm base later in life if it did not grant this early on. We can see these triggers in a major daśā of the 4th house, either early in life or much later. Either way, the lessons of the home come back during sub-daśās of the 4th house throughout life.

5TH HOUSE – DHARMA

Keywords: children, creativity, romance, investments, intelligence, heart and solar plexus, including the stomach, liver, gallbladder, pancreas, and spleen.

The 5th house sees you reaching out to others once you have developed a sense of self and happiness, a sense of what would make you happy. Of course, if you are not happy, then you may seek that in others. The 5th house is your children, your lovers, or whatever you love. It is creative and future orientated. It shows you leaving your nest and seeking something to enjoy. You want that thing, more than anything. And you will do anything for it. You will even disturb your mental equilibrium for it! You have no choice but to share your deepest longings, to go on a journey to find what will set you alight.

The 5th house is indicative of Jupiter and the sign Leo. It shows your blessings, the past life credit you have accumulated from a Vedic philosophical perspective. This comes as blessings such as children, abundance of all kinds, creativity, and love.

The 5th has some things in common with the 4th. Both rule education and the heart. The 4th is formal education, while the 5th shows how you apply your intelligence and further your studies. Life is a process of creation. Having children is one very obvious expression. But you may have a sense of living life creatively, with no obvious tangible things to point to, such as children. The 5th house shows how you progress from your home environment and early education, to think creatively for yourself. It shows how you apply your intelligence.

The 5th, like the previous houses, is very personal. You hold it close to your chest. It shows the early stages of love, the romantic phase of a relationship. This has some obvious connotations. If you are experiencing a major or sub-daśā of the 5th house, you will probably think about these relationships. Having a partner and children may be at the forefront. If not, you may think about your followers and/or students, even if it is just your online following.

The 5th house reflects your sense of self and purpose, what you have to contribute. We all want to express our unique gifts to the world, whatever they may be. The more grounded in the 4th house you are, the safer you feel, and the more you can express your unique gifts with others. The more you can express love, the easier it is to find a lover.

The 5th house is where you want some fun. It represents speculation of all kinds, the life you would like to create. These issues will be paramount in a 5th house major or sub-daśā.

6ᵀᴴ HOUSE – ARTHA

Keywords: self-inflicted problems and health issues, accidents, addictions, weaknesses and vices, enemies, work and daily routines, competition, obstacles, and the intestines.

The 6th house is an area you must improve. Unlike the 3rd house, which is more about fighting for your share, the 6th house becomes a bigger fight for something or someone you love. It represents your day-to-day work. This can create problems because others are usually involved, including co-workers. This may include others who would challenge you. Love may live in the 5th house, with hate in the 6th. One can become the other, as you move from the 5th to the 6th. Or you may move through the house in reverse order, from the challenges of the 6th to more love in the 5th. Either way, you must face your demons in a 6th house daśā. You cannot point the finger and expect to resolve anything at the 6th house stage. It's an inside job. You must tackle these issues within yourself.

The 6th house is indicative of Mars, Saturn, and the sign Virgo. These show problems, but also what you need to overcome them. There is a need to improve your life. It shows problems you create by not dealing with your weaknesses, or overdoing it, creating more problems. It shows any friction with others. You may see everyone and everything as something you must overcome. Your daily habits, including diet and routines, may show problems you create for yourself. The illnesses of the 6th house are usually acute and resolved with some lifestyle hacks.

Planets placed in this house will show how you are dealing with your weaknesses, and if you have any vices or addictions. The 6th shows perceived enemies, people who seem hostile towards you. This may include co-workers and or employees, or both. If you recall the people you argue with, you will see a lot of those coming from work environments. Family can also show this, as the 6th is the 3rd from the 4th. This shows the efforts required at home, the cleaning and chores required to keep the peace.

Workplace issues can become harder to deal with at the stage of the 6th house. You have no choice but to deal with the problems if you would like to improve your life. Either way, the 6th house is about facing down your inner demons.

The work of the 6th house can be a bit of a chore. The 5th house shows what you love to do, while the 6th house shows your willingness to work for it. You may wish to have a child but must change your child's nappies.

The 5th house represents your stomach. While you may have no problem eating what you love to eat, the 6th house shows how well you can digest it. The same goes for any kinds of experiences. If you cannot assimilate an experience, it can show up as a problem later – when the 6th house is active. These undigested experiences may become a problem during its daśā. An enemy points to your own inner demons, the things you haven't fully dealt with. So you may feel challenged at this stage. But it is an opportunity to overcome these issues. If you work on these, you can transform the 6th house from a knee jerk reaction to something altogether more rewarding. You develop 'the strengths of your weaknesses'.

The position of the 6th house ruling planet will show the potential for problems. These are all self-made, although you may not always acknowledge this. This could even result in accidents if you are not conscious of the needs. The 6th house and ruling planet shows where you are more prone to accidents. So it is best to be mindful of impulsive behaviour in its daśā.

The 6th house is both the problem *and* the solution. While this can be a lot more challenging than the 3rd house, the challenges themselves can give you enough impetus to make improvements. If you eat a certain diet and observe a certain routine, despite the allure of your weaknesses, you can improve your life. The 6th house is all about your vices, but it is also the house of your psychic powers or *siddhis* according to Vedic astrology.

There are 6 weaknesses of the mind according to Vedic thought – 6 weaknesses shown by the 6th house – mapping out the challenges you face because of an attachment to a false sense of self. These are greed, arrogance, anger, lust, envy, and delusion. You have your own weaknesses, as seen in planets ruling or aspecting the 6th house in your birth chart. The 6 weaknesses can be associated with planets. Rāhu can be seen to represent greed; Saturn and Sun can be seen to represent arrogance, depending on their strength and position; Mars can be seen to represent anger; Venus, lust; and Mercury, envy. Ketu removes the delusion of a false sense of self.

The planets that influence the 6th house show the weaknesses you must overcome. Rāhu in your 6th house may show greed is the problem. It is the greed that drives one to create excesses, and the greed which eventually leads to losses. Likewise, Saturn connected to the 6th house can show you have the strength of your weaknesses.

Saturn teaches humility through some health issues or challenges. This fuels important change. Saturn is well-placed in the 6th house for this reason. In the same way, each weakness regarding each planet is a way to better yourself through the challenges of the planet.

7ᵀᴴ HOUSE – KĀMA

Keywords: marriage, partners (romantic or business), contracts, passions, desires, pleasures, and the pelvic region.

The 7th house represents your commitment to someone, or something. It represents a stage of being responsible for your life and how you engage with others. The 7th is your doorway into the world and where you must compromise. This is the stage you give up your fighting, i.e., the 6th house. This is the case if you experience the daśās in direct order. When in reverse, it may bring up issues with others after a period of more compromise in the 7th house.

Like the 1st and 4th houses, the 7th anchors you to the world around you, in the present, through your relationships. This is a search for happiness, through others, and in the world of things. While you can also get lost in the other, or in things, it can also balance your tendency to focus too much on yourself.

The 7th house is indicative of Venus and the sign Libra. This is where you form relationships, either with someone or some entity, as in a contractual agreement. Most often, we can see this represents the contract of marriage, where you make an important bond. This house is desirous, as it is opposite your 1st house of self. Whatever you are looking at, you probably want, of course. Why else would you be looking at it? All planets have a direct sight to the house opposite and desire that thing. All signs of the zodiac desire its opposite for balance. More about aspects later.

Aries, for example, the sign of the self, desires another, reflected in Libra. These are the natural 1st and 7th signs of the zodiac. We also see business agreements in the 7th house, so you better be aware of who you are getting into bed with in business, too.

The 7th house is a 'killer' house, and we can understand this when we see longevity in the 8th house. The 7th is the 12th (loss) from the 8th (longevity), which could show a drain on one's longevity. And who drains your longevity more than anyone else? Your partner, of course. But anyone else can drain your energy. Best to find someone you can devote yourself to and give willingly.

The 7th house shows what or who attracts you, and this can be seen in every 7th house from any sign. The stable Taurus desires the hidden depths of Scorpio, even if they don't admit to it. The insecure Scorpio desires the stability of Taurus. Intellectual Gemini desires the higher knowledge of Sagittarius. The instinctual and sensitive Cancer desires the detachment of Capricorn.

If you are experiencing a 7th house major daśā, it is likely you are either beginning a new relationship or are committing more to one. This may occur in a sub-daśā of the 7th, but we should consider this along with other indications. Even if you are not getting into a relationship, you are likely dealing more with others.

8TH HOUSE – MOKṢA

Keywords: death, change, longevity, obstacles, partner's or other people's money and values, inheritance, secrets, research, mysticism, the genitals, and anus.

The 8th house shows the messy part of being in a relationship. This brings with it vulnerability, as other people have their own agenda, separate to yours. You are not in control of this agenda and must face the fact that you cannot predict the outcome. You are likely to resist the inevitable change that must occur. The 8th house shows changes and obstacles, unexpected events you hadn't planned for but must accept.

The 8th house is indicative of Saturn and the sign Scorpio. This represents some of the more challenging aspects of life. The most challenging and ultimate change is that of our death. Yet there are many deaths you experience in life as you reinvent yourself over and over. The 8th house represents longevity. Every moment is dying to create the next, so this house shows where you must change so you can continue living and thriving.

It is easy to get fixated on the things that are passing and struggle with the obstacles of the 8th house. But there is also great depth to this house, including research and mysticism. Any time you are investigating something beyond the surface level, you are activating the 8th house. This would include astrology. So, you are activating the 8th house by reading this book!

The 8th house is the 2nd from the 7th, that which feeds the partner, including the partner's family, wealth and values. Any blocks here would show challenges in dealing with the in-laws. The 8th house also shows inheritance, or any wealth from others that you do not earn yourself. You accumulate these earnings in the opposite 2nd house, which shows your own values, and your valuables. The 8th house shows other people's valuables, which is another reason this house can be challenging. An example of this is dividing up deceased family members' estates.

The 8th house is a hidden area of life. It represents the genitals and anus. It holds your secrets and is full of intrigue. This is the only area of our body we don't expose when in public. The 8th house shows any scandals and controversy. It is the car crash of the zodiac you cannot help but slow down to see, or the sex scandal you pore over in the news.

If this house gets triggered in a major or sub-daśā, you are likely dealing with any or all of the above. How you deal with these secrets and uncertainties is another matter. But with awareness, you can channel the more positive aspects and go deeper than the surface level. It may be uncomfortable, but facing your fears leaves you feeling more powerful than if you had stayed in your comfort zone.

9TH HOUSE – DHARMA

Keywords: father, teachers, tradition, religion, philosophy, faith, beliefs, principles, higher mind, knowledge, good luck, opportunity, growth, long-distance travel, adventure, the hips, and thighs.

Once you have gone through the changes of the 8th house, you develop a philosophy to live by. This gives your life meaning and purpose. If you experience the signs in reverse, this may express itself as first finding some meaningful pursuit. A daśā of the 9th house daśā brings a sense of what your purpose in life is. By being tested in the 8th, you develop a strong faith in the 9th. Or perhaps it is action taken in the 10th house (the next house) that helps you find your purpose. The 9th house gives you a sense you were born with a unique purpose that gives your life meaning, when you do that thing you were born to do. You may connect with that purpose through a lineage or a teaching in a 9th house daśā. You may meet a teacher who has journeyed there before you.

The 9th house is indicative of Jupiter and Sagittarius, where you expand your horizons, either through travel or study. The father is the first teacher, and a signification of the 9th house according to Vedic astrology. Any blocks to the 9th can show problems with gaining a higher knowledge and awareness, as well as problems with your father. Having access to higher knowledge gives you a sense of order. With order comes growth. When there is disorder, there is decay.

The 9th house shows the tradition or teaching you follow. It shows the beliefs you hold. The 9th house will show if you move away from what is traditional and take on other beliefs and traditions.

The 9th expands your horizons. Yet you don't have to leave home. You may experience this through some form of higher education or higher learning if travel is not an option. The 9th and its ruler will give insights into what you like to study, as well as where you like to travel. This area of life brings good luck and a sense of purpose. All these indications will be important in a daśā of the 9th house.

Being a 'trinal' house, like the 1st and 5th, there is a sense of purpose in your life. Unlike the future projections of the 5th, the 9th house represents the past, the traditions and beliefs you take with you into the future. These have a direct impact on your future, and future generations, as you pass on your beliefs.

10TH HOUSE – ARTHA

Keywords: career, profession, boss, social status, recognition, reputation, the back, and knees (the parts of the body that have to work hard).

The 10th house shows the work that is your unique purpose in life, leading on from the 9th house, or from the 11th house of having visualised a goal. The 10th is the work, apart from the everyday chores of the 6th, that thing you do that no one else can do, or in the way you do it. And because you have journeyed far and been through so much to achieve it, you sometimes get recognised for this work. Many times, you get on with it whether acknowledged for it or not. This is the highest you will climb before you must make your descent and return. Your position in life is one of your anchors. Along with the 1st, 4th, and 7th houses, the self, home, and relationship, this gives you a sense of being present in your life.

The 10th house is indicative of Mercury, the Sun, Saturn, and Jupiter, as well as the sign Capricorn. Why so many planets? Well, we place a lot of emphasis on our status and position in life and this requires many supports and skills. Mercury is the primary indicator for a career because it represents skills. Without skills you cannot work, although you may get a job if the Sun indicates such. The Sun represents your resources, given to you by others in power, such as a boss or government. Saturn represents the work itself, your ability to work hard. Jupiter represents opportunities.

There may be a problem gaining employment if any of these is lacking. You may have many skills, but unless you have support and opportunity, you are unlikely to be successful. Even then, if you are not willing to put in the work, you are not likely to be successful.

The 10th house is the highest house in the chart, the place above your head when you were born. It represents your public life and how high in life you will reach. Although it represents work and career, it may not always represent paid work, as in someone not having to work; instead, volunteering. Either way, the 10th house is the most visible part of the chart and your life.

The 10th house represents the actions required to fulfil your destiny, your highest potential. This helps you overcome your inherited weaknesses, as seen in the 8th house. The 10th house is the 3rd from the 8th, where your inherited problems lie. By making more effort (3rd), you can overcome these.

Work will be a big part of your life during a major or sub-daśā of the 10th house. Planets here or influencing can either help or hinder your career.

11TH HOUSE – KĀMA

Keywords: gains, income, rewards, older siblings, friends, associates, associations, groups, ambitions, aspirations, legs, and ankles.

The 11th house shows the rewards for the work you do in the 10th house. The more friends and associates you have, an important part of this house, the more people you have to impress, of course. But the more you gain, too. This is very much a house of give and take, within a larger context. While you may lose a sense of your own unique purpose to please the group, you can blend with the crowd more at the 11th house stage. And when you can combine your purpose with others, you can move mountains.

The 11th house is indicative of Jupiter and the sign Aquarius. This shows your interaction with groups of people and how you share your ideas. It shows how you get along with others in society and in your community, and whether a common vision and worldview inspire you.

This house shows the gains because of the work you do, as the 11th house is the second from the 10th, representing financial gains from your career. It also represents the support from your social network. If you have a group of people you can connect with, it is one of the greatest supports, giving you the support you need in finding paid work. And getting paid for the work you do supports your ongoing work. The 11th house represents all kinds of gains, be it social prestige or the ability to give back after you have been fortunate in your career.

The 11th shows how big you can dream and how far you can reach, with the help of a social network and friends. This house represents your legs which support you in life, the calves, shins, and ankles that are either built on solid foundations or made of sand. If there are any problems in this area of life, if you don't feel supported, you may not dream as big.

The 11ᵗʰ house is opposite the 5ᵗʰ house, where you love something very dear to you. The 11ᵗʰ represents your desire to share your gifts and the things you love with your community. Yet the 11ᵗʰ is the 6ᵗʰ from the 6ᵗʰ. This can show even more complex problems. The 11ᵗʰ is *bādhaka*, a 'block', 'hinderance', and 'troublemaker'. This can show psychological blocks, as well as bigger issues related to society. You may disown and project these problems onto others. As the natural 11ᵗʰ house, Aquarius is the natural blocker, ruled by Rāhu, the biggest psychological block. Its connection to the 11ᵗʰ house of gains, although promising a great deal, can actually create the most problems. Be careful what you wish for!

The 11ᵗʰ (along with the 3ʳᵈ) relates to your ability to listen. If you are aware of any problems, you will work harder at improving the situation. You may have to listen to others who can see your problems more objectively. Like the 3ʳᵈ, 6ᵗʰ, and 10ᵗʰ houses, the 11ᵗʰ house improves with time and effort. You usually get better at listening to others with time. And you gain much by doing so.

All these issues and complexities, as well as the rewards, are up for grabs in a daśā of the 11ᵗʰ house. As long as there are not too many hinderances, you can achieve a great deal. Even with the biggest block that is Rāhu involved, you can achieve so much. It's just you may not feel satisfied with whatever you do. Usually, the 11ᵗʰ house is time to gain something in life, in whatever form that comes in.

Think of the group therapy session which helps you see your problems within a larger framework. Even without attending groups, you may see the benefit of having others to bounce ideas off. Others help you see the bigger picture. You can align with universal themes and trends. When you align with the right people, those who have the right skill sets to help, you can improve your life and the lives of others.

12ᵀᴴ HOUSE – MOKṢA

Keywords: retreat, meditation, spirituality, bed pleasures, secret enemies (including the subconscious), long-distance travel, foreign residency, debts, losses, confinement, expenditure, and the feet.

The 12th house is where you must pay it all back, let it all go, no matter how much you have gained along your journey. Sometimes, the 12th house is actually the 2nd daśā experienced early in life. This occurs if your count goes in reverse. In that case, you may experience loss early in life, either directly or indirectly. Yet this can add a richness to your life that would not have been felt otherwise.

If you experience this daśā towards the end of your life, there is a need to let it all go at a later stage. Whatever knowledge, status, or relationships you have established, you must surrender it all. You must allow yourself to dissolve back into a state of being. By doing so, you are more open and ready for another round of the zodiac, either in this life or the next.

You begin again at the 1st, as you awake each morning, having slept in the 12th house. You awake to your unique nature, back into your body, which is now more imbued with a sense of presence. Each time you take on the journey, you have a deeper sense of self. From a state of dissolution, you return to your body.

Past, present, and future all combine in moments of clarity and unity in the 12th house. You may experience this through spiritual practices and meditation. Or you may experience it through substances that transport you somewhere else. You drop your individuated perspective, in favour of a universal one.

The 12th house is indicative of Saturn and the sign Pisces. It is where you come full circle, where you end something in your life. The 12th house represents the need to give of yourself. This includes spending money, time, and energy. If you have a prominent 12th house, you may be very giving, but you may be a spendthrift. This is something to be mindful of in a daśā of the 12th house. The 12th and last house of the zodiac shows your self-undoing. It can also show hidden enemies, bringing them out into the open in its daśā.

The 12th represents bed pleasures, i.e., sex and sleep. It represents the 'little death' experienced in orgasm. It shows the loss of your everyday self, like when you are in a foreign land. You may feel you can be somebody else when you are away from your usual routines. The 12th house is opposite the 6th house of everyday problems. It shows your desire to let things be.

If you drift into the 12th house too much, you can see all kinds of problems, either using spiritual practices or substances to avoid reality. You may end up in either an ashram or a hospital, depending on what you delve into. The 12th house is about letting go of your worldly concerns, your ability to surrender to the Divine. This takes you back into unity with all that is. This space of surrender is an alive, fertile ground from which to start again.

If this daśā occurs early in life, you may feel you have not found your feet until after this daśā has passed. But when you do, you have a firmer footing in something other than the more obvious world of things.

Outer rim

      Inner joy

         Time elapsed

           Open

              Fixed

Becoming more   All

          Am I?

        I am

PART 2: PATTERNS

K Ā R M I K   P A T T E R N S

Karma represents what you have brought into this life from previous lives. The word *karma* means 'action'. You are always acting. Your actions always have an impact. Not doing something is itself the act of not doing. You can sometimes see the results of actions in what you experience immediately following an action. Mostly, you do not recall all of your past in this life, let alone past lives. You do not see the correlations – the results of previous lives' actions that are bearing fruit now. Your horoscope is a map to help you navigate these. It is a map of the results of actions that are bearing fruit in this lifetime.

Every thought, word, and action has consequence. You weave a tangled web as you go. Whatever you think, say, or do impacts your future self. Your current actions will at some point bear fruit, as seen in your future daśās. The daśās you are experiencing now are because of what you did in the past. You are always reacting to current daśās, and likely recreating similar patterns. You may not change certain patterns, but you can observe how your perceptions are changing with the help of astrology. The more conscious you become of your patterns, the more opportunity you have to view it differently. By doing so, you change your relationship to what is happening, even if you cannot change what is.

While the philosophical framework of Indian astrology includes the belief in reincarnation, you need not believe it to see your birth chart as a ripening of the past. If you look at any pattern in your life, or those of family members, you will see familiar patterns. If you ponder it long enough, you come to realise that whatever you experience is a pattern you have woven on some level. From a Vedic philosophical perspective, your birth chart is a pattern your soul has woven over many lifetimes. You decide your life experience on some level, in that your soul decided what it wanted to experience this time around. This is reflected in the map of the heavens at the time of your birth. This is your kārmik blueprint.

This is a more mature expression of your karma, beyond all the 'you get what you deserve' notions. It's your soul that keeps account of your previous actions, anyway. You are not making the choice consciously. Your soul has already decided what it wishes to experience. You could probably do with a little coaxing.

You can work with your map by first becoming more conscious of it. The less conscious you are of your blueprint, the less influence you have on it–and the more influence it has on you. The less aware you are of something, the more of a hold it has.

Let us take the nodes of the Moon as an example. These patterns are deeply ingrained and often harder to see. This makes them more impactful, yet less obvious why. With the help of astrology, you may see the tendency for you to fall back on patterns of the past, reflected in Ketu, and an impulsive rush to develop new ones with Rāhu. The positions and patterns formed by Rāhu and Ketu are areas where you are likely to experience some level of unconscious behaviour. The more conscious you can make these patterns, the more likely you can impact the outcome. At the very least, you can change your perspective.

Every planetary configuration is a pattern, and you can view every pattern from different vantage points. This is what makes astrology so useful. If you are having difficulty accepting something, you can view it from another angle until you can accept and evolve beyond it.

Some may wish to proclaim, "I create my reality", and deny their true nature, as if the past no longer has a hold on them. And while you always move forward, you must question if you have moved on from something you may not have fully acknowledged and integrated. Astrology is not merely a bunch of labels that would pigeonhole you to create self-fulfilling prophecies; rather, it is a freedom to be yourself while transcending certain things you must.

One area some struggle with in particular is Saturn's placement. Saturn can show feeling 'less than' in some area of your life. Sometimes, you may wish to avoid the issues altogether. Saturn represents the thoughts, words, and actions from your past that were not helpful to others. Its placement shows where you have taken and must pay back. You may experience this as a feeling of losing out when Saturn daśās come around. If you are willing to pay back, it becomes easier to let go of whatever it is. You are unlikely to do so easily, of course. If you accept that you have indeed taken in the past, or withheld something, including your love, it becomes easier to relinquish something in favour of the bigger picture.

In our modern era, Saturn and acceptance of our fate tend to be demonised. We're often told we should not accept everything; rather, we should make our own fate. While you can take actions that produce more positive results, you must accept certain things you cannot change. Unless you can do this, you are unlikely to operate outside your pre-conditioning. If you cannot make peace with the past, and make amends, you are unlikely to create the future you want unimpeded. Saturn can so often represent things you think, feel, and do that seem to be against your own best interest. This can be seen in a daśā of Saturn. The more willing you are to pay it back, the easier Saturn daśā becomes.

All your thoughts, words, and actions are stored in your subtle body and show why you came forth into physical form at the time you did. The configuration of all the planets, not just Saturn, as well as their subsequent movement, ensures that you fulfil their wishes. Each daśā expresses each planet's nature through your subtle, or 'causal' body, which, in turn, influences your mental-emotional body and life force. This influences your physical body, so that you are impelled to take actions.

Your densest body is, of course, your physical body. The signs of the zodiac show your physical environment, what is more obviously experienced. Subtler than your physical body is your 'energy body', and subtler still, your 'mental-emotional body', as seen in the lunar mansions. You are also a spiritual being; you have a subtle blueprint that has an intelligence of its own, a causal or 'soul body' that keeps account of all your past lives. This shows the kārmik imprints on your soul from lifetime to lifetime. The causal body is the most subtle, and yet the most influential precisely because of its subtlety. This is what is in direct communication with the planets. From a simplistic astrological view, you have a body (ascendant), mind (Moon), and soul (Sun).

Your previous thoughts, words, and actions, stored in your causal body, produce results at certain times throughout your life. We can see this in your various daśās. Thus, there are always many things ripening. Once the results of your previous actions have come to fruition, you are directed to think a certain way, which is the planet's influence on your mental-emotional body. This influences your life force so that you have, or are denied, the energy to live out the results of these through your actions or by your inability to act. This plays out in relation to the planetary daśās and transits of the planets, in alignment with your kārmik blueprint in your birth chart.

BEING - SUN

The 1st level or major daśā of any daśā represents the level of the soul, lasting many years, even decades. This level is represented by the Sun. These daśās can last for many years, showing experiences and circumstances over a longer period. The longest daśā is that of Venus, at 20 years, while the shortest is of the Sun, only 6 years. These daśās trigger bigger life lessons, but you may or may not be aware of these. It's as if they were operating on such a subtle level that they become like a background noise you may not always hear. The first time you may have heard it was likely at the very beginning of the major daśā, which also corresponds to the same planetary daśā on all 3 levels. This is when your heart and mind are on the same page as your soul's desire.

FEELING - MOON

The 2nd level or sub-daśā of a major daśā shows the level of your mind and emotions, represented by the Moon. This shows how life's circumstances are reflected in your mind, rooted in your heart. It shows how you are feeling about what is happening, as the light of the Sun is reflected in the Moon. This may last from a few months to about 3 years. It represents the people you meet that help you learn the bigger life lessons of the soul. The 2nd level is usually more conscious than the 1st, although that is not a guarantee. This is more impactful, as it shows how you feel, despite what may or may not be happening.

DOING - ASCENDANT

The 3rd level or sub-sub-daśa of a major daśa shows how you are reacting to all the above, the decisions you make based on these reactions. This relates to your ascendant, as well as Jupiter, representing your intelligence. It shows how you are applying your intelligence to any situation. This level reflects decisions based on emotional reactions (2nd level) to your circumstances (1st level). The ascendant represents how your body reacts to each moment, moment-by-moment. We can see this level for fine-tuning events in your life, as you decide based on how you feel about what is happening. See APPENDIX for a list of sub-sub daśas and their duration.

When we view all three levels of experience, we can make more accurate assessments of your experience. When we add the influence of transits to this, overlaying them on your birth chart, this will show the trigger for events, if there are to be any. All these layers give you a fuller picture of what is experienced.

To recap, the major daśa is like a constant background noise. The 2nd level is how you are feeling. This may conflict with your soul's desire and current circumstance. The 3rd level shows how you react and decide based on all these influences.

Sometimes, all three levels are on the same page, while at others, getting even two of them to cooperate may be a task. You may want something (2nd level) but decide something (3rd level) that may conflict with this need. Or you may experience something (1st level) you would prefer not to (2nd level). Sometimes, you may be completely out of sync with what your soul desires. Your head and heart may be on a different page. At other times, everything may work in tandem, and life seems to flow with ease.

THE QUESTION OF FREE WILL

The daśās and transits show your ever-changing and evolving life experience. An analogy Pearl Finn used was to think of your birth chart as a boat on an ocean. The boat has the wind blowing its sails and the undercurrents taking it along. The boat is like your individual blueprint. This is the snapshot of the planetary alignments when you were born. The winds are like the transits of the planets. These are pushing against you or taking you to where you wish to be. The sea is like the daśā. Your planetary daśās show what is coming up from within, whether or not you are conscious of it. The sea will have its way with you. Transits may or may not assist. You may have the wind at your back or pushing against where you want to be.

One of the first things many ask when they see their whole life mapped out in a timeline is: "Do I not have free will to choose?" Well, you cannot choose the weather, can you? Or the way the tides turn? You may not even have a choice in how you react to what is unfolding. But you can view it from a different perspective. With a cosmic view, you can change how you see your life. And this may be all that's needed to change its trajectory.

Astrology allows you to be more objective about what is happening, so you may have some space between what is happening and your reaction. It opens up another possibility. The choices you make based on what is unfolding dictate where you end up. Even if you don't believe you have the freedom to choose absolutely anything, you still make choices. And even if everything that ever was, is, or will ever be, already exists in a cosmic sense, making decisions about your life is part of that, too. By altering your perceptions, perceptions that reinforce patterns in your birth chart, you can set a course for somewhere new.

Tantrik scholar Christopher 'Hareesh' Wallis writes in his article, *Near Enemy #11: You can choose how to respond,*[1] "If you're in a sailboat in the middle of the ocean, there's only one little thing you can choose, which is the angle of your rudder ... which makes no difference at all to your experience one minute from now, and very little difference one day from now or one week from now. But

---

[1] Christopher Wallis, 'Near Enemy #11: You can choose how to respond', Hareesh [web blog], 30 August 2019, https://hareesh.org/blog/2019/8/30/near-enemy-11-you-can-choose-how-to-respond (accessed 14 June 2022).

eventually, it makes all the difference in the world: it determines whether you make landfall in Australia or Siberia." The choices you make based on what is unfolding now dictate where you eventually end up. With a little or a lot of effort, you can make adjustments that make all the difference in the end.

When you have an awareness of the influences of the tides and weather - the astrological weather - you have an awareness of where you are on the vast ocean of your life. With this awareness, you realise there is a bigger picture and part of you that is on board with all that is. This awareness brings a sense of calm whatever is going on. Even if you know a period in your life is going to be stormy, you know when to batten down the hatches and ride it out. At the very least, knowing when a period is ending brings an enormous sense of peace, no matter what you must face. You can take full advantage of the winds that are taking you out of choppy waters and to calmer seas.

Taking all three indications: your boat, the winds, and the tides, you can make more accurate assessments of your experience. We see this in the dance between the daśās, transits, and your birth chart. When you add the influence of the transits to your planetary daśās, this gives a fuller picture of what is going on for you.

The 3 things to ask yourself in relation to any planetary daśās you are currently experiencing are:

1. What configurations are in my birth chart?
2. Are these configurations activated in daśās, and how are the planets involved?
3. Are my current planetary daśās triggered by a transit of those same planets?

Someone with Venus ruling the 7th house of relationships does not get into a relationship every time they enter a Venus sub-daśā. Although Venus and the 7th house both represent relationships, it is not a guarantee. It would mean a new relationship many times if that were the case. We may see a relationship if someone were in a Venus daśā and if Venus were also transiting a relationship space. This is more likely to show the beginning of a relationship - if they are not already in one. If they are, it may show a better experience of that relationship. If Venus were strong and the sign of a relationships active in a sign-based daśā, we can be more assured of it.

We all experience transits in our own unique way. Yet we also experience transits, as a family, a nation, and global. We cannot separate our lived experience from others' experiences. The sequence of planetary daśās tells a story we are all familiar with.

NATURE OF PLANETS
FOR EACH SIGN

Each rising sign experiences the planets in their own unique way. For each sign, a planet may be crueller or kinder, depending on what houses it rules. While a planet may be kind, it may rule certain challenging houses for you. This will alter its nature, based on the position of the planet in your birth chart. If you have a cruel planet ruling a cruel house, placed in another cruel house, this can actually be a positive indication, a 'double-negative', creating a positive outcome. It may challenge you to overcome something where you end up in a positive situation through significant effort.

The cruel houses are the 6th, 8th, and 12th, while the 3rd is cruel to a lesser degree. If well-disposed, the 8th or 12th houses can give good results, as Parāśara states these are neutral. The 2nd house is also neutral, although the 2nd and 7th can show health challenges. Although the 11th house is the house of gains, it can show challenges. This is especially the case if a planet rules the 11th alongside one of the cruel houses. The 11th house is the 6th from the 6th; the 3rd house, the 8th from the 8th; the 2nd, the 12th from the 3rd, and the 7th, the 12th from the 8th. The 2nd and 7th can show certain issues around health, as they are 12 away from the houses that represent longevity, i.e., the 3rd and 8th.

Some of the planets' maleficence may seem confusing at first. Here is one rule given by Parāśara: "When a malefic [cruel] or benefic [kind] rules an angle, they lose their potency." So, a cruel planet will lose some of its cruelty, while a kind planet will lose some of its kindness. Therefore, Venus is a cruel planet for Taurus, although it rules the sign. It's a kind planet ruling an angle, while it also rules the 6th house.

Combining all these indications, each sign experiences each planet differently. Although Jupiter is a kind planet, it may bring challenges for some signs. The cruel Saturn may actually become a kinder planet, depending on the rising sign.

According to Parāśara, each planet is considered as the following for each rising sign (Rāhu and Ketu are not included):

- For Aries: Mars (ruler), Sun and Jupiter are kind; Mercury, Venus, and Saturn are cruel; Moon is neutral.
- For Taurus: Sun, Mercury and Saturn are kind; Moon, Venus, and Jupiter are cruel; Mars' nature depends on its associations.
- For Gemini: Venus is kind; Sun, Mars and Jupiter are cruel; Mars is inauspicious, while the Moon is less so; Mercury (ruler) is auspicious.
- For Cancer: Moon, Mars and Jupiter are kind; Mercury and Venus are cruel; Saturn is inauspicious; Sun's nature depends on its associations.

• For Leo: Sun, Mars and Jupiter are kind; Mercury, Venus, and Saturn are cruel; Moon's nature depends on its associations.

• For Virgo; Mercury and Venus are kind; Moon, Mars and Jupiter are cruel; Saturn's nature is mixed; Sun's nature depends on its associations.

• For Libra: Mercury and Saturn are kind; Sun, Mars and Jupiter are cruel; Venus is neutral; Mars is inauspicious.

• For Scorpio: Moon and Jupiter are kind; Mercury, Venus, and Saturn are cruel; Mars is neutral. Sun is auspicious.

• For Sagittarius: Sun and Mars are kind; Venus is cruel; Moon and Jupiter are neutral; Saturn is inauspicious; Mercury's nature is not given. Although kind, Mercury rules two angles, losing some of its kind nature.

• For Capricorn: Mercury and Venus are kind; Moon, Mars and Jupiter are cruel; Sun is neutral. Saturn (ruler) is auspicious.

• For Aquarius: Venus and Saturn are kind; Moon, Mars and Jupiter are cruel; Mercury gives mediocre results; Sun is inauspicious.

• For Pisces: Moon and Mars are kind; Sun, Mercury, Venus, and Saturn are cruel; Jupiter's nature depends on its associations.

HOUSE DIVISIONS

There are many ways of dividing up the signs of the zodiac into houses, and several reasons for doing so. Indian astrology traditionally divides the zodiac into 12 equal parts, no matter the location or time of year. This is the *Rāśi Cakra*; *rāśi* (Sun signs), meaning a 'measure' of degrees, and *cakra* meaning 'wheel'. The 360-degree zodiac divides into 12 sections of 30 degrees each. This is the 'natural zodiac' used by most ancient systems of astrology. The Rāśi, or 'whole-sign house' approach in Indian astrology, uses each sign as a house, no matter where the ascendant degree falls. If you were born with Pisces rising, no matter the degree, Pisces is your 1st house, Aries, your 2nd, Taurus, your 3rd, and so on.

There are many other ways to divide the chart using the houses in astrology. This depends on time and location, including the Indian KP house system, akin to Placidus, and Sripathi, much like Porphyry. Others include Koch, Regiomontanus, Morinus, Alcabitius, Campanus, Topocentric, Meridian, and Vehlow.

There are three ways used in traditional Indian astrology: the *Rāśi*, *Bhāva* and *Calit Cakras*, the 'sign', 'house' and 'moving house' systems.

The Rāśi division, or Sun sign division, is most often used. I refer to this throughout this book. The Bhāva Cakra, or 'House Chart' divides the zodiac into 12 equal signs, but usually places the rising degree in the middle of the first house. You can also use this degree as the beginning of the house, but this is not as common. Bhāva means 'state' and shows how we experience each sign. In this context, it means 'house', i.e., where we experience a sign. The Bhāva Cakra calculates the 1st house by taking the exact rising degree, usually mapping out 15 degrees on either side of this point. If you were born with the latter degrees of a sign rising, your 1st house would take in the latter half of that sign and the first half of the following sign. This is the 1st house, *not* the first sign. You cannot have two rising signs. The Bhāva Cakra reflects how you view yourself in relation to the natural order of signs. This can differ from the natural zodiac, i.e., the Rāśi Cakra. The Bhāva Cakra may or may not reflect the natural zodiac position, how things are.

We cannot use rulership and sign aspects, or any combination of these, the same way we would with Rāśi. We can use planetary aspects. Rulership would confuse, as we could end up with two rulers for your rising sign if you were born at the beginning or end of a sign. If you were born with late Cancer rising, you would end up with the Sun and Moon ruling your rising sign. This is not practical for our purposes of timing with daśās.

If you were born with the last degree of Cancer rising, that is your rising sign, no matter how you calculate the houses. If you were born at the very beginning or end of a sign, it will draw on either the previous or following sign. Someone with the first degree of Libra rising would have the latter half of Virgo as their first house in the Bhāva Cakra. Someone with the last degree of Libra rising would incorporate the first half of Scorpio. The Bhāva Cakra shows how you perceive yourself, which is often different from the natural zodiac, unless you were born with the middle of a sign rising.

This makes a significant difference when calculating the placements of planets. You may have the Sun in the 1st house in the Rāśi, but this may be in the 12th or 2nd house when using the Bhāva. This would change how and where you experience the Sun, despite the sign remaining the same.

There is another calculation called the *Bhāva Calit*. *Calit* means 'movement', which, in this context, considers the movement throughout the globe and time of year. Using this calculation, the signs are of different lengths, depending on the time of year and location. This calculation places the rising degree at the centre of the 1st house and the Midheaven at the centre of the 10th house. It then divides the remaining houses according to the constellations' actual sizes. Some signs are much bigger than others. Scorpio is the smallest. Virgo is the biggest. This way of dividing up the houses is not common in Indian astrology. Many calculations, such as lordships, combinations, as well as planetary aspects, will not work. You can only factor in exact planetary aspects and close orbs. Think about it as if the hands on a clock and imagine that hours were of different lengths, changing throughout the year and when travelling about. It would not be an easy clock to read!

There is a growing trend to use a 'true sidereal' zodiac. They use this to calculate transits through the various sized constellations. I do not know exactly how they use it other than for discussing transits. The calculations for houses are different, of course. Signs differ from houses; constellations are not signs. Although you may superimpose the houses onto signs, the signs of the zodiac are signs, *not* houses, and do not change. Whatever way you experience the signs, it does not alter their natural order.

DṚṢṬI (ASPECTS)

Planets look at, and thus, influence, other houses and planets in one way or another. There are certain aspects, *dṛṣṭi*, or 'sight', that have a stronger impact, according to Indian astrology. All planets look at the 7th whole sign from where they are, though the closer the orb of influence, the stronger the impact. All planets influence the opposite house with 100% strength. This shows the desires of a planet. If Venus were in your 1st house, its sight to your 7th house would show the desire for a relationship. Whatever opposes Venus shows the kinds of partners you are attracted to.

All planets have a desire for something. Sun desires power; Moon desires safety and security; Mars desires action; Mercury desires information; Jupiter desires knowledge and meaningful connections; and Saturn desires detachment. Rāhu is the most desirous. Its opposite, Ketu, wishes to renounce everything, which is itself a desire. The lunar nodes show more complexity around the issue of desire.

Apart from the 7th house, there are special planetary sights given to Mars, Jupiter, Saturn, and Rāhu. These are more active at certain portions within their daśās. More about portions of daśās in PART 3. Whatever the planet, its strength or position, aspects show desires. They are not a guarantee of anything. They simply show the desire. Sign daśās show whether your desires are fulfilled, what is available in your environment. Sometimes, all that may show up is the desire.

All planets look at the 7th house with 100% strength; the 3rd and 10th houses with 25% strength; the 5th and 9th houses with 50% strength; and the 4th and 8th houses with 75% strength, except for Saturn, Jupiter, and Mars.

Saturn looks at the 3rd and 10th houses with 100% strength; the 5th and 9th houses with 25% strength; and the 4th and 8th with 50% strength. Jupiter looks at the 5th and 9th houses with 100% strength; the 3rd and 10th with 75% strength; and the 4th and 8th with 25% strength. Mars looks at the 4th and 8th houses with 100% strength; the 3rd and 10th houses with 50% strength; and the 5th and 9th with 75% strength.

Many Indian astrologers consider Rāhu to aspect the same houses as Jupiter, the 5th and 9th, but counted in reverse. Not that it makes a difference technically, as you end up in these houses whichever direction you count. Some astrologers add that Rāhu has a sight on the 12th house, counting in reverse, i.e., the 2nd house counting in zodiacal order. *Bṛhat Parāśara Horā Śāstra* does not include Rāhu's aspects. As always, the lunar nodes have their controversies. They are not physical bodies, they are shadows. Many Indian astrologers do not regard Ketu as having any aspect, as sight show desires, and Ketu ultimately represents liberation from all desires.

ARGALĀ

Argalā means 'bolted down'. This is a way of looking at how planets in certain houses lock certain results in place. We can observe argalā from various houses or areas of life. This is especially relevant when timing events using planetary and sign-based daśās. Argalā shows the support that is given to that area of life, or if there is something blocking your objectives. Planets are usually doing one or the other, helping or hindering.

It is easiest to start with your 1st house (ascendant), to see if your objectives are supported, or if these are blocked. You can then do this for any planet or house, especially when that planet or house is active in a daśā.

The 2nd, 4th, 5th, 8th, and 11th houses from any house will help the objectives of that house. If this is your 1st house, i.e., your rising sign, this will show what is supporting you. If it is from your 10th house of career, it will show professional supports. The 12th, 10th, 9th, 6th and 3rd can block these indications – in that order. We always count this in zodiacal order, unless Ketu were in the sign you are considering. Ketu reverses the count.

The 2nd house shows things that sustain you, including food, wealth, and resources. This includes what you value and how you value yourself. The 4th house shows your home comforts, happiness, and safety; the 5th house, your future speculations, including children and creative thinking; the 8th house, your longevity; the 11th house, your goals and gains. The activities of the 12th, 10th, 9th, 6th, and 3rd houses block these indications.

An example of this is when you spend more (12th house) than you can save (2nd house). Another is when you cannot stay at home (4th) because of work responsibilities (10th). The 9th house blocks the 5th house to a degree, although this is seen as a secondary argalā. The 9th house is your past, and the 5th is your future. What you experienced in the past impacts what you experience in the future. The 9th house represents your beliefs, which have a direct impact on what you think is possible.

Things you do daily (6th), or things you don't do and probably should, decrease your longevity (8th). The unhealthy habits you cannot overcome impact your life span. The 3rd house of pleasure-seeking blocks the 11th house, and your ability to earn money. You gain more when you spend more time earning a living than you do enjoying yourself. The 3rd house shows a selfish need, which impacts your ability to do what a group of people, or society, wants of you (11th). Yet there is an upside to having a cruel planet in your 3rd house. It shows your ability to get what you want, whatever it takes.

The 7th house can either give or block, depending on the signs and planets involved. The 1st house can block the 7th if there are more planets in the 1st. This may block relationships, as there is more focus on yourself than on finding a partner. If there are more planets in your 7th

house, this shows more of an emphasis on others, which may mean neglecting your own needs.

While any of these indications may show the focus, the results can be 'good' or 'bad' based on the whole chart and what the focus is. You may have more planets in the 12th house of spending than the 2nd house of savings. Yet you may be a spendthrift who laments never having enough or someone who is very giving, living a life of servitude.

Every house impacts every other. Every area of our life impacts every other. Your health, home, relationships, and career are the 4 pillars of your life. These have an enormous impact on each other. The past impacts what you see as possible in the future. Thus, the houses of the past, the 12th, 9th, 6th and 3rd, have a direct impact on the houses of the future, the 2nd, 5th, 8th and 11th.

LUNAR MANSIONS

You should, at this point, be somewhat familiar with the 12 Sun signs: Aries, Taurus, Gemini, etc. These divide the zodiac into 30° segments. But what of the 27 star signs or lunar divisions? These are the *nakṣatras*, or lunar mansions, of Indian astrology. The lunar mansions divide the zodiac into 27 segments of 13° 20'. The Sun relates to your circumstances and physical resources, while the Moon relates to your mental and emotional resources. You can use both the Sun and Moon signs to see many things. The Moon signs give more insights and depth to the Sun signs, as they represent the 'fixed stars' beyond the zodiac.

Knowing what sign the Moon is transiting on any day helps you plan your life. This is what ancient cultures used astrology for, i.e., timing appropriate activities. The Moon transits one Moon sign in approximately one day, taking about 27 days to travel through the entire zodiac.

Each Moon sign has a prominent star or cluster of stars, as well as their own mythology and symbols. Each lunar mansion has a ruling deity whose mythological stories become the stories of your life. The names of the Moon signs to follow are in Sanskrit, but I have given simple translations to help gauge the nature of each.

You can use the lunar mansions to understand yourself and others, what your 'Moon sign' says about you or anyone else. The Moon's placement says a lot about *what* you do, while the lunar mansion that was rising (ascending) says a lot of about *how* you do it.

Some lunar mansions are fully contained within one Sun sign, with some bridging two Sun signs. Both Sun and Moon signs end at the end of Cancer, Scorpio, and Pisces, beginning new Sun signs and lunar mansions at the beginning of Aries, Leo, and Sagittarius. These 3 sections, between Cancer and Leo, Scorpio and Sagittarius, and Pisces and Aries, are sensitive junctures in the zodiac. They are like voids, in a sense, reflected in shifts in awareness and complex dynamics during periods of transition when active in daśās and transits.

Each lunar mansion corresponds to a planet, and thus, a planetary daśā. Each will have different lengths of time. I have taken the names and spellings of each lunar mansion from Sanjay Rath's *Bṛhat Nakṣatra*[2], although you may come across spelling variations in various texts.

The 3 sections from Aries to Cancer, Leo to Scorpio, and Sagittarius to Pisces, relate to the 120 year-long viṁśottarī daśā. The Sun signs show your circumstances, while the lunar mansions add how you feel about it. Yet how you feel about your life has a big say in what happens. Both the Sun signs and lunar mansions tell the story of your life.

---

[2] Sanjay Rath, *Bṛhat Nakṣatra*, (New Delhi: Sagittarius Publications, 2008).

Table 2.1

#	Lunar Mansion	Sidereal Degrees
1	Aśvinī	0° 00' – 13° 20' Aries
2	Bharaṇī	13° 20' – 26° 40' Aries
3	Kṛttikā	26° 40' Aries – 10° 00' Taurus
4	Rohiṇī	10° 00' – 23° 20' Taurus
5	Mṛgaśirṣā	23° 20' Taurus – 6° 40' Gemini
6	Ārdrā	6° 40' – 20° Gemini
7	Punarvasu	20° 00' Gemini – 3° 20' Cancer
8	Puṣya	3° 20' – 16° 40' Cancer
9	Āśleṣā	16° 40' – 30° 00' Cancer
10	Maghā	0° 00' – 13° 20' Leo
11	Pūrva Phālguṇī	13° 20' – 26° 40' Leo
12	Uttara Phālguṇī	26° 40' Leo – 10° 00' Virgo
13	Hasta	10° 00' – 23° 20' Virgo
14	Citrā	23° 20' Virgo – 6° 40' Libra
15	Svātī	6° 40' – 20° 00' Libra
16	Viśākhā	20° 00' Libra – 3° 20' Scorpio
17	Anurādhā	3° 20' – 16° 40' Scorpio
18	Jyeṣṭhā	16° 40' – 30° 00' Scorpio
19	Mūla	0° 00' – 13° 20' Sagittarius
20	Pūrvāṣāḍha	13° 20' – 26° 40' Sagittarius
21	Uttarāṣāḍha	26° 40' Sagittarius – 10° 00' Capricorn
22	Śravaṇa	10° 00' – 23° 20' Capricorn
23	Dhaniṣṭhā	23° 20' Capricorn – 6° 40' Aquarius
24	Śatabhiṣāj	6° 40' – 20° 00' Aquarius
25	Pūrva Bhādrapada	20° 00' Aquarius – 3° 20' Pisces
26	Uttara Bhādrapada	3° 20' – 16° 40' Pisces
27	Revatī	16° 40' – 30° 00' Pisces

Table 2.2

#	Lunar Mansion	Longitude of the Moon	Daśā	Length of Daśā
1	Aśvinī	0° 00' – 13° 20' Aries	Ketu	7 years
2	Bharaṇī	13° 20' – 26° 40' Aries	Venus	20 years
3	Kṛttikā	26° 40' Aries – 10° 00' Taurus	Sun	6 years
4	Rohiṇī	10° 00' – 23° 20' Taurus	Moon	10 years
5	Mṛgaśirṣā	23° 20' Taurus – 6° 40' Gemini	Mars	7 years
6	Ārdrā	6° 40' – 20° Gemini	Rāhu	18 years
7	Punarvasu	20° 00' Gemini – 3° 20' Cancer	Jupiter	16 years
8	Puṣya	3° 20' – 16° 40' Cancer	Saturn	19 years
9	Āśleṣā	16° 40' – 30° 00' Cancer	Mercury	17 years
10	Maghā	0° 00' – 13° 20' Leo	Ketu	7 years
11	Pūrva Phālguṇī	13° 20' – 26° 40' Leo	Venus	20 years
12	Uttara Phālguṇī	26° 40' Leo – 10° 00' Virgo	Sun	6 years
13	Hasta	10° 00' – 23° 20' Virgo	Moon	10 years
14	Citrā	23° 20' Virgo – 6° 40' Libra	Mars	7 years
15	Svātī	6° 40' – 20° 00' Libra	Rāhu	18 years
16	Viśākhā	20° 00' Libra – 3° 20' Scorpio	Jupiter	16 years
17	Anurādhā	3° 20' – 16° 40' Scorpio	Saturn	19 years
18	Jyeṣṭhā	16° 40' – 30° 00' Scorpio	Mercury	17 years
19	Mūla	0° 00' – 13° 20' Sagittarius	Ketu	7 years
20	Pūrvāṣāḍha	13° 20' – 26° 40' Sagittarius	Venus	20 years
21	Uttarāṣāḍha	26° 40' Sagittarius – 10° 00' Capricorn	Sun	6 years
22	Śravaṇa	10° 00' – 23° 20' Capricorn	Moon	10 years
23	Dhaniṣṭhā	23° 20' Capricorn – 6° 40' Aquarius	Mars	7 years
24	Śatabhiṣāj	6° 40' – 20° 00' Aquarius	Rāhu	18 years
25	Pūrva Bhādrapada	20° 00' Aquarius – 3° 20' Pisces	Jupiter	16 years
26	Uttara Bhādrapada	3° 20' – 16° 40' Pisces	Saturn	19 years
27	Revatī	16° 40' – 30° 00' Pisces	Mercury	17 years

CALCULATING YOUR DAŚĀS

If you know your Moon's degree using sidereal calculations, you can estimate where you are in the planetary daśās. If you only know your Moon sign, and not the degree, the following will only be a rough guide. Take your Moon's degree by sign in Table 2.2. If you were born when the Moon was at the very beginning of a particular lunar mansion by degree, you would have experienced most of the daśā during the beginning of your life. If, however, the Moon were at the very end of a lunar mansion, you would only have experienced that daśā briefly, before the next one in the sequence began soon after your birth. If the Moon were somewhere in the middle of the lunar mansion, you would have experienced approximately half of your first daśā.

LUNAR MANSIONS & PLANETS

Each planet associates with 3 different lunar mansions. These highlight certain themes based on the myths and symbols of each. You experience each planetary daśā in your own unique way, based on all the various planetary configurations in your birth chart.

Although you may experience a Venus daśā, you experience it in relation to the lunar mansion associated with Venus, as well as Venus' placement and rulership in your birth chart. If the Moon were in Aśvinī when you were born, you would have experienced a Ketu daśā first, followed by Venus, Sun, Moon, etc. Associated lunar mansions define your planetary daśās. With Moon in Aśvinī, a Ketu daśā will highlight Aśvinī themes more than Maghā or Mūla, although they too will bring their themes at various times. Venus will highlight Bharaṇī themes more than Pūrva Phālguṇī or Pūrvāṣāḍha, and so on. All the associated lunar mansions' themes will play out.

If a Venus daśā were active, you experience the lunar mansions associated with Venus, but also the planet associated with where Venus is. If Venus were in Punarvasu, a lunar mansion associated with Jupiter, you have an experience of Jupiter along with Venus. This shows the overall circumstances in your life, but also how you feel about them and what you would like to happen.

You experience the planetary daśās based on what each planet rules by house position. But you also experience this from the Moon's lunar mansion position, and the house position of each planet from the Moon. If you had Leo rising, Venus rules your 3rd and 10th houses of effort and career. If you also had the Moon between 3° 20' and 16° 40' Cancer, in Puṣya lunar mansion, then Venus rules the 4th and 11th houses from the Moon, representing home and earnings. Although you may experience a Venus period as a time for making more effort in career, (3rd and 10th) you will do so for a content home and more earnings (4th and 11th). Or it may be your siblings (3rd house) that are making headways in career (10th), so they can build a new house (4th) with their earnings (11th). You express the planetary daśās in many ways, some of which are beyond the scope of this book.

To follow are the 9 planets and the 3 lunar mansions associated with each. Find where your Moon is in this list and see the associated planet. This is where your planetary daśās began when you were born. You can then work out approximately where you are in your daśās by comparing your age against the daśās listed. If you were born when the Moon was in Citrā (Mars), you began somewhere within Mars daśā. The time would depend on how far into Citrā the Moon had transited. Mars is a 7-year daśā, followed by Rāhu, Jupiter, Saturn, and so on.

Aśvinī, Maghā & Mūla – Ketu Daśā

Ketu daśā can confuse and confound, but also offer a unique perspective and insight into your spiritual nature. Ketu will do so in diverse ways, depending on which of these 3 lunar mansions is more active. We place the most active lunar mansion after your Moon; at least at the beginning of the daśā. If the Moon were in Pisces in your birth chart, a Ketu daśā would activate Aśvinī more, as Aries comes after Pisces, and this is where Aśvinī is.

Aśvinī intensifies the impulsiveness of Aries, making it sharper, even reckless. This may also show an interest in alternative health and methods of gaining strength.

Maghā intensifies the power and dominance of Leo, showing leadership qualities and past life merits. You may experience this through some inherited power or position. Mūla in Sagittarius intensifies the need to uproot anything that stands in the way of finding the truth.

Bharaṇī, Pūrva Phālguṇī & Pūrvāṣāḍha – Venus Daśā

Venus represents the basic needs of shelter, food, and support from family and/or community. When there is excess energy, it shows sensual pleasures. Venus represents beauty and art, an appreciation of the finer things in life, and a wish to feel appreciated. A Venus daśā brings with it many pleasures, but how you go about fulfilling these would depend on the signs activated.

Bharaṇī brings a Venusian flavour to Aries, intensifying passions and creativity. You cannot create anything without discipline. You need to destroy anything that stands in your way. As the saying goes, 'You cannot make an omelette without breaking some eggs'.

Pūrva Phālguṇī adds a flavour of Venus to Leo. This shows a need to express yourself, reflecting an enjoyable and creative cocktail of love and creativity.

Pūrvāṣāḍha adds a flavour of Venus to Sagittarius. This shows a need to rise above animal instincts, for laws and culture to express the absolute best of the human spirit. This reflects a search for meaning in beauty, a search for truth.

Kṛttikā, Uttara Phālgunī & Uttarāṣāḍha – Sun Daśā

The strength of the Sun offers a natural sense of confidence and self-esteem. You can access your Higher Self through a connection to a greater source of power, resulting in a confidence that is unshakable. This is available to anyone, regardless of whether you may have a weak or strong Sun in your horoscope. The route to finding it will vary, depending.

Kṛttikā brings a sharpness to Aries and Taurus, adding heat and purity to dispel any negativity.

Uttara Phālguṇī intensifies the solar impulse in Leo and Virgo thoughtfully. This shows a need to share your many gifts with the world.

Uttarāṣāḍha brings a flavour of the Sun to Sagittarius and Capricorn. This reflects an application of knowledge gained. It's about sharing your insights in a down-to-earth manner, for the sake of a worthwhile goal.

Rohiṇī, Hasta & Śravaṇa – Moon Daśā

Once you connect to yourself, you develop a need to connect with others. You wish to nurture your relationships. Your family and community supports you in this process, through whatever brings comfort. The Moon is the archetypal mother and shows how and where you seek comfort. Caring for others becomes part of the process. This can challenge your mental and emotional well-being if this process is disturbed.

Rohiṇī brings a flavour of the Moon to Taurus. This shows a nourishing and sensual environment, creating many enjoyable moments.

Hasta adds a flavour of the Moon to Virgo. This grants skills in healing yourself and others. It highlights a practical application and management.

Śravaṇa brings a flavour of the Moon to Capricorn. This instils a need to let others shine, to place others on your strong shoulders. There is a need to share all the knowledge that has guided you this far.

Mṛgaśirṣā, Citrā & Dhaniṣṭhā – Mars Daśā

A Mars daśā is about developing strength, although you may see some friction. You may feel this in your relationships or in competition. Mars represents your courage, your willingness to do what it takes to destroy your weaknesses. In a Mars daśā, you end up fighting some battle or other, whether external or internal. These challenges ask you to grow stronger, no matter the battle you choose.

Mṛgaśirṣā brings a flavour of Mars to Taurus and Gemini. This adds passion, inquisitiveness, and playfulness to whatever your chosen art.

Citrā brings the passionate flavour of Mars to Virgo and Libra. You can express your beauty and art for the world to appreciate.

Dhaniṣṭhā brings a flavour of Mars to Capricorn and Aquarius. This sees you break through your glass ceilings, beyond what others think is possible.

Ārdrā, Svātī & Śatabhiṣāj – Rāhu Daśā

Rāhu is a thrill-seeking daśā. You have an insatiable appetite for something you feel you haven't experienced. And you will do anything to get it. You may even do things you thought you were incapable of doing. This brings out your shadow side. Life can become like a beast that needs to be tamed. Rāhu is depicted as a head of a serpent. When released, it can unleash energy that you must learn to control if you are to make the most of the potential buried deep within you.

Ārdrā adds a flavour of Rāhu to Gemini. This intensifies mental stimulation. It can shift you in and out of the eye of emotional storms that help you see what needs clearing out.

Svātī brings a flavour of Rāhu to Libra. This intensifies passions, increasing the need for freedom and idealism. This represents the invaluable dark side of love and artistic expression.

Śatabhiṣāj intensifies Aquarius with a double dose of Rāhu, as Rāhu is associated with this lunar mansion and Sun sign. This shows a need to break free from restriction, carving out alternative paths for yourself and others while healing the body and mind.

Punarvasu, Viśākhā & Pūrva Bhādrapada –
Jupiter Daśā

Jupiter daśās are a time for expansion. Study or travel are often on the agenda, expanding your life and worldview. Expansion can happen on a physical level, too. You may get married or have children, expanding your family. Or you may put on weight. It may be an internal expansion through study and higher knowledge. Jupiter represents righteousness. Its daśās usually uphold natural laws and ways of living. You can see this in having a family or joining a tradition of learning.

Punarvasu adds a flavour of Jupiter to Gemini and Cancer. This increases compassion and a need to nourish the mind and body.

Viśākhā brings a flavour of Jupiter to Libra and Scorpio. This focuses you on deeper aspects of your being. You are looking for meaning in whatever path you choose.

Pūrva Bhādrapada intensifies Jupiter's influence in Aquarius and Pisces. This shows a need to dream bigger than anyone before you have dared. It asks you to look beyond this life for guidance.

Puṣya, Anurādhā & Uttara Bhādrapada –
Saturn Daśā

Saturn represents a reality check, a need to knuckle down and focus on something that is important to you. Saturn is the part of you that has an eye on the bigger picture. It can show a need to take on more responsibilities, more demanding work. Saturn asks you to be present with whatever you are doing, to work for work's sake, regardless of whether the rewards are clear from the outset.

Puṣya adds a flavour of Saturn to Cancer. This brings a keen sense of responsibility, and a hard coating that hides a soft inner nature which needs protecting.

Anurādhā brings a flavour of Saturn to Scorpio. This grants you the ability to guide others from the depths of your being and devotion to a cause.

Uttara Bhādrapada brings a flavour of Saturn to the depths of Pisces. This brings together extremes of both love and fear. Here, there is an understanding that these are inseparable sides of the same coin.

Āśleṣā, Jyeṣṭhā & Revatī – Mercury Daśā

Mercury's daśās return you to a child-like innocence and curiosity. Mercury represents practical concerns, such as work and business. These can bring many choices and distractions, too. The strength of Mercury is your ability to discriminate between what you should and shouldn't be doing. If there are too many choices, you may need more stillness to decide on your next route.

Āśleṣā brings a flavour of Mercury's intellectualism to the emotional nature of Cancer. This mixes things up in an ever-changing mental loop, helping you to channel feelings in more practical ways.

Jyeṣṭhā brings a flavour of Mercury to the depths of Scorpio. This results in deep insights and practical skills. These help you overcome your vulnerability, especially when you experience the inevitable changes.

Revatī brings a flavour of communicative Mercury to Pisces. This instils in you the ability to say what needs saying. You may help calm and comfort others who may feel lost at sea, helping you bring your own soul home.

27 MANSIONS OF THE MOON

To follow is a description of each of the 27 lunar mansions and their ruling deities, starting from the beginning of Aries. Pay attention to the lunar mansion the Moon was in when you were born, and each subsequent lunar mansion in each associated planetary daśā. The myths and symbols of the lunar mansions show how the planetary daśās are unfolding in your life. Whatever planet is active in any daśā, you can read this from your Moon and ascendant. This will give you a fuller picture of what the daśā is about, as will the planet associated with each lunar mansion in each daśā. This gives you two things to look at: the planetary daśā itself, and the planet associated with the lunar mansion.

You may be in a daśā of Venus, but the planet associated with the lunar mansion Venus is in will give you other themes based on that planet. The relationship between both planets will show the bigger picture. One straightforward way to remember which planet is associated with each lunar mansion is to list each planet associated with each lunar mansion from 1 to 27, starting with Ketu and Aśvinī: Ketu: 1 – 10 – 19; Venus: 2 – 11 – 20; Sun: 3 – 12 – 21; Moon: 4 – 13 – 22; Mars: 5 – 14 – 23; Rāhu: 6 – 15 – 24; Jupiter: 7 – 16 – 25; Saturn: 8 – 17 – 26; Mercury: 9 – 18 – 27.

1. *Aśvinī:* The Swift One
0° 00' – 13° 20' Aries

Aśva means 'horse', which is one of this lunar mansion's symbols. This reflects its swiftness, power, and driving force. If this is active in a Ketu daśā, or a planet placed here, you may start something new and be eager to move on. Yet you may be a little impulsive, even reckless, less interested in following through. 'Act first, think later' is its motto. This is a time to be courageous. It may challenge you to develop courage, though.

The ruling deities are the twin horsemen and physicians to the gods, Aśvinī-Kumāra. *Kumāra* means a youth. Together with the horse, this represents primal energy and vigour. Its swift nature promotes swift recovering after an illness or surgery. You may have an interest in exercises that give you a sense of vitality and youthfulness. One pitfall is overdoing it and injuring yourself. Accidents are possible if you are overdoing the impulse to move.

This impulse can work for you in any situations where you need more intensity to focus. This may be through more intense sporting activities, or anything that spikes adrenaline. As long as you are mindful, you can channel its energy to achieve whatever you set your mind to. The precision and directness that are possible can make you achieve anything you want. It is already done, in a way. All you need is to line up with what you have already asked for on some level.

Apart from an interest in health and vitality, travel and adventure may interest you. You will, at the very least, need to sense your life is moving forward. It's all about taking on new and exciting adventures. Be mindful of running away from your problems, though. Ketu represents the past catching up with you. Sexual adventures may be another theme and interest. You may get into all kinds of adventures besides.

With the Moon in Aśvinī, themes of movement and travel may be prominent throughout your life. You began your life in a Ketu daśā. Ketu here can show an impulsiveness that leads to losses. Yet it could show gaining something far more important from a spiritual perspective. This can show a deeper connection to spirit, and to more energy and vitality.

The Sun exalts in this lunar mansion, so a Sun daśā, if placed here, would bring out the Sun's strength. The twin horsemen were born of the Sun deity in myth, so this is fitting. You may move up in the world in a Sun daśā. Yet you must acknowledge a deeper connection to what gives you power: your spiritual self. Mars here could show accidents, as it triggers Ketu in a daśā. You may need to be more conscious of what you are doing, unless you are older and wiser—and slower—in your movements. A Mars-Ketu connection can be quite volatile unless you know what you are doing. Even then, you must accept when things seem to happen for no reason.

Mercury may challenge you, as Ketu is beyond the rational mind. Ketu is the headless part of the serpent in Vedic myth. It may confuse you about what to direct your attention towards. Mercury may show a need to get practical, yet Ketu shows a need for something beyond the physical. Jupiter here may bring discernment. Yet, it could expand on the themes mentioned, increasing risk-taking. Jupiter may show you being lucky in whatever you do, no matter how you do it. Any planet here is likely to be more impulsive.

Even Venus, a planet that represents receptivity, may be more proactive. This may show you going for what you desire with more gusto. Yet this could show problems in getting what you want. Venus requires more compromise and receptivity than this sign suggests. Saturn requires restraint but may find this difficult in impulsive Aries.

This can challenge you to keep healthy boundaries, either pushing too hard, too soon, or not pushing at all.

Rāhu can wreak havoc here, leading to all kinds of irrational and impulsive behaviours. Despite your need to move ahead, any reckless actions take you back to the past, to atone for your missteps.

Whatever the planet, you are likely to go for whatever it suggests. Yet you must accept the past and your past actions that are bearing fruit now. Be mindful of overreacting, creating more problems than is necessary. You may regret it later. There are no mistakes from another perspective, only bigger lessons.

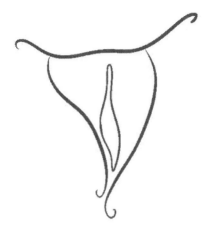

2. *Bharaṇī:* The Productive One
13° 20' – 26° 40' Aries

Bharaṇī translates as 'she who bears'. The expressions 'to bear' or 'to bear down' have connotations of childbirth, and the sign's symbol is the *Yoni*, or vulva. This represents the power of creation, the forbearance needed to produce anything. Yet where there is life, there is death. Everything that has a beginning must have an end.

Its ruling deity is Yama, the 'god of death'. Big themes of life and death are likely to play out in a Venus daśā or of a planet placed here. Yama is sometimes referred to as the 'god of restraint' or the 'god of discipline'. This reflects a need to discipline yourself in anything you wish to achieve. It also requires acceptance when it is over. Yama is the deity that keeps account of all your past deeds. In

Classical Yoga, the yamas are the moral disciplines. Yama is the 'Lord of Dharma', of righteousness. He decides what happens to us in the next life. But you don't have to believe in an afterlife for this to be relevant to you now. Whatever you are creating now becomes your future.

If this sign is active, either in a Venus daśā, or any planet in the sign, you may be interested in creativity, family planning, sexuality, and death. Yet you must relinquish something to achieve whatever you wish to produce. Once you have given birth to something, you are a changed person. When you have a child, you have become a parent. Creating something changes you forever more.

After the previous lunar mansion brought impulsiveness, this one requires more consideration. Creation is a dance between wilfulness and allowing. The creative urge springs forth whenever it wishes. Yet, as any creative person is aware, there is a lot of demanding work required before any kind of spontaneity is possible. There is a lot of effort required before something becomes effortless.

With the Moon in Bharaṇī, themes of productivity and creativity may stay with you throughout your life. Your life began in a Venus daśā and you are likely to discipline yourself to get what you want. You are a force to be reckoned with. Yet you are likely to attract the resources you need to make something happen. Venus here shows receptivity. Venus in Aries could pose problems if you are striving too hard to achieve what you could do with allowing. If you are so focused on making something happen, you may not stop to appreciate what you have already asked for.

The Sun is strong here, but it needs more discipline to see something through to completion. You must also accept when it is over. This is often the hardest part of the creative process; letting it go. You may have to say goodbye to your children so they can find their way in the world. Or it's that masterpiece you have worked on for years. Mars is strong here, as it rules the sign Aries, where this lunar mansion is. Yet Mars must adhere to compromise and restraint. The more you can channel your energy through a discipline, the better off you will be – and the more you can achieve.

Mercury is challenged here, although Venus helps it out, as a friend. This shows the possibility of cooperation. Jupiter may struggle to find the meaning in what may seem like very sexual themes. Yet it may express itself in bigger themes of life and death. Jupiter here can find purpose in helping those dealing with births and deaths. Expanding your own family may also be a theme.

Saturn here may challenge you to find the time and energy to produce anything. Or you may not know when to quit. This may show not knowing what to do, how much effort to put in. It may show up as too much restraint or not enough, leading to an ill-timed, lacklustre response. You may work towards your goals but may doubt whatever you are doing. This can fuel more arduous work until you get it right.

Rāhu could exaggerate and distort these themes all the more. This may express itself in all kinds of extremes during the creative process. You may have many great insights and creative outlets, yet you may not be consistent. Ketu here could challenge your process to go deeper. Either lunar node could bring up complexities around themes of life and death, judgement and redemption.

Venus and Mars, planets associated with Bharaṇī, reflect a need to find a balance between doing and allowing. Some planets do better with one or the other. You may find your way to achieving a great deal with more or less effort.

3. *Kṛttikā:* The Sharp One
26° 40' Aries − 10° 00' Taurus

Kṛttikā means 'to cut' and one of its symbols is a blade. Words such as 'critical' and 'critique' express its nature. The blade, a symbol of the sign, reflects a need to cut out any negativity from your life. Its ruling deity is the god of fire, Agni. Agni represents the transformative nature of fire. It represents a purification, an inner clarity once you have removed any imperfections. This shows a need to remove anything that is not true, or beneficial, for yourself or others. Fire can either warm or burn, blades can heal or kill. You may do both. You may have to be cruel to be kind.

Kṛttikā's nature is both sharp and soft. You may help others get rid of things, removing blocks for them to improve their lives. Yet you may have to sacrifice something. If you help someone else out, you must sacrifice your time and energy. In looking out for those less fortunate, you must know your own needs. This may show up as animal rescue or attempting to rescue someone in your life. But the question to ask yourself is: How much can I give? There is a need to find a balance between what you can and cannot do for others.

With the Moon in Kṛttikā, themes of purification may stay with you throughout your life. You may even be interested in fire rituals. You began your life in a Sun daśā. The Sun's clarifying nature reflects the benefits of ridding yourself of negativity. The Moon is lit up by the Sun, drawing on its energy for sustenance. This may mean having the resources that ease your mind, to care for others less fortunate. Yet this could also show lofty ideals where life does not always meet your expectations. Despite the stability and security, you may wish for more. This may be the case if you wish to help others who have less. Yet you cannot help everyone. The Sun here shows a time for purification, to bring more clarity and purpose.

Mars can cause problems here, more so in the Taurus division, as Mars is about selfish pursuits. This expresses itself better in the Aries division, where your sharpness and selfishness can do wonders. In Taurus, there's a need for at least a little compromise to acknowledge your true source of power.

Mercury does better in the more stable Taurus than in Aries. Its association with the Sun can show proper discrimination, to see what you or others need, and when. Taurus supports Mercury, the intellect, to deal with the practicalities. Jupiter here can show many blessings, as the Sun's association with Jupiter is positive. Yet the downside is thinking you can take on more than you can, including other people's problems. Jupiter's strength is the ability to discern who needs help and how much.

Venus is happy in the Taurus division, as it rules the sign. It may be too sharp in the Aries division. There is always the possibility of sharpness that can leave others hurt. Saturn's association with the Sun may challenge your confidence. You may learn this by trying to help and not being able to, or trying too hard, leaving yourself with nothing to give.

Rāhu in Taurus can show an ability to amass a great deal of resources. Yet any association of the nodes with the Sun may show other complexities. Powerful relationships and urges may distort the need to do good. You may gather so many resources yet may still be wanting. More recognition, more power, and resources; it's never enough for Rāhu. There are no planets debilitated in Taurus unless you count Ketu. Ketu may show a neglect or rejection of the basics in life. Ketu here requires you to notice your saboteur, your shadow self. It may throw a spanner in the works.

All planets here must blend with the Sun, highlighting the themes of the planet. The more elevated you can be, the more you can purify it for everyone's benefit, including your own.

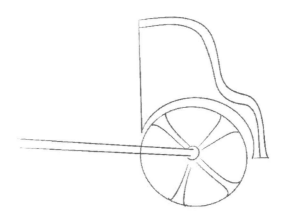

4. *Rohiṇī:* The Comfortable One
10° 00' – 23° 20' Taurus

Rohiṇī means 'reddish woman', representing passions and growth. This has a connotation of sex, but it also reflects growth in all aspects of life. You can direct your sexual energy into something that is long lasting. Rohiṇī is sensual and nourishing, a fertile ground for creating something beautiful. It represents an appreciation of the finer things in life. One downside may be overindulging. It may also show a life cut off from your spirit, beyond all the finer things you are likely to accumulate. But when it's this good, how could you deny yourself?

Its symbol is a chariot, a symbol of wealth and comfort. Home comforts and luxury items are likely to play a part, either in a daśā of the Moon or a planet placed here. Prajāpati, the god of creation, rules it. This reflects a need to create something long lasting, to use your creative strengths to increase and accumulate assets.

The Moon is the most comfortable in this sign. In Vedic myth, the Moon had 27 wives, the 27 lunar mansions, but preferred to stay with this one the most. The Moon was cursed to wax and wane because of giving Rohiṇī more attention than the others. This reflects the ebb and flow of enjoyments, the ups and downs of pleasure. But who would blame the Moon? This is a very enjoyable sign!

With the Moon in Rohiṇī, themes of enjoyment may stay with you throughout your life. You began your life in a Moon daśā. It is likely that you have a sense of warmth and well-being. You are also likely to gather around you many things you enjoy, with people you enjoy them with. It may challenge the Sun because the Sun is about purpose and your Higher Self. Connecting with others after you have fully connected to yourself is necessary. Mars may challenge here. While you may gather resources to enjoy, your relationships might suffer from your selfish pursuits. Things are more enjoyable when you share them with others.

Mercury is happy in Taurus, although there may be complications because of its relationship to the Moon. Mercury is the illegitimate child of the Moon in Vedic myth. This points to the intellect's needs to address emotional and instinctual impulses. Jupiter may deliver the goods, but pleasures can be meaningless with something deeper. Jupiter may grant many blessings here all the same. You may even find meaning in basic pleasures.

Venus is delighted here, as it rules Taurus. Combined with the Moon, there are relationships to cherish and many things to enjoy. Venus is likely to show some compromise and the many benefits of being able to do so. Venus and Rohiṇī are both about sensual enjoyment. The downsides of this are when you overdo any sensual enjoyments. Saturn may dry beautiful things up. It may lessen enjoyments in favour of responsibilities. Yet it may also show you delaying gratification in favour of doing the right thing. Saturn daśās demand a clear out. The analogy of having to clear the land to build a house should not be lost on you.

Rāhu might be happier here, as it exalts in Taurus. Yet Rāhu is never happy, in another sense. It represents obsessions and a lack of satisfaction, no matter how much you get. This is the inherent problem when Rāhu is so powerful. It is more powerful to create problems. Rāhu expresses extremes, which lead to a block of the very thing you wish to accumulate. It may be a case of feast or famine, gaining much and then losing it all. Or you may lose interest when it cannot please you. It may block the flow of resources because of hoarding. Ketu isn't interested in even the basics. It's a part of you that has no interest in such frivolity. Yet this is not frivolous to someone who doesn't have even the basics, only to those who have plenty. The basics may be the most important thing if Ketu were here. What happens when you don't get what you want, or you get everything you thought you ever wanted? You are likely to search for something beyond. Ketu deepens your relationship to your spiritual essence. This may be due to not getting what you want. Or you get everything you ever wanted and still feel you are lacking.

Whatever the planet, it must learn to attract the people and resources to create something beautiful. There is always a 'give and take' required to keep the flow of good things coming.

5. *Mṛgaśirṣā:* The Curious One
23° 20' Taurus – 6° 40' Gemini

Mṛgaśirṣā means 'deer's head'. Like a deer, this brings a fondness for roaming about, exploring new avenues of adventure. There is an innocent curiosity during a daśā of Mars. It is creative and intellectual. Yet you may be overly stimulated and become hyper-vigilant to any changes in your environment. You may become more socially attuned, more curious, and wish to travel or explore your mind. It's also a sexually curious sign, egged on by the youthful and adventurous Mars.

Soma, the Moon god, rules Mṛgaśirṣā. This emphasises its gentle nature. It may represent an interest in healing herbs and treatments. It may also express itself in some intoxicating substances and hallucinogens. Soma represents a cure, an elixir of youth, which you may chase. You may explore the interests of your youth or maintain youthfulness. You are likely to feel more energised and excitable.

With the Moon in Mṛgaśirṣā, themes of adventure and curiosity may stay with you throughout your life. You were born in a daśā of Mars. Whether you wander about travelling, or go on 'trips' by taking substances, you will be in the mood to explore. Any planet mixes with Venus and Mercury, because of Mṛgaśirṣā's split between Taurus and Gemini. Together with Mars, these planets can show a lot of stimulation and fun. Your energy needs a healthy outlet.

Mars itself may challenge you in either Taurus or Gemini, as selfishness and recklessness can bring mental strain. Venus and Mercury need compromise and negotiation. If you express an opinion without taking others' opinions into account, it doesn't matter if you are right. What matters is that these relationships may not support your needs. The Sun can challenge relationships with superiors. Your immediate superiors at work or in government may dictate how far and free you can roam. There is a need to compromise.

Mercury is happy in this realm, especially in the Gemini division. Mercury in Gemini expresses itself with lots of enthusiasm and an eagerness to explore. This may be through travel, business, or communication. The deer's antlers reflect your mind, considering many options. One pitfall is not being able to make your mind up when you have so much to choose between. Jupiter may find it challenging to find something more meaningful here. Even if you win the debate, there is a need to connect to something deeper beyond right and wrong. Winning an argument is unlikely to win you friends.

Venus is happy here, especially in the Taurus division. The Gemini division gives even more things to enjoy and share with others. Without others to share things with, life can become a little dull. Saturn may be good for building something enjoyable, especially in the Taurus division. It may show something to enjoy in Gemini, as long as there is due respect given to your elders and the rules of the game.

Rāhu is likely to expand and exaggerate on all these themes, creating many difficulties as it does so. You may gather resources in Taurus, but experiences are the focal point for Gemini. This can lead to all kinds of mental stimulation that leave you ungrounded. Ketu is least likely to entertain these notions, unless you are engaging in a way that does not neglect your spiritual essence.

Whatever the planet, you can enjoy life's simple pleasures. This doesn't mean you have to neglect your spiritual essence. This may actually make these experiences all the more enriching.

6. *Ārdrā:* The Clarifying One
6° 40' – 20° 00' Gemini

Ārdrā means 'moist' and its symbols are a teardrop and jewel. This represents the role of tears in creating a new sense of clarity, much like after a 'good cry'. If this sign is active in a Rāhu daśā, you can overcome negative thoughts with courage and conviction. This shows the difficulties faced by an overactive mind. But it also points to the clearing of the air as you deal with the issues.

Its ruler is the god of storms, a fierce form of Śiva named Rudra. The mythological story tells of how Rudra did not have a name at birth and cried until Brahmā named him Rudra, meaning 'to cry' or 'to howl'. He was given different names. You may go through name changes if this sign is active in a Rāhu daśā, or of any planets placed here. This may mean a change in position or status. Other interests may be detoxification therapies or renovation. It may be a suitable time for a clear out.

With the Moon in Ārdrā, themes of clarifying issues may stay with you throughout your life. You were born in a daśā of Rāhu. You may re-invent yourself over and over. Rāhu here is likely to blow all these stimulations, and simulations, out of proportion. You may not know who you are and what you are about. Your life may be about finding answers to questions you have not yet formulated. You may search your whole life for more information, more interaction.

The Sun can bring clarity after emotional storms, once they blow over, at least. Connecting to yourself, and confidence from knowing your role, may be one expression. Yet you may be lost in the need for recognition, either in a position you hold or a role you play. Mars here may challenge you as it mixes with Rāhu, and Mercury, the ruler of Gemini. Both can block to your willpower and drive with excessive thinking. Rāhu exaggerates and depletes Mars, while Mercury can get into all kinds of debates about what to do. Having one cup of coffee may get you going, but after ten you cannot function!

Mercury is right at home in Gemini, although that is no guarantee of a peaceful life. In fact, it may be so stimulating, with so many things to choose between, that you cannot choose anything. Limiting mental stimulation or interaction with others may help lessen this tendency. Jupiter may find it hard to find its centre of the storm of this sign. You may wish to connect to something more intuitive. If you are changing your mind about who you are, and what you believe to be true, you may need to tune within. Yet it could offer the discernment to communicate deeper truths.

Venus is happy to indulge others, as well as your sensual and sexual appetites. Be aware of the potential for overdoing it. This may challenge your relationships if you crave more stimulation than one partner can give you. This lunar mansion is about having more roles, more interactions, more of everything. Saturn may challenge you to focus your attention instead of scattering it. It may do this by reminding you of a need to be still. Saturn in Gemini may need more restraint, in social engagements and in role playing. It's helpful to know where your boundaries lie, what you can and cannot do.

Ketu is the calm at the eye of the storm. You can always find your centre. It helps ground Rāhu in what is real, beyond mental stimulation or virtual worlds. Ketu may show a need to renounce all that is frivolous and distracting to your spiritual quest. This can tap you into something beyond the limits of the intellect. It can bring forth a deeper knowing, yet it may also cloud your judgement. Ketu can show a mindlessness, an erratic impulse to do whatever comes to mind.

Whatever the planet, the scattering of energy can clear a way forward. Confusion eventually leads to clarity and a sense of purpose.

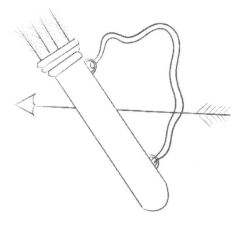

7. *Punarvasu:* The Truthful One
20° 00' Gemini – 3° 20' Cancer

Punarvasu means 'light again'. After the storms of the previous Rāhu daśā, Jupiter brings clarity. Its symbol is an arrow returning to its quiver. This reflects repeating patterns. Light returns after a storm; clarity comes after confusion. This is when you wish to make some sense of the patterns in your life. This lunar mansion has a benevolent nature and is pure and virtuous, kind and forgiving.

Its ruler is the infinite goddess and mother of all creation, Aditi. She represents the underlying pattern of order and cohesion behind all creation. The truth of this will make itself known to you in a daśā of Jupiter. Jupiter is like the lightning bolt that cuts through your doubts. The Sun shines through the clouds. When active in a daśā of Jupiter, you may find yourself in a search for truth. You may wish to protect and care for your family and community. Other interests may be healing, education, travelling, and study.

With the Moon in Punarvasu, themes of truth and righteousness may stay with you throughout your life. You were born in a Jupiter daśā. You may look for the hidden connection behind all things, discovering the magic behind all creation. Jupiter is moving towards its exaltation in the Cancer division. You may be on a quest for truth and wish to impart this to others. Or you may seek the truth from others, such as teachers or mentors. There is likely a deep connection to something beyond the intellect. This taps you into something more profound beyond the mind. The emotions are the first port of call. Yet you must also transcend these to go beyond fluctuations towards stillness.

The Sun here may lead to more clarity about what is true. Its connection to Jupiter, Mercury, and the Moon can bring many realisations. Mars can be a problem here, especially in the Cancer division. This can show an attempt to negotiate with your emotions but lacking the will to rise above them. Mars may challenge intellectual debate. You cannot ignore how you feel. You may replace action with emotional considerations. If you want to do something, you will. If not, then you won't. Yet new perspectives mean putting aside impulsive actions so you can think about it.

Mercury is happy in the Gemini division but must acknowledge something deeper. You must go beyond the noise to see your patterns, to be still. In the Cancer division, Mercury has to deal with instincts and emotions it may not process. Some emotions and feelings may leave you at a loss about how to express yourself. Yet there is the possibility of communicating your truth, even if you cannot explain it rationally.

Venus is happy to hang out in Gemini, although its relationship with the Moon and Jupiter is more complex. The enjoyments of Venus need to combine with more meaningful pursuits. Saturn may be a little too direct or detached in its approach in Cancer, although Gemini suits its nature more so. Mindful communication, from the heart, may be a better way to express Saturn's detachment.

Rāhu can show issues with truth, as it distorts perceptions. Yet Rāhu can also show deeper insights if you can organise your thoughts into a more coherent whole. This may also show fear of dealing with emotions, which only makes them seem more challenging. Ketu can show a loss of rationality and a challenge to truth-finding. But it may also show a deeper truth, beyond words, feelings or instincts. Ketu is a knowing that comes from some other place altogether.

Whatever the planet, there is a need to settle into stillness. There is always stillness within, beneath the fluctuations at the surface of the mind.

8. *Puṣya:* The Nurturing One
3° 20' – 16° 40' Cancer

Puṣya means 'flowering' and 'nurturing'. Its symbols are a flower and a cow's udder. This reflects its nourishing and flourishing nature. Feeding a child or offspring is one expression, as is anything that feeds your body, mind, and soul. If this were active in a Saturn daśā, there is a need to look at what nourishes and how wholesome it is.

Its ruler is the priest to the gods, Bṛhaspati. This is a representation of the planet Jupiter. Although Saturn associates with this lunar mansion, Jupiter shows a balance between both. This usually means finding a healthy balance between attachment and detachment in Cancer. You may take on a role of teacher, guide or adviser, or parent. Or you may meet with guides and advisers. You may develop an inner awareness of truth through spiritual means or by questioning.

With the Moon in Puṣya, themes of nourishment may stay with you throughout your life. You were born in a Saturn daśā. You may have to look more closely at what you are subjecting yourself to. It requires more objectivity. Saturn shows more responsibilities in your life, be it a child, students, whomever you have an impression upon. Saturn teaches you to do the right thing by everyone.

The Sun here is strong in its association with the Moon, the ruler of Cancer. And yet, its association with Saturn may challenge your confidence. Yet Saturn may temper overconfidence and self-centeredness, so that you can think about others. Mars is not happy in debilitation in Cancer. If you don't feel restrained by Saturn, you may feel many things you would rather not because of the emotional landscape of the Moon. Actions you take now must take on others' needs. Yet you may not always want to do what needs to be done.

Mercury is less effective because of its association with Cancer. Emotional considerations may make rational communications a challenge. Yet Saturn's influence can show the much-needed objectivity. Jupiter exalts here. It shows a life connected to others, to community, to nourish others. There are lofty ideals, though, so you may find that life doesn't always match your expectations. Venus can get confused about what a healthy adult relationship looks like. One partner may treat the other as a child.

Rāhu exaggerates these themes, adding more emotional extremes. There may be a fear of feeling all your emotions, and yet you feel them all the same. When combined with the Moon and Saturn, Ketu can bring complexity. It may show you running for the hills! Ketu in Cancer shows a need to find stillness at your centre. Ketu requires a deep dive beneath emotional fluctuations or compensations. It shows a need to be still, whatever you are feeling. Whatever the planet, you must find a balance between what you think and how you feel. Any planet needs to find space for everyone, you included.

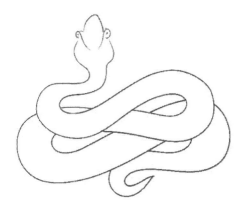

9. *Āśleṣā:* The Regenerating One
16° 40' – 30° 00' Cancer

Āśleṣā means 'embracing' and 'clinging'. It reflects attachment issues and skills in mental and emotional manipulations – for good or ill. This may mean manipulating others for your own needs, or it may show a cultivation of your energy through spiritual practices. You may be more aware of the negative and positive expressions of attachment during this daśā. It expresses this understanding through Mercury.

The Sarpas, the serpent deities, rule this lunar mansion. Its symbol is a coiled snake, representing the hidden energy at the base of the spine called *kuṇḍalinī*. This untapped energy may wake up during a daśā of Mercury if triggered. This may mean unleashing an energy that needs management. You may have more of an interest in occult knowledge and mystical practices. Or you may have an interest in healing diseases of the body or mind, either through modern medicine or spiritual states and plant medicines. Snakes represent hidden knowledge and spiritual awakening, as well as poisons. This may show an interest in black magick. You may do little or nothing with any of the above. Yet you may still have to experience the fluctuations of the mind and learn to tame them. You may not be conscious of the manipulations as you deal with your attachment issues in your adult relationships.

With the Moon in Āśleṣā, themes of emotional attachments may stay with you throughout your life. You were born in a Mercury daśā. You may find your way to healing modalities or simply an interest in these. Mercury can show attachments to one's ideas. You must acknowledge these manipulations if you are to navigate your way to the best outcome for all concerned. Mercury placed here would double up on Mercury themes, including alchemical processes and secret knowledge. Understanding where you get stuck will help you with undoing some of your entanglements, even if you stay in relationships that were once co-dependent.

The Sun shines a light on all these manipulations, healing relationships. Emotional and energetic entailments, even sexual, can be an enlightening experience. Mars is least happy here. This is where it is debilitated by exact degree. There are emotional attachments to deal with. Mars' youthful energy can jar with the impulse to care. You cannot simply do what you want. Combined with Mercury, there are too many considerations to be that effective in anything you do. Yet you can certainly channel the energy in spiritual disciplines and methods that teach you to manipulate your energy in more productive ways. Any feelings of victimhood or martyrdom are an opportunity to take charge of your life.

Jupiter offers great connections here. It must combine with Mercury in a daśā, though. This may mean having to process emotions through more productive means. It may mean connecting with others in practical ways, while tapping into something more profound.

Venus combining with the Moon and Mercury can show an intense desire for physical, mental, and emotional entanglements. Any kind of co-dependency would spoil a perfectly good relationship, so be mindful of why you do whatever you do for others. Saturn here may show a need to withdraw from any entanglements. There is such a thing as a loving detachment.

Rāhu here can create all kinds of emotional manipulations that you may not even be aware of. Or you may meet someone who has such a powerful hold over you and you cannot fathom why. Being mindful of this potential doesn't mean looking at everyone as a potential threat. Yet Rāhu can show a hyper-vigilance that needs modification. Ketu here can be quite a complex affair. You must relinquish your attachments in a Ketu daśā if placed here. And yet, Mercury's influence shows a need to look at life in more practical terms than Ketu would prefer. You may wish to run away, but Mercury will keep you in the world of things.

Whatever the planet, there is a need to observe your attachments and transform them into healthy bonds. By becoming more self-orientated through spiritual practices, you may not cling to others unhealthily. Instead, you realise you connect to everyone in every which way.

10. *Maghā:* The Mighty One
00° 00' – 13° 20' Leo

Maghā means 'magnificent' and 'mighty'. This represents inherited power and entitlement. Its symbols are a royal throne and crown. The ancestors, the Pitṛs, those who grant you any inherited talents, gifts, power, and resources rule it.

Everyone has an entitlement, even if you wish it were something else. You may use your position and entitlements to get ahead in life. Or you may lament not having all you want and strive to get it, because you feel entitled to it. Whatever you were born with, your ancestors made it possible. Recognising this, even if it is not obvious, connects you to those who have given you your greatest gifts.

If this sign is active in a Ketu daśā, you may have to sacrifice something for this privilege. You may have a certain status in a company, your family or community but have to sacrifice something else. Ketu relates to spirits, as well as rituals, which invoke powers from beyond the grave. There is a need to channel this power into ambitious strategies. It may be a suitable time for risk-taking and decisive action. Be mindful of being impulsive, basing your decisions on irrational thoughts. Ask your ancestors for guidance.

With the Moon in Maghā, themes of entitlement are likely to stay with you throughout your life. You were born in a Ketu daśā. You may lead from a place of privilege as a generous king or a ruthless dictator! Ketu intensifies the need to renounce what you did not ask for while going for what you want. This may give you great power in the world, but it may not live up to your standards or please you in any meaningful way.

The Sun is powerful here. It connects you to your ancestors and the power and majesty of the sign Leo. This is where confidence and leadership roles are natural. The Sun here activates Ketu, so you must be mindful of other worldly dimensions. If you come to realise you stand on the shoulders of giants, you're more likely to succeed in anything you do. If not, you may at some point have to relinquish what you have achieved. This is especially if your gains are ill-gotten. Mars is strong in Leo. Yet strength is not only brute force. Although this may indeed be how you express it. Strength here can show inherited gifts that fuels your passions. Ketu suggests a need to be open to losing it at some point, though. Anything you have must one day leave. Yet, with this awareness, you can enjoy it more while you still have it.

Mercury here may challenge your intellect. This may show a lack of comprehension of hidden dimensions. Mercury would prefer to focus on practical application. But you do yourself a disservice if you do not acknowledge the authorities. Jupiter in Leo is usually a gregarious combination. Yet Jupiter's association with Ketu is less certain of itself, or what is true. It's likely to bring a change to your beliefs. Understanding where those beliefs come from may be a more useful exercise. You can change what you believe is possible.

Venus in Maghā may challenge relationships, as Ketu is exacting and relinquishing. This can jar with themes of comfort and enjoyment, bringing something more profound. Saturn brings restraint to where there should be power. This may mean having to accept your weaknesses. Or you may use your weaknesses to get you what you want. You may not have wanted it if you were not denied it in the first place.

Rāhu here can confuse you with where your true source of power lies. Are you seeking success in the world of things, or are you discovering your strengths within? Rāhu, in this lunar mansion, activates the opposite node,

Ketu. The future may pull you forward, only to show you where, and who, you came from.

Whatever the planet, you must acknowledge your true source of power to keep it. Pay homage to those who have gone before you and you are more likely assisted from beyond the grave.

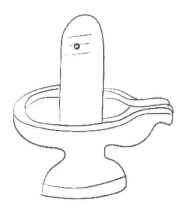

11. *Pūrva Phālguṇī:* The Creative One
13° 20' – 26° 40' Leo

Pūrva means 'former' and *phālguṇī* means 'fruitful'. It is twinned with the next lunar mansion, *Uttara Phālguṇī*, the 'latter fruitful'. Pūrva Phālguṇī is a pleasure-seeking and creative lunar mansion. Its ruler is the god of good luck and enjoyment, Bhaga. This represents your desire for leisure and luxury, for sexual delights. As enjoyable as this is, there may be a tendency to overindulge.

One of its symbols is the *Śiva Lingam*, while another is the foot of the marital bed. This represents the creative urge, the regeneration that is possible using sexual energy. You may express this through having children or some creative expression. The Śiva Lingam represents your ability to 'trans-mutate' the sexual impulse for spiritual purposes. This is like rocket fuel to bring you to higher states of awareness. This may also express itself in the arts, through luxury, relationships, and enjoyable pastimes. A daśā of Venus is likely to be enjoyable. You may not be making art, but your life is a work of art. You may not always be making love, but this is usually an enjoyable lunar mansion.

With the Moon in Pūrva Phālguṇī, themes of pleasure may stay with you throughout your life. You were born in a Venus daśā. It is likely to show up as an artistic sensibility, even if you do not express it through art. Whatever you do, there is a need to enjoy the experience. Yet it requires resources from those in power, in Leo. You may have to negotiate with those who have all the connections to create what you want.

The Sun can be very enjoyable here, as the Sun is strong in its own sign, Leo. It mixes Venus themes up with the Sun. This means having to compromise what you want, to please another, to get what you want. Mars may be strong in Leo, but its association with Venus shows a need for more compromise. Whatever art you are passionate about expressing requires an audience.

Mercury brings many wonderful things to talk about, and to stimulate the senses. Jupiter is less interested in sensual indulgence, which may seem meaningless. Yet this is also about transmutating the sexual urge into something higher.

Saturn brings many responsibilities to areas of life that should be more enjoyable. It does so because of more serious considerations. Its association with Venus, no matter how pleasant, requires more detachment. Instant gratification will not cut it for Saturn! If you can take a step back and focus on the bigger picture, you can make the most of this combination.

Rāhu exaggerates enjoyments to the point of hedonism. It combines with Venus in ways that see you chasing your tail. You may get many opportunities for sensual gratification but they may not satisfy. Ketu's association with Venus can challenge relationships and sensual indulgence. It may point to a need to relinquish someone or something for the sake of something more profound. Yet it is because of losses that your gifts are so much more meaningful. If you lost nothing, you would not enjoy it as much. Absence makes the heart grow fonder.

Whatever the planet, there's a need to attract wealth and resources into your life to achieve all you desire. Relationships can be enjoyable, as can channelling your sexual energy into creative pursuits.

12. *Uttara Phālgunī:* The Committed One
26° 40' Leo – 10° 00' Virgo

Uttara means 'latter' and *phālgunī* means 'fruitful'. Twinned with the previous lunar mansion, Pūrva Phālgunī, which is about the pleasure of relationships, this one is about agreements and commitment. It bridges the sign Leo and Virgo, representing the need to share your gifts, wealth, and resources. One of the sign's symbols is the head of the marital bed.

Its ruler is the 'god of friendship' and marriage, Aryaman. This represents cooperation and commitment to a partner, or anything. If this is active in a daśā of the Sun, you are likely to form committed partnerships. It may also be about committing to yourself. You may get into business and/or a romantic relationship. If you're already in a relationship, it may show more commitment.

You may even think about marriage. When the Moon transits here each month, it is one of the best days to get married.

With the Moon in Uttara Phālguṇī, themes of commitment and agreement may stay with you throughout your life. You were born in a Sun daśā. This would show a need to make more contacts, whether for business or pleasure. The Sun is powerful in the Leo division of this lunar mansion. This doubles up the strength of the Sun as ruler of the sign Leo and its association with Uttara Phālguṇī. The Sun is less powerful in Virgo but more able to share the many resources or take stock of them. This may mean delegating tasks and sharing resources. Mars is strong in Leo. Its association with the Sun is powerful. In Virgo, Mars may be less about sharing and more about gathering the resources you need.

Mercury is powerful in the Virgo division. Its association with the Sun enhances discrimination, to know what you need, and what you can share. The Virgo division is a powerful place for Mercury to do some productive work. Jupiter can expand on the themes mentioned, but it may find it less interesting. This is especially if the resources are only physical. Jupiter requires something more profound. It may let you know this with a spiritual stock-take.

Venus is not thrilled here, especially in Virgo. Its association with the Sun daśā adds to the need for clarification and perfection. And yet, perfection is never reached. Whether you are getting married or looking for a mate, you need to find the best match possible. Yet you must accept someone as they are if you are to be happy. Saturn's association with the Sun shows a contrast between lack and plenty. This contrasts strength and weakness. Saturn here may be about making the most of what you've got. You may feel you don't have as much to share, but you always have more important things than stuff. A Saturn daśā is usually a time to focus on what you have, letting go of what you cannot.

Rāhu's is better in the Virgo division, as Leo can exaggerate the ego and the shadow side of relationships. Instead of magnanimity, you may experience egotism. In Virgo, Rāhu is more stable and practical, a better use of Rāhu's gifts in making progress. Ketu here shows a potential lack, but also a deeper insight and awareness of what matters. Ketu in Virgo may challenge your practical life. If you are open to something greater, you can connect to something beyond. Ketu can be more sincere and committed in relationships, leading to spiritual bonds.

Whatever the planet, there is a need to commit. When you commit to yourself, it's easier to commit to someone, or something, else.

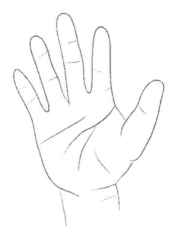

13. *Hasta:* The Skilful One
10° 00' – 23° 20' Virgo

Hasta means 'hand', the symbol for this lunar mansion. It is practical and skilful, whatever the task at hand. It is dexterous, but with a tendency to overthink things, to micro-manage. You can channel this into productive work and many accomplishments. This is a wonderful time for being more efficient and meticulous, to do many things all at once. Yet you may overstimulate yourself.

Its ruler is the Sun god, Savitṛ. This deity grants clarity and illumination. It's about getting all the resources you need to manifest your vision. Savitṛ relates to the early morning Sun, more so, a New Dawn. Indeed, if this sign is active in a daśā of the Moon, you may develop a new skill or are upskilling. It's a suitable time to get your life in order, so you can make something happen. Another area of interest may be health and well-being. Be mindful of seeing the big picture, whatever you are doing.

With the Moon in Hasta, themes of health and orderliness are likely to stay with you throughout your life. You were born in a Moon daśā. You have an orderliness in whatever you do. The Sun connects to this lunar mansion because of the ruling deity. This combines both luminaries in a powerful, yet down-to-earth, manner. This can mean having the resources you need to achieve all your goals, to improve your life and the lives of others. Mars may show a critical nature. It may show a need to balance emotional considerations with being proactive. Mars may get too bogged down in red tape, where acting on impulse must give way to thinking more about your next step.

Mercury is the most powerful here, as it exalts in Virgo and this lunar mansion. This can show a great deal of practical application. Mercury can do its best work, channelling your skills through your heart's desires. When head and heart are on the same page, you are more likely to manifest what you want. Jupiter may be less effective but can expand on these themes. The issue with Jupiter is being able to access something beyond practicalities. Look for meaning in your everyday tasks and you will find all you seek.

Venus is more challenged here. Yet everything is good for something. Venus, in the detail-orientated Virgo, may show a lack of happiness. Something or someone may not be exactly as you would like. If you focus on being happy regardless, you can find happiness in the imperfections. Saturn's seriousness may curtail thinking too grand. Yet this could work for you to make something better. You can learn to work smarter, not harder.

Rāhu is strong in Virgo, as it rules the sign according to some Indian astrologers. Virgo can bring all the ambitions of Rāhu into practical realms of achievement. One pitfall is an obsessive focus on achievement. No matter how much you achieve, you may feel you are lacking. Ketu may challenge the practical side of life. While you may focus on what lies beyond, it may challenge you to do so by taking something away. By tuning into the truth of who you are, beyond all success and failure, you can find the stillness within that does not judge.

Whatever the planet, there is a need to achieve many things now. Knowing when to quit, letting it be as it is, offers an important counterbalance.

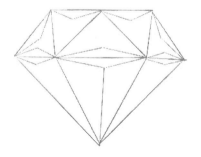

14. *Citrā:* The Bright One
23° 20' Virgo – 6° 40' Libra

Citrā means 'brilliant'. Its symbol is a bright jewel. Its principal star, Spica, is one of the brightest in the night sky. This sign has a keen and refined aesthetic. You are likely to shine in its daśā, to create and show off some talent. After mastering a skill in the previous daśā, you are now at a stage of wishing to share it with others.

Its ruler is the celestial architect, Viśvakarmā. Drawing up plans to build something in your life is what this is all about. This is all about designing your best life. This may reflect a talent, a skill in art and design. At the very least, there may be a need to live in an aesthetically pleasing environment. If this sign is active in a daśā of Mars, you may draw up plans for something new.

With the Moon in Citrā, themes of designing the perfect life may stay with you throughout your life. You were born in a Mars daśā. The Virgo division is meticulous. The Libra division is about finding a balance between exactitude and compromise. Mars here may show a need to find a healthy channel for any frustration when something is not perfect. Mars in Virgo is more exacting, more frustrated. In the Libra division, it may be frustrated, but this may be with others. If the Sun were active in a Mars daśā, this may show compromise, but it may show too much. This may show up as issues around self-confidence and self-esteem. This is especially the case with the Sun in Libra.

Mercury is strong in this lunar mansion and the Virgo division more so. This is the best place to put all your analytical thought and processing. The downside to Mercury is mental overstimulation. Searching for balance are the themes of Libra. You may often overshoot the mark and must backtrack. Jupiter can show fortunate actions that bring excellent results. Yet, in searching for meaning, you may lose yourself in the details. Keep the big picture and meaning behind anything you do to the forefront.

Venus is least happy here, as it is debilitated in this lunar mansion, at the end of Virgo. This can show up as a lack of appreciation or feeling this from others. It may show a longing for love. Yet you may search in all the wrong places. It's about realising you are not only loved –

you *are* love. You were born from an expression of love. While you may not feel this with Venus in Virgo, the lack of love and appreciation can send you on a journey to self-love. In Libra, there is more of a possibility to find balance, between your needs and others. Saturn can bring up issues of when to work hard and when you are pushing too hard. Saturn requires some restraint, although it also requires effort. How much and how often will be big themes throughout its daśā.

Rāhu can bring up issues of how much is enough. It may show your enthusiasm fluctuating when things don't go exactly as you would like. Rāhu brings up your shadow desires, the things that you may hide from even yourself. Ketu can show a need to forgo certain things, so you can connect with something profound within. Ketu can help you be more conscious, especially if you are not getting what you want, as you want it.

Whatever the planet, there is a need to develop skills in the Virgo division. Yet you must couple this with people skills in the Libra division. The perfect life includes imperfect entanglements.

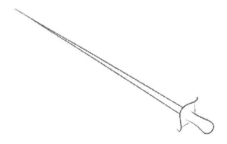

15. *Svātī:* The Independent One
6° 40' – 20° 00' Libra

Svātī means 'independent one'. One of its symbols is a young sprout blowing in the wind. This reflects your need to adapt to new circumstances, to go against the grain. Its ruler is the god of wind, Vāyu, the 'deity of life'. This represents the life-force. The wind blowing a young sprout challenges it to become stronger. Another of the sign's symbols is a sword. This represents a need to break away from the crowd, to go it alone, to figure out your own path on your own terms.

If this sign is active in a Rāhu daśā, you may have to go it alone for a time to find your own way. You may have a heightened sensitivity and artistic nature and may do some precision work. Whatever you do, you must add your own twist.

With the Moon in Svātī, themes of finding your own way may stay with you throughout your life. You were born in a Rāhu daśā. You are a maverick. Yet you must also find a space for others. Rāhu placed here will double up on these themes. Being acquainted with hidden impulses can tap into your untapped potential. The Sun is weaker in Libra. You may get lost in the mix. You may try to figure out yourself in relation to others. By doing so, you may lose a sense of self that you try to regain from them. This may mean looking to others for recognition and acceptance. If you're always comparing yourself to others, you end up feeling less than at some point. Finding yourself in the interaction, and in your relationships, can be the fuel. Mars here can exaggerate irrational actions. You may overdo it or you may stop whatever you are doing to figure out what the other wants.

Mercury here can exaggerate mental stimulation and interaction. This can be very enjoyable. Yet too much stimulation can leave you feeling on edge. Jupiter may block clarity about whatever you are trying out on your own. You may be clear about how to progress, although progress is the point. Jupiter can help balance Rāhu's tendency to do all or nothing. This can bring more coherence and unity if there is too much division.

Venus is at home in Libra, where this lunar mansion is. Combined with Rāhu, this can show all kinds of extremes. It can be extremely enjoyable, of course. You may experience more relationships, for example – at the same time. Or you may explore different art forms and alternative lifestyles. Rāhu and Venus combined can be very enjoyable, but, as always, Rāhu shows a need to rein it in. Saturn is happy in Libra, as it exalts here. Combined with Rāhu, it may challenge, but you are up for it and willing to do whatever it takes. You may need to put your needs aside for others, either a partner or any other. You may serve others' needs in a daśā of Saturn.

Ketu rejects worldly things altogether, including relationships. This is especially the case if your relationships are superficial. Ketu can show complex issues of needing others and yet a need to go it alone.

Whatever the planet, there is a need to find your unique voice and approach, despite the need to be with others - a tricky balancing act.

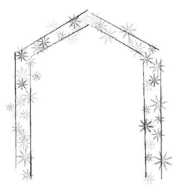

16. *Viśākhā:* The Dedicated One
20° 00' Libra – 3° 20' Scorpio

Viśākhā means 'two-branched'. Its symbol is a decorated archway, representing your chosen path in life. This shows your dedication to what you have chosen, your courage to achieve your desires. Yet it may also show an obsession about what you have set your sights on. This lunar mansion is mostly in Libra. If this sign is active in a daśā of Jupiter, you are likely to focus on your goals. Yet you can compromise to get what you want. In Scorpio, its more obsessive qualities may come to the fore and you are less likely to compromise.

It has two rulers, the god of fire, Agni, and the chief of the gods, Indra. This deity is Indrāgni. This reflects two sides of the coin: decisiveness and indecisiveness. What should you direct your attention towards: material or spiritual? Being split between Libra and Scorpio highlights this dilemma. You will have to find a balance between both.

With the Moon in Viśākhā, themes of decisiveness and indecision may stay with you throughout your life. You were born in a Jupiter daśā. You may weigh up the pros and cons, including other people's needs. Any indecisiveness is but a signal that there is something important to discern – for everyone's sake. Jupiter in Libra is not as sure as its placement in Scorpio. In Libra, Jupiter is looking for advice from others, which may lead you astray. In Scorpio, there is more of an inner knowing.

Sun is weak in the Libra division, as it requires taking others into account. The self must combine with others, your need to shine bonded with others' needs. The Sun is stronger in the Scorpio division. This can show more confidence, a dedication to the path you have already chosen on some level. Mars can show lucky actions, but it also requires a compromise if placed in the Libra division. Mars does better in Scorpio, fuelling your willpower to stick with the decisions you've made.

Mercury is better able to express itself in the Libra division, as it points to an ability to negotiate with others. In Scorpio, there is less compromise, which can challenge relationships. This is especially the case if you focus solely on your need to express yourself.

Venus is strong in Libra but must associate with Jupiter. This means you must listen to that still voice within if you are to make the correct decision. You may get advice from others, but the choice is yours. This is an easier thing to do in the Scorpio division, but the challenge here is not to ignore others' points of view. Saturn is strong in Libra, as it places more emphasis on others for being of service to their needs. In Scorpio, Saturn may challenge you to maintain healthy boundaries. As you push through personal limitations, you may end up pushing people away.

Rāhu can be helpful in Libra, as you discover your shadow in the other. You can face your fears through your engagements. Jupiter's association with Rāhu is an antidote to Rāhu's chaos, channelling it through more productive means. Rāhu in the Scorpio division may exaggerate and distort your perceptions about what is a threat. You may fixate on digging deep and forget to give yourself light relief. This obsessive thinking can grant you great insights, though. Ketu in Libra can confuse others about your motivations. You are likely to confuse yourself. In Scorpio, Ketu is strong in its own sign, so you can tune into what is true within yourself. What is true for you at your core is true for everyone else.

Whatever the planet, there is a need to balance any considerations before reaching a conclusion. Once you do, you can focus all your energy and will power on your chosen path.

17. *Anurādhā:* The Devoted One
3° 20' – 16° 40' Scorpio

Anurādhā, meaning 'after Radha' or 'another Radha', refers to Krishna's devoted lover. This reflects the loyalty inherent in this lunar mansion. It is the most devoted of all. This may express itself in your need to commit to something or someone.

Mitra, the god of friendship, is its ruler. This shows great love and affection, and co-operation. One of its symbols is a lotus flower, highlighting the depth of feeling that allows a blossoming to occur. While all that sounds nice, there are challenging emotions to navigate in Scorpio. You may need to acknowledge jealousy if the subject of your affections does not feel the same. Yet these feelings can allow something even deeper to develop within you. You may develop a divine bond, a deeper love.

If this sign is active in a Saturn daśā, you may have a devotional practice, and be making long-term commitments.

With the Moon in Anurādhā, themes of loyalty and commitment are likely to stay with you throughout your life. You were born in a Saturn daśā. The question to ask yourself is: What or to whom am I committed? Is it wholesome? You may commit yourself to negative thoughts that serve no one. Saturn's association reflects a need to be objective. Saturn in Scorpio may challenge you to do the right thing by everyone, including yourself. It asks you to be responsible for whatever you do, to set healthy boundaries. Yet this may be through having your boundaries challenged. You only have so much time, energy, and resources. A Saturn daśā is a time to cut back.

The Sun is strong in Scorpio yet challenged when combined with Saturn. A Saturn or Sun daśā may bring up issues of identity, even an identity crisis. Mars is strong in Scorpio, yet Saturn shows a need to slow down at the same time. This push-pull combination requires more precision in anything you are doing.

Mercury asks to keep things light and fun in Scorpio. Not a straightforward task. This can show a time to delve into a subject, to do a lot of research. It may lead to obsessions that come from your devotion. Jupiter in Scorpio manifests your deepest desires. The loyalty it suggests points to a worthy cause.

Venus in Scorpio may challenge you to accept the flipside of love and affection. This may include feelings of jealousy and possessiveness. Venus here may be the need for more loving detachment.

Rāhu here can exaggerate your obsessions, taking these to extremes. While this can lead to great insights into what the human mind and heart are capable of, it may leave you vulnerable. Saturn's association can help ground Rāhu in something real. Ketu is at home in Scorpio. Yet its association with Saturn could challenge you to detach in a more responsible way. Ketu may see you running away from any uncomfortable feelings. It may mean changing some fundamental things that have kept you feeling safe. Yet this security may be a prison you can now break free from.

Whatever the planet, your devotion needs a certain amount of detachment. While loyalty to something is admirable, friendships built on trust are as important.

18. *Jyeṣṭhā:* The Secretive One
16° 40' – 30° 00' Scorpio

Jyeṣṭhā means 'eldest'. This refers to skills you gain. It represents the initiation into secret knowledge for the initiated few. Being an elder may mean feeling overlooked and becoming bitter, of course. Yet any bitterness can propel you to even greater heights. Its symbols are an umbrella and talisman. These represent an initiation into secret knowledge and the protection this offers.

Its ruler is the chief of the gods, Indra. Indra was always after power and yet was always losing it. This was especially because of his sexual desires. This is one of the challenging transitions to go through for a spiritual aspirant; that of navigating desires. This may be the desire for sex, or power – or both. And yet, it represents the fuel that propels you to even greater spiritual heights. In myth,

Indra was cursed with 1,000 vulvas all over his body. These were transformed into 1,000 eyes, covering his entire body. This reflects the insights that are available through sexual transmutation. All these themes are likely if Mercury were activating this lunar mansion. Yet you are likely to overcome these obstacles, winning the battle and conquering your demons.

With the Moon in Jyeṣṭhā, themes of power and control are likely to stay with you throughout your life. You were born in a Mercury daśā. Secrets are likely to hold a powerful charge for you. Knowledge is power. Secret knowledge is even more powerful. You may hold many secrets yet may be guilty of over sharing. Research and learning help you overcome challenges in your life.

The Sun is powerful in Scorpio, but not obviously. The Sun brings clarity to the darkest parts of the psyche, leading to many realisations. You are likely to be very aware of the power of your subconscious and of what lies hidden. Mars is at home in Scorpio, yet it requires more skill in communicating from the depths. You must learn to communicate about life's challenges in a way that is palpable.

Jupiter is strong in Scorpio. Its association with Mercury requires more articulation. You may know what is true, but can you explain it? Who is the teacher and who is the student? This may become an issue as you find your own inner guidance through more powerful means.

Venus in Scorpio may challenge you to love all of you, even your dark corners. Despite the vulnerabilities, its association with Mercury can be what's needed. You may be more detached and/or analytical. Talking about your feelings and your desires, no matter how inappropriate or uncomfortable, may be necessary. Saturn in Scorpio asks you to draw a line. Saturn's association with Mercury can bring the much needed objectivity. Communication skills can navigate many complexities.

Rāhu in Scorpio exaggerates and distorts perceived threats. This could lead to all kinds of irrational thoughts. Its association with Mercury can bring more clarity and rationality, if you can be objective now. Ketu is at home in Scorpio, yet it can bring conflicts between spiritual and practical considerations.

Whatever the planet, there is a great power to tap into here. Make sure you are using this power wisely. Otherwise, it may lead to power struggles, with others, and within yourself.

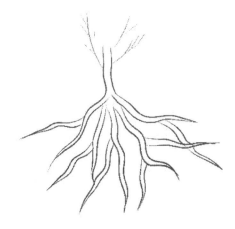

19. *Mūla:* The Penetrating One
00° 00' – 13° 20' Sagittarius

Mūla means 'root' and is one symbol for this lunar mansion. This refers to your family roots, but also our cosmic roots. We can view the centre of our galaxy from this vantage point. Roots bury deep and you are likely to do the same. Yet you may also uproot yourself. You may need to rid yourself of something to get back to your core being if this triggered in a daśā of Ketu. Roots of plants and herbs for healing are also likely to be of interest.

Its ruler is the goddess of destruction, Nirṛti. This shows a need to destroy anything that stands in your way to finding the truth. This may mean having to destroy many things that are not you in a spiritual sense. You may have something you need to relinquish in a Ketu daśā. Any losses remind you of your true spiritual nature, what lies beyond this life. Surgery or purification therapies may also be an interest or a necessity. This is a time to remove things you could do without.

With the Moon in Mūla, themes of getting to the root of an issue are likely to stay with you throughout your life. You were born in a Ketu daśā. Ketu in Mūla is a powerful position. Yet its strength may challenge you to understand things. You may undercover many untruths before you get to the truth of who you are.

The Sun's association with Ketu can bring clarity to the process. There may be a need to renounce worldly success, despite the Sun's power. It taps you into a hidden power that is not always obvious. Mars is also powerful here – at getting to the truth. Yet Mars may also be more volatile and explosive in doing so. This may challenge relationships that are not authentic.

Mercury may help with getting to the truth. Yet it may lead to some confusion if you attempt to intellectualise the process. There are deeper processes at work here. Jupiter is strong in this lunar mansion, and in the sign Sagittarius. This brings clarity. Yet Jupiter's association with Ketu can bring confusion before you reach a state of knowing. Jupiter calms the intensity of Ketu so you can remove all you need without overdoing it.

Venus is more interested in worldly things. Its association with Ketu may bring losses that need understanding. If you are looking for something tangible to bring clarity, it may not be forthcoming. Saturn is more detached about the process, allowing you to take a step back and access from afar.

Rāhu may challenge you to keep perspective about what is the right way forward. In removing blocks, you may focus too much on the removal process and lose touch with the reality of who you are.

Whatever the planet, it requires a deep dive and patience in getting to the truth. It also requires acceptance once the dust settles.

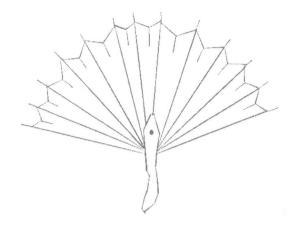

20. *Pūrvāṣāḍha:* The Exuberant One
13° 20' – 26° 40' Sagittarius

Pūrva means 'former' and *aṣāḍha* means 'invincible'. This is twinned with the following Uttarāṣāḍha, or 'latter invincible'. The former reflects an exuberance and joy we most often associate with the sign Sagittarius. It reflects its fighting spirit, and search for the truth.

Its ruler is the goddess of water, Āpas. Water-related themes are prominent. Water is purifying and reinvigorating. After a period of losses in a Ketu daśā, Venus-related themes are a thirst quencher. Yet this lunar mansion shows the potential of going overboard. You may take on more than you are capable. It shows lofty ideals.

If this sign is active in a Venus daśā, it grants more of a sense of optimism and joy. One of the sign's symbols is the elephant's tusk, showing an ability to cut through something. Along with Mūla, it's what makes Sagittarius so frank and to the point. Another symbol is a fan for cooling down passions if you get too heated. Other interests may be herbal remedies and mantras that ward off ill effects.

With the Moon in Pūrvāṣāḍha, themes of purity and truth are likely to stay with you throughout life. You were born in a Venus daśā. Travel and adventure are likely to play a significant role, as are any enjoyable, meaningful excursions. Study is one way to broaden the mind; studying while travelling, the perfect mix.

Sun here is strong and optimistic, bringing clarity of purpose. Mars is also strong here, although more likely to create problems in relationships if you force opinions on others. Mars combined with Venus can show a lot of passion a fan cannot conceal.

Mercury is likely to show frank and open discussions, with a tendency to exaggerate how good it is. Jupiter is at home here, though its connection to Venus may jar with its higher ideals. Venus brings basic instincts and pleasures. Staying high-minded while acknowledging basic drives may be a theme.

Saturn may dampen down enthusiasm. Yet it may also show you working hard on achieving your ideals. Saturn brings Jupiter down to earth. Sometimes, this can be a welcome realisation, at other times, a comedown. Saturn may show an 'attentive optimism'.

Rāhu may challenge high-minded ideals, taking different routes that are uncertain. Going against tradition may be more costly than following a well-worn path. Yet it can bring insights you would not have gained otherwise. Ketu here may be strong. Yet it's complicated by its association with Venus and Jupiter. Jupiter can contain Ketu, bringing out its more beneficial side, helping you get to the truth. Yet Ketu may also challenge worldly things as it searches for something beyond.

Whatever the planet, this lunar mansion's enthusiasm buoys it up. Some planets are prone to going overboard, while others are a sober reflection on what is possible.

21. *Uttarāṣāḍha:* The Unstoppable One
26° 40' Sagittarius – 10° 00' Capricorn

Uttara means 'latter' and *aṣāḍha* means 'invincible'. It is twinned with the previous Pūrvāṣāḍha. It represents a need to use power responsibly. First, you have a goal, (Pūrvāṣāḍha), then you must work at it (Uttarāṣāḍha). It shows what you need to see something through.

The Viśvadevas, the universal gods that govern and control intellectual development, rule it. They represent all the elements needed to see something through to completion. It bridges Sagittarius and Capricorn, taking the lofty ideals of one down to earth in the other. One symbol is the planks of a bed, where you replace comfort with austerity, the ability to endure austerities to reach your goal. The other symbol is an elephant, reflecting your unstoppable force once you begin something. You will stop at nothing to get it done. If this is active in a daśā of the Sun, you are willing to do anything to see your goal to fruition. You are likely to defeat enemies and get the job done.

With the Moon in Uttarāṣāḍha, themes of responsibility and work are likely to stay with you throughout life. You were born in a Sun daśā. This highlights the sense that with power comes great responsibility. You are likely to be responsible for whatever you do. Mars is strong here too, especially in the Capricorn division, moving towards exaltation. This can force you to channel your energy to get much more done. High hopes are one thing, yet nothing happens without action.

It may suit Mercury in the Capricorn division, though it can show practicality in either. Yet Mercury is more suited to the business world of Capricorn than the priestly Sagittarius. This is unlike Jupiter, which is strong in the Sagittarius division but weak in Capricorn. Those lofty ideals crash down to earth with a thud in Capricorn. Jupiter's needs are rarely met while fulfilling ambitions. God is 'out the window' in favour of making a 'quick buck', hope for something better replaced by issues that are unavoidable.

Venus may conflict with the Sagittarius ideals, but it is more suited to Capricorn. This can show a more responsible approach to money and relationships. There is a need to 'get real' in Capricorn. This may be too real, but at least there is a commitment to sticking with something. You are more likely to stick with it in the Capricorn division. Saturn is strong in Capricorn yet doesn't mean it is easy. It is likely to challenge you to make changes. You may not wish for it, but you know it must be so.

Rāhu suits the ambitions of Capricorn, but not the high-mindedness of Sagittarius. It can work in the shadows, doing the necessary to get ahead. Ketu is more suited to the truth-seeking Sagittarius. It is less likely to assist in the business world of Capricorn. Yet you may channel it through more meaningful work that is of service.

Whatever the planet, there must be a responsible approach to making something happen. There must be an acceptance of what it will take to see it through.

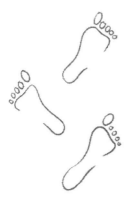

22. Śravaṇa: The Traditional One
10° 00' – 23° 20' Capricorn

Śravaṇa means 'listening'. It represents the ability to connect to knowledge. Traditionally, knowledge was as handed down orally. One of its symbols is an ear. Another symbol is three footsteps, reflecting the need to follow a traditional path. This is symbolic of the three steps of Viṣṇu, restoring harmony to the universe. Viṣṇu is its ruler, the god of preservation, upholding and preserving tradition. Viṣṇu returns a sense of order and upholds truth.

If this is active in a Moon daśā, you may follow a traditional path. This may be through a tradition or advice from others. By doing so, you have access to the wisdom of the ages. This may include the use of rituals, mantras, and music. Even if you never seek advice, the lesson here is to listen within. Viṣṇu represents the consciousness that pervades everything. When you remove all outer noise and distraction, you can hear the truth. Other interests may be education and travel. The myth of Viṣṇu taking three giant footsteps, reclaiming the universe back from a demon, reflects your need to move around and restore harmony. This may be through movement practices or travel.

With the Moon in Śravaṇa, themes of following traditions are likely to stay with you throughout your life. You were born in a Moon daśā. This stresses your ability to hear what is more important, beyond the fluctuations of the mind. Be still and know.

Sun here is not as strong in Capricorn. This is about following others, not yourself. Yet it may show a connection to tradition that fuels a self-confidence in what you learn from others. Mars is powerful here. It can focus your energy on achieving anything. When you follow instructions, you can make anything happen. Taking orders from others is part of the process.

Mercury can teach you that listening is more important than speaking if you wish to learn something. It challenges Jupiter themes in Capricorn. Though it might seem suited to tradition, Jupiter is that 'still voice' within that you may doubt in Capricorn. If you cannot hear it, you may seek many others for advice. You are likely to end up at a loss with so many conflicting reports. The truth lies within you.

Venus here can bring beauty and respect to dealing with those older and wiser than you are. Saturn are those elders and is well-placed here. Saturn represents a part of you that is always older and wiser, no matter your age. It shows a need to listen to those who have gone before you.

Rāhu here can challenge you to follow tradition. You may prefer to go it alone. Yet when you do, you can access more insights. The problems begin when you think you know it all. Ketu is not interested in worldly things, unless it brings you to something beyond these.

Whatever the planet, it must follow the beaten path to find its own way. It must 'stand on the shoulders of giants' to raise itself up.

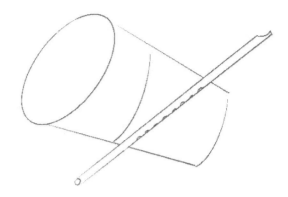

23. *Dhaniṣṭhā:* The Allied One
23° 20' Capricorn – 6° 40' Aquarius

Dhaniṣṭhā means 'wealthy' and 'steady'. It represents being wealthy in every sense of the word. The Vasus rule it. These are the elemental demigods, the allied forces of the polestar, sky, wind, water, earth, pre-dawn, fire, and the Moon. It shows the possibility of achieving all your goals with all the elements it takes to be successful. This reflects your genuine sense of wealth when you are abundant in all aspects of life. Alliances are important when wishing to achieve something.

Its symbols are a drum and flute, reflecting a link to music and the power of sound. It is twined with the previous lunar mansion Śravaṇa, the 'star sign of listening'. This represents the triumphant sound of victory.

If this is active in a Mars daśā, you may bring in all the elements to make something happen in your life. You will stop at nothing until you meet your goal. Be mindful of being too ambitious, recognising others who have helped you get where you are. If you are not getting where you want, recognise the support networks around you. You cannot go it alone now. This lunar mansion bridges Capricorn with Aquarius. It shows your friends and associates that help you get ahead. You rely on others as much as your own work ethic to achieve something.

With the Moon in Dhaniṣṭhā, themes of alliances and wealth may stay with you throughout your life. You were born in a Mars daśā. Mars is strong here. It exalts at the end of Capricorn. This can show your immense focus and energy to achieve something. Success and fame are more likely with Mars' help. Sun here is not as strong because it must adhere to others' rules. This may not come naturally. The Sun reflects your sense of self, which needs to take a back seat in favour of the group. Your own goals may overtake your own capabilities.

Mercury may show an ability to communicate with others, but only after you have listened to them. To get the most out of any engagement, you must see others' points of view. Jupiter is weaker in the Capricorn division, though it's not yet strong in Aquarius. Capricorn loses Jupiter's lofty ideals in dealing with the business of the day, while Aquarius at least shows some other possibility.

This can bring many breakthroughs, although many times after many breakdowns.

Venus here must balance a passionate nature with a cool head if it is to be effective. Otherwise, passions can run riot and make a mess. Respect for others is likely to bring more success than pleasing yourself. Saturn is strong in Capricorn and even stronger in Aquarius. Responsibility and detachment can lead to great leaps forward. If you do not get stuck on how things should be, you are more likely to be successful.

Rāhu is strong in Aquarius, a sign it co-rules alongside Saturn. This shows a more innovative approach. Rāhu can be ingenious, breaking many a 'glass ceiling'. Ketu is only interested in breaking you free from bondage. It reminds you of your past and every time you made mistakes while trying to get ahead.

Whatever the planet, any success and achievement requires help from many others. Yet your true source of wealth lies within.

24. Śatabhiṣāj: The Eccentric One
6° 40' – 20° 00' Aquarius

Śatabhiṣāj means '100 healers' or '100 demons', depending on how you translate the word. This is about healing the psyche as much as the body. This lunar mansion displays many contradictions. It's all about knowing the rules of the game, so you can break them. One of its symbols is an empty circle. This represents the inclusion of all apparent opposites. The empty circle contains everything.

Its ruler is the god of the sea, Varuṇa. This represents the underworld, the darkness of the hidden realms and secrecy, as well as the cosmic realms and enlightenment. Lightness and dark combine in a heady mix. Varuṇa is the guardian of the vast oceans, representing the depth of being and the often-confusing nature of the depths. How can this be true *and* that be true at the same time?

Śatabhiṣāj sees the contradictions as part of the whole equation.

If this is active in a Rāhu daśā, it may show confusion. Yet confusion is as important as the next step: the breakthrough. You are likely to be more interested in philosophy and healing, mind and body. This suggests there is something to heal, or someone in your life that needs healing.

With the Moon in Śatabhiṣāj, themes of healing are likely to stay with you throughout your life. You were born in a Rāhu daśā. Being seen as unusual is likely a common theme also, although you may not label yourself. Others may find you challenging the status quo, or their preconceived ideas. You are likely to push through many glass ceilings – and people's buttons.

Sun here is a challenge to your sense of self, as doing anything innovative requires questioning your motives. You don't see the years of doubting a scientist spends in the lab before making a breakthrough. Even after the breakthrough, the scientist gets back to work on the next thing. It continues to challenge you to push the boundaries of what is possible. It challenges Mars here, as the focus is all over the place. There is so much ingenuity to get into a groove.

Mercury communicates eccentricity with a smile. Yet it may challenge rationality when combined with Rāhu's influence. Jupiter fares better in Aquarius than Capricorn, but it is not out of the woods until it reaches Pisces. This is more like a 'twilight zone' for the planet of clarity. This may bring some 'light bulb moments', but also many a flickering light.

Venus likes to experiment with what is 'normal' here. It may challenge relationships and your boundaries. It's at least an exciting and ground-breaking experience. Saturn is strong here, building on what you have already built. This can lead to more innovations that can stick. Ketu is least interested in the debates that can ensue here. The only thing Ketu questions is the reason for being here at all.

Whatever the planet, this lunar mansion can fuel ground-breaking change. This may lead to progress, yet it may also show doubts about the direction you are heading in.

25. *Pūrva Bhādrapada:* The Visionary One
20° 00' Aquarius – 3° 20' Pisces

Pūrva means 'former' and *bhādrapada* means 'auspicious feet'. This lunar mansion is twinned with *Uttara Bhādrapada*, the 'latter auspicious feet'. This is symbolic of the journey to the next life, the most auspicious step you will ever take.

Its ruler is an unusual one-footed deity called Ajaikapada. This is like a lightning bolt, a form of *Śiva* standing on one leg as a penance. It represents a need to cut through the confusion. This may challenge you to stand on your own two feet as you figure out what is true. This sign has a visionary nature. Its symbols are a man with two faces, a sword, and the front legs of a funeral cot. All these symbolise a cutting away of falsehood. These represent themes of life and death, of making distinctions between what is real and what is not.

If this is active in a daśā of Jupiter, you are likely asking yourself some big and meaningful questions. You may have an interest in education now, especially higher knowledge and spirituality.

With the Moon in Pūrva Bhādrapada, themes of discerning your truth may stay with you throughout your life. You were born in a Jupiter daśā. Jupiter stresses the need for a spiritual orientation. Yet it doesn't mean you cannot have worldly success. Actually, it may mean you do, but that it sends you on a search for some far greater treasure. Jupiter is strong in Pisces, bringing more clarity and meaning.

Sun here is more powerful in the Pisces division, leaving the doubts of Saturn's signs behind. The Sun instils confidence in your search for the truth, despite the sacrifices. Mars is stronger in the Pisces division as well. Aquarius can challenge being proactive when there is so much experimentation. Although stronger in the Pisces division, it can create so much possibility that leaves you wondering where to direct your energy. The two-faced man, the fish swimming in opposite directions (Pisces), shows many contradictions.

Mercury in the Aquarius division can show many interesting ideas, but in Pisces it may show a struggle to make sense of the many dichotomies. The mind attempts to understand what is true and what is false. Yet it may never reach a conclusion.

Venus is happier in the Pisces division, its sign of exaltation. Here it can jump in and enjoy the depth of feeling. Unlike Mercury, it can swim in the sea of possibility, without having to work it all out. Venus in Aquarius may bring many experiments. Breaking boundaries and glass ceilings has its own enjoyments. Saturn is strong in the Aquarius division but is less enamoured with Pisces. It can bring structure to an otherwise diffuse sign.

Rāhu is strong in Aquarius but may challenge you to keep perspective in Pisces. It can exaggerate confusion. Rationality may be harder to come by. Ketu can bring great clarity, diving deep into what is possible. You can realise you are everyone and everything, all at once.

Whatever the planet, it must dive deep into the mystery of life to gain clarity. It must discern truth from falsehood; sometimes, in ways that may seem destructive.

26. *Uttara Bhādrapada:* The Mystical One
3° 20' – 16° 40' Pisces

Uttara means 'latter' and *bhādrapada* means 'auspicious steps'. The previous lunar mansion is twinned with this lunar mansion. It represents a step further towards enlightenment, deeper into the depths of Pisces. This is a stage when the spiritual pursuits of the previous Jupiter daśā become a reality. This may mean having to deal with things which make the spiritual journey more practical. Despite the vague notions of spiritual life, there must be some order.

Its symbol, and its ruler, is a serpent of the deep called Ahirbudhnya. This represents hidden realms, the mysterious depths. This is another form of *Śiva* who removes blocks from the truth. It is emphatic, reflecting your ability to take on everyone and everything. The oceans contain everything, both good and bad, and everything between.

If this is active in a Saturn daśā, you may need more seclusion and self-care. This is so you don't take on everyone else's problems and cannot cope. Saturn daśās are a time for yourself, despite the need to be of service. Other interests may be commitments such as marriage. Yet you may wish to retreat to a place of sanctuary now.

With the Moon in Uttara Bhādrapada, themes of seclusion and spirituality may stay with you throughout your life. You were born in a Saturn daśā. Saturn here stresses the need for retreat. This could be in your day-to-day life, or for extended sabbaticals and pilgrimages.

Sun here highlights the depth of being that can lead to a complete surrender. Mars is strong here, too, but may be unclear where to direct its energy and focus.

We lose Mercury at sea in the middle of Pisces, left without a paddle. The intellect can grapple with figuring out the depth of feelings that can run counterintuitively. Jupiter is strong in Pisces. Yet its association with Saturn can be more real, more grounded in the reality of a daily spiritual life. Venus is moving towards its exaltation, where both pleasure and surrender await. Venus is happy to swim in either direction.

Rāhu may exaggerate feelings here, for good or ill. The depth of feelings can confuse a mind that tries to make sense of its ambitions. You may not be clear about what you want: pleasure or spiritual bliss. Ketu here is at home, deeply embodied and yet ready to let go. Ketu realises to have one, you must have the other.

Whatever the planet, it must dive into the apparent contradiction of being a spirit encased in flesh. Some planets will prefer one over the other, while others make no such distinction.

27. *Revatī:* The Faithful One
16° 40' – 30° 00' Pisces

Revatī means 'wealth' and 'abundance'. Its ruler is the guardian of the living and the dead, Pūṣan, which means 'nourisher'. It represents both material and spiritual nourishment. This is the deity who shepherds his flock from this life to the next. This shows a need to help others on their journey from one life to the next. Yet it shows a need to nourish yourself. It shows a search for seclusion.

This is the last sign of the zodiac, representing a stage of self-realisation. This provides nourishment for your soul to self-realise. Its symbol is a fish, reflecting a faithful nature and spiritual depth, as seen in the Christian faith.

If this sign is active in a Mercury daśā, you are likely to go on a journey, even if only metaphorically. Other interests may be remedies, marriage, and travel.

With the Moon in Revatī, themes of surrender and nourishment may stay with you throughout your life. You were born in a Mercury daśā. Yet Mercury may feel lost here, trying to fathom the spiritual depths, before it can begin again in the next life. This may mean moving from one life stage to another, from one marriage to another, one job to another, etc. It can be a confusing time of endings.

Sun here is a soul ready to let go of all attachments. Yet there is strength in letting go that is not obvious in the world of things. Worldly success may come, but it is not necessarily the goal. Mars is strong in Pisces but, like all planets here, must learn to surrender before it can begin again.

Jupiter is strong in Pisces and willing to surrender for the greater good. In doing so, it finds its salvation and a deeper sense of clarity.

Venus is happiest here, going with the flow, enjoying the scenery. Venus exalts at the end of this lunar mansion and the sign Pisces. It can surrender to spiritual or conjugal bliss, whichever comes first. Saturn can be a container for spiritual life, even if it is a simple life of servitude. Saturn may prefer this to any grand notions of spirituality.

Rāhu may drown in the deep end here. It cannot see that surrender to the divine is the quickest way to get what it wants. Ketu has no such problem and can give you everything. But only once you let go of everything.

Whatever the planet, there is a need to surrender to receive the kingdom. Some planets may have an easier time letting go. Others may confuse tripping out with spiritual release.

INTERCALARY LUNAR MANSION

Abhijit
6° 40' – 11° 13' 20" Capricorn

We sometimes use Abhijit for timing, placed almost entirely within Uttarāṣāḍha. It is only a little over a degree within Śravaṇa. *Abhijit* means 'victorious'. It is an intercalary lunar mansion, which means it gets slotted between two others. Its primary star is Vega, the brightest star in the northern constellation of Lyra. It is extremely far north of the ecliptic. It's sometimes used as a 28th sign for timing auspicious activities, though not used in timing each daśā.

QUALITY OF EACH LUNAR MANSION

Table 2.3 is a quick reference guide to the qualities of each lunar mansion. You can plan your daily activities around these. The Moon transits one lunar mansion every day of the month. You can use these qualities to gauge what activity is appropriate. You will need a calculator or resource to calculate where the Moon is transiting each day. One option is to download the *Timeline Astrology App*. This will calculate where the Moon is on any day. It will also calculate where it was when you were born.

Table 2.3

Fixed	Rohiṇī, Uttara Phālguṇī, Uttarāṣāḍha, Uttara Bhādrapada
Sharp	Ārdrā, Mūla, Āśleṣā, Jyeṣṭhā
Fierce	Bharaṇī, Maghā, Pūrva Phālguṇī, Pūrvāṣāḍha, Pūrva Bhādrapada
Swift	Aśvinī, Puṣya, Hasta
Soft	Mṛgaśirṣā, Anurādhā, Revatī, Citrā
Sharp & Soft	Kṛttikā, Viśākhā
Changeable	Punarvasu, Svātī, Śravaṇa, Dhaniṣṭhā, Śatabhiṣaj

Fixed signs are best for starting something you would like to sustain and flourish, such as a marriage or a new home. When the Moon enters one of these lunar mansions, it's a suitable time to make vows or start the build. Sharp signs are best for gaining insight and clarity, or for removing unwanted things. These are good for overcoming something through some means. This can mean having to have that conversation you've been putting off or ending some behaviour that is no longer appropriate. Fierce signs are best for tackling a problem or behaviour, with even more fierce actions. Soft signs are best for love and friendship, enjoyments, and sensuality. Mixed signs are both sharp and soft, so they offer mixed results. They may be conducive to enjoyments and agreements but need more negotiation. And finally, mutable signs are changeable and best for movement, travel, and study.

STAR PATTERNS

Planetary daśās operate on many levels. Longer daśās show general themes, while sub-daśās pinpoint certain events. Another way to see the indications of the 9 planetary daśās is to break them down into exactly that: 9 daśās. These daśās repeat as sub-daśās throughout your life, though you experience major daśās only once. There are 3 that may be more challenging yet set you on your trajectory forward. These are the 3rd, 5th, and 7th daśās. They may challenge you to change your life's direction. Yet you may neglect what you know you must do. This can create problems if you have strayed off course, although there is no such thing as straying off course from another perspective. Either way, these daśās bring you back on track, although this can prove quite challenging if you have been living out of synch with your life purpose.

There are 3 groups of 9 lunar mansions. This shows repeating patterns based on the 9 planets. The 9 planets associate with 3 lunar mansions each. If one lunar mansion is active in a planetary daśā, it will trigger the other two lunar mansions. It will also trigger any planets placed in any of these lunar mansions. When planets transit any of the 3 lunar mansions, it will reflect its theme. If the 3rd, 5th, or 7th daśās are to bring challenges, they so in the daśā of these planets, or when planets transit these. Table 2.4 shows the 3rd, 5th, and 7th daśās in each star group shaded so you can easily identify them.

Table 2.4

#	Planetary Daśā	Star Group 1	Star Group 2	Star Group 3	Natal Planets
1					Moon
2					
3					
4					
5					
6					
7					
8					
9					

You may wish to fill out your planetary daśās in the first column on the far left-hand column. Add all the planets in the following sequence: Ketu, Venus, Sun, Moon, Mars, Rāhu, Jupiter, Saturn, and Mercury. You may have begun at any point in the above sequence. Input the 1st lunar mansion at birth in the first line of 'Star Group 1'. This is the lunar mansion the Moon was in when you were born. Finally, input all your natal planets in each of their corresponding lunar mansions in the far right-hand column. The Moon usually begins the count, so it goes in the first position.

BEGINNING FROM DIFFERENT STARS

You may also begin the count from different stars, depending on the position of the Moon in your birth chart. If the Moon were in an angle or trine, houses, 1, 4, 5, 7, 9 or 10, you can read it from the Moon as usual. However, if you have the Moon in the 2nd or 6th house, you can also read it from the 4th lunar mansion from the Moon. Enter the 4th lunar mansion from your Moon in the first column under 'Star Group 1' and list the lunar mansions in order. If you have the Moon in the 3rd or 11th house, you can read it from the 5th lunar mansion. If you have the Moon in the 8th or 12th house, you can read it from the 8th lunar mansion. These three ways of reading the daśās are called *kṣema* (Moon in 2nd or 6th), *utpanna* (Moon in 3rd or 11th), and *ādhāna* (Moon in 8th or 12th).

You can use the Moon's lunar mansion as the starting point whether you add any others. Reading it from the Moon's lunar mansion applies to all. It shows events happening in your life, even if you are not consciously creating them. If you have the Moon in the 2nd, 3rd, 6th, 8th, 11th or 12th, the events may be the same, but you may react differently to them. You may be on a different page in the story, although the story is going along at its own pace, as seen in the typical count from the Moon.

Another important vantage point is from the planet with the highest degree, regardless of the sign. This planet is called the Ātma-kāraka, or 'soul significator'. This planet offers important life lessons that you can track with the planetary daśās. You can start the daśās from this planet if the Moon were in this planet's sign. If Jupiter was the planet with the highest degree, and the Moon is in either Sagittarius or Pisces, you can start with Jupiter.

Adding more of these points of reference gives you more perspectives that are based on an oral tradition in India. We should consider these alongside the typical reading of the Moon's lunar mansion and each daśā.

Wherever you begin the daśās, the following is a list of the 9 daśās in sequence and a word I associate with each Sanskrit word.

1. *Janma*: Start
2. *Sampat*: Acquire
3. *Vipaṭa*: Pause
4. *Kṣema*: Secure
5. *Pratyarī*: Challenge
6. *Sādhaka*: Attain
7. *Vadha*: Change
8. *Mitra*: Befriend
9. *Atimitra*: Connect

1. Janma

The 1st daśā you were born within shows the beginning in your life. This is an important planet for your whole life. The birth chart you were born with still impacts who you are, even though the planets no longer form such alignments. The same can be true of your 1st daśā. Every time you enter a planetary daśā of this planet, within the sub-daśās, it will show a new beginning, a reset point in your life. How you experience this depends on your beginnings, as well as the indications during each fresh start. You must take each new beginning in other daśās and transits, although it will highlight a new beginning just the same.

2. Sampat

The 2nd daśā represents a period of growth, as one translation of the word *sampat* means 'to gain'. This planetary daśā represents a period of wealth and prosperity, and some form of blessing. It may be a period when you count your blessings or focus on acquiring more things to be grateful for.

3. Vipaṭa

The 3rd daśā requires patience in achieving your objectives, as it can show obstacles and weaknesses you must overcome. Yet these same obstacles build strength and endurance as you learn patience and forbearance in achieving what you want. The obstacle is the way.

4. Kṣema

The 4th daśā is a more relaxed affair, after feeling challenged in the previous daśā. The word *kṣema* means 'safety', 'tranquillity', 'peace', 'rest' and 'security', offering you a sense of ease and comfort in some form or other.

5. Pratyarī

The 5th daśā can challenge you with a 'well-matched opponent', as we sometimes translate the word to mean. The word *pratyarī* can also mean an 'equally powerful enemy'. These struggles test you. You feel challenged to 'up your game'.

6. Sādhaka

The 6th daśā shows the challenges of the previous daśā were not in vain. After working hard on something, you become an expert; you develop a skill. *Sādhaka* means 'skill' or 'accomplishment', while a sādhaka is someone who attains a *siddhi*, meaning 'power'.

7. Vadha

The 7th daśā challenges you to change direction once you have attained a skill. You should be up for the challenge. *Vadha* means a 'deadly weapon', and the word *vajravadha* from which we derive it can mean 'death by thunderbolt'. This is Indra's weapon of choice. Indra, the chief of the gods, is tasked with changing your life, destroying something, or changing something into something else.

8. Mitra

The 8th daśā brings you into contact with friends and supporters who help you on your path. *Mitra* means 'friend', and this brings back a sense of support after the previous period of change. This period may be a time of contractual agreements, more cooperation, as Mitra is the god of friendships and agreements.

9. *Atimitra*

The 9th and final daśā shows an even greater sense of friendship and agreement. Mitra means a 'friend', while *Atimitra* can mean a 'great friend', reflected in a divine bond, a deeper love and connection to something or someone.

27-STAR PATTERN

The 9 star-pattern repeats 3 times to make up 27 star signs. Each one represents something specific for you, based on the position of the Moon in your birth chart. This is regardless of the general indications of each lunar mansion. There are certain significations for each when counting from the Moon in your chart that do not correlate with the general themes of the lunar mansion in question. The natural 12th lunar mansion is Uttara Phālguṇī and is auspicious, while the 12th lunar mansion from your Moon represents similar themes of commitment. Yet the 12th in a sequence correlates with Vipata that can show challenges to overcome.

Table 2.5 highlights the significations of the 27 lunar mansions, included in a handout during a lecture given by

Sanjay Rath at the British Association of Vedic Astrology in London in 2009.[3]

Table 2.5

Body	Mind	Soul
1. Birth	10. Work	19. Guru, Father
2. Food	11. Marriage	20. *Upasana* [worship] Fortune
3. Trouble	12. Weakness	21. Path
4. Home	13. Security	22. Temple, Arena
5. Struggle	14. Challenge	23. Tests, Heartbeat
6. Learn	15. Achieve	24. *Siddi* [powers], Medicine
7. Slayer	16. Vanquisher	25. Sannyasa [renunciate], Death
8. Helper	17. Colleague	26. Brotherhood, Club
9. Protector	18. Leader	27. Coronation, Goal, Freedom

[3] Sanjay Rath, "Nakshatra Mandala", (lecture handout presented to the British Association of Vedic Astrology, London, received on 7 March 2009), p. 6. English terms in brackets and highlights were added by the author.

The shaded areas in Table 2.5 highlight pivotal turning points in your life. These may challenge you to return to your purpose if you are not already on the right path. Some of the lunar mansions correlate with the 12 houses. The 1st lunar mansion represents your health, a signification of the 1st house; the 2nd, your resources; the 4th, your home; the 10th, your work. Sanjay Rath has also taught that each planetary daśā correlates with each house. So, your 1st planetary daśā correlates with the 1st house, the 2nd planetary daśā with the 2nd house, and so on. Don't be alarmed by some of the language in Table 2.5, such as 'slayer' or 'Death', as this should not be taken literally. And, of course, you only die once. When you experience any of these daśās, you are more likely to experience them as changes in your life direction. These changes are opportunities for growth.

SPECIAL LUNAR MANSIONS

There are some lunar mansions that are given special attention. These include the 1st, 4th, 8th, 10th, 16th, 18th, 19th, and 25th. The 1st begins the sequence and shows your health, the energy you have to do anything. It shows what it is you are doing; what you would like to do, at least. The 1st lunar mansion refers to the Moon's placement, but you could also take any other point as the 1st, including your ascendant. While the Moon shows *what* you would like to do, the ascendant shows *how* you do it. You experience a new beginning every time the 1st lunar mansion is triggered in a daśā or by transit. This is how you began your life. It's a time to start over.

We can see the 4th lunar mansion from your birth Moon for your family life, your background. It shows things that bring comfort. The 8th lunar mansion connects to your mother, so it is a helpful if unafflicted. The 10th lunar mansion relates to career and status. It's also the beginning of the second set of lunar mansions along with the 19th, making it an important one for beginning anything. The 1st, 10th, and 19th lunar mansions represent what you would like to do, and the people that help you do it. The 16th relates to people you associate with, including more intimate relations such as marriage, public relations, and groups; the 18th, to all experiences; the 19th, to circumstances around conception and your father. We give the 25th importance for mental health and well-being. Lunar mansions themselves represent your psychology. The 25th lunar mansion shows how your minds works, the challenges you must overcome, and the mental and emotional resources at your disposal.

1 0 8   P A D A S

We can further divide the zodiac into 108 *padas* or 'steps' of 3 degrees and 20 minutes each. A Sun sign is 9 of these steps. The 9th house represents your father according to Indian astrological analysis. A lunar mansion has 4 steps. The 4th house represents your mother. Your mother and father gave you your life, of course. This highlights the connection between the Sun signs and lunar mansions. The 9 divisions of the Sun signs give a 9th divisional chart to examine for deeper insights into your being. This reflects underlying strength and themes. Both the natal chart and 9th division give a more rounded view, a more wholistic perspective. You may wish to revisit the strengths of planets in each sign at this point (see Table 1.1). The 9th division shows underlying strengths that may not be obvious from your birth chart.

Each pada corresponds to a sign in the 9th divisional chart. When you add these, you get a more intricate view of your chart. Although a planet may be in a weak position in your birth chart, the 9th division may show an underlying strength. The reverse could be true of a strong planet, of course. You may experience the apparent strength, yet it may be weak in the 9th division. This could show an underlying weakness, despite what it may look like on the surface level.

The relationship between the signs in your birth chart and 9th division can be friendly or challenging. Friendly relationships are when planets are in the same or supportive elements. Earth and water support each other. Fire and air are supportive. If you have planets in supportive elements when comparing both charts, it shows an underlying harmony in relation to that planet.

Each step of the lunar mansions correlates with the 4 directions: dharma, artha, kāma and mokṣa. Each of these correlates with an element: dharma with fire, artha with earth, air with kāma, and water with mokṣa. If a planet were in a fire sign in your birth chart, but a water sign in your 9th division, it shows an inner conflict with that planet. If a planet is in the same element, there is more harmony with what the planet signifies.

We would ideally see the 9th divisional chart side-by-side with your birth chart for chart analysis. It gives a more holistic view of the signs. Aries is not simply a fire sign, it is a 'fire-dominant' sign. It has more steps in fire, in dharma, as more signs in the 9th division are fire signs. Likewise, Taurus is an 'earth-dominant sign, as it has more steps in earth, Gemini in air, Cancer in water, etc. (see Tables 2.6 to 2.17).

9 DIVISIONS OF ARIES

Table 2.6

Aries	Degrees	Pada	Direction	Element	9th Division
Aries 1	0° 00' – 3° 20'	Aśvinī 1	Dharma	Fire	Aries
Aries 2	3° 20'– 6° 40'	Aśvinī 2	Artha	Earth	Taurus
Aries 3	6° 40 – 10° 00'	Aśvinī 3	Kāma	Air	Gemini
Aries 4	10° 00' – 13° 20'	Aśvinī 4	Mokṣa	Water	Cancer
Aries 5	13° 20' – 16° 40'	Bharaṇī 1	Dharma	Fire	Leo
Aries 6	16° 40' – 20° 00'	Bharaṇī 2	Artha	Earth	Virgo
Aries 7	20°00' – 23° 20'	Bharaṇī 3	Kāma	Air	Libra
Aries 8	23° 20' – 26° 40'	Bharaṇī 4	Mokṣa	Water	Scorpio
Aries 9	26° 40'– 30° 00'	Kṛttikā 1	Dharma	Fire	Sagittarius

9 DIVISIONS OF TAURUS

Table 2.7

Taurus	Degrees	Pada	Direction	Element	9th Division
Taurus 1	0° 00'– 3° 20'	Kṛttikā 2	Artha	Earth	Capricorn
Taurus 2	3° 20'– 6° 40'	Kṛttikā 3	Kāma	Air	Aquarius
Taurus 3	6° 40 – 10° 00'	Kṛttikā 4	Mokṣa	Water	Pisces
Taurus 4	10° 00'– 13° 20'	Rohiṇī 1	Dharma	Fire	Aries
Taurus 5	13° 20'– 16° 40'	Rohiṇī 2	Artha	Earth	Taurus
Taurus 6	16° 40'– 20° 00'	Rohiṇī 3	Kāma	Air	Gemini
Taurus 7	20° 00'– 23° 20'	Rohiṇī 4	Mokṣa	Water	Cancer
Taurus 8	23° 20'– 26°40'	Mṛgaśirṣā 1	Dharma	Fire	Leo
Taurus 9	26° 40'– 30° 00'	Mṛgaśirṣā 2	Artha	Earth	Virgo

9 DIVISIONS OF GEMINI

Table 2.8

Gemini	Degrees	Pada	Direction	Element	9th Division
Gemini 1	0° 00'– 3° 20'	Mṛgaśirṣā 3	Kāma	Air	Libra
Gemini 2	3° 20'– 6° 40'	Mṛgaśirṣā 4	Mokṣa	Water	Scorpio
Gemini 3	6° 40 – 10° 00'	Ārdrā 1	Dharma	Fire	Sagittarius
Gemini 4	10° 00'– 13° 20'	Ārdrā 2	Artha	Earth	Capricorn
Gemini 5	13° 20'– 16° 40'	Ārdrā 3	Kāma	Air	Aquarius
Gemini 6	16° 40'– 20° 00'	Ārdrā 4	Mokṣa	Water	Pisces
Gemini 7	20° 00'– 23° 20'	Punarvasu 1	Dharma	Fire	Aries
Gemini 8	23° 20'– 26°40'	Punarvasu 2	Artha	Earth	Taurus
Gemini 9	26° 40'– 30° 00'	Punarvasu 3	Kāma	Air	Gemini

9 DIVISIONS OF CANCER

Table 2.9

Cancer	Degrees	Pada	Direction	Element	9th Division
Cancer 1	0° 00'– 3° 20'	Punarvasu 4	Mokṣa	Water	Cancer
Cancer 2	3° 20'– 6° 40'	Puṣya 1	Dharma	Fire	Leo
Cancer 3	6° 40 – 10° 00'	Puṣya 2	Artha	Earth	Virgo
Cancer 4	10° 00'– 13° 20'	Puṣya 3	Kāma	Air	Libra
Cancer 5	13° 20'– 16° 40'	Puṣya 4	Mokṣa	Water	Scorpio
Cancer 6	16° 40'– 20° 00'	Āśleṣā 1	Dharma	Fire	Sagittarius
Cancer 7	20° 00'– 23° 20'	Āśleṣā 2	Artha	Earth	Capricorn
Cancer 8	23° 20'– 26°40'	Āśleṣā 3	Kāma	Air	Aquarius
Cancer 9	26° 40'– 30° 00'	Āśleṣā 4	Mokṣa	Water	Pisces

9 DIVISIONS OF LEO

Table 2.10

Leo	Degrees	Pada	Direction	Element	9th Division
Leo 1	0° 00'– 3° 20'	Maghā 1	Dharma	Fire	Aries
Leo 2	3° 20'– 6° 40'	Maghā 2	Artha	Earth	Taurus
Leo 3	6° 40 – 10° 00'	Maghā 3	Kāma	Air	Gemini
Leo 4	10° 00'– 13° 20'	Maghā 4	Mokṣa	Water	Cancer
Leo 5	13° 20'– 16° 40'	Pūrva Phālguṇī 1	Dharma	Fire	Leo
Leo 6	16° 40'– 20° 00'	Pūrva Phālguṇī 2	Artha	Earth	Virgo
Leo 7	20° 00'– 23° 20'	Pūrva Phālguṇī 3	Kāma	Air	Libra
Leo 8	23° 20'– 26°40'	Pūrva Phālguṇī 4	Mokṣa	Water	Scorpio
Leo 9	26° 40'– 30° 00'	Uttara Phālguṇī 1	Dharma	Fire	Sagittarius

9 DIVISIONS OF VIRGO

Table 2.11

Virgo	Degrees	Pada	Direction	Element	9th Division
Virgo 1	0° 00'– 3° 20'	Uttara Phālguṇī 2	Artha	Earth	Capricorn
Virgo 2	3° 20'– 6° 40'	Uttara Phālguṇī 3	Kāma	Air	Aquarius
Virgo 3	6° 40 – 10° 00'	Uttara Phālguṇī 4	Mokṣa	Water	Pisces
Virgo 4	10° 00'– 13° 20'	Hasta 1	Dharma	Fire	Aries
Virgo 5	13° 20'– 16° 40'	Hasta 2	Artha	Earth	Taurus
Virgo 6	16° 40'– 20° 00'	Hasta 3	Kāma	Air	Gemini
Virgo 7	20° 00'– 23° 20'	Hasta 4	Mokṣa	Water	Cancer
Virgo 8	23° 20'– 26°40'	Citrā 1	Dharma	Fire	Leo
Virgo 9	26° 40'– 30° 00'	Citrā 2	Artha	Earth	Virgo

9 DIVISIONS OF LIBRA

Table 2.12

Libra	Degrees	Pada	Direction	Element	9th Division
Libra 1	0° 00'– 3° 20'	Citrā 3	Kāma	Air	Libra
Libra 2	3° 20'– 6° 40'	Citrā 4	Mokṣa	Water	Scorpio
Libra 3	6° 40 – 10° 00'	Svātī 1	Dharma	Fire	Sagittarius
Libra 4	10° 00'– 13° 20'	Svātī 2	Artha	Earth	Capricorn
Libra 5	13° 20'– 16° 40'	Svātī 3	Kāma	Air	Aquarius
Libra 6	16° 40'– 20° 00'	Svātī 4	Mokṣa	Water	Pisces
Libra 7	20° 00'– 23° 20'	Viśākhā 1	Dharma	Fire	Aries
Libra 8	23° 20'– 26°40'	Viśākhā 2	Artha	Earth	Taurus
Libra 9	26° 40'– 30° 00'	Viśākhā 3	Kāma	Air	Gemini

9 DIVISIONS OF SCORPIO

Table 2.13

Scorpio	Degrees	Pada	Direction	Element	9ᵗʰ Division
Scorpio 1	0° 00'– 3° 20'	Viśākhā 4	Mokṣa	Water	Cancer
Scorpio 2	3° 20'– 6° 40'	Anurādhā 1	Dharma	Fire	Leo
Scorpio 3	6° 40 – 10° 00'	Anurādhā 2	Artha	Earth	Virgo
Scorpio 4	10° 00'– 13° 20'	Anurādhā 3	Kāma	Air	Libra
Scorpio 5	13° 20'– 16° 40'	Anurādhā 4	Mokṣa	Water	Scorpio
Scorpio 6	16° 40'– 20° 00'	Jyeṣṭhā 1	Dharma	Fire	Sagittarius
Scorpio 7	20° 00'– 23° 20'	Jyeṣṭhā 2	Artha	Earth	Capricorn
Scorpio 8	23° 20'– 26°40'	Jyeṣṭhā 3	Kāma	Air	Aquarius
Scorpio 9	26° 40'– 30° 00'	Jyeṣṭhā 4	Mokṣa	Water	Pisces

9 DIVISIONS OF SAGITTARIUS

Table 2.14

Sagittarius	Degrees	Pada	Direction	Element	9th Division
Sagittarius 1	0° 00'– 3° 20'	Mūla 1	Dharma	Fire	Aries
Sagittarius 2	3° 20'– 6° 40'	Mūla 2	Artha	Earth	Taurus
Sagittarius 3	6° 40 – 10° 00'	Mūla 3	Kāma	Air	Gemini
Sagittarius 4	10° 00'– 13° 20'	Mūla 4	Mokṣa	Water	Cancer
Sagittarius 5	13° 20'– 16° 40'	Pūrvāṣāḍha 1	Dharma	Fire	Leo
Sagittarius 6	16° 40'– 20° 00'	Pūrvāṣāḍha 2	Artha	Earth	Virgo
Sagittarius 7	20° 00'– 23° 20'	Pūrvāṣāḍha 3	Kāma	Air	Libra
Sagittarius 8	23° 20'– 26°40'	Pūrvāṣāḍha 4	Mokṣa	Water	Scorpio
Sagittarius 9	26° 40'– 30° 00'	Uttarāṣāḍha 1	Dharma	Fire	Sagittarius

9 DIVISIONS OF CAPRICORN

Table 2.15

Capricorn	Degrees	Pada	Direction	Element	9th Division
Capricorn 1	0° 00'– 3° 20'	Uttarāṣāḍha 2	Artha	Earth	Capricorn
Capricorn 2	3° 20'– 6° 40'	Uttarāṣāḍha 3	Kāma	Air	Aquarius
Capricorn 3	6° 40 – 10° 00'	Uttarāṣāḍha 4	Mokṣa	Water	Pisces
Capricorn 4	10° 00'– 13° 20'	Śravaṇa 1	Dharma	Fire	Aries
Capricorn 5	13° 20'– 16° 40'	Śravaṇa 2	Artha	Earth	Taurus
Capricorn 6	16° 40'– 20° 00'	Śravaṇa 3	Kāma	Air	Gemini
Capricorn 7	20° 00'– 23° 20'	Śravaṇa 4	Mokṣa	Water	Cancer
Capricorn 8	23° 20'– 26°40'	Dhaniṣṭhā 1	Dharma	Fire	Leo
Capricorn 9	26° 40'– 30° 00'	Dhaniṣṭhā 2	Artha	Earth	Virgo

9 DIVISIONS OF AQUARIUS

Table 2.16

Aquarius	Degrees	Pada	Direction	Element	9th Division
Aquarius 1	0° 00'– 3° 20'	Dhaniṣṭhā 3	Kāma	Air	Libra
Aquarius 2	3° 20'– 6° 40'	Dhaniṣṭhā 4	Mokṣa	Water	Scorpio
Aquarius 3	6° 40 – 10° 00'	Śatabhiṣāj 1	Dharma	Fire	Sagittarius
Aquarius 4	10° 00'– 13° 20'	Śatabhiṣāj 2	Artha	Earth	Capricorn
Aquarius 5	13° 20'– 16° 40'	Śatabhiṣāj 3	Kāma	Air	Aquarius
Aquarius 6	16° 40'– 20° 00'	Śatabhiṣāj 4	Mokṣa	Water	Pisces
Aquarius 7	20° 00'– 23° 20'	Pūrva Bhādrapada 1	Dharma	Fire	Aries
Aquarius 8	23° 20'– 26°40'	Pūrva Bhādrapada 2	Artha	Earth	Taurus
Aquarius 9	26° 40'– 30° 00'	Pūrva Bhādrapada 3	Kāma	Water	Gemini

9 DIVISIONS OF PISCES

Table 2.17

Pisces	Degrees	Pada	Direction	Element	9ᵗʰ Division
Pisces 1	0° 00'– 3° 20'	Pūrva Bhādrapada 4	Mokṣa	Water	Cancer
Pisces 2	3° 20'– 6° 40'	Uttara Bhādrapada 1	Dharma	Fire	Leo
Pisces 3	6° 40 – 10° 00'	Uttara Bhādrapada 2	Artha	Earth	Virgo
Pisces 4	10° 00'– 13° 20'	Uttara Bhādrapada 3	Kāma	Air	Libra
Pisces 5	13° 20'– 16° 40'	Uttara Bhādrapada 4	Mokṣa	Water	Scorpio
Pisces 6	16° 40'– 20° 00'	Revatī 1	Dharma	Fire	Sagittarius
Pisces 7	20° 00'– 23° 20'	Revatī 2	Artha	Earth	Capricorn
Pisces 8	23° 20'– 26°40'	Revatī 3	Kāma	Air	Aquarius
Pisces 9	26° 40'– 30° 00'	Revatī 4	Mokṣa	Water	Pisces

G U Ṇ A S

There are 3 underpinning *guṇas* or impulses, 3 modes of being that influence everything, be it an event, a thought, or an emotion. These 3 states are pulsating in everything, at various ratios at various times throughout your life. They are in a constant flux throughout every moment of every single day, intermingling all the time. We know these 3 impulses as *rajas*, *sattva*, and *tamas*, Sanskrit words that translate as 'creation', 'destruction' and 'preservation'. These 3 impulses are ever present in varying ratios in everything. Everything has a beginning (rajas), middle (sattva), and an end (tamas).

Table 2.18

Exalted, own sign	Awake
Friend, neutral sign	Dreaming
Enemy sign, debilitated	Sleeping

The 3 impulses relate to the 3 states of being, the awake, dreaming, and the deep sleep states (see Table 2.18). Planets in their own or exalted signs express more sattva, i.e., more clarity and wakefulness. Planets in a friendly or neutral sign are more rajas, i.e., more dream-like. Planets in an enemy sign or debilitated are more tamas, i.e., they are less able to function and need some help in waking up.

Yet even in the deepest state of deep sleep, there is access to pure consciousness. We cannot separate the impulses out from one another. You have a body that will move through different states during the day, from feeling inert, to more energised, to more balance, and back to inertia. Planets reflect these different states within you, too.

While being aware of the timing of your daśās, you always have access to your timeless being. No matter what state of being you currently find yourself in, this is always available. That is why you sometimes hear of people who go through the most intense depression, and how it wakes them up to their true spiritual nature. You do not have to be 'spiritual' to awaken, but it is easier to feel a state of ease when you are in a more balanced state. Yet it is also easy to get lost in a spiritual state of being, to forget that it, too, is a state, that there is something beyond all states.

Mercury, Venus, and the movable signs, Aries, Cancer, Libra, and Capricorn, relate more to rajas; Mars, Saturn, Rāhu, Ketu, and the fixed signs, Taurus, Leo, Scorpio, and Aquarius, relate more to tamas; Sun, Moon, Jupiter, and the dual signs, Gemini, Virgo, Sagittarius and Pisces, relate more to sattva.

These 3 impulses are the bedrock of Indian astrological analysis. Everything is a combination of them; every planet and sign of the zodiac has a predominant impulse or mode of being (see Table 2.19).

Table 2.19

Venus and Mercury (Rajas)	Sun, Moon and Jupiter (Sattva)	Mars, Saturn, Rāhu and Ketu (Tamas)
Creative, agitated, energised	Inspired, clear, balanced	Destructive, unconscious, inert

RAJAS – MERCURY & VENUS

Rajas is the energised impulse. It's self-motivated and has an outward, goal-seeking drive. Its energy moves out and to the sides, as if looking around for stimulation and pleasurable release. Mercury and Venus express this impulse more so. Mercury rules the sign Gemini, which represents the neck, arms, and hands. The neck moves the head from side-to-side, offering a variety of options, while the hands grasp for more. Mercury also rules Virgo, which is prone to overdoing the details. It shows being mentally agitated when attempting to micromanage. Venus rules the sign Taurus, the most sensual sign of the zodiac. This can be a more stabilising influence. Although Venus is excitable, Taurus is a fixed sign. Venus also rules Libra, where there may be more excitement. This is because Libra is about relating to others and the world. This shows more of a rajas nature.

The rajas impulse breaks any stagnation of the previous periods to Mercury and Venus, i.e., Saturn and

Ketu. Yet it is not long before this impulse creates its own problems through overstimulation. At some point, this leads to exhaustion, i.e., tamas, as and when Mercury leads the way to Ketu. There is the possibility of moving from inertia to a more balanced state. You can always use the desire and agitation, and more energy, to break up the stagnation to move you into a more balanced state of being.

TAMAS – MARS, SATURN, RĀHU & KETU

Tamas has a poor reputation. We tend to demonise Saturn, Mars, and the lunar nodes. These are the cruel planets. Life can sometimes be a struggle within their daśās. Yet if you do not look at what these periods are good for (everything is good for something), you cannot see the possibilities. They represent the results of past negative actions you must overcome now, or negative actions you take that impact your future. They have important lessons to teach you.

The tamas impulse reflects a need to bring all things to an end. You must remove some things so as not to create further problems. Yet you may get so fixated on what is ending, and not on what you are free to experience. You may keep looking at the doors that are closing and not at the opportunities presenting themselves. This is especially the case in a Saturn daśā. One image Vedic astrologer Komilla Sutton uses to highlight this dynamic is Saturn as a steel door you keep pushing against. Eventually, you realise the door opens towards you! When you learn to let go, all the things you were working hard for, on the other side of the steel door, opens to you. Yet you may push against the steel door for much of a Saturn daśā. In doing so, it can block your connection to a more balanced state of being. While it may be more obvious when Saturn and Mars do this, Rāhu and Ketu, the 'shadow planets', do so in ways you may not fathom. Rāhu represents your subconscious need to protect a self that is not even real to begin with. Ketu can help you remove false notions. Yet this may mean losing something tangible.

We often translate tamas as death and decay, which is true, of course, but it is also prominent when you sleep. You can't live without sleep. Without death, there is no life. Without rest, without ending things, you cannot start over. If you did not remove anything from your life, you would suffocate under the weight of all that you have accumulated. This may be an emotion, a thought or belief that is no longer true. Saturn is like the garbage man who comes to take away your excess. It's the accountant who lets you know what is due in taxes. This allows you to balance the books. Saturn may bring up blocks, but it also grants you the opportunity to remove them. Rāhu is a lot more complex because it creates as many blocks as it does success. Actually, success is one of those blocks. Rāhu is a challenge to overcome because you may not realise there is a problem. The block could be anything at all, but the removal always leads to the same thing: a connection to your true self. Rāhu may obscure your true self in worldly pursuits.

You may be within a major Saturn daśā, a time of seclusion and renunciation, but other impulses may dominate on the 2nd and 3rd levels. These levels represent your emotions and reactions. This would show what you would like to happen and how you are reacting to what is happening. You may or may not be on the same page as a Saturn major daśā. You may have lots of desires, despite the deeper need to withdraw – in a Saturn-Venus-Mercury daśā, for example. Saturn shows a need to spiritually reorientate. Venus and Mercury represent sensual and worldly desires. Sensual desires are prominent on the 2nd level, or sub-daśā of Venus, while practical considerations are prominent in a Mercury sub-sub-daśā. Yet a Saturn daśā may block these. Planetary daśās are a mixed bag of many levels of experience, which, when combined, show a truer, more complex picture than I am painting here.

Mars creates inertia because of acts of destruction. That destruction could be of your blocks, of course. You may get so focused on protecting your egoic needs, on winning. Mars is about finding courage to overcome your weaknesses. Often, you may find yourself focused on the problems life is presenting, or the people you are having a problem with. The strength of Mars lies within. Mars is your courage and the effort you are making to improve yourself.

Saturn and Mars both represent a need to protect the ego. You must protect yourself, of course. But if you are only concerned with protecting yourself, you never reach beyond this inert state. The higher expression of Mars is protecting others, while Saturn's highest expression is humility through loss. It is the recognition that we are all in this together, in shared experiences of grief. Even in the most inert of states, you can always find your true source of power. And you can always start over. This is usually what you experience after a major daśā of Saturn, as Mercury's daśā begins.

The 'shadowy planets', Rāhu and Ketu, obscure light. They have a dark quality that eventually leads to clarity. A Rāhu daśā leads to a Jupiter daśā. A Ketu daśā leads to a Venus daśā. Jupiter and Venus are the two guiding planets. Rāhu and Ketu bring up the blocks so you can remove them. Rāhu is the block, and Ketu removes it. Yet Ketu can remove too much, leading to losses, such as someone renouncing everything. Ketu is a spiritualising daśā. Yet if something does not orientate you towards spirit, you may have a sense of disillusionment. This can even lead to the most extreme expression of annihilation apart from the renunciate life, i.e., suicidal ideation. You may experience Ketu as a sense of uncertainty and vulnerability. There may be many changes occurring that you have no apparent control over. The best thing to do is to lean into the uncertainty a little more, as you remove the blocks to self-realisation.

SATTVA – SUN, MOON & JUPITER

If other impulses do not obstruct them, the Sun, Moon, and Jupiter uplift. The need is to find balance and inspiration. You might find blocks to this if other planets get in the way. Jupiter and the luminaries illuminate. They usually bring clarity and inspiration. This impulse expresses itself through a state of intelligence. This energy has an inward and upward motion, bringing about the awakening and development of an 'inner intelligence'.

When you are under the influence of the luminaries, you will seek people and experiences that keep you in a state of balance, as it is not possible to stay agitated or inert forever. You can always learn to achieve more balanced states, even during particularly inert or agitated periods. It is much easier to stay balanced when you find yourself balanced; at least until you move into another planetary period. And once you are out of balance, you will seek things that keep you imbalanced. Most are not conscious of the tamas impulse. It is dark, unconscious. To be conscious is to make more positive changes in your life. This reflects the harmonious Jupiter and the luminaries. These are your guiding lights, offering you a deeper sense of purpose and meaning.

The Sun represents the universal spirit, while the Moon represents your experience of an embodied spirit. The Moon represents the duality of the mind, the ever-changing emotional landscape. This can obscure reality, especially when the Moon eclipses the Sun. Yet it is during periods of stillness that it can reflect your true self, just as the Moon reflects the light of the Sun.

Jupiter inspires and uplifts, especially if well placed in your birth chart. It represents the natural order of things, a sense of cohesion, unless it is weak in your horoscope. If so, it can bring a sense of lack, a lack of cohesion and unity, a lack of growth. For growth to occur, whether inner or outer, there needs to be some organising principle at play. A strong and unobstructed Jupiter expresses this harmonising principle.

Each planetary interaction, be it a planet in a sign, or a planet influenced by or conjunct another planet, results in a certain impulse. To find out which impulse is dominant, we must first look at each planet and sign individually. We can then put them back together holistically. Table 2.20 is adapted from Freedom Cole's *Science of Light Vol. 1*[4], a helpful guide in ascertaining each sign's nature when we consider the sign's ruling planet.

[4] Freedom Cole, Science of Light Vol. 1, (Nevada City: Science of Light LLC. 2018), p. 105.

Table 2.20

Sign	Ruler	Planet's Nature	Objective of Sign	Possible Outcome
Aries	Mars	Tamas	Rajas	Sattva
Taurus	Venus	Rajas	Tamas	Sattva
Gemini	Mercury	Rajas	Sattva	Tamas
Cancer	Moon	Sattva	Rajas	Tamas
Leo	Sun	Sattva	Tamas	Rajas
Virgo	Mercury	Rajas	Sattva	Tamas
Libra	Venus	Rajas	Rajas	Rajas
Scorpio	Mars	Tamas	Tamas	Tamas
Sagittarius	Jupiter	Sattva	Sattva	Sattva
Capricorn	Saturn	Tamas	Rajas	Sattva
Aquarius	Saturn	Tamas	Tamas	Tamas
Pisces	Jupiter	Sattva	Sattva	Sattva

Table 2.20 shows the impulse of each sign and the outcome for each once we include the sign's planetary ruler. This gives a more comprehensive view of the signs. The planet Venus is rajasic. It is desirous and sensual, which can energise and agitate the mind, seeking sensual fulfilment. Venus' position in your birth chart will show how this plays out. If Venus were in exaltation, this may show a very idealistic expression of love. This is a much less agitated impulse, and more of a balanced state of being. This may be an unconditional and universal love for humankind. An example of this may be someone

joining groups, religious or otherwise, to express their love of humanity through a life of servitude.

Venus rules both Taurus and Libra. Taurus is a fixed sign, which means it is more tamasic, while Libra is a moveable sign and is more rajasic. When we include Venus' rulership, Taurus becomes sāttvika, while Libra remains rajas. This is because Taurus is a fixed sign and has fewer objectives than Libra. Taureans are usually more content with their lot. Because Venus has lots of energy and desires, it reaches the sign's objectives with plenty of energy to spare. Taurus may become more balanced and harmonious, more sāttvika. Libra may remain agitated with more objectives. Libra's desires together with Venus can agitate the mind even more. We can observe this with those more influenced by Libra seeking an ideal they may never fully realise. The result is a residue of desires that continue to agitate.

To keep it simple, you can view each of the moveable signs as rajas, the fixed signs as tamas, and the dual signs as sattva. Then, looking at the positions of planets in these signs, depending on the planet's nature, it will garner different results. For example, Mars is more tamas in a tamas sign, e.g., Mars in Aquarius, than it is in a sattva sign, e.g., Mars in Sagittarius.

The three impulses influence each planetary or sign-based daśā. These three are ever present in varying ratios in your life because of the patterns of shorter planetary daśās within longer daśās. These are in a constant flux every moment of every single day. We break each major daśā down into shorter and shorter sub-daśās. This shows how your life is unfolding, minute-by-minute, year-on-year. A daśā you experienced for a few weeks ten years ago may repeat in some context all next year, or for a week next month. Although places and faces have changed, there is a common theme that keeps cropping up.

Venus and Mercury daśās usually bring some sort of excitement, i.e., rajas. This may be through some mental agitation during a Mercury daśā or some sensual indulgence in a Venus daśā. The Sun, Moon, and Jupiter usually bring more balance and inspiration, more sattva. This usually brings more inspiration. At the very least, it brings a need for more harmony. The lunar nodes, Rāhu, and Ketu, as well as Saturn and Mars, usually bring some obstruction, or some unconscious behaviour, as expressed through tamas. Yet it wouldn't be helpful to think of tamas as simply wrong, as it represents a necessary ending most times. Saturn daśās are about endings, ridding yourself of something, so you can feel unburdened. Likewise, Mars daśās are destructive in some form, but it is not the full story. Mars gives you the energy to overcome something, although it may lead to overdoing this impulse, destroying more than is necessary. Thus, relationships can suffer in a Mars daśā. The lunar nodes can show issues because of their tamasic impulse. They are shadows, and unlikely to be experienced consciously. As the lunar nodes are subconscious, you are likely to get triggered by them. Yet you can always make them more conscious, even elevate their impulse to become more balanced. This is more likely if dignified, balanced planets influence them.

Each planetary daśā can dominate in one of these impulses, depending on its position in your horoscope. You may also be one more than the other. Whether you are more energetic or more inert, the various planetary daśās and sub-daśās will change this to a degree. If you are more inert overall and you experience a daśā of Saturn, you will experience more inertia. This may express itself as a need to slow down, which may create excessive inertia, even depression. If you are more energetic, an inert Saturn daśā may calm you down. We must interpret this in context, in your birth chart, observing the many levels of daśās activated.

These impulses are ever present in various ratios on every level of your being, from the microcosmic to the macrocosmic. You can see these interact from the infinitesimally small to the awe-inspiring vastness of being. They represent the continual unfolding of birth, sustenance, and decay. Every living thing has a beginning, middle, and an end.

You may enjoy the excitement of having your desires fulfilled in a Venus or Mercury daśā; feel inspired as things settle down in a Sun, Moon, or Jupiter daśā; or feel a need to end something in a Saturn, Mars, Rāhu, or Ketu daśā.

URANUS, NEPTUNE & PLUTO

Uranus, Neptune, and Pluto are not visible to the naked eye, although Uranus is visible at certain times. Pluto was not discovered until the 1930s. Thus, they are not included in traditional Indian astrology and the planetary daśās. I explore their transits in Part 3. Yet we can still correlate them with the 3 impulses: rajas, tamas, and sattva.

We can liken Uranus to the impulse of rajas. This is the impulse to create, often translated as individuality, freedom, and rebellion in a modern context. Uranus is the Greek God of the Sky, which we could compare to the Vedic deity Prajāpati. We can liken Neptune to the impulse of sattva, which is to preserve life, no matter the form. The form keeps changing, yet something remains the same. Neptune is the impulse to sustain something, often translated as spirituality and ideology in a modern context. Neptune is the Greek God of the oceans, which we could compare to the Vedic deity Varuṇa. We can liken Pluto to the impulse of tamas, i.e., to transform, to change, and transcend. Pluto is the 'lord of the underworld' in mythology, so we can see its correlations with Yama, the 'god of death' in the Vedic pantheon.

If we look at the outer planets as the 3 impulses, although far from us on earth, they represent something closer than our own breath. They are the outer expressions of something deep within us. Regardless of whether ancient astrologers knew of their existence, we can always welcome an expanded view of who we are. We can do so through the lens of the outer planets. Seeing into the depths of space it expands our inner depths.

Indian astrologers often substitute Rāhu and Ketu for Uranus, Neptune, and Pluto. Uranus rules Aquarius in modern astrology; Rāhu rules Aquarius in traditional Indian astrology. Pluto rules Scorpio in modern astrology; Ketu rules Scorpio in traditional Indian astrology. Both Rāhu and Ketu have some attributes of Neptune, in that they can obscure, and yet, reveal, our true spiritual nature. Some Indian astrologers give Ketu rulership of Pisces. Thus, we could compare Ketu with Neptune, its modern ruler.

When these 'invisible' planets engage with a visible planet, they manifest their results more obviously. Yet they play a significant role, based on their house position by transit, as an ongoing phenomenon, albeit in a much subtler way.

URANUS

William Herschel discovered Uranus with a telescope in 1781. It was observed before that but was not categorised. This discovery occurred as he was trying out a new telescope. This is apt. Modern astrological interpretations of Uranus include ingenuity, invention, and all things brand new. The discovery of Uranus came during a period of revolution and invention. America gained independence, and the French built a new society. These are both Uranus-type significations.

We can see the impulse of creativity, of rajas, in the modern significations of Uranus. Modern interpretations of Uranus go one step further. It reflects shocks, unexpected surprises, and volatility. Creation is often shocking, of course, as something new disturbs the status quo. Creation is also often unexpected. It is often volatile, as anything new struggles into existence. Uranus, and rajas, represent an agitation, a desire for something new.

NEPTUNE

Neptune came into conscious awareness in 1846, when it was first discovered with a telescope. There was a growing interest in spirituality around the globe, a sort of melting pot of philosophies from East to West. It is no wonder Neptune represents something not clearly defined. It is blurry and vague. Think about the 'you' you think of as you in your everyday life, the person you identify with that others see at a certain distance. Now zoom in until your outline becomes blurry, a patch of skin and obscure shapes. Neptune goes deeper still, into You that is truly You, a Self beyond all narrow definitions. This is the only 'thing' that is maintained always, i.e., your spiritual essence.

Neptune's transits bring a vagueness which, from a spiritual perspective, is who you truly are. Yet from a practical point of view, this can show some confusion.

Neptune rules intoxicants such as drugs and alcohol in modern astrology. The balancing act of being in the world, while orientating yourself to your spiritual nature, is the impulse of sattva. This is the higher impulse of inspiration, reflected in Neptune.

PLUTO

Pluto was first discovered with a telescope in 1930. This marked the beginning of a decade of greater understanding of destruction and of energy, the building blocks of matter, the constituents of the atom. This is like the impulse of tamas, representing the material realm and destruction. Tamas is dark, inert, and decaying, as everything material must one day die. In the late 1930s, with the atomic bomb, we saw the release of massive amounts of energy in this destructive process.

The discovery of these capabilities, along with the planet Pluto, is not a coincidence to an astrologer. Pluto has taken on this expression in a more conscious way since its discovery. Yet may I point out an obvious, yet often overlooked fact: Pluto, Neptune, and Uranus have been there since the formation of our solar system.

Although Pluto transits out in the far reaches of our solar system, it reflects our innermost core. This is one reason I find it hard to believe that ancient seers and higher minds did not at least have an inkling. And they may indeed have known of their existence.

In his article, *Pluto: A Neo-Vedic View*, [5] Dennis Harness recounts a meeting with Indian astrologer Narendra Desai. Desai claimed he saw an ancient Vasistha Nadi palm leaf in a museum in Madras, India, predicting three important planets would be discovered by the jyotishis of the Kali Yuga. He writes that, "according to the ancient palm leaf the names of the planets would be Prajapati, [the god of creation]; Varuna, [the god of sustenance], and Yama, [the god of death]." We can see the correlation among these three gods and the modern astrological significations of Uranus, Neptune, and Pluto.

What if ancient cultures knew of them through other means? This is not so incredulous when we see how modern planets are discovered. Astronomers do so by observing visible planets around them. They study how planets behave because of the influence of other planets.

In modern astrological analysis, the destructive release of energy is analogous to Pluto's destruction of the ego. This also represents the immense energy such a transformation creates. If you do not identify with your ego, it frees up a lot of energy to be, instead of holding your old story together. This type of energy release follows massive changes to your perception of who you are, destroying all that you are not. It is fitting that Pluto

---

[5] Dennis Harness, 'Pluto: A Neo-Vedic View', Denis Harness, [web blog], Date Unknown, https://dennisharness.com/articles/pluto-a-neo-vedic-view/, (accessed 14 June 2022).

had been categorised as a planet and then demoted as a dwarf planet. Pluto disintegrates the structures that make us who we are on an egoic level. This is something quite fragile, something life tears down, much like our fragile egos. The debate around Pluto's classification is ongoing.

Although Pluto came late to our astrological family, it completed a stage of evolution. This stage required destruction for fresh growth to occur. It blew apart many limiting factors in relation to how we could see ourselves, too. This included the range of our destructive capabilities. We may focus solely on the destruction process involved. It can be a painful experience when things are blown apart. Yet, if you are aware of the need to dismantle a part of yourself, you release massive amounts of energy. You could either mourn the loss of who you thought you were, or you could free your soul and soar like a phoenix from the flames. Once you remove your story or identification (Pluto), you feel inspired (Neptune) to tell a different story (Uranus).

GUṆAS & DAŚĀS

Each planet has natural impulses and inclinations, although this changes based on their position in a particular sign and planets associating with them. You can see the impulse that dominates in a particular daśā by viewing the planet's nature, the nature of the planets that have a sight or aspect, as well as the nature of the sign it is in. Or you could simply ask yourself the question: Am I more energised, inert, or balanced right now? What would bring me back into balance, a more ideal state of being?

You may experience a Moon daśā, for example, which can be more balanced. Yet if the Moon were conjunct Rāhu, in debilitation in Scorpio, the Moon's balance may be obstructed, reflected in an absence of peace of mind. In this case, you could address Rāhu's impulse, which often brings confusion, to find more balance. Jupiter remedies the disorders of Rāhu, bringing clarity when there is confusion. Taurus can help balance the tendencies of a Scorpio Moon, feeding the mind with positive, life-enhancing qualities. Emotions stabilise when having good nutrition and friendly, supportive relations.

The advantage of having a timeline of these impulses is to work with what is, to find more balance within the predominant impulse. Too much of anything is not good long term, except for balance. Too much energy or inertia always leads to problems, and a lack of balance.

If you are in a period of the Sun, and it is unobstructed and strong in your birth chart, you may not need as much help to find balance. But if the Sun were weak and obstructed by Saturn, then working with the impulse of Saturn may help you see the light, by removing the negative impact of Saturn. To develop confidence, you can incorporate Saturn disciplines. Thus, exercise, a signification of the Sun, when done in a disciplined way (Saturn), is one of the best ways to tackle depression, a signification of Saturn.

Being more active balances any sense of inertia in a Saturn daśā. But it works the other way around also. Inactivity can help balance an overly stimulated Mercury or Venus daśā – if you feel you are too stimulated, that is. It may be that Mercury or Venus are themselves blocked from expressing this natural impulse, due to either a conjunction with Saturn or a sight from Saturn, for example.

If you were to feel blocked in some way, once you get moving, if you stay in that state, there is only one result: exhaustion, more inertia. Many people live their lives moving between two imbalanced states of being: agitation and inertia; too much activity and not enough. They may overcompensate for the inertia by taking stimulants, thus setting the scene for further inertia.

An unobstructed Sun, Moon, or Jupiter may reflect a balanced state. It does not mean the other planets cannot bring balance, but they usually create problems along the way. Saturn, Mars, and the lunar nodes tend to create obstructions, even if they are also strong and influenced by a strong Sun, Moon, or Jupiter. The difference is they may also bring many great experiences once the person steps up to the challenges. Overdoing anything, even if it was a good move to begin with, leads to imbalances.

Recognise where you are in the daśās and impulses to see if you can offer a counterbalance. You can achieve this through more active pursuits if you are feeling more inert, and more rest if you are too active. It's a basic premise, but one I see many people skip over when looking for more complex answers in their birth charts.

There are always opportunities to squeeze out as much balance as possible out of life. This can result in more peace and harmony no matter what daśā you find yourself in.

DAŚĀ SANDHI

When you move from one major daśā to another, these are more complex junctures in time (sandhi). The end of a major daśā is like a joint in time. Any juncture in time is weaker, just as joints in the physical body are weaker. Yet it is the joints that allow movement and adaptability. You can change and adapt. This is when life circumstances may completely change, depending on the configurations in your birth chart. If there is a strong link from one daśā to another, it may not be as big a change. However, it is still a change. The ending daśā loosens its grip and another begins to take hold. This can be a major time of upheaval. It's at least at time of adjustment.

Tamas is likely to increase as you resist the change. With an awareness of your daśās, you can at least know when it's time to let go, even if you have a hard time doing so. At the same time, a new daśā and chapter in your life begins, and you are likely to experience an increase of rajas, expressed in excitement and energy for something new. Yet you may describe this as feelings of agitation and frustration, as it doesn't necessarily come quickly. You may have many conflicting emotions as you grieve the loss of something but feel the excitement for something new. As both tamas and rajas increase, there is little time for balance and harmony, as the old you gives way to a new you.

Try not to force changes or hold on to how things were. Sometimes it takes many months, or even a few years, before you settle into your new way of being. Try not to add complications; instead, keep life as simple as possible. Once you have settled into the new daśā and circumstance, you can find more balance.

You can calculate a chart for the beginning of a new daśā (daśā praveśa), observing the position of the new daśā planet's placement from your ascendant. Simply calculate a chart for when the same degree is rising as your birth at the start of the new daśā. Or you can simply observe the transits of planets during the beginning of the new daśā. Another technique is to calculate a chart for the exact beginning of the daśā, although this requires a very precise time of birth to be accurate.

You could use transits to the daśā planet you are just beginning by observing the transit of the Sun and planets to this planet in your birth chart. The planet's transit itself should be looked at for triggers. If you're beginning a Saturn daśā, for example, and Saturn is placed in your 10th house, Saturn's transit to your 10th house, or in a house that has a sight on the 10th, may also be a trigger. Anytime you experience a transit that lines up with a placement in your birth chart, it reignites that theme in your life. More about transits in PART 3.

All major daśā transitions are complex periods; most have the potential of creating challenges. Ketu-Mercury, Venus-Ketu, Sun-Venus, Mars-Moon, Rāhu-Mars, Jupiter-

Rāhu, and Mercury-Saturn, can be especially complex. The other transitions, Moon-Sun and Saturn-Jupiter, may also be challenging, depending on your birth chart, but they are generally not as complex. Saturn and Jupiter are neutral to one another, and Jupiter's sub-daśā at the end of Saturn's 19-year long daśā is usually a time of relief for most people. It's usually a time of more balance and hope after much inertia and doubt.

The last sub-daśā is an ending phase pointing you back to the major phase in your life many years previous. These periods represent the ripening of your actions (karmas). At the tail end of a major daśā, they bring back past issues to deal with before you can move onto the next major daśā and chapter in your life. This transition can take from a few months to almost 3 years. At the end of a 17-year Mercury daśā, there is a sub-daśā of Saturn. The Mercury-Saturn daśā lasts 2 years, 8 months, and 9 days. The next longest is the Saturn-Jupiter period. A Jupiter sub-daśā at the end of a 19-year Saturn period lasts 2 years, 6 months and 12 days. The next longest is Jupiter-Rāhu, lasting 2 years, 4 months, and 24 days. The shortest is the Moon-Sun daśā, lasting 6 months, while the Mars-Moon daśā lasts 7 months. All other transition periods last about a year.

Each period has its own rewards and challenges, no matter how long or short. Each sub-daśā points back to the previous major one. You can only move forward once you have resolved the past. Yet the past is never done, just as the future already exists on some level. And while you experience these transitions in your own way, depending on the many variables in your birth chart, there are some common themes.

In times of transition, remind yourself there is a non-changing part of you that is always present. This 'non-self' is always observing what is happening. The constant changes do not perturb it. Tune into that 'part' if you are currently in a major period of transition, while recognising it as a time to let go of the old and get ready for the new. Use this time as it's meant to be used: as a steppingstone, a platform to spring forth from.

In India, priests offer prayers for those going through transitions. This is especially so if the impulses themselves are more challenging to manage when combined. Longer transitional periods can be more challenging because of the longer time periods. It is going to take longer to move from a major daśā of Mercury to Ketu, from the practical concerns of Mercury to the spiritualising world of Ketu. It is Saturn's job to help with the transition, i.e., Mercury-Saturn daśā, and Saturn is slow in teaching anything. It's going to take some time for Jupiter to heal the hurts of a major Saturn daśā in Saturn-Jupiter daśā. You need time to open to something new and exciting once a major Mercury daśā begins. It's Jupiter's job to open your mind to the new possibilities and opportunities. This is a more hopeful period before you take on a new Mercury adventure. It will take a few years for Jupiter to prepare you for such a change.

One of the more complex transitions is that of Jupiter-Rāhu. This period lasts about two and a half years. It is Rāhu's job to remind you of what you have not tasted in the previous Rāhu major daśā. In Jupiter-Rāhu, it takes one last swipe at success. You may jostle with this desire. Yet you know it will not satiate you. It is a period to let go of the ideals of Jupiter. The approaching Saturn daśā is about getting real, to be at peace with what is. Rāhu's hunger for more becomes a challenge to be still. This could occur in Jupiter-Rāhu daśā at a younger age. Yet someone who has tasted more may feel more jaded by it than a youth starting out. A youth may not have experienced a Rāhu major daśā previous to the Jupiter daśā, as Jupiter is 16 years. The lesson of letting go of your obsessions is the same whatever age you are in Jupiter-Rāhu daśā. The only way you can completely let go after a period of Rāhu is to experience it all and realise it will never be enough. After a daśā of Jupiter-Rāhu, you come to rest in a major daśā of Saturn.

Rāhu-Mars daśā is generally more challenging, as it emphasises the shift from darkness to more inspiration and cohesion in the next phase of Jupiter. But only after a heavier dose of darkness and destruction in a Mars sub-daśā. Kishori once relayed this to me in conversation as if it were like "squeezing the last bit out of the tube." Rāhu-Mars creates one last push and desire for Rāhu to fulfil.

A Mercury-Saturn period may be easier. You may have exhausted all your excitement in the Mercury daśā, and now need to recuperate. A Saturn transitional time offers some rest before going deeper into a Ketu major daśā. This means becoming orientated to spirit. Yet you couldn't re-orientate overnight after many years of practical concerns in a Mercury daśā. You need Saturn to slow you down and look within. A Jupiter daśā is usually a balanced and expansive state. A slower period in a Saturn daśā comes next. This can create some confusion, as Jupiter gives way to Saturn. This occurs in a Rāhu sub-daśā, i.e., Jupiter-Rāhu. Table 2.21 shows all the major and sub-daśās of the planets.

Table 2.21

Ketu	Venus	Sun	Moon	Mars
Ketu-Ketu	Venus-Venus	Sun-Sun	Moon-Moon	Mars-Mars
Ketu-Venus	Venus-Sun	Sun-Moon	Moon-Mars	Mars-Rāhu
Ketu-Sun	Venus-Moon	Sun-Mars	Moon-Rāhu	Mars-Jupiter
Ketu-Moon	Venus-Mars	Sun-Rāhu	Moon-Jupiter	Mars-Saturn
Ketu-Mars	Venus-Rāhu	Sun-Jupiter	Moon-Saturn	Mars-Mercury
Ketu-Rāhu	Venus-Jupiter	Sun-Saturn	Moon-Mercury	Mars-Ketu
Ketu-Jupiter	Venus-Saturn	Sun-Mercury	Moon-Ketu	Mars-Venus
Ketu-Saturn	Venus-Mercury	Sun-Ketu	Moon-Venus	Mars-Sun

Rāhu	Jupiter	Saturn	Mercury
Rāhu-Rāhu	Jupiter-Jupiter	Saturn-Saturn	Mercury-Mercury
Rāhu-Jupiter	Jupiter-Saturn	Saturn-Mercury	Mercury-Ketu
Rāhu-Saturn	Jupiter-Mercury	Saturn-Ketu	Mercury-Venus
Rāhu-Mercury	Jupiter-Ketu	Saturn-Venus	Mercury-Sun
Rāhu-Ketu	Jupiter-Venus	Saturn-Sun	Mercury-Moon
Rāhu-Venus	Jupiter-Sun	Saturn-Moon	Mercury-Mars
Rāhu-Sun	Jupiter-Moon	Saturn-Mars	Mercury-Rāhu
Rāhu-Moon	Jupiter-Mars	Saturn-Rāhu	Mercury-Jupiter
Rāhu-Mars	Jupiter-Rāhu	Saturn-Jupiter	Mercury-Saturn

GOLDEN RATIO

As you observe your daśās in Table 2.21, are there any obvious patterns that you can pick out? The most obvious is that the daśās are in a particular order: Ketu, Venus, Sun, Moon, Mars, Rāhu, Jupiter, Saturn, and Mercury. This repeats in the sub-daśās. Actually, this repeats on many levels, up to 6 different levels, right down to the minute. I have begun the sequence from Ketu, as it represents the still centre from which we experience the beginning of the zodiac, the lunar mansion within the beginning of Aries.

The last sub-daśā within any major daśā is the same planet as that of the previous major daśā. For example, the last sub-daśā within Jupiter's major daśā is that of Rāhu, i.e., Jupiter-Rāhu, and Rāhu is the previous major daśā to Jupiter. The daśā before Rāhu is Mars, the previous major daśā to Rāhu, and so on. This pattern points to how our lives are repeating patterns. Although we each experience these patterns through different lenses, they bring the same themes. It is natural that a period of clarity follows a period of excess and confusion, as Rāhu leads to Jupiter. Or, as the poet William Blake so eloquently put it: "The road to excess leads to the path of wisdom."

Once we observe the same patterns repeatedly in our lives, we can assimilate these through various scenarios. We do so within different contexts and with different people. It may be easier to see other people's patterns, as we're usually our own biggest blind spot. Once we have lived long enough, we can see the same story, told over and over. Places and faces may change but the patterns remain the same.

This pattern is a spiral pattern. Our lives unfold in an ever-increasing spiral from a central point. It helps to orientate yourself on a map by starting from a starting point. That starting point is the time at which you were born. Astrology gives you a map of the terrain and the tools to help you navigate a path you have chosen on some level. One thing to remember, as Kishori has said in our conversations, "The map is not the territory." Your astrology chart is not you - it is a map to help you understand yourself better.

By realising the influences set forth because of the circumstances of your birth, you can work with what you've got with more skill. Having a map of your life helps you to better plan an easier route. There are certain things laid before you which you would prefer to avoid, I'm sure. But you can choose to work with any obstructions. Turn even the most negative experiences into positive opportunities for growth. You can take advantage of more obvious opportunities that present themselves. Keep your eyes open for opportunities that are on the horizon in upcoming daśās. Having a map and timeline of when the difficulty will pass is enough many times. Sometimes it's all you need. This is the benefit of astrology. At its most practical level, it helps you effectively plan your life.

The Golden Ratio is a mathematical language that describes the axiom, *As Above, So Below* - in number form, as does, *As Within, So Without*. The Fibonacci sequence is a sequence of numbers that increase by adding the two previous numbers, starting from 1. So, 1 added to 1 is 2, added to 1 is 3, and so on. By doing so, we end up with the following sequence of numbers: 0, 1, 1, 2, 3, 5, 8, 13, 21, 34, 55, 89, 144, and so on. When we take any two successive numbers, the ratio is remarkably close to the Golden Ratio, or 1.618033988749.... The bigger the number, the closer it gets to the Golden Ratio.

This pattern is everywhere. It is within all natural patterns and many times in art and design. Ancient designs use it. Whether the Parthenon of the Acropolis, the petals of a flower, or the spiral galaxy, the divine proportion shows up everywhere. We can see the Fibonacci sequence everywhere in astrology. So, it should come as no surprise that it shows up in your birth chart and, yes, in your planetary daśās.

Our lives are part of a divine plan, mapped out in the heavens. You are like a musical instrument, attuned to the orchestra of the universe. Your life is a sacred pattern, expressed in your thoughts, feelings, dreams, and aspirations. All these are of a divine proportion. All your thoughts, feelings, and actions are in line with the Golden Ratio. By studying your patterns, you can see the perfect symmetry of your life existence, an intricate tapestry in the stars.

If you add up the length of the planetary daśās, starting with different planets and dividing them in different ways, you end up with an approximation of the Golden Ratio. Astrologer Rafael Gil Brand explained this concept in a British Association of Vedic presentation titled "Decoding Vimshottari Dasha".[6] He described the many ways the Golden Ratio shows up in planetary daśās. We can do this by making different lists of the planets but keeping them in the order of the daśās. Starting with Saturn, and separating the planets in two friendly groups, we get the following sequence:

Saturn-Mercury-Ketu-Venus + Sun-Moon-Mars-Rāhu-Jupiter

The nodes are, as always, anomalies. Adding each planet's length in the daśās, you can add them in each grouping. Saturn (19), Mercury (17), Ketu (7) and Venus (20) add up to 162 years. Sun (6), Moon (10), Mars (7), Rāhu (18) and Jupiter (16) add up to 159 years. The Golden Ratio is 1.62. It's close, but still only an approximation. Another way to divide the daśās is to take the two friendly groups of planets, starting with Ketu and drawing a wavelike pattern, placing Mars in the middle of the wave.

---

[6] Rafael Gil Brand, "Decoding Vimshottari Dasha", British Association of Vedic Astrology online lecture, 16 September 2012.

Ketu-Venus-Sun-Moon-Mars-Rāhu-Jupiter-Saturn-Mercury

Leaving Mars out of the count, Ketu, Venus, Sun, and Moon daśās add up to 43, while Rāhu, Jupiter, Saturn, and Mercury daśās add up to 70. 70/43 = 1.63 - another approximation, but a more accurate representation of the Golden Ratio. Let's add Mars' 7 years to its adjacent daśās, Moon (10) and Rāhu (18). 7 + 10 + 18 = 35. Divide this by the next two planets on either side, Sun (6) and Jupiter (16), 6 + 16 = 22. 35/22 = 1.6. Do it again, this time adding Venus (20) and Saturn (19), divided by the furthest out, Ketu (7) and Mercury (17), and you end up with the exact Golden Ratio, 1.62. 39/24 = 1.62.

Just as with the Fibonacci sequence, which gets closer to the exact Golden Ratio the more you add up the numbers, the planets further from Mars in the planetary daśās add up to the exact number of the Golden Ratio.

The pairing of these planets is an important consideration in the planetary daśās. Thus, each pair of planets, when combined in a daśā, is a crucial time in a person's life. The pairs of planets are Ketu-Mercury, Venus-Saturn, Sun-Jupiter, and Moon-Rāhu. When you experience Ketu-Mercury or Mercury-Ketu, Venus-Saturn or Saturn-Venus, Sun-Jupiter or Jupiter-Sun, Moon-Rāhu or Rāhu-Moon, these are important periods in your life. Each of them represents a momentous time of change.

Another pattern that is observable in these daśās is their correlation with the four directions in life: dharma, artha, kāma and mokṣa. Generally, Sun-Jupiter and Jupiter-Sun daśās are periods of dharma, along with daśās of Mars; Venus-Saturn and Saturn-Venus daśās are periods of kāma; Moon-Rāhu and Rāhu-Moon daśās are periods of artha; and Ketu-Mercury and Mercury-Ketu daśās are periods of mokṣa.

As astrologer Andrew Foss points out in his book, *Yoga of the Planets*,[7] the three dharmic planets are Sun, Mars and Jupiter. These come in 3rd, 5th, and 7th place in the order of the natural daśās, starting with Ketu and ending with Mercury. These daśās, although dharmic (righteous), often challenge you to get back on the right path if you have strayed. The 3rd, 5th, and 7th daśās challenge you to return to the right path for you. The 3 lunar mansions in the natural order that are associated with these 3 daśās are the only ones that bridge two different Sun signs. Kṛttikā is the natural 3rd lunar mansion and correlated with the Sun, bridging both Aries and Taurus; Mṛgaśirṣa (5th) is correlated with Mars, bridging Taurus and Gemini; Punarvasu (7th) is correlated with Jupiter, bridging Gemini and Cancer; Uttara Phālguṇī (12th) is correlated with the Sun, bridging Leo and Virgo; Citrā (14th) is correlated with

---

[7] Andrew Foss, *Yoga of the Planets* (Virginia, USA: ShriSource Publications, 2016). pp. 500 – 517.

Mars, bridging Virgo and Libra; Viśākhā (16th) is correlated with Jupiter, bridging Libra and Scorpio; Uttarāṣāḍha (21st) is correlated with the Sun, bridging Sagittarius and Capricorn; Dhaniṣṭhā (23rd) is correlated with Mars, bridging Capricorn and Aquarius; and Pūrva Bhādrapada (25th) is correlated with Jupiter, bridging Aquarius and Pisces.

The other lunar mansions are contained within just one Sun sign, so their daśās may not challenge you to change course as much as the 9 lunar mansions that bridge two. Some may challenge you in other ways, but the challenges of the 3rd, 5th, 7th, 12th, 14th, 16th, 21st, 23rd, and 25th may be more obvious. These show major periods of change in your life, as the spiral pattern takes a turn in ways that can make you feel your life is moving in another direction. You are exactly where you need to be, on a path back to your centre.

An insoluble problem is seldom solved on its own terms; rather, it loses its urgency through the dawning of a new way of life.

- Carl Jung

PART 3: TRENDS

STAGES OF LIFE

There are natural stages of life we all experience at the same age apart from our personal daśās (see Table 3.1). Each stage corresponds to the planets, Sun, Moon, Mars, Mercury, Jupiter, Venus, and Saturn. Rāhu and Ketu are not included in these stages as they run against the natural order of things (retrograde).

Table 3.1

Planet	Age
Moon	0-1
Mars	1-3
Mercury	3-12
Venus	12-32
Jupiter	32-50
Sun	50-70
Saturn	70+

The first year of your life relates to the Moon, a time when your caregiver, usually your mother, is the most important person. This is when you bond, or not, depending on the strength and position of the Moon in your birth chart. This has a profound impact on your whole life. Regardless of what planetary daśā you experience from the beginning, the first year of life is an important time for bonding.

The next couple of years relate to Mars, when you assert your independence and wilfulness-the 'terrible twos'! This is when you seek freedom from your caregiver and wish to express your will. This is also when your care givers may get you to behave in a manner they see fit. Depending on Mars' strength in your birth chart, this may be an enormous task for them, or managed more easily. This stage has a profound impact on how you assert your will throughout your life, as seen in the position of Mars in your birth chart.

Mercury relates to the period from three to twelve years of age. You learn the skills of reading and writing during this time. This represents your practical life lessons, as well as early schooling, which help you in life in a practical way. This is when you develop your rational thinking and analytical skills. You go to school to learn and develop various other skills.

Venus relates to the period from twelve to thirty-two. This period is when you experience puberty and develop relationships into adulthood. This is the stage of life when romantic relationships are the most important part of your development.

Jupiter relates to the period from thirty-two to fifty. This period is usually about raising children or pursuing something that is meaningful to you. Jupiter shows both. You are looking to expand. It could be through raising a family or through an inner expansion. It's a stage when you look for a purpose in life, which, of course, may challenge you if you cannot find it. This would depend on the strength and position of Jupiter in your birth chart.

After the age of fifty, and until the age of seventy, you experience your 'golden years', as represented by the Sun. This is the stage of life you may have 'found yourself' and what is important to you. Many people retire or change direction once they have found a sense of self and purpose. If the Sun were strong in your birth chart, there is a sense of confidence. Yet you can always develop a sense of confidence having lived a full life, even if the Sun was weak.

The last stage of life, after the age of seventy and until you die, relates to Saturn. This is when you begin to recede from the world. Saturn represents the ageing process, a withdrawal from distractions to your true calling; that of finding your spiritual nature. This can offer enormous peace when it's time to let go.

While these natural stages show general themes, you experience them in your own unique way. Consider the planets' strengths, and the planetary and sign-based daśās, alongside these.

MATURATION OF PLANETS

Each planet matures at a certain age, reflecting the aspect of your being that matures after this age. This is explored in *Lal Kitab*, the 'red book'[10]. These positions are given in Table 3.2. Consider this alongside any daśā you experience. Although you may experience a Saturn daśā, a period that is all about maturity, Saturn's maturity doesn't kick in until after the age of thirty six. So while Saturn represents maturity, its full maturation may not fully express itself until after that age. Likewise, Venus matures at twenty five, reflecting the need for a relationship. A Venus daśā before then may not reflect maturity around relationships.

Rāhu, the north lunar node, and Ketu, the south lunar node, develop later. These show more complex dynamics. But they are also the most rewarding when you make peace with the dichotomy of these apparently separate extremes. Rāhu is the head of the serpent in Vedic myth, the part of you that is hungry for life experience. Rāhu is insatiable. No matter how much you get during a Rāhu daśā, you want more. Anything you get is but a temporary relief from wanting. The hunger returns in another, even bigger, form. This matures after the age of forty-two. This is when you realise you cannot get it all and begin to settle down. Yet it may express itself as trying to get everything

---

[10]   B. M. Goswami., L.K. Vashisth, *Lal Kitab*, (New Delhi: Motilal Banarsidass Publishers (Pvt. Limited), 2003), p. 72.

you think will make you happy. This is the 'mid-life' crisis. This is not always an easy maturation and can show an attempt at filling the void.

Table 3.2

Planet	Age
Jupiter	16
Sun	22
Moon	24
Venus	25
Mars	28
Mercury	34
Saturn	36
Rāhu	42
Ketu	48

Ketu shows the need to renounce the world altogether. This can lead to feelings of disillusionment. Ketu matures at forty-eight, which is the age when you may become disillusioned with life. Ketu shows a need to go beyond, and within, to realise that nothing can satisfy in any worldly sense. It teaches you to have a different orientation. Yet its maturation may be a period of change that is not always easy. In a study by Dr Blanchflower of

Dartmouth College in New Hampshire,[11] 109 data files of happiness statistics from around the world were compared. His findings showed a "happiness curve" reaching its perigee at 47.2 years. This reflects Ketu's maturation at 48. The good news is that after this final planetary maturation, the happiness curve takes an upward swing once more.

---

[11] David G. Blanchflower, *Is Happiness U-shaped Everywhere? Age and Subjective Well-being in 132 Countries* (NBER Working Paper No. 26641, 2020).

5 ELEMENTS OF TIME

Each of the 5 elements, fire, water, earth, space, and air, correspond to the 5 visible planets and the 5 divisions of time. These are solar days, including hours (fire), lunar days (water), half lunar days (earth), Sun-Moon yogas or combinations (space), and lunar mansions (air). The position and strength of each associated planet affects each of the associated areas of life, as listed in Table 3.3. Observe these planets' daśās to see their relevant themes.

Table 3.3

Element	Planet	Division of Time	Indications
Fire	Mars	Solar Days	Health and vitality
Water	Venus	Lunar Days	Love and relationships
Earth	Mercury	Half Lunar Days	Work and skills
Space	Jupiter	Sun-Moon Yogas	Harmony and order
Air	Saturn	Lunar Mansions	Life-force and disease

FIRE ELEMENT: SOLAR DAYS

Each planet rules a day of the week. Certain days are more conducive to certain activities based on the planet. Each day has its own distinct energy. The fire element is associated with the day of the week, which is related to Mars, the planet that represents your energy and vitality. Each day's energy is based on the planet that rules it. We divide each day into 24 hours, and each hour relates to a certain planet and energy as well. When you take both together, you get a feel for the energy in any hour, on a particular day of the week.

The day of the week you were born on says a lot about your energy levels and vitality. The planet that rules this day of the week is an important planet for your health and vitality. This is more relevant during a daśā of this planet.

Sunday – Sun's Day

For many, Sunday is the day for worship, even if going to a place of worship is not for you. Whatever you worship, it is but a reflection of the higher self. Spending time in nature helps to deepen this connection, and Sunday is often the day many take to the countryside for a walk. Physically exposing yourself to the Sun can help, of course, giving you more of a sense of this connection. Music and dance are other ways to tap into the Sun's energy, as the Sun represents the rhythm we live our lives by. The Sun moves one degree a day, and one zodiac sign each month, giving you a sense of time through the seasons of the year.

On Sundays, you may wish to pay more attention to the rhythm of your life by keeping a steady pace. Whatever way you tap into the Sun's energy, know that you are a bright spark from our one source of light.

Monday – Moon's Day

The Moon's day is conducive to resting your awareness at your heart. If you have been relying too much on your intellect to navigate your life, it helps to root your awareness in something deeper. This will help you access the stillness of your being. The more time you spend here, the more you can access a deeper awareness of self, beyond the fluctuations of the mind. Spending time by the water may also help bring you into more of a connection to nature and balance the fire element that day. Discovering the waxing and waning phases of the Moon will help you go with the ebb and flow. Being still at the New and Full Moons can help with any exaggerated emotions. The waning phase is a time of letting go, while the waxing phase allows for full expression on a theme.

Tuesday – Mars' Day

You may wish to be more active and express yourself on Tuesdays. This is a good day for taking on a challenge or competition. This is when to take on a task that you may have been putting off. Use the courage of Mars to tackle something uncomfortable. Yet this is not an auspicious day for any new beginnings. If there is something you need to improve or remove from your life, then this would be a good day for it. Sometimes, you have to do things that do not feel good. This is necessary if you wish to destroy the things that keep you feeling weak or held back. Tuesday is the day to just do it.

Wednesday – Mercury's Day

You may wish to learn something new or upskill on Wednesdays. This can be a mentally stimulating day, a time to study something. If you can do so with others, all the better. Mercury represents communication and interaction. You may wish to use this day to deal with your practical life. This may mean doing things which on other days may seem too trivial or tedious.

Thursday – Jupiter's Day

On Thursdays, you may wish to expand. You may learn something meaningful, anything that will broaden your horizons. You may travel somewhere you haven't been before to broaden your mind. This is a good day to explore. This can give you a profound sense of what is possible, and more hope and optimism to further expand upon.

Friday – Venus' Day

Fridays are a good day to enjoy yourself, whatever you find pleasurable. Social engagements, parties, and lovers are all ways to enjoy Venus for the weekend. Do whatever makes you happy and gives you a sense of contentment. Be mindful of overindulging, of course. You will only have to work harder at paying back tomorrow if you do. Being content with what you have is the best expression of Venus. The ability to be happy for no reason is Venus' greatest gift.

Saturday – Saturn's Day

Saturday is the best day for clearing any excesses brought about in the week prior. This may be through food fasting, or mentally fasting with the aid of meditation. But while Saturn is all about a clear out, it is also about working hard. Saturday is best for doing the chores. As Gurdjieff used to say to his followers, "Work consciously. Suffer voluntarily." Deliberately inviting limitations into your life is one of the best ways to mitigate Saturn-type issues. You may not have to experience as much of the negative expressions of the planet of restrictions, delays, and obstructions. Fasting allows you to experience restriction, leaving you feeling lighter and refreshed for the week ahead. Give something up for Saturn on Saturday, and Saturn will give back to you in kind.

CHUNKING YOUR DAYS

The Sun rules the Day and the Moon rules the Night. It may seem obvious, but the Sun has prominence during the day and the Moon at night. There is a daily pattern of productivity and rest we all experience. Metabolism has a solar and lunar component. Catabolic hormones break down molecules to release energy during the day; anabolic hormones build molecules at night to repair the body after the exertions of the day.

We can divide the Day into eight parts of three hours each: four parts during the day, and four during the Night. The first part begins at sunrise. A second round of four parts takes place at Night, after sunset. The timing of the Day and Night begins at sunrise and sunset specific to your location and time of year, although a mean calculation is used across the board. Thus, you can chunk your day based on the planets and their themes. The following times show the most conducive activities according to each planet's significations:

Sun: 6 am – 9 am

Mars: 9 am -12 pm

Jupiter: 12 pm – 3 pm

Mercury: 3 pm – 6 pm

Venus: 6 pm – 9 pm

Saturn: 9 pm – 12 am

Moon: 12 am – 3 am

Rāhu: 3 am – 6 am

Early mornings are best for connecting to the Sun and your essence through ritual, prayer, and meditation. Before you start with the work of the day, take time to reflect on this connection. Once you have done so, your day can run smoothly, as you 'get out of your own way'. The more connected you are to the Sun energy around sunrise, the more you can align with your purpose.

Mid-mornings are best for getting work done, as reflected in Mars. Work is about digesting whatever you are doing, which peaks as Mars' time of day kicks in. Mars rules the brain and nerves. It is an important time of day to build strength, to focus on the task at hand.

Afternoons are for 'Jupiterian' things. This may come as an afternoon nap after a heavy meal, as Jupiter is the largest planet in our solar system. Jupiter is about feeling comforted. You may wish to do something meaningful or connect with others who comfort you, such as a teacher or mentor, or study something more profound.

Late afternoons are for Mercury, a suitable time of day for learning and play. You learn better when you are playing, of course. If you are in a good mood, you are open and curious about trying out new things. This is a suitable time of day to be more dexterous, to coordinate more elements, to communicate with others.

Evening times are for Venus. This is the best for entertaining friends and being with your partner. It's a time to enjoy each other's company.

Late evenings are best for Saturn-type activities. This means less is more. Saturn's time of day is best kept to a minimum. Avoid taking on too much, whether mental stimulation or food, as the clearing out begins.

The Moon's period comes in the early morning hours. This is a time for deep sleep, to rebuild and repair through the release of anabolic hormones. It is also a time to dive deep into your subconscious.

Rāhu's period is a transition between Night and Day, those twilight hours that can sometimes disturb the mind. A lowered blood sugar and elevated levels of cortisol may wake you up, but it is the random thoughts that keep you awake longer. If you sleep through it, it's a deep dive through which you emerge with the dawning of a new day and a return of the light of the Sun.

HOURLY RULERS

Each planet rules an hour of the day, beginning with the first hour at sunrise of the planet, which rules that day. So, for example, the Sun rules the first hour after sunrise on Sunday, the Moon on Monday, Mars on Tuesday, and so on. There is a discrepancy among astrologers about how to calculate the exact hour. Some astrologers use 06.00 am across the board, while others use the exact time of sunrise each day. This changes throughout the year. However, it may make more sense to use 06.00 am, as certain latitudes and times of year would alter Table 3.4 so that it may not be of any practical use.

Table 3.4

Hour	Sun	Mon	Tues	Weds	Thurs	Fri	Sat
1	Sun	Moon	Mars	Mercury	Jupiter	Venus	Saturn
2	Venus	Saturn	Sun	Moon	Mars	Mercury	Jupiter
3	Mercury	Jupiter	Venus	Saturn	Sun	Moon	Mars
4	Moon	Mars	Mercury	Jupiter	Venus	Saturn	Sun
5	Saturn	Sun	Moon	Mars	Mercury	Jupiter	Venus
6	Jupiter	Venus	Saturn	Sun	Moon	Mars	Mercury
7	Mars	Mercury	Jupiter	Venus	Saturn	Sun	Moon
8	Sun	Moon	Mars	Mercury	Jupiter	Venus	Saturn
9	Venus	Saturn	Sun	Moon	Mars	Mercury	Jupiter
10	Mercury	Jupiter	Venus	Saturn	Sun	Moon	Mars
11	Moon	Mars	Mercury	Jupiter	Venus	Saturn	Sun
12	Saturn	Sun	Moon	Mars	Mercury	Jupiter	Venus
13	Jupiter	Venus	Saturn	Sun	Moon	Mars	Mercury
14	Mars	Mercury	Jupiter	Venus	Saturn	Sun	Moon
15	Sun	Moon	Mars	Mercury	Jupiter	Venus	Saturn
16	Venus	Saturn	Sun	Moon	Mars	Mercury	Jupiter
17	Mercury	Jupiter	Venus	Saturn	Sun	Moon	Mars
18	Moon	Mars	Mercury	Jupiter	Venus	Saturn	Sun
19	Saturn	Sun	Moon	Mars	Mercury	Jupiter	Venus
20	Jupiter	Venus	Saturn	Sun	Moon	Mars	Mercury
21	Mars	Mercury	Jupiter	Venus	Saturn	Sun	Moon
22	Sun	Moon	Mars	Mercury	Jupiter	Venus	Saturn
23	Venus	Saturn	Sun	Moon	Mars	Mercury	Jupiter
24	Mercury	Jupiter	Venus	Saturn	Sun	Moon	Mars

It is useful to be aware of the hour when something happens. If you keep a list of planetary hours by the phone, see if you can figure out what the issue will be before you answer! You could reverse engineer it with the hours and day of the week. You could plan your activities based on the day and the hour. If you are applying for a job, you could send the application in the planet's hour that rules your 10th house of career.

WATER ELEMENT: LUNAR DAYS

We calculate the lunar days based on the separation of the Sun and Moon. The lunar day shows a distinct quality of time based on their degrees of separation during the waning and waxing phase of the Moon. This relationship, the lunar phase, says something about the way you relate on any given day (see Table 3.5).

There are 30 lunar days altogether, 15 days of the bright half of the Moon phase, including the Full Moon, and 15 in the dark half, including the New Moon. The lunar days reflect relationship dynamics, as the Sun and Moon relate to each other in different ways in each of the Moon phases. Each planet rules a lunar day. The lunar day and planet that rules it have an impact on your relationships each day. The planet that rules the lunar day you were born on, as well as the element associated with it, says something about how you approach your relationships.

The Moon moves about 13 degrees each day of the month, while the Sun moves one degree each day. This means the Sun and Moon are always either separating or coming together by increments of 12 degrees every day. Each lunar day is associated with a planet. This planet says something about your relationships, its position and strength affecting the way you relate. This is more relevant during a daśā of the planet.

Table 3.5

Moon Phases	Ruling Planet	Element
1	Sun	Fire
2	Moon	Earth
3	Mars	Space
4	Mercury	Water
5	Jupiter	Air
6	Venus	Fire
7	Saturn	Earth
8	Rāhu	Space
9	Sun	Water
10	Moon	Air
11	Mars	Fire
12	Mercury	Earth
13	Jupiter	Space
14	Venus	Water
Full Moon	Saturn	Air
New Moon	Rāhu	Air

Each lunar day has an associated element. The 1st, 6th, and 11th lunar days are associated with fire, the 2nd, 7th, and 12th with earth, the 3rd, 8th, and 13th with space, the 4th, 9th, and 14th with water, and the 5th, 10th, Full and New Moon days with air. Each one shows how you approach your relationships.

The fire element can disrupt relationships due to excessive passions, while air can show emotional volatility and instability. Fire and air don't mix well with water, the overall element of the lunar days. Earth is a good container for water and tends to sustain relationships. If you were born on the 2nd, 7th, or 12th lunar day, you are more likely to sustain relationships. While we must address other indications in your horoscope, this shows an underlying support. The space element is a good container for relationships, as this element is about 'holding space' for others. The water element itself may mean emotions overcome you, as water combined with water can show highly emotional relationships. This may be good or bad, depending. Whether it's good or bad, it's likely to be intensely so.

EARTH ELEMENET: HALF LUNAR DAYS

We divide each lunar day in half to show more practical concerns. The half lunar days show how you do things, even the type of work you do. This is associated with Mercury and the earth element, the most practical element. Specifically, the planet associated with each half lunar day will show how you go about doing anything. We examine the half lunar day when you were born to see how you approach your work, the associated planet affecting your professional life.

As each lunar day is 12 degrees, the difference between the Sun and Moon each day, the half lunar days must be half that, i.e., 6 degrees. Therefore, there are 60 of these each month, twice that of the lunar days, 30 in the bright half of the lunar month, and 30 in the dark half. Each of the seven half lunar days repeat eight times throughout the month. The planets associated with each run in the order of the days of the week, which are the Sun, Moon, Mars, Mercury, Jupiter, Venus, and Saturn. Rāhu and Ketu are added to the end and very beginning in the lunar month (see Table 3.6).

Table 3.6

Lunar Day	Bright Half		Dark Half	
1	Ketu	Sun	Moon	Mars
2	Moon	Mars	Mercury	Jupiter
3	Mercury	Jupiter	Venus	Saturn
4	Venus	Saturn	Sun	Moon
5	Sun	Moon	Mars	Mercury
6	Mars	Mercury	Jupiter	Venus
7	Jupiter	Venus	Saturn	Sun
8	Saturn	Sun	Moon	Mars
9	Moon	Mars	Mercury	Jupiter
10	Mercury	Jupiter	Venus	Saturn
11	Venus	Saturn	Sun	Moon
12	Sun	Moon	Mars	Mercury
13	Mars	Mercury	Jupiter	Venus
14	Jupiter	Venus	Saturn	Rāhu
15	Saturn	Sun	Ketu	Rāhu

SPACE ELEMENT: YOGAS

The yoga formed between the Sun and Moon when you were born shows which planet is a unifying force in your birth chart. The exact degree that is calculated based on the combined degrees of the Sun and Moon is called the 'yogi point'. The planet associated with this lunar mansion is the 'yogi planet'.

There are 27 types of relationships that are possible, based on the 27 lunar mansions and the Moon's transit each day of the month. Each day has a certain quality of time that is either conducive to holding things together or challenges a sense of order. This is reflected in the planet that rules the daily yoga. This planet's position at the time of your birth says a lot about how blessed you feel, while the daily yoga shows the level of cooperation for each passing day (see Table 3.7).

The Moon transits one lunar mansion a day, a distance of 13° 20', either towards the Sun or away from it, showing 27 different relationships that are possible between the luminaries. This links the lunar mansions to the Sun's and Moon's combined degrees.

To calculate your Sun-Moon yoga, take the number of the lunar mansion for your Sun and Moon and subtract 1. Someone with the Sun in Maghā (10) and Moon in Anurādhā (17) would have the 26th yoga. Maghā is the 10th lunar mansion and Anurādhā is the 17th. Adding both together and then subtracting 1, we get 26 (10 +17 − 1 = 26).

Some yogas are less helpful for a general sense of order and protection. These less auspicious and thus, less binding combinations are the 1st, 6th, 9th, 10th, 13th, 15th 19th, and 27th. All other yogas or combinations are more auspicious for activities that require more cooperation, and for a sense of protection.

We link the element of space to this limb of time and Jupiter is the planet that is associated with space. Jupiter holds everything together–in space. This is quite literally the case, as Jupiter is the largest of the planets, exerting a huge gravitational pull, so that it does not orbit the Sun exactly; instead, both the Sun and Jupiter orbit around a point in space (barycentre).

Each planet is associated with three yogas each, just as they associate with three lunar mansions. The list of daily yogas given in Table 3.7. begins from Puṣya lunar mansion, which is associated with Saturn. The planet that rules this in your birth chart is your 'yogi planet'. This planet generally brings prosperity in its daśā. As the overall representative of this yoga, Jupiter represents abundance, the 'glue that binds things together', enabling more growth and prosperity to occur.

The planet that rules the Sun sign the yogi point is found is also an auspicious planet (duplicate yogi), and another beneficial planet and daśā. On the other hand, the 6th lunar mansion from your yogi point is your 'avayogi'.

The planet associated with the 6th lunar mansion from your Moon is an inauspicious planet in a general sense, although this cannot be the only thing to consider when ascertaining the role of any planet.

Table 3.7

Yoga	Yogi Planet
1, 10, 19	Saturn
2, 11, 20	Mercury
3, 12, 21	Ketu
4, 13, 22	Venus
5, 14, 23	Moon
7, 16, 25	Mars
8, 17, 26	Rāhu
9, 18, 27	Jupiter

AIR ELEMENT: LUNAR MANSIONS

The lunar mansions show how energy moves through your birth chart, as the vital energy of the Sun signs are divided into lunar divisions. The lunar mansion the Moon is in relates to Saturn and the air element, reflecting how energy moves through your birth chart. The air elements impacts your mental-emotional and prāṇic (energy) bodies. It shows the energy of each day as an ongoing phenomenon, what's 'in the air' that day. The lunar mansion the Moon was in at your birth says a lot about your moods, your overall health and well-being.

The 3 sections of 9 lunar mansions relate to the 3 impulses or guṇas. See shaded portions in Table 3.8.

Table 3.8

#	Lunar Mansion	Sidereal Degrees	Daśā
1	Aśvinī	0° 00' – 13° 20' Aries	Ketu
2	Bharaṇī	13° 20' – 26° 40' Aries	Venus
3	Kṛttikā	26° 40' Aries – 10° 00' Taurus	Sun
4	Rohiṇī	10° 00' – 23° 20' Taurus	Moon
5	Mṛgaśirṣā	23° 20' Taurus – 6° 40' Gemini	Mars
6	Ārdrā	6° 40' – 20° Gemini	Rāhu
7	Punarvasu	20° 00' Gemini – 3° 20' Cancer	Jupiter
8	Puṣya	3° 20'– 16° 40' Cancer	Saturn
9	Āśleṣā	16° 40' – 30° 00' Cancer	Mercury
10	Maghā	0° 00' – 13° 20' Leo	Ketu
11	Pūrva Phālguṇī	13° 20' – 26° 40' Leo	Venus
12	Uttara Phālguṇī	26° 40' Leo – 10° 00' Virgo	Sun
13	Hasta	10° 00' – 23° 20' Virgo	Moon
14	Citrā	23° 20' Virgo – 6° 40' Libra	Mars
15	Svātī	6° 40' – 20° 00' Libra	Rāhu
16	Viśākhā	20° 00' Libra – 3° 20' Scorpio	Jupiter
17	Anurādhā	3° 20' – 16° 40' Scorpio	Saturn
18	Jyeṣthā	16° 40' – 30° 00' Scorpio	Mercury
19	Mūla	0° 00' – 13° 20' Sag	Ketu
20	Pūrvāṣāḍha	13° 20' – 26° 40' Sag	Venus
21	Uttarāṣāḍha	26° 40' Sag – 10° 00' Cap	Sun
22	Śravaṇa	10° 00' – 23° 20' Cap	Moon
23	Dhaniṣṭhā	23° 20' Cap – 6° 40' Aquarius	Mars
24	Śatabhiṣaj	6° 40' – 20° 00' Aquarius	Rāhu
25	Pūrva Bhādrapada	20° 00' Aquarius – 3° 20' Pisces	Jupiter
26	Uttara Bhādrapada	3° 20' – 16° 40' Pisces	Saturn
27	Revatī	16° 40' – 30° 00' Pisces	Mercury

The beginning of Aries, Leo, and Sagittarius brings a change of impulse. Aries is a movable sign; Leo is a fixed sign; and Sagittarius is a dual sign. The beginning of movable Aries to the end of movable Cancer represents the impulse of initiation (rajas); the beginning of fixed Leo to the end of fixed Scorpio represents the impulse of stagnation (tamas); and the beginning of dual Sagittarius to the end of dual Pisces represents the impulse of harmony and balance (sattva).

We can divide the lunar mansions into trends based on where the Moon is in your birth chart, apart from the 3 shaded areas. The placement of the Moon at your birth is the beginning of the 1st part. Count 9 lunar mansions from here. The first 9 lunar mansions reflect more of your present circumstances (1-9). The next 9 lunar mansions will show your future (10 – 18), while the last 9 will show your past (19 -27).

We can divide your current planetary daśā into 3 parts, and then further into 4 parts, or padas. First, divide your current planetary daśā into 3 sections. If you were born with the Moon in Maghā, the 1st third of Ketu's major daśā would last for 28 months, as Ketu is 7 years in total or 84 months (12 months x 7 years). Dividing 84 by 3, we get 28 months. Each 28-month period would correspond more to the lunar mansion in question, starting from the first lunar mansion from where your Moon is. Maghā themes are highlighted more so in the first 28 months, Mūla in the next 28 months and, finally, Aśvinī in the last 28 months. We can see this trend for all planetary daśās.

Simply multiply each major period in years by 12 months. Then, divide by 3.

Each part highlights certain themes according to the lunar mansion, but it will also highlight themes based on its position. You can begin by observing the house position counting from the Moon in your birth chart to see the areas of life that are triggered. You can then add your rising sign. Each part will focus on certain areas of your life based on these indications. You can then look at this from the Sun, or any other planet, to get a more rounded view.

We can further break these 3 phases down into 4 padas or steps, to show the more immediate changes within the overall themes. Using the Maghā example, we can break the first 28 months down into 4 sections, by dividing 28 by 4. This would show each 7-month period shifting sections in the 9th divisional chart. This would also show the underlying support of the 9th divisional chart, based on its corresponding sign. We convert each section of your birth chart into a sign in the 9th divisional chart, to show the underlying themes of dharma, artha, kāma and mokṣa.

Table 3.9 is a breakdown of all planetary daśās into 3 sections, and further into 4 divisions, corresponding with the 9th divisional chart. Each major period in years corresponds to the same number of months.

Table 3.9

Planetary Daśā	Major Period in Years	3 Phases in Months	4 Divisions in Months
Ketu	7	28	7
Venus	20	80	20
Sun	6	24	6
Moon	10	40	10
Mars	7	28	7
Rāhu	18	72	18
Jupiter	16	64	16
Saturn	19	76	19
Mercury	17	68	17

PORTIONS OF EACH DAŚĀ

You should not expect a longer daśā to produce the same results throughout its period. There must be a way of dividing the whole period up into phases, apart from each sub-daśās. We do this by first looking at one third portions within each daśā based on the nature of the planet.

We can divide each planetary and sign-based daśā into different periods, as different portions within the complete daśā bring out certain significations. We do this based on the nature of the planet and the sign, as the nature of a sign is impacted by the planet that rules it.

Jātaka Pārijāta explains how to divide the daśās of planets. Each planet gives its results in different portions of their major daśās. This depends on whether the planet is cruel or kind. The 1st and 2nd portions are divided up differently for these planets. All planets, whether cruel or kind, express their desires and aspects more so in the last portion of their daśās, whether in a major or sub-period.

The general nature of the planet will also have a say in how you experience the whole daśā, based on whether it is cruel or kind. While cruel planets can do wonders, as they challenge you to improve your life, kind planets may not always be the best thing for you. As cliché as it may sound, sometimes you have to 'be cruel to be kind', while at other times, you are 'killed with kindness'. Either way, don't simply take cruel to mean 'bad', or kind to mean 'good'. Everything is good for something.

CRUEL PERIODS

The 1st third of the major planetary daśā of a cruel planet, the 1st 3 sub-daśās, expresses more of the planet's strengths and weaknesses. This includes strengths across all divisions of the sign. So, while a planet like Saturn may be strong for one area, it may pose a challenge because of some weakness in a certain division. Actually, even when strong, Saturn can pose a challenge. Still, it is usually more helpful to have a strong planet in a powerful position, as it shows the strength to overcome the challenges – even if it also brings them. A strong Saturn may mean having the ability to take on more, to be more responsible because of the very responsibilities it brings.

While you may experience Saturn as strong in your main birth chart, there may be an underlying weakness in the 9th division. So, while you may show a more responsible approach in your outer demeanour, you may not access it as easily within. These issues may be there from the very outset of Saturn's major daśā, the sub-daśās of Saturn-Saturn, Saturn-Mercury, and Saturn-Ketu.

The 2nd third shows what Saturn represents for you, the houses and areas of life Saturn rules, as well as the house it is in. Saturn rules Capricorn and Aquarius. Look to the house positions of these signs in your birth chart. Saturn reflects a need to be more responsible about these areas. This would especially be the case in the sub-daśās of Saturn-Venus, Saturn-Sun, and Saturn-Moon.

The 3rd and final third of the daśā reflects yet another trend. This is when Saturn's sight and aspects are more active, as well as aspects from other planets. All planets have desires, even Saturn, which impresses upon you the need to restrict yourself in some areas of your life. But Saturn shows a desire to work hard also. Many times, Saturn periods delays things, so that you end up focusing a lot more on it. In Saturn daśā, it should be quite clear to you what your options are. You are likely to simplify your life because of the restrictions. By removing other options, you can focus on what is possible and achieve a great deal.

Saturn's 3rd house aspect shows where you withheld in a previous life. This shows where you must make efforts to pay back this time round. Saturn's 10th house aspect shows where you may feel punished but also where you have a lot of work to do. The 10th house is the 3rd house from the 8th. This shows the work you must do (10th), the effort you must make (3rd), to overcome your kārmik debts (8th). Saturn's 7th house aspect shows the desire for detachment, often in relationships, as well as who you are likely to feel separated from. These aspects become more apparent in the last third of Saturn's major or sub-daśā.

Mars is also a cruel planet. Like Saturn, its strengths and weaknesses are more apparent in its first 3 sub-daśās, i.e., Mars-Mars, Mars-Rāhu, and Mars-Jupiter. You either experience a great deal of power, or a certain sense of timidity and lack of energy. A strong Mars reflects your ability to digest a great deal of life experience. Mars reflects a need to develop strength and courage. A weak Mars may show a lack of drive and motivation to just do it. Yet it can also express itself as an overcompensation. This may become clear in the first few years of Mars' daśā.

It may express itself as an initial inability to do something you know you must, or through a relationship with someone who challenges you to do so.

The next 3 sub-daśās of Mars, i.e., Mars-Saturn, Mars-Mercury, and Mars-Ketu, express what Mars represents in your chart more specifically. This portion shows the impact of where it is in your birth chart, the house positions of Aries and Scorpio, and the house is it in. Mars may represent your partner, your child, your boss, or your parent. It may represent your home life or work life, your future direction, or your past. It depends on what Mars rules by house position in your chart. Whatever it is, you may meet with some challenge you must overcome. If Mars were strong, you are likely to be up for the challenge and willing to do what it takes. Yet a strong Mars may show you create more problems than you solve, as Mars is the part of you that doesn't know when to quit. Mars can sometimes show more destruction than is necessary, a burning of many bridges that you have built in the previous Moon daśā. Some of these bridges may need burning, of course. It may be time to challenge yourself to get out of your comfort zone.

The last 3 sub-daśās of Mars, i.e., Mars-Venus, Mars-Sun, and Mars-Moon, bring out Mars' aspects more so, as well as aspect to it. This phase shows what Mars desires, what you desire. Mars looks at the 4th house from where it is. This relates to the home environment and safety. Mars is the part of you that wishes to protect your peace of mind and safety - at any cost. During the last few years of Mars' daśā, it's important to protect the things you hold dear.

Mars' influence on the 8th house, the house of debts and disease, shows the need to remove any problems. If there is anything that increases debts or reduces your life span, Mars's impulse is to remove these problems. It's about getting rid of bad habits, introducing healthier ones. Mars' influence on the 7th house can show a lot of passion and drive. Yet this may actually create problems in your relationships and is something to be mindful of as you continue to improve yourself.

Mars and Saturn are about protecting your interests, but they do so in unique ways. Saturn protects you through fear. It restricts you, so you don't overdo anything. Mars protects you through anger, fuelling a sense of rage when you don't get your way. Both feelings ensure you are thinking more about yourself and your needs. This can create problems with others, though the need is more unconscious (tamas).

Rāhu is also cruel. Its strengths and weaknesses expresses itself more so in its first 3 sub-daśās, i.e., Rāhu-Rāhu, Rāhu-Jupiter, and Rāhu-Saturn. Rāhu's strengths can be a little hard to manage, reflecting a lot of chaos for a time before everything settles down. This is especially the case in the Rāhu-Rāhu daśā, where the mythological head of the serpent raises its head so it can devour some experience. The issue is not being able to digest all that you experience. Yet you may not be consciously aware of this. This can create all kinds of interesting dynamics, including manipulations that are projected onto others. You may meet with those who push your buttons, when truly you are seeking to push your own boundaries on some level.

At the beginning of Rāhu daśā, it may feel as if life is a beast that needs taming. It's important to note that whatever your experience of Rāhu, it is your subconscious desire. It may create situations you would never consciously choose. Until you withdraw your projections, you are likely to project your shadow onto others who challenge you. This is whether Rāhu were strong or weak in your birth chart. In one way, having a strong Rāhu can create as much trouble as a weak one, though we think of a cruel planet in a weaker position as even crueller. It's as if a roguish part of you feels hard done by and acts out all the more.

The next 3 sub-daśās of Rāhu daśā, i.e., Rāhu-Mercury, Rāhu-Ketu, and Rāhu-Venus, bring out what Rāhu rules in your chart, the house placement of the sign Aquarius. This phase also emphasises the house placement of Rāhu, as well as any planets it associates with. While any planet must adhere to the sign it is in, this is even more relevant for the lunar nodes, Rāhu, and Ketu. That's because they are not physical entities. Instead, they are shadows that need a physical planet to express themselves through. So, the sign and house position of Rāhu becomes even more important in determining its expression. It is better to have Rāhu expressed through its antidote, i.e., Jupiter. It is especially helpful when Jupiter influences, and thus, tames the chaotic energy of Rāhu. Jupiter represents order and clarity. Although Jupiter itself reflects your life after a major daśā of Rāhu is complete, it is helpful to antidote it for the duration of the daśā. The area Aquarius represents by house position will experience a hunger and thirst for experience. This will be the case during the 2nd third portion of 3 sub-daśās more so. But it will also bring up complications around these issues, especially during Rāhu-Ketu sub daśā. This is because Ketu is opposite Rāhu. Despite the hunger for some experience, Ketu can show losses. The second phase within the major daśā of Rāhu will show a thirst for life experience and success. Yet whatever you deem success to be comes with a price. Rāhu can block the experience as much as it creates the opportunity. Mostly, it does both. You may hunger for something so much that no matter what success you achieve, it never is enough.

The last 3 sub-daśās of the Rāhu daśā, i.e., Rāhu-Sun, Rāhu-Moon, and Rāhu-Mars, show a waning daśā. But it can be a beast that rears its head in more powerful ways towards the end. The last sub-daśā of Rāhu-Mars intensifies your hunger for something, a last-minute push for success and achievement. The whole phase, from Rāhu-Sun, can show a need to achieve some power. Rāhu represents the ego, and the ego can feel powerful even when you are experiencing challenges. In fact, the ego loves the challenge, and a role, whether a powerful one or a victim. It needs a role with which it can identify. Rāhu reflects a distorted view of yourself and of what you are capable.

In this last portion of Rāhu daśā, its aspects kick in more so. This fuels a need for some experience you haven't had yet. Or a replacement need when you have all you thought you ever wanted. Rāhu looks at the 5th and 9th houses, counting in reverse. This shows Rāhu's need to twist and contort reality to suit its agenda. The 5th is the future, while the 9th is the past. Rāhu twists even this. You may think all you need is in your future, not realising that your future creates your past as much as your past creates your future. Think of it this way: Whenever you think of your past, you are recreating it over and over. Depending on how you feel, you create all kinds of different situations in the past, in your mind's eye. Likewise, when you contemplate what may happen in the future, you do so based on what you experienced in the past, a past that makes you feel a certain way. The more present you can be in a Rāhu daśā, the less of a hold it has on you. Irrational fears cannot take hold in the present moment.

Both Rāhu and Ketu show this loop in time and perception, a loop you can get caught up in during the later phase of Rāhu's daśā. This is because you experience all 3 sub-daśās of the previous major daśās at the tail end of Rāhu, i.e., Sun, Moon, and Mars, but only if you have lived long enough before entering a Rāhu daśā. This may distort the past as much as it can instil profound insights. It may do both at this stage.

Rāhu influences the 12th house from where it is in your birth chart, according to some astrologers. This shows you looking back over your shoulder to see the area it has been, as if it leaves a shadow behind it. This shadow is your distorted sense of self. When looking at Rāhu's aspect to the 12th, count in reverse. Rāhu looks backwards, and thus, it influences the 2nd house in zodiacal order. Imagine Rāhu were in Aries. This means Rāhu would influence Taurus, the 2nd sign from Aries, although it is actually Rāhu's 12th

sign when counting in reverse. Once Rāhu moves into Pisces in reverse motion, it will influence Aries. Rāhu's 12th house sight can show up as subconscious blocks, as the 12th house is the subconscious. You must deal with these blocks at the very end of Rāhu's 18 year-long daśā. This can offer you a profound sense of what lies ahead, as you prepare for more clarity in Jupiter daśā.

We also see Ketu as cruel. Thus, it will show its strengths and weaknesses in the 1st phase of its major daśā, the first 3 sub-daśās, i.e., Ketu-Ketu, Ketu-Venus, and Ketu-Sun. But here's the thing: Ketu is not like all the other planets. It is not a planet at all, but an eclipse, a shadow. It behaves differently than even the other shadow, Rāhu. Unlike Rāhu, it has no desire – for anything. It's dis-embodied and uninterested in creating any more action. While its initial phase can pack a punch, it's at the very end of the daśā astrologers warn clients of its cruel nature. Ketu is the tail of the mythological serpent in Vedic lore, unleashing its poisons at the later part of the daśā. Yet I have seen the beginning of Ketu to be as troublesome for clients. Many feel a bit lost at this stage. They are looking for any kind of surety and sense of purpose in all the uncertainty.

The next 3 sub-daśās of Ketu, i.e., Ketu-Moon, Ketu-Mars, and Ketu-Rāhu, may bring out its rulership of Scorpio more so. Whatever area of your life Scorpio represents may not be obvious to you. That is the nature of Scorpio, anyway. This is a more complex period. It is useful to notice what the sign Scorpio represents for you by house position. If you can make this need conscious, you can lessen the uncertainty. Ketu-Rāhu is especially complex, bringing up the dynamics of both nodes. The past points you to the future, while the future points you to the past.

The last 3 sub-daśās of the Ketu phase, i.e., Ketu-Jupiter, Ketu-Saturn, and Ketu-Mercury, offer their own complexities. Ketu's need for liberation reigns supreme. Yet Ketu does not have any sight. It is a 'headless' part of you. But the other planets have their desires, of course. Jupiter, Saturn, and Mercury, all wish for something, even while Ketu wants for nothing. Any planets looking at Ketu would show a desire. If either Jupiter, Saturn, or Mercury influence, this would be more prominent during their sub-daśās. Even if they don't, they will all bring their wishes to the table at the tail end of Ketu. The very last sub-daśā, that of Ketu-Mercury, is more complex. This shows a need to deal with certain existential questions, while also dealing with the practical side of life. The Ketu daśā loosens its grip after Ketu-Mercury, and you find yourself in a Venus daśā. The losses that were inevitable may have shaken any sense of certainty, but you are now prepared to trust in life again.

The Sun is also cruel. Yet the Sun is also more harmonious (sattva) than the other cruel planets. Planets become angry because of being too close to the Sun (combust), yet there are benefits to the Sun beyond its cruelty. When the Sun creates a challenge, it can show a more philosophical response, and more clarity. The 1ˢᵗ 3 sub-daśās in a Sun daśā, i.e., Sun-Sun, Sun-Moon, and Sun-Mars, bring out the strengths and weaknesses of the

Sun. This is in relation to your birth chart and divisions of the sign. It may be strong in a more outward way, as expressed in your birth chart, but you may also lack a sense of confidence deep down, as seen in the 9th division. Either way, the initial phase of the Sun's daśā brings out its highs and lows.

The next 3 sub-daśās of the Sun daśā, i.e., Sun-Rāhu, Sun-Jupiter, and Sun-Saturn, are more complex because of the other planets involved. Rāhu and Saturn mixing with the Sun are especially complex. Your light and shadow mix up in interesting ways. Wherever the sign Leo is, this will become more active in this portion, along with where the Sun is in your chart. This eventually make the issues of the Sun, of confidence and self-esteem, clearer. You will find out at this point what are the areas of your life you need to work on to feel more self-assured.

The last 3 sub-daśās of the Sun daśā, i.e., Sun-Mercury, Sun-Ketu, and Sun-Venus, have their own complexities. The Sun's influence on the 7th house adds to these complexities. Sun-Venus can create complexities around relationships, while the Sun also looks at the 7th house of relationships. This may be a tricky period to negotiate your own sense of self-worth and self-esteem, while having to consider someone else's needs.

KIND PERIODS

The 1ˢᵗ 3 sub-daśās of Jupiter, Jupiter-Jupiter, Jupiter-Saturn, and Jupiter-Mercury sub-daśās, bring up specific lessons based on what Jupiter rules in your chart. Jupiter rules Sagittarius and Pisces. Whatever houses these signs fall under, it shows what the focus is. You are likely to sense this as positive, or at least see the benefit if it is not. Jupiter is kind. If you feel blessed, it is Jupiter's blessing. It brings comfort to whatever area of life it impacts. Sometimes, of course, that comfort is too much of a good thing and can lead to problems. Usually, though, it is a welcome relief, a sense of growth, an inner growth and/or an outer expansion. You can connect more with the areas Jupiter rules in the first 3 sub-daśās, as well as where it is in your chart. This may be because of some bounty or a sense of heightened awareness.

The next 3 sub-daśās of Jupiter-Ketu, Jupiter-Venus, and Jupiter-Sun bring out Jupiter's strengths and weaknesses more so. This is reflected in your birth chart and its divisions. The strength of Jupiter is the ability to discern truth. It shows an ability to organise your life and usually gives a more coherent and peaceful experience. It brings faith in the workings of the universe, in the many opportunities that are likely presenting themselves. When weak, Jupiter may not deliver on these, although the experience of expansion, even if only in your mind, is always available. Yet a weak Jupiter can show a lack of faith, a lack of trust in your own intuition, and an over-reliance on those who would lead you astray, whether they mean to or not. This can lead to not knowing what to do, or feeling as if life has lost meaning. Yet you can get it back, of course, and you will. Yet you must work at it if Jupiter were weak in your chart. But it is likely stronger in some respect, so there is bound to be somewhere you feel more faithful.

The last 3 sub-daśās of Jupiter-Moon, Jupiter-Mars, and Jupiter-Rāhu bring with it Jupiter's desires. Jupiter desires knowledge and truth. This triggers Jupiter's special aspects in your chart, the 5th, 7th, and 9th houses from its position. This shows a need to grow and expand on these areas. Jupiter brings a sense of good luck and opportunity. Whether you take on these opportunities is another matter, of course.

Jupiter's influence on your 5th house can show many future possibilities, including children if you so desire. Its sight on the 9th brings blessings from the past in some form of guidance. Its sight on the 7th house can bring harmony to your relationships. You may experience a new relationship or relationships, where you can connect to others more deeply. This will be especially useful in the last phase, i.e., Jupiter-Rāhu, as others can help you through a complex period with some sage advice.

All the other kind planets, Venus, Mercury, and Moon, go through this same sequence in each of the 3 sub-daśās. The houses these planets rule will be prominent, followed by their strengths and weaknesses in their signs and divisions. Finally, in the last 3 sub-daśās, their 7th house sight is more prominent, including any planets that aspect them back.

Venus, Mercury, and the Moon all have many desires to negotiate. Because they do not look at other houses as much as the 7th, they focus a lot on relationships. Yet it may not always mean an actual relationship, unless they are in the 1st house. There is the desire for the opposite in any of their daśās, whatever, or whomever, lies opposite in your birth chart.

Whatever the focus, these planets show a lot of desire to negotiate during the last 3 sub-daśās. The opposite of Venus shows what you desire in a partner, anyway. Any planets in this sign, or ruling, will show what kind of partner attracts you. This attraction will be more relevant in this last phase of Venus. Mercury desires worldly things. It wants success. The Moon shows all your likes and dislikes. This shows an attraction, and attachments, to certain people and things.

SIGN TRENDS

Each sign rises with its head or back. This shows when the sign will bear fruit, either in the beginning (head) or end (back) of the daśā (see Table 3.10). There are 3 portions for sign-based daśās, when the sign, its ruler, or its aspects, are more prominent. The relationship between signs that are active on two levels in a sign-based daśā is important, too. This shows whether there is comfort or struggle involved in the themes presented in each portion.

Each sign represents a theme or area of your life, but this may or may not work well with other areas. If a planet is well-placed in a sign that is active in a daśā, it will give excellent results. Parāśara states, "If a sign is posited with exalted or own planet, the Daśā of the sign will afford sensuous enjoyment and wealth. If the sign is devoid of any planet, the Daśā of the sign will be unfavourable and defunct."[12]

The translator of this text adds a note to explain that defunct in this case is to mean 'uneventful'. We can see the possibility of less activity when there are no planets in a sign. Yet no area of life is ever completely uneventful, so we must take this interpretation in context. A better expression may be 'less eventful'. Whether a sign has a planet, there are always planets influencing the sign. And the sign has a ruling planet that is also doing something in

---

[12] Girish Chand Sharma, *Brihat Parasara Hora Sastra Vol. 2* (New Delhi: Sagar Publications, 1995), p. 162.

your chart. The planet ruling the active sign will be more active at a certain point in the daśā, too.

Table 3.10 shows the signs in relation to the part of the body rising for that sign. All back-rising signs, Aries, Taurus, Cancer, Sagittarius, Capricorn, and Aquarius are stronger during the Night. All head-rising signs, Leo, Virgo, Libra, and Scorpio are stronger during the Day. Gemini is an exception. Although it's a head-rising sign, it's stronger during the Night. Pisces is strong during the Day, although it rises with both the head and back.

Signs that rise with the head, i.e., Gemini, Leo, Virgo, Libra, and Scorpio, give their results in the beginning third of the daśā more so. The back rising signs, Aries, Taurus, Cancer, Sagittarius, Capricorn, and Aquarius, give their results during the last third. Pisces is both a head and back-rising sign (think of the two fish swimming in opposite directions). It gives the results of the sign itself in the middle third of the complete daśā.

For example, Aries rises with its back. When Aries is active in the daśās, it gives its results more so in the last 4 sub-daśās of the major daśā (we divide each major daśā into 12 sub-daśās, based on the 12 signs). The next step is to find out when the ruler of the sign, as well as planets placed in the sign or aspecting (influencing), will give their results. Refer to Table 1.2 for signs and their ruling planets.

Cruel planets give their results more so at the beginning of the sign's daśā. Thus, Mars, Saturn, Rāhu, and Ketu, as well as the Sun, give their results at the beginning of their sign's periods. Kind planets, Jupiter, Venus,

Mercury, and a waxing or Full Moon, give their results more so later.

Table 3.10

Sun Sign	Part Rising	Day/Night Strength
Aries	Back	Night
Taurus	Back	Night
Gemini	Head	Night
Cancer	Back	Night
Leo	Head	Day
Virgo	Head	Day
Libra	Head	Day
Scorpio	Head	Day
Sagittarius	Back	Night
Capricorn	Back	Night
Aquarius	Back	Night
Pisces	Both	Day

Mars rules Aries, so Mars will give its effects in the first 4 sub-daśās. The sign Aries itself, its house position, will be more active during the last 4 sub-daśās. This leaves the middle 4 sub-daśās for any planets in the sign Aries, or aspecting, to give their results. Planets placed in or aspecting are more active during the middle third of the daśā. If an Aries daśā were to last for 12 years, these three phases would last 4 years, based on the division of 12 signs. Mars' position and strength would show its impact for the first 4 years. Then, planets' strength in the sign or influencing will impact during the next 4 years. Finally, the sign itself will give its full impact in the last 4 years.

Taurus rises with its back, so gives the sign's results more so in the last 4 sub-daśās. Venus rules Taurus and is a kind planet, so it will give its results later. This is in the middle part of the whole daśā. That leaves the first part of a Taurus daśā for any planets placed in or aspecting.

Pisces gives the sign's placement by house position in the middle portion of the daśā. Its ruler, Jupiter, is a kind planet and gives its result more at the end. Thus, the first 4 sub-daśās give the results of planets in or aspecting.

These are general trends. See them alongside more specific indications, including how signs on the 1st and 2nd levels combine to give a result.

G O C H Ā R A (T R A N S I T S)

Planets' transits impact each Sun sign and lunar mansion. Certain transits are more relevant if you are also experiencing a daśā of that planet or of the sign being transited. Transits are like the seconds hand on the clock, fine-tuning events. *Gochāra* refers to the movement (chara) of planets through the divisions of the ecliptic (go). Otherwise, transits show general themes. But because you experience all the planets on many different levels of different daśās, you experience all the transits on some level, every moment of every day of your life. Though not all transits reflect events in your life, they all show general themes you experience on some level.

We all experience transits in different ways, as well as there being a global phenomenon, a collective experience. Transits trickle down into your individual experience in many ways and to varying degrees. The celestial oceans flow into rivers, as rivers flow into streams, filtering into your life experience. You can see the more relevant transits by looking at your planetary and sign-based daśās. The transit of these planets are the ones to watch. More especially, when you experience a daśā of a planet or sign for many years, that planet or sign leaves its mark on life events, as a transit is bound to trigger events at some point within longer time periods. Otherwise, transits are a useful tool to see general trends. This is how any astrology column or transit report can be of any use to everyone.

While we couldn't deny the impact of all the transits, the focus on an individual's life must focus on transits of planets active in daśās. Use all the other transits to see mundane, or worldly, events.

Whatever daśā, this imprint was at one time a transit. Different transits are active at different times in your life. Yet the seed potential was there from the beginning. Daśās may be more impactful than transits, in that they show something already set in motion, i.e., an imprint in your birth chart was once a transit. The current transits trigger events by triggering something that is already within you, which you are ready to experience on some level.

If you are experiencing a Venus daśā, for example, and Venus represents a certain relationship, its current transit is more important to watch for timing the beginning of that relationship. Venus daśās get triggered at different times in your life, as Venus may be active on any level, whether you are conscious of it or not. Once Venus transits a planet or degree in your birth chart that shows a relationship, it can bring what is promised in your birth chart. Other transits are important apart from this, of course, but perhaps not as much at Venus.

While transits represent trends that are part of our collective experience, your experience of global trends is unique. You can observe trends through transits, in a general sort of way, so that you can take from it what is relevant and useful.

Transits colour your experience of life, but it is the houses of astrology that make astrology more personal to you. Houses make sign transits more specific to you, showing the area of your life that is impacted by a particular transit.

The influence of planets changes because of the alignment of the signs throughout the day. Planets don't stop moving, and neither do you. You are forever changing, evolving. Although you were born with an imprint in your horoscope, the planets have not been in the same position ever since. While their position at your birth shows an ongoing influence throughout your life, you must see this along with ongoing transits.

The houses do not move in relation to where you are. Instead, the signs move in relation to the houses. The different signs of the zodiac are in various locations throughout the day as the Earth spins on its axis. As each sign rises in the East, the relationships between signs change, based on their house position. These houses show how astrology becomes more relevant to you, relative to their position in your birth chart.

The 10th house is the highest in the horoscope, appearing above your head. Yet the sign that is in the 10th house will change throughout the day. The 10th house remains above your head, whatever your location or time of day. Likewise, the 4th house remains below you, the 7th on the western horizon, and the 1st house or rising sign on the eastern horizon. It is the signs that change, altering your experience in each area of your life. The houses fix your experience of the planets and signs, giving them a particular quality and expression.

The word 'planet' comes from Greek, meaning 'wanderer', but houses do not wander about. Work is where you left it. Your home is where you go after work every day. Your experience of these changes because of planets and signs changing in relation to the houses, your desires change around these areas of your life.

We can also observe general trends in relation to various countries, institutions, or events based on transits. We do this by drawing up a chart for the beginning of that country, institution, or event. So, where a country has declared independence, or the signing of a company's legal documents, the 'birth' chart has certain indications we could call trends. Everyone within that country or company experiences them. The country you live in has a lot to say about how you experience life. Two people with the same horoscope, living in different countries, will have very different life experiences. Then there are family dynamics, and groups of people who share similar themes. We must consider these when reading your personal chart, as you are not separate from your environment.

Trends offer general indications for masses of people. These show general indications of anything from fashion to the economy. Some astrologers focus on financial markets, while many observe general trends by observing news media. I have received a lot of insights into current transits by watching movies released at the time of a particular transit. Transits reflect the themes, as much as the stories that make headline news.

Each transit you experience has its distinct flavour. The same is true of a country's chart. Each nation experiences the different effects of each of the transits, and this impacts the nation's population. You must take this into consideration when looking at your birth chart, based on where you were born and where you currently live. Yet without knowing the specifics of your birth chart or planetary daśās, the transits provide only a general idea of themes based on your location.

TRANSIT TIMES

The slower-moving planets' transits have more of a profound impact because of the slowness of their orbits. The faster-moving planets bring sudden experiences that may or may not stick, depending on the details. Thus, the outer planets offer subtler, yet more profound, influences because of the distance and their lengthy transit times. The Moon takes only two and a half days to transit through each Sun sign. Saturn takes approximately two and a half years to travel through a Sun sign. The Moon's influence is more immediate, while Saturn's influence stays with you for the long haul, leaving a deeper impression. Your moods change constantly (Moon), as you continue to age (Saturn). Table 3.11 shows how long it takes for each planet to transit a 30-degree sign, or through the entire zodiac.

Table 3.11

Planet	30°	360°
Moon	2.5 days	1 month
Mercury	1 – 2 months	1 year
Venus	1 – 2 months	1 year
Sun	1 month	1 year
Mars	2 months	2 years
Jupiter	1 year	12 years
Rāhu/Ketu	1.5 years	18.6 years
Saturn	2.5 years	29.5 years
Uranus	7 years	84 years
Neptune	14 years	164 years
Pluto	10 – 20 years	248 years

TRANSITS TO LUNAR MANSIONS

The Moon transits one lunar mansion in approximately one day, but it is not exactly a day. Thus, to track the Moon's movement, you must use a Moon calculator. Planets' transits to the lunar mansion will depend on the speed of the planet. Saturn takes approximately one year to transit one lunar mansion. The following list shows the approximate transit times for each planet through each lunar mansion:

Moon ~ 1 day
Sun ~ 12 days
Venus ~ 12 days
Mercury ~ 12 days
Mars ~ 24 days
Jupiter ~ 4 - 6 months
Saturn ~ 1 year
Rāhu ~ 8 months
Ketu ~ 8 months

We can break down transits to lunar mansions into padas or steps within each, highlighting the 9 divisions. This shows underlying strengths for each transit, despite outer appearances. We connect each of the 4 steps in each lunar mansion to the 4 elements and aims in life: dharma (fire), artha (earth), kāma, (air) and mokṣa (water). The approximate transit times for each planet through each step are as follows: Moon ~ 6 hrs; Sun ~ 3 days; Venus ~ 3 days; Mercury ~ 3 days; Mars ~ 6 days; Jupiter ~ 40 days; Saturn ~ 100 days; Rāhu ~ 60 days; and Ketu ~ 60 days.

SUN, MOON & STARS

You can look at the house being transited by the planets from your ascendant, Moon, or Sun. You can view these three points of view altogether, to get a more holistic picture. Mars transiting Taurus may be in your 10th house of career from your ascendant. This is a great place to direct Mars' attention. But it may also be in the 7th house from your Moon, creating problems in your relationships. You may feel challenged to get along with others while you are ambitious at work (10th house). Mars may be in the 8th house from your Sun. This could show more deep psychological changes you are undergoing. This could create all kinds of power dynamics in your interactions with others. When you observe all three transits together, it paints a more accurate picture.

Transits from your rising sign show the impact on your physical environment. Transits from your Moon sign show the impact on your thinking and emotions. The Sun is the least obvious level of awareness when looking at transits, in a way. Yet it has a profound impact on your being. It shows your essence nature, which may or may not impact your physical (ascendant) or mental-emotional (Moon) nature. By taking all three into account, you will get a well-rounded view of what is going on in any transit.

You can look at transits from any perspective. You could consider the transits from all the planets. In the beginning, it's best to observe your rising and Moon sign. The rising sign changes every couple of hours or so, while the Moon takes over a couple of days to move through a

Sun sign. The Sun takes a month to move through a Sun sign.

All three give you a view from your body (rising sign), mind (Moon sign), and soul (Sun sign). The Moon's transit to different houses and lunar mansions is a helpful way to gauge your day-to-day experience. You could also track the transit of the Moon from your natal Moon, or the Sun from your natal Sun. The Moon's transit to the 8th house from your natal Moon is a couple of days to pay particular attention to. Each month, this may show you are feeling a little vulnerable. It's best to keep these days for quiet contemplation and self-care routines. It's at least a good time to be aware of the potential emotional complexity.

The Sun's transit from your Sun sign is also a good way to track the year, and your birthday, of course. When the Sun returns to where it was in your birth chart, this is your solar return. This is an important reset point in the year. It is a time to recharge yourself, a reminder of where you can share your unique talents and gifts with the world. This is a time to tap into your higher purpose and sense of self. The Sun's transit through the Sun signs is an important consideration. This helps you see how each area of your life is being reinvigorated at different times of the year. You may find more of an emphasis on partners in the summer (Sun in 7th), which would mean more of an emphasis on yourself in the winter (Sun in 1st). Or you may find more of an emphasis on home life and happiness in the spring (Sun in 4th), which would mean more work-related emphasis in the autumn (Sun in 10th).

PLANETS' TRANSITS TO EACH HOUSE

Planets transiting signs impact certain houses or areas of your life. The 'outer planets' Uranus, Neptune, and Pluto take so long that you will not experience them in all the houses. Uranus takes approximately 84 years to transit the entire zodiac, so you may experience all of its transits. Neptune and Pluto take approximately 164 and 248 years to transit all the houses.

Planets' transits impact different houses and areas of your life, depending on what you are looking at. To begin with, you can observe the transits from your ascendant or rising sign. This shows the more objective circumstances unfolding. You can then add transits to your Moon to see how you feel about it. Finally, you can observe the transits from your Sun sign, or any other points of interest. Planets' transits are impacting you in many different ways.

Planets transiting a house will also impact any planets you have in those houses. While certain house transits show particular themes and experiences, you may also have planets in those houses. These would represent other areas and themes. Transits shows how your life is unfolding through the lens of your birth chart, along with your planetary daśās.

PLUTO TRANSITS

Pluto's transits how a need for change. Pluto's change usually shows an ending of something initially. Pluto transits ask you to change something about your life, in whatever area it impacts by house position. Its transits are about removing old ways of being, to unburden yourself of what you have accumulated. As long as you do not focus solely on the loss, but see it as an opportunity, you can make the most of Pluto's transits. The changes Pluto brings may not at all be obvious from the beginning. They may occur in the background mostly.

Pluto in the 1st

Those with Pluto rising in their birth charts are always burying deep to find their core issues. Yet they can bury so deep they lose perspective. While the excavations may prove fruitful on some level, they may be a blind spot. With Pluto transiting the 1st house, there is something you must release so you can find more energy, and a new you. This is the quintessential 'phoenix from the flames' transit. Yet if you cannot see yourself as you are, it becomes harder to see what you are not, and drop what needs to go. This is a time to drop whatever is no longer you, so you can gain new perspectives and ways of being in the world.

Pluto in the 2nd

Pluto transiting your house of finances and family can show a change of something you once thought of as secure. This can show up as a change in your financial situation. It may show a change in what you value, especially if things you relied upon before are no longer reliable. Changes could occur in your family dynamics, too. You may need to mitigate any sense of insecurity by making practical changes while adjusting. These changes point to profound new perspectives on what's important to you now. Your diet could probably do with a tweak.

Pluto in the 3rd

Pluto transiting the area of communications can show changes in how you express yourself. This may mean changes in how you think. Stepping back from social media or social interactions may be helpful in figuring out how to communicate what you stand for. By pausing communications, you can get clear about what you are trying to say. This may include dropping some ideas in favour of others. Your relationships with your siblings and people in your vicinity are likely to go through changes. These people are going through their own changes, which may mean you have to engage with them differently.

Pluto in the 4th

Pluto's impact on your home environment may show a change of house, or a need to renovate. It may represent a need to dig deep into your past, to remove any emotional blocks or issues from your childhood. You may need to have some tough conversations with family members, especially your mother. You may look more closely at this relationship and how it has shaped how you feel about yourself. Your personal life is likely to go through changes.

Yet it may not be obvious what needs to change, at least not from the outset.

Pluto in the 5th

Pluto impacting romance, children, and creativity could show up as a need to let go of someone or something dear to you. This may mean becoming an 'empty nester' for some, or a need to end a romance or creative project. For others, it might show having to change your relationship to those people and things, so you can find a better expression. Either way, there is something to relinquish, so you can free up some room to invite something or someone new into your heart. The 5th house is about the life you are creating for your future self. Pluto will let you know what stands in the way.

Pluto in the 6th

Pluto brings changes to how your everyday life works. If something isn't working, Pluto will let you know through some problem that needs to be addressed. It may be through some difficulty at work or with your health routines. It does this so you can make the adjustments, either to your routine or to your diet. Yet this may create some conflicts at work, as you make the changes. If you are unwilling to make the adjustments, you may avoid conflict with co-workers but may end up creating problems for yourself or your colleagues.

Pluto in the 7th

Pluto impacts relationships profoundly. You can no longer relate the same. This may even mean big changes for your partner. This could be a romantic or business relationship. It shows a need to meet with the world in a new way and change how you interact with others. These relationships may go through a lot of changes and you must adjust to their needs. Many old forms of relating may need to be relinquished.

Pluto in the 8th

Pluto and the 8th house go hand-in-hand. They both represent change. Yet this may be change you resist, unexpected change that is harder to accept when you haven't planned it. The sooner you can get on board with what's necessary, the better. This may mean a change in your financial situation, or for your partner. Either way, it impacts you both. The 8th house brings money to you from others, either from your partner or through some form of financial assistance. Your in-laws may go through a lot of changes now, too. As with any Pluto transit, the changes may not be obvious at all. This is especially the case for the 8th house. It represents deep psychological change which no one, not even yourself, may be clear about in the beginning.

Pluto in the 9th

Pluto in the 9th house is a time to let go of old beliefs and ways of doing things. This is so you can free yourself from the ways things used to be. Pluto reminds you to find meaning in the inevitable changes life brings. Once you get on board with what beliefs much change, you can change what you believe is possible. This can open up more opportunities for growth, as long as you are willing to shed the excess weight of the past. This pruning allows for fresh shoots of growth to emerge. Your relationship with your father will be one that highlights the internal changes going on for you. He may go through more obvious changes.

Pluto in the 10th

Pluto can alter the direction of your life in your 10th house, changing how you work, even where you work. At the very least, this may show a need to adjust to some recent developments in your career. You may have to take on a different approach to whatever you were doing. It may show up as obstacles in your path, but this is so you can free up energy to use in furthering your career prospects. Relationships with superiors at work needs to change. This may mean your boss or superiors are going through their own changes, to which you must adjust.

Pluto in the 11th

Pluto influencing your friends and social life can show a need to alter your networks. It may show substantial changes happening to these people, too. You may need to let go of some associations so you can make room for more. This will change your worldview. A new or trimmed back social circle can help with that. You may have to let go of certain aspirations or alter them. You may have to move on from friends who used to share these aspirations. This is so you can dream up a new dream.

Pluto in the 12th

Pluto's transit through your 12th and final house shows a time of endings. Yet it may not be obvious to you what needs to end. This can show a deep sense of inner transformation. You may experience this through some form of therapy that uncovers subconscious blocks. You can remove these. Pluto's transit here is about letting go and moving on. You can concentrate on letting go of things that lie buried deep within. These things are no longer useful for your development. A fresh start can begin once Pluto has finished in your 12th house.

NEPTUNE TRANSITS

Neptune transits can be a little vague and idealistic. You may have an idea in your mind's eye, but whether you can make it a reality is another matter. Neptune transits can confuse, depending on the details of your chart and how you approach it. It may be a little fantastical. If you remain open to what is, there is much that is possible with the help of dreamy Neptune. This can show you a picture you wish to make real. Yet you may have to accept it is not in focus from the outset. As Neptune transits your houses, you may keep some dream alive in your imagination, whether you actualise it. Keep an open mind and dream your dreams. Just make sure you know which has the potential to become real and which is pure fantasy.

Neptune in the 1st

Those with Neptune in the 1st house at birth can have quite an idealised view of themselves. They may not see themselves as others do, preferring to keep their rose-tinted glasses on. This can create an uncertainty about who they are, a blurry boundary when dealing with others. These themes will be prominent as Neptune transits your 1st house. While it may be a time to dream about who you could be, it may also warrant a reality check when confronted by the reality of your situation. The most obvious expression of this is in your ageing body. You may not see your body as a problem, or you may simply wish to ignore problems so you can live out the fantasy. It's time to dream about the possibilities, but to also keep a close eye on what is actually true about yourself.

Neptune in the 2nd

Neptune transiting your 2nd house can bring ideals to your finances and values. It may even represent a fantastical notion about what you are worth. This may show a fantasy about your financial situation that needs a reality check. Family life may be another way you experience idealism. If your family life or finances are not what you would like, this transit may show what is possible. This can keep a vision alive in your mind's eye until you can make these visions a reality. The ideal situation that makes you feel safe, one that nourishes your soul, may be something you are imagine.

Neptune in the 3rd

Neptune in your 3rd house can show a dream of doing what you want, expressing yourself in some idealised way. The 3rd house is all about communication and opinions. It shows how you communicate with yourself and others. It's the voice inside your head. This voice may be a little vague right now. Yet there is something important you can hear through the process of reflection. This can bring great clarity about what is possible with a little effort. Neptune may confuse you about how much effort is required, of course. The image can be a little blurry to begin with. Eventually, you figure it out and apply the effort to achieve your desires. Relationships with siblings and neighbours may reflect these themes.

Neptune in the 4th

Neptune can blur the picture of your home environment. This may mean a dream home, or the dream of an ideal private set-up. This may bring idealism about your mother and how you feel about her. Even if she is no longer with you, it may show you keeping her alive in your mind's eye. This transit may show an unrealistic approach to someone who is human, with all their own shortcomings. Your mother has her own faults, which you may completely disregard. Neptune shows an idealised version of a person with her own problems. It can show you reaching for the ideal rather than dealing with what is. Yet this is also an opportunity to integrate and heal something so you can feel more secure and cared for. Caring for your mother and/or home life may form part of the picture.

Neptune in the 5th

Neptune can show an ideal future situation and creative self-expression. It may show a longing for children or some creative or romantic outlet. This can show a need to enjoy yourself, especially with children or a romantic partner. Romance itself may seem more idealised, which may cause problems in dealing with the real person. If you meet someone new, it may be a romanticised version of an actual person you may not truly see. Likewise, you may not see your children as they truly are, but how you wish they were.

Neptune in the 6th

Neptune may seem at odds with your everyday life and work commitments. Neptune represents an idealised version of your life that may not suit your everyday chores. Yet you could create the ideal life in your mind's eye, even if you struggle to get your life in order. Health issues would need a good dose of reality now. Otherwise, the reality of your health may jar with what you wish were true. Any kind of involvement with people you perceive as less than ideal may prove difficult. You may have your rose-tinted glasses on in relation to any problems, which may not be the best way of dealing with them. But at least it can show creative solutions to issues you may get too caught up in otherwise.

Neptune in the 7th

Neptune can influence your relationships in a way that is not at all in touch with the real person in front of you. Your partner could experience your idealised projection, but they may not know that. This may mean relating only to a fantasy, rather than with who the person is. Anyone you come into contact with now, in any meaningful way, may experience this projected idealism. And while it is sometimes good to take the rose-tinted glasses off in a relationship, it may be good to see the best in them. This way, you can encourage the best from them, an ideal version you hold in your mind's eye.

Neptune in the 8th

Neptune can show an idealised vision of your in-laws and your partner's financial situation in the 8th house. Yet the picture you have in your mind's eye may be in stark contrast to what is true. This can bring conflict with others around joint resources. This is especially if you are not willing to be open to what's important to others. The 8th house brings uncertainty and change at every turn, change which you may not be clear about now. Intimacy is a big part of the 8th house. Yet Neptune can sometimes make things unclear, where healthy boundaries are harder to maintain.

Neptune in the 9th

Neptune and the 9th house may seem to be a better fit than most other areas of life. The 9th represents your philosophies and beliefs. Yet it could create an unreal belief that has no bearing on reality. This may show you being more philosophical than usual. Yet this needs a good dose of practicality, too. If you can get the balance right, you can apply any new ideas in a way that organises and expands on possibilities. The more you believe is true, the more can be true, on some level, at least. Your relationship with your father may bring out some of these themes. You may reminisce about your relationship, especially if he is no longer with you in physical form. Travel and study may be things you dream about.

Neptune in the 10ᵗʰ

Neptune can show an ideal you wish to achieve in your professional life. This may or may not line up with the reality of what is happening. You may have your wishes, but your boss has his or her own ideas. This may mean having to work at what you wish to make happen with what you have at your disposal. The 10ᵗʰ house requires action, actions that will let you know how realistic your dreams are. By acting, it will become clear what dreams are fantasy. You may aim so high at this point and hope for the recognition reserved for the very few. Yet who knows, you may indeed be one of the chosen few!

Neptune in the 11ᵗʰ

Neptune and the 11ᵗʰ house can show you are dreaming bigger than ever, with bigger groups you associate with. Yet your friendships may become so idealised that you may not see them for who they are. While these interactions can fuel a better future vision for all concerned, you must marry this with what is possible. Not to worry, there may be someone in the group keeping you well-informed! This transit can show grand plans for your future, a wish for something you dare to dream.

Neptune in the 12ᵗʰ

Neptune and the 12ᵗʰ house go hand-in-hand. The 12ᵗʰ house is all about sleep and dreaming, an area Neptune has covered. While this may show a tendency to slumber in dream states, spending hours in daydreams, there comes a time to wake up to the reality of your life. Neptune in the

12th house may show a need to retreat from the world. It may also show up as fantastical notions about your spending habits, as the 12th house represents expenditure. This is something to be mindful of if you are on a budget. Otherwise, Neptune in the 12th may be a time to let go a little more. And to realise the dreams you dream exist in some reality, always.

URANUS TRANSITS

Uranus transits may show your need to disrupt the status quo, all on your own terms. It may bring a need for freedom and an original approach to the area of your life impacted. This can disorientate, especially if it also impacts a planet in the house in question. Uranus transits a sign for approximately 7 years. This gives you plenty of stimulation and change in each area. Expect the unexpected. Be open to change and you can make the most of the potentials of its transits.

Uranus in the 1st

Uranus can bring surprising changes to who you are and how you express this to others. For anyone with Uranus in the 1st at birth, there is a need to express an originality that doesn't always sit comfortably with others. Still, there is a need to find some new way to present yourself as Uranus transits your 1st house. You may be more rebellious than usual or changing things about yourself that you thought were set in stone. This is a time to keep an open mind about who you are and what you think is possible.

Uranus in the 2nd

Uranus can bring changes to what once seemed stable and fixed. The 2nd house represents those things that bring comfort and security, such as family, money, and resources. These may go through a shake up with Uranus transiting here. It may bring more innovation and changes in how you store wealth, or even what you value. Your finances may go to fluctuations, which unsettles what may have been more secure previously. Go with the changes, so you can make the most of the new opportunities cropping up. Your family dynamics may go through some changes, too. This may be part of the process of financial restructuring that is going on, new ways of approaching what makes you feel secure.

Uranus in the 3rd

Uranus brings changes to how you communicate and interact while transiting your 3rd house. After you have figured out your new value system in the 2nd house, Uranus in the 3rd expresses your unique point of view. You now stand for something else, so your communication must reflect this. This should include a change in how, not just what, you are communicating. This can show a new way of exchanging ideas and new ways and means to travel about. It may bring new ways of interacting with your siblings and neighbours, as well as alternative approaches to getting what you want in life.

Uranus in the 4th

Uranus shakes things up in your home environment while transiting your 4th house. This can bring a house move, renovation or some change to its occupants. The 4th house represents your formal education. There may be some disruption or change to your studies if you are currently in school. The 4th house represents your mother, so you may find changes are happening for her, or in your relationship with her. She may surprise you! It is always best to go with the flow with Uranus, so you can make the most of the opportunities presenting themselves. This may include moving home or finding new ways of finding happiness. Your relationship with your mother reflects this quest.

Uranus in the 5th

Uranus can bring changes in how you express your creative side, as well as changes to what you have already created. This may include children or projects and plans already begun. This suggests a change in how you relate to your children. It may also represent a new romantic partner. It may show a complete change in how you relate to what you love, and how you go about creating the future you want. Keep an open mind about how it will all work out. Holding it close to your heart keeps what's important to the forefront at all times. Feel the inspiration for something new.

Uranus in the 6th

Uranus can shake up your everyday life, bringing increased opportunities to do things differently. If you don't have a steady routine, you may initiate one. You may experiment with your work routines. You must consider this in relation to deadlines or when working for someone else. This could create friction at your workplace if the changes you must make upset your colleagues. Uranus in the 6th can also show a need to change your diet and health routines, including any exercise regimes. Best to keep some sense of order here, as it can lead to all kinds of erratic energy that won't sustain daily habits. Learning new things about your health is always positive, as long as you can implement them daily.

Uranus in the 7th

Uranus can show surprises in your relationships. It can, at the very least, show a change in how you relate to others. This may mean a new lover or new business contacts. All these people can bring a new flair and surprising insights into how you negotiate what you want from others. If you are already in a relationship before Uranus enters the house, your partner may keep you on your toes. If you meet someone new during this transit, it's likely to be exciting. New and exciting adventures await you when engaging with Uranus through other people. Just be sure you are aware of your need for freedom, a need that you may project onto others who may seem unavailable.

Uranus in the 8th

Uranus can bring unexpected developments while transiting your 8th house. Yet these changes must take place all the same. You may look back and be thankful for them in hindsight. The 8th house can show a fresh approach to your partner's financial situation and/or their family. The most obvious expression is an inheritance or finances coming to you from an unexpected source. There may be even bigger surprise in how you relate with your partner, requiring you both to adapt to how you come together. While we typically see the 8th house for relationship problems, it can also deepen certain relationships and bonds of intimacy. But only if both parties are open to doing it differently once Uranus calls.

Uranus in the 9th

Uranus can show a need to think about things differently while transiting your 9th house. This may mean you are thinking more 'outside the box' while it transits the house of philosophy and principles. You may have new insights now that change what you believe to be true. This may bring changes for your father or a teacher or mentor, anyone who has a significant impact on what you believe. Uranus brings a need to stay open-minded about how you've always done things, leaving room for a more innovative approach. Your father may experience something new, or you may experience him in a new way.

Uranus in the 10th

Uranus shakes up your career and professional trajectory while transiting your 10th house. This may impact the actions you take now and the direction your life is taking you. This change of direction can bring unexpected opportunities at work. These may not always seem like opportunities from the outset, as change is sometimes hard to adapt to. Yet these changes are necessary for your continued growth. Keeping an open mind will help you adjust to the radical changes happening in your life.

Uranus in the 11th

Uranus can show a need for new friends and social circle. This may mean getting involved in new groups and associations, people who open your mind to new points of view. This may create more opportunity to think even bigger than you thought before. It may show radical thoughts you must incorporate into how you see the world and what is possible. It can show new ways of connecting to groups and networks. This brings more gains and rewards. Be the change you want to see in the world.

Uranus in the 12th

Uranus in the 12th and last house can show the beginning of the end of something in your life. This could show new ways of ending your day, or how you end something in your life. This can show a disturbance to your sleep patterns, while new insights bubble up from your subconscious. It may show a new way of spending money and energy, and in how much you have to spend. It can show new ways of retreating from the world, new ways and places to surrender.

SATURN TRANSITS

Sade sati, meaning 'seven and a half', is one of the most talked about astrological components of Indian astrology today. This refers to Saturn's transit to the signs surrounding one's Moon, the time it takes Saturn to move through the 12th, 1st, and 2nd signs from the Moon. This can be a challenge, as Saturn brings some form of distance. Saturn transits a square position from itself every 7.5 years, 'the seven-year itch'. This may bring issues you have not dealt with previously.

Its impact on your Moon is especially important and why Indian astrologers pay more heed to this transit. The slowest visible planet influencing the fastest shows a need to slow down and pay attention. Detached Saturn gets you to look long and hard at your attachments. Sometimes, it does this by removing them; sometimes, by distancing you from them. Yet Saturn's influence can give you the detachment you need. This would impact you more if you were also in a daśā of Saturn, especially a Saturn-Moon or Moon-Saturn daśā. This is because you experience a Saturn-Moon daśā as if it were a conjunction of these two. What is being impacted depends on what both these planets rule in your chart.

I have observed that once Saturn moves into the 12th from the Moon; it triggers many to make substantial changes. Although the advice is usually to not make any major life changes, that is indeed the impulse. This is a way for you to fulfil the results of your previous actions. You may not be conscious of this, of course. The changes you make when Saturn enters the 12ᵗʰ house from your Moon have consequences. You may wish to move home, change jobs or country, or end a relationship. Often, all three things can happen at the same time. You may feel something is not right with your life. By making these changes, you experience further changes as Saturn transits your Moon in a few years. This is usually the most intense period of sade sati. It can show more detachment, losses, or even betrayal. Many people betray themselves, of course, by doing the very thing that lands them in trouble. Yet this is Saturn's way for you to fulfil your debt. Usually, this means feeling isolated once Saturn transits your Moon.

The last phase of the 7.5 years begins once Saturn moves into the 2ⁿᵈ from your Moon, for the last 2.5-year phase. This is usually a phase of tying up loose ends after a testing time. Saturn's transit to the 2ⁿᵈ house from your Moon may seem as if this is the end. But that would depend on the daśās you are experiencing during this last phase. A Saturn-Moon daśā may still create a need to withdraw, or to finish something up at this stage. You may do the very thing you needed to when Saturn first transited the 12ᵗʰ from your Moon. You may leave a relationship that is unhealthy. The issue is not what you did, but how you are feeling, as it is the Moon's perspective. Feelings of isolation are common in any Saturn-Moon connection. The last phase of Saturn's transit to your Moon may bring up issues of sustenance. This is often the case with monetary wealth, but it is also an issue of emotional support. Saturn's transit to the 2ⁿᵈ house from your Moon means it looks at the 11th house of earnings. Family issues may be prominent, as would your relations at home.

Relationship issues would also be important once Saturn transits your Moon sign, or opposite to your Moon, or any other planet. This could be more of something you want if you are experiencing a Saturn daśā. If you are not experiencing a Saturn daśā during its transit to your Moon, you may not want to give up what it is asking you to.

It's always worth noting wherever Saturn is by transit in any year. This is the area of life to do some work, while letting go of all that is no longer possible or appropriate. Less is always more for Saturn transits. Sometimes, this means having to do more with less.

Saturn in the 1st

Saturn is not well-liked in the 1st house, and for obvious reasons. Any kind of restriction, whether physical (rising sign) or mental-emotional (Moon sign), is not usually welcome. This is a time to draw your focus and energy inward, not to scatter it all about. That would leave you feeling depleted. A slower, more mindful approach would do wonders, as would a more stoic take on life. It may be best to simplify your life and do without some things you don't need. If you restrict yourself, you may not have to experience the restrictions of Saturn in more challenging ways. Yet you may have to accept certain impositions. If you accept the heavy workload, yet work for work's sake, you will have an easier time with it.

Saturn in the 2nd

After a close look at yourself with Saturn in your 1st, Saturn's 2nd house transit is all about what you stand for. It's all about what you value. This may lead to a reduction in your valuables, initially impacting your stored wealth and resources. There is a lesson to be learned from this temporary influence, which is to look at what you value beyond assets. This gets you to look at how you are earning and how best you can direct your energy. Work smarter, not harder. This will allow you to be more resourceful, which is Saturn's lesson in the 2nd house. Your family life may also feel Saturn's impact. You may have to step away, or someone in your family may feel they wish to withdraw. Again, this is a valuable lesson about the values your family instilled in you from the beginning. The question to ask is: Do I value what you taught me to? If not, what do I value?

Saturn in the 3rd

Saturn is well-placed in the 3rd house, although it requires a little more effort on your part to see results. Saturn in the 3rd is asking you to look at how and what you are communicating. This may challenge you to be clear, perhaps because you are not or because you haven't spent the time thinking about these things. The 3rd house is that voice in your head. Saturn's transit here is about changing old patterns and beliefs that are no longer helpful. Listening is as much part of communication, an important part of communication and a signification of the 3rd house. Saturn will get you to listen more so you can hear what is being said. It may be time to speak less, so you can hear something. Saturn has something important to impart.

Saturn in the 4th

Saturn in the 4th shows a need to get clear about how you feel, which may include not being clear for a while. Saturn asks you to take a long, hard look at yourself and ask yourself: Am I happy? Your well-being and home life will be a huge focus now, so make sure the focus is productive. You may feel down or even depressed if you are not deliberate about it. Saturn casts its eye to your 1st house while in your 4th. This transit has an enormous impact on you. Your relationship with your mother, her way of relating to you, may be the focus. Whether your mother is alive, this is about how you care for yourself and others. Saturn asks you to look at what nourishes you, what you care about. It may be a time to feel the consequences of not caring for yourself. Now would be a time to look after yourself.

Saturn in the 5th

Saturn can bring more focus to your children as it transits your 5th. This includes your relationship with them. They may either be moving away, or you may have a new child and need to focus on them. This may include you worrying about them, too. If you don't have children, you may focus on your future, your legacy. It may be a creative endeavour you are planning, or some project you wish to see through. Be mindful that Saturn in the 5th can sometimes cloud your thinking. Therefore, it's not always the best time to make speculative investments. It may not be a time to try your luck. Playfulness you once enjoyed may feel like work, or you may not bother with it. How about trying to incorporate play as a strategy for a more balanced life? Life is already hard work. Don't make play feel like work, too!

Saturn in the 6th

Saturn can do some magnificent work in the 6th, but it may also feel as if Saturn were 'doing a job on you'! Saturn is a hard taskmaster. You may experience this as a need to deal with some problem you've been putting off. This could be a health issue, a work problem, or some debt. There is no avoiding the issues with Saturn. This period will get you to improve yourself. Anything less than optimal may be Saturn's way of cleaning up your act. This may be a better way to look at any health or life challenges you may deal with now. Whatever it is, you can make improvements with some effort.

Saturn in the 7th

Saturn can show a need to commit to or break up with someone when it transits your 7th house. It depends on the details of your chart and circumstance. Sometimes, it may show a need to pull away–if the relationship is not working. It may show a need to step back and reassess, even if it is. Saturn can bring a distance from your partner. It may even express it in a physical distance, as he or she may need to move away from you. Saturn will let you know if your relationship is working or not. Its transit won't allow things to continue as they are. You must make some changes; do the right thing – by everyone. You may feel forced into deciding something about your relationship, in taking it to the next level of seriousness. If you are dating, it may mean getting serious and committing to marriage. If you are already married, it may mean your relationship feels more pressurised, with more serious issues to deal with. Yet Saturn is well-placed in the 7th house to help you make these big decisions. Its eye on your 1st and 4th houses ensures you feel the negative repercussions if you do not do what you must.

The pressures Saturn brings to bear shows whether a relationship was already on shaky ground or built to last. Your relationship will either become fortified or break apart, depending.

Saturn in the 8th

Saturn can challenge you to make some big psychological changes in the 8th. If you began a relationship recently, this transit gets you to go deeper. If you ended one, this would get you to ask some big questions about your very existence. Yet any recent challenges in relationships can lead to deeper levels of intimacy at this stage. Yet it may also show you unwilling to 'go there'. The 8th house is all about what you don't always reveal. It represents chronic issues, whether physical or mental, that don't have simple solutions. Saturn in the 8th can show a need to focus on these issues, which can feel scary. As the saying goes, 'Everything you want is beyond your fears'. This may be the opportune time to tackle your fears, especially around intimacy. It may be a time to be more open to feeling vulnerable around unexpected changes. Stepping back and assessing any trauma that you have not dealt with may be appropriate.

Saturn in the 9ᵗʰ

Saturn in the 9ᵗʰ can show you questioning any guidance. Nothing wrong with an enquiry, of course. But the issue with Saturn, especially in the 9ᵗʰ house, is that you may question just for the sake of it. Saturn can show a distrust. You may never believe anyone or anything. By questioning everything, you may leave yourself without a paddle or clear direction in life.

Saturn in the 9ᵗʰ shows a need to give up your antagonism but it's not about being anyone's fool. You must question those who are misleading you. But you must also trust those who have your best interest at heart. Saturn's influence can show issues with trusting, doubting everyone and everything. And yet, doubt is as important to your journey to a stronger faith. It gets you to think about what you believe. Your relationship with your father may challenge now. He may experience something himself that is hard to deal with. Yet this is also an opportunity to strengthen your bond, to get real about your relationship.

Saturn in the 10ᵗʰ

Saturn can show you are working hard while transiting the 10ᵗʰ house. It can be a time for many accomplishments, for some promotion that is due - as long as it's due, of course.

Saturn may reveal you have not put the work in and have to work ten times harder to get anywhere at this stage. This may impact your life in lots of ways as the 10th house is a prominent house. Its eye on your 4th and 7th can lead to problems with those nearest and dearest. This will be especially the case if you are bringing your work issues home with you. Best to leave the office politics where it belongs, while working towards a goal. That will focus the Saturn energy on what it does best. Saturn is best expressed through demanding work and commitment, even if the rewards don't seem to be forthcoming. Saturn teaches you to work for the sake of it, not for the rewards. They come later.

Saturn in the 11th

Saturn is well-placed in the 11th house. This shows the possibility of taking the broad view, to focus on your long-term objectives. This will impact what you think is possible, as you inspect the bigger picture. You may find some things are not worth the effort, of course. Some people you associate with may no longer fit your ambitions. Even close friends may feel your icy stare and detachment. While this suggests a need to look at your objectives, your goals, and aspirations, it also suggests a need to factor others into the equation. You may need to drop some people to make the equation work out for everyone. Questioning your ambitions may lead to earning less than you did before. If that is the case, Saturn often does a demolition job for good reason. It's about building something from the ground up with a solidity it might not have had before. Whatever new financial dealings, they are likely to be stronger in the future.

Saturn in the 12ᵗʰ

Saturn's journey through the zodiac has reached a completion as it enters your 12ᵗʰ house. This means having to let go of something, to finish something up in the next couple of years. While it's common for someone to do just that, especially if this is from your Moon sign, there may be a tendency to hold on. This is when Saturn's transit to the 12ᵗʰ may lead to problems, either in your sleep patterns, or your ability to shut off when you cannot let things go. The 12ᵗʰ house represents your subconscious, which may call to you with important messages.

This phase may be about letting it all go, but it's also about working hard at what must remain when something is ending. This is your spiritual essence, your true self. The more tapped into your essence you are, the more you can assuage any confusion about what comes next. A new beginning awaits you in the years that follow this transit, so make the most of the clear out so you can start afresh, unburdened by what has gone before.

RĀHU- KETU TRANSITS

Rāhu and Ketu bring up many complexities as they transit a sign for a year and a half. They transit the signs opposite each other, moving retrograde or backwards through each. Rāhu and Ketu do not offer simple-to-follow guidelines and are not at all obvious. If you are currently in a daśā of either, the issues are complex. This is because either daśā activates your shadow. They represent your evolution. Yet it could also bring up irrational thoughts and feelings. Both can bring up survival instincts.

Rāhu points you forward. You are eager to get more, as you feel you don't have enough. Ketu shows a part you may reject. Ketu points you back. This could be your history, or your essence nature, your true spiritual self. Rāhu is eager for worldly experience. It is simply the experience. Ketu represents the one who experiences.

Rāhu shows a primal fear. When triggered, it can bring up all kinds of irrational responses. These responses are usually not based on any reality, in the present, at least. They are based on what you imagine being the case, about an unlikely future. Rāhu doesn't exist in the present moment. It thrives on driving you forward. Ketu is on the other end of the spectrum, bringing with it irrational responses because of the past. Usually, you must deal with some past issue because you haven't dealt with it before. Ketu can show losses as an indicator of the past. It can show a wish to get away from where you came from.

You are more likely to experience unusual events when Rāhu and Ketu transit houses in your birth chart.

This is especially the case when they line up with the Sun and Moon and create an eclipse. Eclipses, either a solar (New Moon) or lunar (Full Moon), show a reset is due in that area of your life. Solar eclipses are especially potent for new beginnings, while lunar eclipses are a more immediate time of culmination and change.

If the eclipses are near one of your planets, you may experience change in relation to what the planet represents in your chart. This includes house positions of the eclipses, as well as the houses the planet rules. Rāhu and Ketu show what you must give up (Ketu) so you can evolve (Rāhu). Usually, Ketu eclipses show losses, while Rāhu eclipses show something gained. Yet it is never that straight-forward with the lunar nodes. Many times, whatever you lose, there is a gain, and vice versa. Rāhu may show the need for something, some experience, but it often comes at a price. You may get something, but you have to deal with the complex repercussions. Ketu may show loss, but you gain a deeper perspective. You gain a more spiritual orientation, or re-orientation. Ketu simplifies your life. Rāhu complicates it.

There is always a more evolved expression of the nodes towards which you can move. You can always move away from the more primal instincts and irrational reactions to an unreal threat. By doing so, you can express the best of what these catalysts for change can do for you.

Rāhu and Ketu's transits take a year and a half in each house. The areas Rāhu transits usually show a need for some experience, for more of that thing, whatever the house shows. It usually shows some gains. Yet you may have to sacrifice something in relation to the opposite area, as seen in Ketu's transit. Another possibility with Ketu is to deepen your connection and awareness. This is what loss does for you. When you lose something or someone close, you gain a deeper understanding of your true nature, as, at its core, you and everything else are the same.

Rāhu in the 1ˢᵗ – Ketu in the 7ᵗʰ

Rāhu transiting your 1ˢᵗ house shows a need to change yourself, to evolve. Yet Rāhu exaggerates and distorts, so you may have a distorted sense of who you are. Or you may need to express your individual needs more now. The downside to this is that you may neglect others, as shown by Ketu in the 7ᵗʰ. Ketu can show some neglect or even rejection of others, in favour of yourself and your need for more independence and freedom. You may be afraid of what you could be and yet not conscious of it. Instead, you may project your fear of the unknown onto others, rejecting them on some level.

Rāhu in the 2ⁿᵈ – Ketu in the 8ᵗʰ

This can be a complex transit, as Rāhu may bring up primal fears around the basics of life. There is a need for safety and security. Financial concerns and family matters are pressing. Rāhu may want more, but it may squeeze the life out of the very thing you want. Any obsession about getting more eventually leads to a sense of lack. Ketu in the 8ᵗʰ may show you rejecting others' help, whether emotional or financial. Or you may experience a loss of support and must now rely on your own resources. Rāhu in the 2nd may show a time of being more resourceful. It's a time to figure out what you stand for, apart from what others have to say about it.

Rāhu in the 3rd – Ketu in the 9th

Rāhu is well-placed in the 3rd. The 3rd house is interactive and playful, a placement Rāhu can enjoy itself in. This may mean expressing your opinions more, exaggerating yourself and your self-interests. Ketu in the 9th may show a neglect or rejection of the advice others wish to give you. You may not be as interested in anyone's wise counsel, preferring instead to work it all out on your own. While there are advantages to this, there are some obvious pitfalls, as you try but fail at certain things while you work it all out for yourself.

Rāhu in the 4th – Ketu in the 10th

Rāhu is looking for home comforts and safety in the 4th house. This may mean a change of house or a change in your home environment. You are likely on a quest to find more happiness. Be aware of Rāhu's ambitions getting out of control. If you are always looking to be happy, you are telling yourself you are not on some level. Ketu in the 10th may show a neglect of your work commitments and responsibilities as you search. This may occur as you chase some ideal state of well-being, which is not always found at work. And yet, Ketu in the 10th is a time to deepen your connection to what you do, to find more meaning in your work.

Rāhu in the 5ᵗʰ – Ketu in the 11ᵗʰ

Rāhu in the 5ᵗʰ can be very enjoyable. It can be more creative, but also more expensive. Rāhu can overdo it in the 5ᵗʰ house, as it can anywhere. This may show up as taking one too many speculative risks. It may also show up as a need for having children or creating some new thing. Ketu in the 11ᵗʰ can show a change in your earning power, as well as your friends circle. This may show a rejection of certain friends that no longer fit the mould. Friends circles often change when you have children. Ketu's need is to deepen relationships, as opposed to outright rejection. But if you cannot deepen them, you may indeed neglect or reject them on some level. In doing so, you are cutting yourself off from the group and leaving yourself without the gains that are more readily available when you are more connected.

Rāhu in the 6ᵗʰ – Ketu in the 12ᵗʰ

Rāhu may obsess about the details, the problems that need solving in the 6ᵗʰ, and not allow you to take a break from the day-to-day drudgery. You may focus so much on a problem that you lose all perspective. Ketu in the 12ᵗʰ can show your inability to shut off, to take some time off and retreat from all your responsibilities. There is always a balance to maintain with Rāhu and Ketu transits, a balance that can go awry all too often. The balance between the 6ᵗʰ and 12ᵗʰ is being able to focus on the details and then letting them all go, resting fully, so you can emerge from your slumber ready to fight another day.

Rāhu in the 7th – Ketu in the 1st

Rāhu can magnify your desire for a partner in the 7th, whether or not you currently have one. If you are in a relationship, this can increase the need to experience more. If you are not, you may jump head-first into a relationship before considering the consequences. Or, on the other end of the extreme, you may obsess about someone you haven't even met yet! You may fantasise about a partner that does not exist. Ketu in the 1st can show a neglect of your own needs, in favour of another's. A better expression of this would be to deepen your awareness of you who are, while staying open to others. Either way, this points to very personal changes you make that will impact who you are and how you relate to others.

Rāhu in the 8th – Ketu in the 2nd

Rāhu in the 8th can show your need to deal with your traumas, to get therapy or go through some transformative experience. These experiences and therapies can completely transform you. Rāhu's tendency to exaggerate and obsess can cause problems, of course. You may focus solely on the trauma. If you are always going through some transformative experience, you do not allow things to settle in any kind of stability. You will need plenty of rest. Ketu can be challenging in the 2nd house. It can show a loss of security and stability while you are going through so many deep psychological changes. Best to keep things on an even keel while you do the work you need to make the changes.

Rāhu in the 9th – Ketu in the 3rd

Rāhu in the 9th can show you are going on some journey, whether a literal journey, a pilgrimage, or an inner journey of the mind. You may begin higher studies. These may explore your higher nature, either a more philosophical course, or furthering your formal education. The likelihood of being so wrapped up in whatever you are doing could lead to Ketu expressing itself in its less evolved state in the 3rd. This could show up as a rejection of your own points of view, for some higher goal, or tradition. You may not feel you can form an opinion when others seem more knowledgeable. This is how you learn, how you become an adept.

Rāhu in the 10th – Ketu in the 4th

The 10th house of career and status is an effective use of Rāhu's talents. This fuels a strong need to get ahead in the world. This may show a neglect of your home life and responsibilities as Ketu transits the 4th. As long as you are aware of the pitfalls of overreaching for worldly success, you can achieve a great deal of success that is long-lasting. Rāhu and Ketu in these cornerstone houses can show tremendous changes in your home and work life. More than anything, it reflects a need to find your work-life balance. You can only grow as tall as your roots are deep.

Rāhu in the 11th – Ketu in the 5th

You can put Rāhu to effective use in the 11th, by increasing your connections in your community. This could be through new friends and associates, new contacts and networks in your professional life. Ketu in the 5th may show a neglect of your heart's desires, especially if you focus only on the group's wishes. While it's all too easy to get lost in the noise of this transit, you can place your hand on your heart and listen to what you desire. When you connect with your desire, you can share your gifts with others.

Rāhu in the 12th – Ketu in the 6th

Rāhu in the 12th can show a need to get away for a while, for a retreat or long-distance travel. If this is not possible, you may find other ways to get away from your everyday responsibilities. Some of these ways may not be so wholesome. Rāhu in the 12th may show a need to tune out, either through drugs, alcohol, or sex. Ketu in the 6th may show a neglect of things you probably should address. You may wish to run away from your problems. A more evolved expression of this may be to rid yourself of your problems while learning to shut off. If you can turn off, you can awaken refreshed and ready to tackle the day again.

JUPITER TRANSITS

Jupiter's expansive transits are an antidote to Saturn's restrictions. Jupiter is the 'big jolly giant' of the planetary line-up. It often brings a sense of blessing and prosperity. This counteracts Saturn's more limited focused approach. Together, they bring a counterbalance. Jupiter brings the ideals, while Saturn brings these down to earth. Jupiter transits a sign for about a year. Its transits usually offer a great deal of comfort. Jupiter is the in-breath to Saturn's out-breath. Jupiter is expansive, comforting and hopeful. It represents life. Saturn is restrictive and doubtful. When both are active, either by transit or in a planetary daśā, they can balance things out for each other. Jupiter is the ideal, a hope for something better, while Saturn makes you work hard for it. Jupiter shows the opportunity, while Saturn shows the need to focus. When both are active, they bring a balance that can create a great deal of momentum in your life.

On its own, Jupiter transits can bring comfort, even if you are not experiencing a Jupiter daśā. Even in a Saturn daśā, you can find moments of expansion within what seems to be restrictive. This is because you will experience Jupiter on some level in the many years of Saturn, even if it's only for a few weeks or months at a time. It's at these times that you could do with a boost and should take full advantage of these more buoyant times. Knowing when Jupiter's daśās are coming, even if only for a few weeks or months, is an opportunity to find more ease within all the hard work of Saturn.

Jupiter's transits can expand in ways you wouldn't always welcome, of course. If Jupiter were transiting your rising sign, you may put on weight. But if Saturn has already been transiting through your rising sign before, a Jupiter transit would be a time to heal any hurt caused. Jupiter is like the much-needed balm to help heal any divisions. It represents a more cohesive period after Saturn has broken things apart or slowed things down. Jupiter offers a way to reconnect. It organises your life. From this organisation and coherence, more growth can occur.

Jupiter in the 1st

Jupiter brings a sense of comfort, sometimes too much so, to the 1st house. This may mean you put on weight if you overindulge. Yet the comfort Jupiter brings is more than just food – it's the hope, the possibilities you now sense. Jupiter offers great protection and strength here during a time of healing. Jupiter can broaden your world and worldview as you tap into your inner knowing. It can be a time of growth and many opportunities. It's a time for more awareness and travels. You may feel you can breathe easy, finding space in your life, even in your body, as you drop into the experience of simply being.

Jupiter in the 2nd

Jupiter can bring a sense of bounty to the 2nd, either through wealth and resources or through a family dynamic that is more supportive. This is a wonderful time to connect to family and community, to what you value.

This is because your family, your tribe, instils in you a profound sense of security. Your resources are likely to increase because you feel so supported. You attract the people and things into your life to reflect this sense of abundance. The only downside is much like the 1st house transit, where you may overindulge in 'good' foods. This may reflect too much of a good thing.

Jupiter in the 3rd

Jupiter can be a bit more playful in the 3rd, or it can show you having to fight for something important to you. Jupiter is the part of you that doesn't wish to fight for anything, though. This can create problems when you must fight for something that is right and just. You may shy away from going for it or doing what you know you must. Yet, on a higher level, it can show a deep sense of knowing, and trusting, that all is well and taken care of. Jupiter's transit to the 3rd house may need a little more effort on your part. Your relationship to those around you, including your neighbours and siblings, is likely to improve despite the problems you may create for yourself. That is because you are not likely to fight for what you want, and everyone else feels you are more peaceful and approachable, at least.

Jupiter in the 4th

Jupiter's transit to the deepest part of your chart brings a sense of peace and calm, a time for healing old hurts. Your home life will enjoy the breath of fresh air, either through some home improvement, an extension or house move.

You may simply feel you have more space at home, whether you actually move or extend your house. There may be a sense of your home life being more organised and peaceful. Your relationship with your mother can be a source of comfort now, even if she is no longer with you. If she is still alive, this can show a comfort in her life, too.

Jupiter in the 5th

Jupiter may bring a child if you are thinking about having a family now. It's a great time for prosperous speculations, for thinking about your future. Jupiter does well in the 5th, as it can express itself in many more opportunities for growth, in obvious, and less obvious, ways. This may come through an experience of inner growth and expanded awareness, apart from the more obvious external expansion. If you are not planning on children, you may create something else. Either way, it's about leaving your legacy behind for the next generation. This is also likely a lucky time for speculation, either financial or otherwise, unless you express the extremes of Jupiter and take on one too many ventures. Otherwise, this is a great time for fun and games, literally. If you already have children, you are likely to connect more deeply with them during this transit.

Jupiter in the 6th

Jupiter in your 6th is a time to deal with any unhealthy habits, and anything negative you have accumulated. Jupiter's expansive nature may create problems if you end up accumulating more vices, of course. This is best utilised by improving your health and daily life. It may be a time for healing any damage already done. This may be through some sort of therapy or a healthy lifestyle. This can be a wonderful time to connect to your day-to-day life in more meaningful and productive ways. Your work life and relationships with colleagues should improve under this transit, as you are less likely to cause strife for others. You are more likely willing to get along and connect with others than fight. And while this means you may be a pushover, getting on with others will help you get what you want in the end.

Jupiter in the 7th

Jupiter in the 7th can show opportunities for a relationship. Or it may deepen your connections to your current partner. This can be a great time to heal past hurts and to connect more with your partner or partners. It's a better time to connect to others, as you are likely to feel more connected to yourself. This sense of expansion, of possibility, is likely a comforting experience. Anyone you meet is likely to bring a sense of hope and idealism into your life. Even if you had not sensed this from your partner before, you can see the best in them now and grow together. If you are not married, this may be a good time to sign on the dotted line. If you are, this may be a time for that second honeymoon! You are likely to feel positive and generous during this transit, as one leads from the other.

Jupiter in the 8th

Jupiter in the 8th is a time to heal any trauma so you can change your life. Deepening your relationships to your partner through more intimacy and connection may play a big part in your healing process. This is an opportunity to go deeper into hidden drives that benefit from your increased awareness. You may join the dots with complex issues you may have been unaware of until now. Practically, it can be a great time for increasing your wealth through some inheritance or through your partner. Partners, whether personal or business, may bring you more money to you at this stage. The conversations you are likely to have are around other people's values and valuables. You are likely making some big changes in your life besides. While it may show more unexpected changes, expect some pleasant surprises along the way.

Jupiter in the 9th

Jupiter and the 9th house of good luck and positive growth go hand-in-hand. This can be a time to learn more about life, to travel and to take up higher studies or a more philosophical mindset. This can be a very positive transit, so much so that the only downside may be that you may take on too much as you travel far and wide. It may only show up as a need to travel within, to uplift yourself through some meaningful studies. You may wish to further formal studies. If you have a Masters, you may embark on a PhD. If you are not interested in formal studies, you may meet a teacher of some spiritual tradition that deepens your awareness. Either way, you are likely to ponder life's bigger questions. This is more likely to expand your horizons, whether you leave the house or not. Your father is likely to experience this as a positive period if he's still alive. Your relationship with him can improve, even if he is not. You sense a deeper connection to your past, to who and what has shaped you, that you are more likely to make better decisions about your future.

Jupiter in the 10the

Jupiter can increase work prospects in the 10th. This may show new opportunities for a more positive career advancement. Whether this is actually the case on paper, you may find you are more prosperous in your workplace. This will also likely show up in your elevated status. You may find opportunities to be more visible as Jupiter transits the most public area of your chart. Any actions you take now are likely to feel lucky, although this is simply Jupiter's way of bringing you the rewards you deserve. Your superiors are likely to benefit from your work, and your relationship to them can improve. You are likely to sense a deeper connection to your place in the world and the purpose behind whatever you are doing.

Jupiter in the 11th

Jupiter and the 11th work well together. You may experience this as some sort of gain. Although these may not always be obvious gains, such as financial rewards, you are likely to feel more positive about what you are achieving at this point. You may indeed increase your income, or you may gain in other ways that are more meaningful. You are likely to increase your social connections and circle of friends. Connecting more to others in your community is likely, whether new friends or old acquaintances. This can be a wonderful time to connect to those who you kept at the periphery until now. It may be a time to heal some divisions. It's certainly a fun time to make new connections, either in your personal or professional life. Either way, you are likely to feel more connected to a larger group with this transit.

Jupiter in the 12th

Jupiter in the 12th house of losses can show up as spending more, after a period of gains. If you have recently gained more, you have more to spend. It may not be about wealth. It may be about spending energy. This is a time to give, and to trust that whatever you give comes back to you, tenfold. You may wish to spend more time away now, either on retreat, or on some far-flung beach of paradise somewhere. It may mean wishing to take time out of your busy schedule for more rest. This is a wonderful time to delve into more spiritual practices, to find more connection and meaning in your everyday life, by being able to drop into the flow more. Meditation is one obvious example of what's possible now. But whether you ever sit on a meditation cushion, you can experience whatever you do more meditatively. You are more willing to surrender, which means more profound meditations and better sleep. This leaves you feeling refreshed and regenerated, ready for another spin around the zodiac.

SUN TRANSITS

The Sun transits one 30° sign a month. This occurs from mid-month, according to current sidereal calculations. These are different to the tropical calculations, based on the Solstices and Equinoxes, the reference points for the tropical zodiac. The dates in Table 3.12 are based on the Sun's transit through each Sun sign according to the sidereal zodiac. This aligns more with the actual constellations we can see in the night sky. But it is an approximation. The signs of the zodiac are different to the actual constellations, which vary in size. The signs do not vary according to traditional astrology. They are a way of dividing the zodiac into 12 equal 30° divisions, much like a clock for timing.

Table 3.12

Sun in Aries	Apr 14 - May 14
Sun in Taurus	May 14 - Jun 14
Sun in Gemini	Jun 14 - Jul 16
Sun in Cancer	Jul 16 - Aug 17
Sun in Leo	Aug 17 - Sep 17
Sun in Virgo	Sep 17 - Oct 17
Sun in Libra	Oct 17 - Nov 16
Sun in Scorpio	Nov 16 - Dec 16
Sun in Sagittarius	Dec 16 - Jan 14
Sun in Capricorn	Jan 14 - Feb 13
Sun in Aquarius	Feb 13 - Mar 14
Sun in Pisces	Mar 14 - Apr 14

If you were born on any of the days the Sun moves signs, double-check which sign the Sun was in. Most astrology software and online calculators will give you this information.

As the Sun transits through each house, it lights up that area of your life, highlighting the themes for a month. Depending on the strength of the Sun in each sign, the transits can be a more positive emphasis. Either way, the Sun's transits bring more awareness of the need for more energy and vitality. They shine a spotlight on each area of your life, reinvigorating each part of you throughout the year. Table 3.12 shows the approximate dates for the Sun's entry into each sidereal sign for Universal Time. This may change by a day based on your location.

MARS, VENUS & MERCURY TRANSITS

Mars, Venus, and Mercury move faster than the other planets and usually stay in a sign for just a few weeks. They do not impact one area of life by transit for long, unless they are retrograde within one sign. If they retrograde in one sign, they can spend many months. Retrograde transits show bigger themes over a longer period. More about retrogrades later.

Mars usually spends a couple of months in a sign. It can bring an acute experience to that area of your life. It's good to know where you are impacted, because if you are not on board with Mars, it can create havoc in some area of your life. Mars is the selfish part of you unwilling to compromise. It's that childish part of you that wants it now! Mars' natural stage of life is between the ages of 1 and 3, when you may have stomped your feet to get your way. How this period develops says a lot about how you go about getting what you want throughout your life. As Mars transits signs, it shows where you are more selfishly focused. It shows where you have more energy to get things done. If you are not getting something done, it may cause problems. Sometimes, this can show issues with others. As you go for what you want, others may have something to say about it.

Some houses are more conducive to Mars, such as the 3rd and 6th houses. This is about fighting for something you want, doing whatever it takes to get it. Yet the issue with Mars is not knowing when to quit, creating problems for yourself and others. Mars in the 3rd may show you having problems communicating effectively. You may state your case so strongly that no one is actually interested in what point you were trying to make. Mars in the 6th can show you overdo any improvements, to the point it may no longer be helpful. It may be like taking on a healthy eating habit that leads to an unwillingness to negotiate at the dinner table. Strife with others may ensue in either case, although you may feel good about yourself. Likewise, Mars in the 1st house can show you have a lot of energy to do things, but it may just as easily lead to accidents if you overdo it. This may also be the case for either the 3rd house or 6th house. Mars requires an outlet, so there's no use trying to quench the desire. Doing so would simply create more problems than it solves. The best is to find a healthy outlet and do something with it, mindfully.

In all other houses, Mars can create even more issues, as you may run into problems with others, either your family (2nd house), mother or home (4th house), children or lovers (5th house), partner or others in general (7th house), in-laws (8th house), father or advisors (9th house), boss or superior (10th house), friends or associates (11th house), or those you think are on your side but are working against your best interests (12th house). The 12th house is a problematic transit for Mars because it may reflect you sabotaging a situation. Although a time to see your otherwise hidden blocks, it can show you 'shooting yourself in the foot'. There is a part of your subconscious that may work against your conscious needs. You may end something you later regret or have a run in with someone you thought was on your side, and then deem them to be the enemy. Mars externalises things but is hidden from you in the 12th. Its transit here can create all kinds of power dynamics that are difficult to fathom.

Venus usually just spends a month or two in a sign. This shows where you are looking for pleasure and happiness, but also, unlike Mars, where you may be willing to compromise in getting it. Venus is one of the kindest planets, so you are likely to enjoy whatever Venus impacts, as long as there are no other transits or natal positions blocking this. Usually, Venus transits offer something to enjoy, either some activity or person who makes life enjoyable. Without Venus, life would be unbearable. When life is hard, it makes it tolerable. When it's already enjoyable, the joy becomes bliss. And while there are pitfalls to overindulging sensual pleasure, a key signification of Venus, it usually brings a great deal of stability and comfort by transit.

Venus does well in most houses, bringing some sense of enjoyment to every area of life. One transit that may not be so enjoyable is the 6th house. This is the least conducive place for Venus, which may make you feel as if life is a struggle. It's difficult to find the enjoyment or anything to appreciate with Venus in the 6th. You may find it's all work and no play. You may criticise yourself and others for their lack. Until this transit is over, you may have to put off enjoyments and focus on work for a while. It's usually not a long transit, so nothing to worry about for too long. And even while you may be challenged to extract some enjoyment from Venus in the 6th, you can certainly learn to appreciate the efforts you're making to better yourself. It may, however, seem as if you're not getting the attention and love you crave.

Mercury is the fastest moving planet, apart from the Moon. The intellect is very simulating and changeable, although that doesn't change as often as how we feel, as represented by the Moon. Mercury's transits stimulate different areas of your life as it transits through the houses. Whatever place Mercury is transiting, you may think more about the topics involved. The added mental stimulus can create its own problems, of course. If you try to work things out in your head, you realise the intellect has limitations. You may be out of touch with how you feel in this area, as there is just too much to think about. You are likely to have more options to choose from.

Mercury's transits are usually so fast that it can move into 3 different signs in just one calendar month. So, there's usually no long-standing issue in relation to any house. Changeability is an issue with Mercury. The problem is it cannot focus on any one thing for long enough to sort it out. The only time this occurs is when it retrogrades. Otherwise, Mercury zips through your life, exciting your mind into reacting immediately to stimuli. As Mercury transit through your chart, it asks you to think about each, to figure things out in a practical way. This can lead to great strides forward in some areas, or many detours that go nowhere in others.

The 12th house issues are problematic for the mind to grapple. Mercury here can show a mind lost in reverie and daydreaming, unable to function in the day-to-day. But it may also show a mind that can dream up all kinds of creative thoughts while it wanders, eventually flowing back to the conscious mind for assimilation. This transit may evoke many feelings that do not allow the mind to settle and rest. We could add the 4th house transit to this as well, as Mercury refuses to sit quietly at home. Mercury is that wayward, child-like part of you that gets bored easily. Likewise, Mercury's 7th house transit may not allow your attention to settle on one thing or one person, flittering about as you engage with many.

Mercury's transits bring the communication skills that help smooth out life's misunderstandings, apart from the retrograde phases. This can lead to many enjoyable interactions and much understanding about yourself and your life.

TRANSITS & PLANETARY DAŚĀS

When two or more planets are transiting together in the same sign, one impulse wins out over the other, depending on the strength of the planets involved and your current daśās. If you are currently experiencing a Mars daśā, Venus' transit will not completely assuage your need to get something for yourself. While this may cause challenges in relationships, especially if Mars were transiting your 7th house, a concurrent Venus transit in your 7th may at least soften the blow for others. Mercury's child-like influence on your 1st house may lead to an improvement in learning something new, but if Saturn were also transiting here, your uptake may be slower than it would have been otherwise. You must consider all transits at the same time. More so, you must consider your current planetary daśā and follow that planet as it transits your chart. These planets' transits are the ones to watch.

TRANSITS FROM THE MOON

You can read planets' transits from your rising or Moon sign but it's helpful to know what you are looking for with either. The rising sign, and houses counted from your rising sign, show what is happening in your environment. Transits to these places show the areas of life impacted. But there are differences between transits to the houses from your rising sign and Moon. What you would like is reflected in the transits calculated from your Moon. Transits to your rising sign show what is happening, whether you like it or not. Transits from your Moon show what you are feeling, while transits from your rising sign show what's happening. You should read the transit from both, as you are likely to make certain things happen based on what you would like to happen. This is like when planetary daśās, calculated from your Moon, show what is happening to an extent. Transits to your Moon show what you make happen, based on your desires.

Each planet has certain houses it benefits from by transit from the Moon. Each planet gives points to others based on their relative positions. You may benefit from a transit to your rising sign, but the Moon shows how you feel about it. When a planet transits a certain house from the Moon in your birth chart, there are other transits that can impede the result, too. Table 3.13 shows the beneficial transits from the Moon, including houses that can impede excellent results if other planets transit here at the same time.

Table 3.13

Transiting Planet from Moon	Beneficial Transit	Obstructing Transit
Sun	3	9
	6	12
	10	4
	11	5
Moon	1	5
	3	9
	6	12
	7	2
	10	4
	11	8
Mars	3	12
	6	9
	11	5
Mercury	2	5
	4	3
	6	9
	8	1
	10	8
	11	12
Jupiter	2	12
	5	4
	7	3
	9	10
	11	8
Venus	1	8
	2	7
	3	1
	4	10
	5	9
	8	5
	9	11
	11	6
	12	3
Saturn	3	12
	6	9
	11	5

When planets transit obstructing signs during a planet's transit from the Moon, it will show some block to the benefit that is possible. It may bring the experience but there is also likely some block. Yet the Sun and Saturn do not obstruct each other, nor do the Moon and Mercury. For all other planets, if they line up in obstructing houses from the Moon, we must question the benefit of any transit.

Moon is best in houses 1, 3, 6, 7, 10, and 11 from itself. From the Moon, Sun is best in houses 3, 6, 10, and 11; Mars is best in houses 3, 6, and 11; Mercury is best in houses 2, 4, 6, 8, 10, and 11; Jupiter is best in houses 2, 5, 7, 9, and 11; Venus is best in houses 1, 2, 3, 4, 5, 8, 9, 11, and 12; and Saturn is best in houses 3, 6, and 11.

AṢṬAGAVARGA

Another way of assessing the strength of planets, either in your birth chart or by transit, is to look at their relationship to other planets. Sun, Moon, Mars, Mercury, Venus, Saturn, Jupiter, and the ascendant are 8 focal points, *aṣṭakavarga*, or '8 divisions', used to calculate strength. We do not include Rāhu and Ketu here. Each planet and ascendant can receive up to 8 points. This is used to analyse house strengths in your birth chart, as well as the strength of planets' transits. Though not the only factor to determine strength, it is a quick guide to see if a planet or house is supported.

Each planet gives points based on house positions from the other planets and the ascendant. Adding up all points for all planets shows the overall strength of a house. When planets transit powerful houses, it shows more favourable indications for that area of life. Yet, these totals are difficult to calculate accurately. You will need a computer software to do so. There are other, more complex, calculations apart from the best positions I have listed. These include making deductions based on points obtained by signs within the same element, as well as signs ruled by the same planet. We add up the points each planet gives for each house; a total for each calculated to get a sense of strength for each area of your life. Note, this is a general indication of strength and needs to be qualified by other things in your birth chart.

Kind planets have more points to give. Cruel planets are less cooperative and have less points to give. Jupiter has the most, at 56; Mercury has 54; Venus has 52; Moon has 49; and Sun has 48. Mars and Saturn have only 39 points each to give. The ascendant has 49 points to give. As an example, Mars is best in houses 3, 5, 6, 10, and 11 from the Sun, and picks up a point in any of these houses – from the Sun. Mars does not give any points to the remaining houses. The total of all these best positions for all planets is 386. Dividing this number by 12, for the 12 houses, comes to 32. Anything above 32 for any house is above average. Each planet can receive a maximum of 8 points in any house, including a point a planet can give to itself. Anything above 4 for a planet is above average. The higher the score, the more the strength. The lower the score, the lower the strength. Don't worry if you have a 0 score for a planet, or less than 32 total for any house. There are other things to factor in arriving at an overall picture of strength.

The following is a list of best placements for each planet in relation to all other planets. Vedic astrology software programs will calculate the total scores for you.

Sun is best in:
1, 2, 4, 7, 8, 9, 10, 11 from itself
3, 6, 10, 11 from Moon
1, 2, 4, 7, 8, 9, 10, 11 from Mars
3, 5, 6, 9, 10, 11, 12 from Mercury
5, 6, 9, 11 from Jupiter
6, 7, 12 from Venus
1, 2, 4, 7, 8, 9, 10, 11 from Saturn
3, 4, 6, 10, 11, 12 from ascendant
Total points: 48

Moon is best in:
1, 3, 6, 7, 10, 11 from itself
3, 6, 7, 8, 10, 11 from Sun
2, 3, 5, 6, 9, 10, 11 from Mars
1, 3, 4, 5, 7, 8, 10, 11 from Mercury
1, 4, 7, 8, 10, 11, 12 from Jupiter
3, 4, 5, 7, 9, 10, 11 from Venus
3, 5, 6, 11 from Saturn
3, 6, 10, 11 from ascendant
Total points: 49

Mars is best in:
1, 2, 4, 7, 8, 10, 11 from itself
3, 5, 6, 10, 11 from Sun
3, 6, 11 from Moon
3, 5, 6, 11 from Mercury
6, 10, 11, 12 from Jupiter
6, 8, 11, 12 from Venus
1, 4, 7, 8, 9, 10, 11 from Saturn
1, 3, 6, 10, 11 from ascendant
Total points: 39

Mercury is best in:
1, 3, 5, 6, 9, 10, 11, 12 from itself
5, 6, 9, 11, 12 from Sun
2, 4, 6, 8, 10, 11 from Moon
1, 2, 4, 7, 8, 9, 10, 11 from Mars
6, 8, 11, 12 from Jupiter
1, 2, 3, 4, 5, 8, 9, 11 from Venus
1, 2, 4, 7, 8, 9, 10, 11 from Saturn
1, 2, 4, 6, 8, 10, 11 from ascendant
Total points: 54

Jupiter is best in:
1, 2, 3, 4, 7, 8, 10, 11 from itself
1, 2, 3, 4, 7, 8, 9, 10, 11 from Sun
2, 5, 7, 9, 11 from Moon
1, 2, 4, 7, 8, 10, 11 from Mars
1, 2, 4, 5, 6, 9, 10, 11 from Mercury
2, 5, 6, 9, 10, 11 from Venus
3, 5, 6, 12 from Saturn
1, 2, 4, 5, 6, 7, 9, 10, 11 from ascendant
Total points: 56

Venus is best in:
1, 2, 3, 4, 5, 8, 9, 10, 11 from itself
8, 11, 12 from Sun
1, 2, 3, 4, 5, 8, 9, 11, 12 from Moon
3, 5, 6, 9, 11, 12 from Mars
3, 5, 6, 9, 11 from Mercury
5, 8, 9, 10, 11 from Jupiter
3, 4, 5, 8, 9, 10, 11 from Saturn
1, 2, 3, 4, 5, 8, 9, 11 from ascendant
Total points: 52

Saturn is best in:
3, 5 ,6, 11 from itself
1, 2, 4, 7, 8, 10, 11 from Sun
3, 6, 11 from Moon
3, 5, 6, 10, 11, 12 from Mars
6 ,8, 9, 10, 11, 12 from Mercury
5, 6, 11, 12 from Jupiter
6, 11, 12 from Venus
1, 3, 4, 6, 10, 11 from ascendant
Total points: 39

RETROGRADE TRANSITS

All planets retrograde every year. Because of the way Earth orbits the Sun, all planets appear to move backwards against the backdrop of stars. And while this is an apparent motion because of our own planet orbiting the Sun at different speeds to the planets, they do actually move back through the signs from our perspective.

It is quite common to see at least one or two in a birth chart. If you were born when a planet was retrograde, it becomes a signature for your life. When planets appear to move backwards, the planet's expressions are more unusual, the significations not so clear-cut. There can be a certain imbalance expressed, an all-or-nothing approach. Mars represents courage, so its retrograde may show swinging between brute force and timidity, for example. Whether you have a retrograde planet in your horoscope, you will experience a retrograde planet in transit at different times.

Retrograde motion offers great strength, but this creates complexities apart from whether a planet is strong. A retrograde planet is not easily expressed, although there may be a strength within. This may mean not being able to express yourself clearly if Mercury were retrograde, for example. If Mars were retrograde, it may mean not being able to do the necessary when required. Although there is a hidden strength to retrograde motion, you may not express it as easily as a direct planet.

Retrograde transits point to a time to restore and renew. You must deal with unfinished business, as retrograde doesn't mean you are not moving-it just means you must move in a different direction for a while. Retrograde transits offer you a way to slow down and move inwards as you concentrate and reclaim your energy to prepare for moving forward with more self-awareness once the retrograde is complete.

We give special attention to planets' stations, either when they are stationing retrograde or direct again. This means the planet doesn't appear to be moving at all. These periods are important to slow down with regards the significations of the planet in question. Retrograde planets are powerful. Stationing planets are even more powerful. They have a tremendous impact on the areas of life they represent.

MERCURY RETROGRADE

Mercury retrogrades most often, as it only takes 88 days to transit around the Sun. It retrogrades on average for about 24 days. When Mercury is retrograde, communications are not straightforward. You may have to listen more, using the time to re-evaluate what you are expressing and how you are expressing it. Mercury represents our most practical concerns: money, work, security, communication, travel, health, and daily routines. When it moves retrograde, you must re-check all the above. Your mind may need to go offline so you can work it all out.

We give special attention to Mercury retrograde, as it does so more than any of the planets; three, sometimes four times a year. Yet Mercury is one of the kind planets.

It doesn't always cause problems; certainly not as many as Mars and Saturn. It does, however, cause some issues when it's not operating at full capacity. When your mind has to take on too much, you may not operate as effectively or efficiently.

Things don't run as smoothly when Mercury appears to stop moving and then backpedals from our perspective. This can be a nuisance at the very least, or a complete and utter meltdown, especially if you are already on the verge. Mercury represents your everyday life and communications, how well everything functions. It's only when things stop functioning that you may pay them any heed. What seems so trivial at other times takes on a whole other dimension during its retrograde. Losing your keys, getting locked out of your house, missing flights, misinterpreting what someone meant and taking offense, computer malfunctions, missed calls, accidentally deleted emails - these are quite common under a Mercury retrograde period. Most of the time, you get over it by clarifying the issue. Sometimes, they set something off that has lasting repercussions.

Mercury retrograde periods are at the very least a detour. They represent periods when you must slow down and pay attention. If you miss your turning on the motorway because you were thinking too much about something else, it reminds you to be present. Of course, it adds more time to your journey. Many times, Mercury retrograde is a liminal state of being. If you miss your train and have to wait a few hours for the next one, what do you do? You could fret about it, or you could enjoy the time for which you hadn't planned. Mercury retrogrades are an opportunity to take some time out. If you must plan, keep an open mind about whatever you are doing. Mercury is the most adaptable planet, so that's usually not such a problem.

It's a good idea to keep a sense of humour, to stay light on your feet and be ready for the next change you must make. Humour is really an important tactic to detach emotionally from what is going on, to view the situation from another perspective, one that eases the feeling of mental pressure. Mental pressure is really a trick of the mind. It's all about the perception of time.

Remind yourself that it is all in your mind. The dangers in a Mercury retrograde period are not serious on their own. Usually, you can laugh off the petty annoyances. But when you add a misunderstanding or misstep to other, more challenging indications, it might worsen things. If you are dealing with some challenges, and you add an overworked mind into the mix, you are likely to create more problems. Best to take a step back at this stage and tread carefully. You are likely to misunderstand something and create an even bigger problem in your mind. It's a better time to review something. If you try to move ahead with something new, the winds are not at your back. You will struggle every step of the way. Use the time for what it's good for: a review.

Pay close attention to the signs involved. You must include Gemini and Virgo in your deliberations, as Mercury rules these signs. Gemini and Virgo represent our everyday communications and routines, which can go a little haywire during Mercury retrograde. Pay attention to what is happening in the moment. If you notice your mind wandering too far off course, bring it back to the present. Focus on something that is always present. You could use your senses, the breath, or some task you are doing to come back to what is happening now. Whatever insights you gleam from this period, you can move forward with a new plan and impetus once Mercury stations direct. Use the time to your advantage, redoing, reworking, rethinking your entire approach to the areas of your life impacted.

VENUS RETROGRADE

Venus takes 225 days to travel around our Sun. It is retrograde every 18 months for about 40 days. This is a time to re-evaluate the things and people in your life you hold dear. In a general sense, Venus represents money, comforts, love, relationships, art, beauty, pleasures, enjoyment, entertainment, femininity, and sexuality. It would be wise to take counsel before deciding about relationships or expensive purchases during its retrograde. It may tempt you! An old love may revisit you, for example, or you may simply dwell on things you used to value; bringing them back into your life through your imagination. There is nothing wrong with this, of course. Yet you may not pay attention to the here and now. It may be wise to delay making any definite decisions about such matters while Venus is retrograde.

Venus, like all planets, shows the possibility of you losing balance. This may mean alternating between sensual fixations and a lack of interest or expression. You may express a more unusual side of your desires. Venus retrogrades by transit are about reflecting on what and who you value, as well as how you go about fulfilling your desires.

MARS RETROGRADE

Mars takes approximately 2 years to travel around our Sun, moving retrograde every 26 months or so, from 55 to 80 days. Mars retrograde represents the courage to act based on previous experience. This builds inner strength and resolve. It's a time to hold your nerve. Strength trainers know that strength has more to do with the nervous system than anything else. The increase in muscle - a tissue ruled by Saturn - is merely a by-product of a nervous system that can manage the task at hand. You may do things you used to do to gain more strength, whether physically, mentally, or emotionally, as you tap into vast reserves of strength within. But you may just as easily find yourself at a loss, as if your system were in shutdown mode because you cannot manage the extra energy that has no apparent outlet.

Mars retrograde can be all or nothing about energy, leaping up in bounds and dropping as dramatically. You may hold back what you want to say or do, only to leave it so long that you explode at something for stopping you from doing it. Those who are not used to Mars being so twisted and internalised may find its retrograde frustrating if they cannot release the build-up of energy. You may bite your lip. It may build into an unavoidable hot mess when it erupts. Take a lesson from Mother Nature as she releases a build-up of pressure through earthquakes and volcanoes. Find healthy ways of releasing the excess energy that seems to have nowhere to go, as you notice where you need to strengthen your defences.

Energy can come in bursts that can just as quickly take a dive. It may challenge you to find a balanced approach.

JUPITER RETROGRADE

Jupiter takes approximately 12 years to travel around the Sun, moving retrograde every year for about 120 days. Your ideas and ideals may get themselves into all kinds of twists while Jupiter is retrograde. Jupiter retrograde behaves a bit like Rāhu, which is always retrograde according to traditional Indian astrology, although the 'true' nodal positions do station direct. Rāhu is all about innovation and change. Jupiter is usually the antidote to this impulse, bringing coherence and order. Its retrograde by transit may show a lack of order for a while. Jupiter retrograde is a time to reassess laws, policies, beliefs, and practices that keep a sense of order and coherence. While Jupiter is not behaving in the usual manner when retrograde, it can lead to a lot of confusion. You may reconsider your guiding principles and may struggle to sense the right way forward. Mistakes are very possible in the immediate period, although from a larger perspective there are no mistakes - only bigger lessons.

Your faith may be tested. Or you may hesitate. At other times, you may overstate your case. You may reflect more on what is meaningful. This may lead to delays in expanding whatever areas of your life are impacted, as you seek more cohesive thoughts on the issues. Growth doesn't occur without some sense of order. Jupiter retrogrades reorder your life, as you figure out what your purpose is. Once you figure that out, growth is inevitable. Growth may feel stunted with Jupiter retrograde, but it is an opportunity to turn your attention inward and deepen your awareness.

SATURN RETROGRADE

Saturn takes approximately 29.5 years to travel around the Sun, moving retrograde every year for about 140 days. Saturn is the planet of time and form. As it moves backwards, it shows a need to renegotiate your boundaries; to find out where your limits lie. This may be through finding out what you can, and can no longer, commit to. You may discover you no longer have the time or the energy to continue down a certain path. This may be a time to draw a line and to make it clear to others, and to yourself, where that line is. As Saturn stations direct once again, the line has taken a definite form. This process can last up to nine months every year when we include Saturn's shadow phases. Shadow phases are the periods when a planet transits over the point to which it will return once the retrograde phase is complete. In the end, you may find you have less energy for something, or that you can no longer do that thing you had been doing if you are to remain healthy and well-adjusted.

You may find it a challenge to keep healthy boundaries. You may overwork, eventually leading to you having to take time off. You may over-commit and then completely pull back, as you try to find the right amount of responsibility you can take on. It's a lengthy process and one that you go through every year, so there's no rush in figuring it all out. Keep the bigger picture, your long-term objectives, in view at all times.

When Saturn stations at a point in the zodiac, it can feel as if that area of life has ground to a halt. Saturn, or any planet, stationing on a point, drills down into it. You cannot avoid the pressing issues. With Saturn, it may feel more pressured. This may be a job, a relationship, an idea. Whatever it is, it is asking you to take a long, hard look at it. Some things and people may not withstand the force, while other relationships are fortified. If already built on firm foundations, it will further strengthen the bond. If not, it may break it apart, so you can move on and build elsewhere.

URANUS RETROGRADE

Uranus takes about 84 years to travel around the Sun, moving retrograde every year for about 150 days. These periods are a time to catch up with any unexpected changes that have occurred in the world around you. As it retrogrades, it offers you an opportunity to make some internal adjustments to these more obvious outer changes.

Uranus retrogrades may show you reflecting more on these changes. There may be more changes to deal with. It changes your perceptions and intensifies your attention on the issues. Retrograde planets are already more unpredictable. Uranus retrograde is doubly so. If you have Uranus retrograde from birth, you are more likely used to this and make the adjustments quickly. If not, you may take longer to adjust.

NEPTUNE RETROGRADE

Neptune takes about 165 years to travel around the Sun, moving retrograde every year for about 160 days. Neptune retrograde transits are about finding a balance between truth and fantasy. You may wonder about what is true in relation to the sign impacted. You may reflect on what could easily become confusing. The best use of Neptune retrograde is to keep an open mind while thinking more creatively about solutions.

PLUTO RETROGRADE

Pluto takes 248 years to travel around the Sun, moving retrograde every year for about 160 days. Pluto's retrogrades are a time to reflect on deep-seated change you may resist. Yet resistance itself is a part of the process of change. If you stall, it may help to think about this strategy as a way you prepare for the inevitable changes. You may be familiar with your 'inner saboteur', or what you may call procrastination. Either way, the extra time to work things out on a more hidden level brings you far greater change than if you were to act on the first impulse to change.

Time stays long enough for anyone who will use it.

- Leonardo da Vinci

PART 4: EXAMPLES

TIGER WOODS' CAR ACCIDENT 2021

Tiger Woods was born at 10.50 p.m. on December 30th, 1975 in Long Beach, California. Chart 4.1 shows his South Indian-style birth chart using sidereal calculations (Citrapakṣa Ayanāṁśa) and whole sign houses.

Tiger Woods D1

Jp21°58' 7 Pis	Ke25°47' 8 Ari	Ma24°3' 9 Tau	10 Gem
6 Aqu			Sa7°36' 11 Can
Me2°55' 5 Cap			12 Leo
Su15°27' 4 Sag	Ne18°59' Mo28°52' Ve5°1' 3 Sco	Ra25°47' Ur12°50' 2 Libr	Pl18°8' As0°54' 1 Virg

Chart 4.1

The planets and ascendant are abbreviated as follows: AS: ascendant or rising sign, Su: Sun, Mo: Moon, Ma: Mars,

Me: Mercury, Jp: Jupiter, Sa: Saturn, Ra: Rāhu, Ke: Ketu, Ur: Uranus, Ne: Neptune, and Pl: Pluto.

While every birth chart is an intricate weaving together of many potentials and possibilities, any of which we could focus on and interpret differently, there is no denying what happened to Tiger Woods on February 23rd, 2021. He experienced a car crash after which he ended up in hospital. Thankfully, he is making a good recovery, although he was still using crutches many months later.

Mars Major Daśā: 06 Jun 2020 - 06 Jun 2027
Sub-daśās:
  Mars: 06 Jun 2020 - 4 Nov 2020
  Rāhu: 4 Nov 2020 - 22 Nov 2021
  Jupiter: 22 Nov 2021 - 30 Oct 2022
  Saturn: 30 Oct 2022 - 08 Dec 2023
  Mercury: 08 Dec 2023 - 04 Dec 2024
  Ketu: 04 Dec 2024 - 30 Apr 2025
  Venus: 30 Apr 2025 - 01 Jul 2026
  Sun: 01 Jul 2026 - 08 Nov 2026
  Moon: 08 Nov 2026 - 06 Jun 2027

Timeline 4.1

The first thing to examine is what is being triggered in his chart, looking at the planetary and sign-based daśās. Timeline 4.1 shows his planetary daśās (Viṁśottarī Daśā).

He began the major daśā in June 2020. That is already a red flag and a potential problem, although not everyone who enters Mars daśā will have an accident, of course. For most, it may simply mean some challenge to find strength. There must be indications of an accident as an expression. Mars rules the 3rd (Scorpio) and 8th (Aries) houses, as he has sidereal Virgo rising (ascendant) in his birth chart. The 3rd and 8th are both challenging areas. It blends short travels (3rd house) with the potential for obstacles (8th house). But it is not all Virgo ascendants that will experience this as an accident, of course, even in a Mars daśā. If we look further into his chart, we can see why this is indeed the case for him.

First, Mars is in the 9th house, Taurus. Thus, Mars combines the significations of the 3rd and 8th houses with the 9th house of travel. The 3rd is brief trips, while the 9th is long distance travel. Venus, the planet that rules Taurus, and where Mars is, is in Scorpio, Mars' sign. This means Mars and Venus are swapping signs, the 3rd and 9th signs, a 'mutual exchange', mixing up a cruel house (3rd) with the house of good luck (9th). This shows more problems and a loss of luck while travelling. The 8th house is the 12th from the 9th, and another sign of the loss he experienced.

Another way to read the chart is to take the planetary daśā ruler, in this case Mars, and use that as the 1st house, delineating results from this new position. Reading the chart from Mars, Saturn in the 3rd is opposite Mercury in the 9th, with Rāhu in the 6th. Saturn can show some restriction in travel in his 3rd house and opposite the planet that represents travel: Mercury, placed in the 9th house of travel. The Moon, the ruler of the 3rd from Mars, where Saturn is placed, is in Scorpio, in debilitation. Mars daśā has the potential to create problems for him, especially when active in a planetary daśā. But we couldn't say that all his Mars daśā, from 2020 to 2027, would lead to accidents. We need to do some fine-tuning. We can do this by looking at sub-daśās within the major Mars daśā.

Mars-Rāhu began in November 2020 and lasted until November 2021. This period has more potential for accidents for him, not only because the combination of Mars and Rāhu often shows problems, but because Rāhu rules Aquarius, his 6th house. The 6th house can show issues such as illness and wounding from accidents or surgeries. Mars and Rāhu are also in a conflicted relationship, further highlighting the potential for a problem. If you count inclusively from Mars to Rāhu, it is 6 signs away, while counting back from Rāhu to Mars, you get 8. This 6/8 relationship is inimical. Rāhu is said to block the energy of Mars, but it often does so after it has exaggerated its actions, as if lashing out because of feeling restrained. This further emphasises the possibility of an accident for him between November 2020 and November 2021.

We can then break this period down further, into a sub-sub-period, to show how he is reacting to all the above indications. This fine tunes the timing of the accident. Saturn, the planet that co-rules Aquarius, his 6th house, along with Rāhu, was active from February 19, 2021, just a few days before his accident on February 23. The planetary daśā on all 3 levels was Mars-Rāhu-Saturn. Saturn can show up as issues around being restricted. This can be especially frustrating in Mars daśā, egged on by Rāhu, i.e., Mars-Rāhu-Saturn. Here, all three of the cruellest planets, Mars, Rāhu, and Saturn, were active in his birth chart.

Mars' 4th, 7th, and 8th house aspects were triggered in its daśā; thus, influencing his 12th house of loss and hospitalisation, his 3rd house of travelling and his 4th house of vehicles. Mars' influence tends to disturb.

The Moon is in the 3rd whole sign house of his chart; thus, we can also calculate his planetary daśās starting with the 5th lunar mansion (utpanna) from the Moon's position in Jyeṣṭhā. The 5th lunar mansion from Jyeṣṭhā is Śravaṇa, which is associated with the Moon. We can calculate his planetary daśās beginning with the Moon. This is shown in Timeline 4.2.

He had begun Saturn in this interpretation, the 5th lunar mansion and daśā in this sequence. The 5th can show challenges. Breaking down Saturn's 17-year long daśā into sub-periods, we see he was experiencing a Saturn-Mercury daśā at the time of the accident using this technique (see Timeline 4.3).

This shows Saturn's and Mercury's positions from his natal Moon are an important piece. This way of reading the daśās based on the house position of the Moon is more telling of how someone is responding to events, as seen in the Moon's position. Saturn is in the 9th from his Moon, with Mercury in the 3rd. Both houses relate to travelling, while the 3rd is about brief trips.

Vimshottari (Utp)

Start Date			Age	Dashas
3/	11/	1966	-9.2	Mo
2/	11/	1976	0.8	Ma
3/	11/	1983	7.8	Ra
3/	11/	2001	25.8	Jp
3/	11/	2017 n	41.8	Sa
3/	11/	2036	60.8	Me
3/	11/	2053	77.8	Ke
3/	11/	2060	84.8	Ve
3/	11/	2080	104.8	Su
4/	11/	2086	110.8	Mo
3/	11/	2096	120.8	Ma
5/	11/	2103	127.8	Ra

Timeline 4.2

Vimshottari (Utp)

Start Date			Age	Dashas	
3/	**11/**	**2017**	**41.8**	**Sa**	**Sa**
6/	11/	2020 n	44.9	Sa	Me
17/	7/	2023	47.5	Sa	Ke
25/	8/	2024	48.7	Sa	Ve
25/	10/	2027	51.8	Sa	Su
6/	10/	2028	52.8	Sa	Mo
8/	5/	2030	54.4	Sa	Ma
17/	6/	2031	55.5	Sa	Ra
23/	4/	2034	58.3	Sa	Jp
3/	**11/**	**2036**	**60.8**	**Me**	**Me**
1/	4/	2039	63.3	Me	Ke
29/	3/	2040	64.2	Me	Ve

Timeline 4.3

Though we can make quite good predictions using the planetary daśās alone, we can look further to examine a sign-based daśā to see what was triggered. In this example, I have included Chara daśā (see Timeline 4.4).

Chara					
Start Date			**Age**	**Dashas**	
31/	12/	2015	40.0	Tau	Ari
30/	6/	2016	40.5	Tau	Pis
30/	12/	2016	41.0	Tau	Aqu
1/	7/	2017	41.5	Tau	Cap
30/	12/	2017	42.0	Tau	Sag
1/	7/	2018	42.5	Tau	Sco
30/	12/	2018	43.0	Tau	Libr
1/	7/	2019	43.5	Tau	Virg
31/	12/	2019	44.0	Tau	Leo
30/	6/	2020	44.5	Tau	Can
30/	12/	2020	45.0	Tau	Gem
1/	7/	2021	45.5	Tau	Tau

Timeline 4.4

He was born when the sign Virgo was rising, so Virgo was his first sign daśā. Virgo runs in a clockwise direction, to Libra, Scorpio, and so on. Taurus was active from December 2015, and until July 2021. This is because Venus, the planet that rules Taurus, is 7 signs away in Scorpio. By counting forward from Taurus to Venus, and subtracting 1, you get a count of 6 years for Taurus daśā.

This has the potential to cause problems. The previous Aries daśā would show the potential as the 8th house, except that he did not begin his Mars planetary daśā until June 2020. All daśās must be looked at together to get a more accurate picture. Taurus daśā was active at the same time as Mars-Rāhu-Saturn. This shows more potential for accidents, as Mars is in Taurus, while Rāhu and Saturn both rule Aquarius, his 6th house of accidents. If we read the chart from Aquarius, the ruler of the 3rd house from here is Mars, placed in the 4th. The 3rd represents short travels, while the 4th represents vehicles. Because Taurus was active, and because it houses Mars, this would show the more probable timing.

The planetary and sign-based daśās clearly show the potential for an accident in February 2021. But there still is one more layer to evaluate: the transits on the day of the accident. This shows the exact timing of the accident, the crucial last piece in the analysis.

Chart 4.2 is for the time of the accident, which was reported to have taken place at 07.12 a.m. on Tuesday February 23rd, 2021, in Los Angeles, California. The first thing to know is that Mars, the planetary daśā planet, had just moved into Taurus, his 9th house, as ruler of his 3rd house, of travelling. This alone is a trigger for his natal Mars in Taurus. Rāhu was also transiting Taurus, a Mars-Rāhu conjunction, at a time in his life when both Mars and Rāhu were active in planetary daśās, while the sign Taurus was also active.

The sign rising at the time of the accident was Aquarius. Not only is Aquarius his 6th house, but the ruler, Rāhu, was with Mars, while the sign was being transited by Venus as the 9th house ruler, and the Sun as the 12th house ruler. The 12th house represents losses and the potential for hospitalisation. The crucial part here in relation to the accident was that Mars, as the current planetary daśā, rules the 3rd from Aquarius, and was transiting the 4th

(representing his vehicle) with Rāhu, the sub-daśā planet. Saturn, the sub-sub-daśā planet, also shows the timing of hospitalisation, being placed in the 12th house from Aquarius.

Tiger Woods Crash D1

2 Pis	Ur$_{13°16'}$ 3 Ari	Ma$_{0°57'}$ Ra$_{21°52'}$ 4 Tau	Mo$_{24°22'}$ 5 Gem
Ne$_{25°55'}$ Su$_{11°5'}$ As$_{25°51'}$ Ve$_{3°28'}$ 1 Aqu			6 Can
Jp$_{21°14'}$ Sa$_{13°44'}$ Me$_{17°15'}$ Pl$_{1°45'}$ 12 Cap			7 Leo
11 Sag	Ke$_{21°52'}$ 10 Sco	9 Libr	8 Virg

Chart 4.2

Could we have known that Tiger would have his accident on February 23rd without a doubt? At the very least, someone looking at these trends may have been able to advise him to slow down when driving. While it is an astrologer's role to assuage as much hardship as possible, many times, a reading is simply about easing someone's hardship by accepting what has already occurred. It's all happening perfectly. It may not be something we wish for always, but it's all happening perfectly in the grand scheme of things.

There are other things I could add to show a confluence of factors that would further suggest some mishap. But just using these important three layers: 1) planetary daśās, 2) sign-based daśās, and 3) transits, it shows the potential and timing. I may add that it occurred on a Tuesday, ruled by Mars, or that Venus, as ruler of the 9th house of good luck, was in its most challenged position in the 6th house. Venus in the 6th house is called *maraṇa*, a Sanskrit word to suggest 'death', but really it means the planet suffers in that place. As ruler of the lucky 9th house, Venus in its death-like place shows luck was not on his side that day.

JOE BIDEN'S ELECTION WIN 2020

Joe Biden was born at 08.30 a.m. on November 20th, 1942 in Scranton, Pennsylvania. Chart 4.3 shows his South Indian-style birth chart using sidereal calculations (Citrapakṣa Ayanāṁśa) and whole sign houses.

	Joe Biden D1		
	Mo7°56'	Ur9°44' Sa16°54'	
5 Pis	6 Ari	7 Tau	8 Gem
Ke6°40'			Jp2°5' Pl14°11'
4 Aqu			9 Can
			Ra6°40'
3 Cap			10 Leo
	Ve5°31' As10°9'Su4°31'	Me28°29' Ma19°33'	Ne8°28'
2 Sag	1 Sco	12 Libr	11 Virg

Chart 4.3

Although Joe Biden's time of birth may not be exact (A-rated news report), it will not alter his planetary daśās very much if the time is off by a few minutes. And it will not at all alter his sign-based daśās. That is because the progressed signs used are based on the rising sign at birth, whether the very beginning or very end of the sign was rising. The rising degree was 10 degrees of sidereal Scorpio at 08.30 a.m. on the morning of his birth. It does not change signs, even if we adjust the time by 2 hours later or 50 minutes earlier. We can be almost certain his rising sign is sidereal Scorpio and use the sign-based daśās. The planetary daśās may change by some weeks, even months, depending on the adjusted time. The first thing to check are Joe Biden's major planetary daśās (see Timeline 4.5).

Major Daśās:
    Ketu: 19 Sep 1938 - 19 Sep 1945
    Venus: 19 Sep 1945 - 19 Sep 1965
    Sun: 19 Sep 1965 - 20 Sep 1971
    Moon: 20 Sep 1971 - 19 Sep 1981
    Mars: 19 Sep 1981 - 19 Sep 1988
    Rāhu: 19 Sep 1988 - 20 Sep 2006
    Jupiter: 20 Sep 2006 - 20 Sep 2022
    Saturn: 20 Sep 2022 - 19 Sep 2041
    Mercury: 19 Sep 2041 - 20 Sep 2058

Timeline 4.5

Joe Biden was in Jupiter-Rāhu daśā during the election in November 2020. More precisely, this was Jupiter-Rāhu-Jupiter. Jupiter, the planet of expansion, is in his 9th house of fortune and good luck. Although exalted in Cancer, it is retrograde. On the one hand, it brings him the blessings; on the other, it shows a mixed bag of results. Rāhu is in the prominent 10ᵗʰ house, the powerful Leo, while the Sun, the ruler of Leo, is in Scorpio, his rising sign. This is a powerful combination, one which saw him come into power.

Jupiter Major Daśā: 20 Sep 2006 - 20 Sep 2022
Sub-daśās:
Jupiter: 20 Sep 2006 - 06 Nov 2008
Saturn: 06 Nov 2008 - 18 May 2011
Mercury: 18 May 2011 - 26 Aug 2013
Ketu: 26 Aug 2013 - 01 Aug 2014
Venus: 01 Aug 2014 - 29 Mar 2017
Sun: 29 Mar 2017 - 17 Jan 2018
Moon: 17 Jan 2018 - 18 May 2019
Mars: 18 May 2019 - 22 Apr 2020
➢ Rāhu: 22 Apr 2020 - 20 Sep 2022

Timeline 4.6

His 10ᵗʰ divisional chart (Chart 4.4) is used to hone in on the 10ᵗʰ house of career. This chart divides up each sign in his birth chart by 10. Thus, there are ten 3-degree portions for each sign that correlate with a sign in the 10ᵗʰ division. We draw another chart to give an in-depth view of his career. The 1ˢᵗ sign in the 10ᵗʰ division is Libra with Rāhu placed therein, unless he was born more than 5 minutes earlier or 10 minutes later. Rāhu sub-daśā triggered this career chart, thus, we can me more assured his time of birth is around 8.30 am as reported. Rāhu is the planet with the second highest degree (counting in reverse for Rāhu) in his natal chart. This technique is called

Charakāraka, or 'moving significators', where planets take on different roles based on their degrees, regardless of sign placement.

Jp20°58' 6 Pis	U̲r̲7°22' Ma15°32' K̲e̲6°43' 7 Ari	8 Tau	**Mo**19°28' **Sa**19°9' 9 Gem
5 Aqu			Me14°59'Ne24°46' P̲l̲21°53' 10 Can
4 Cap			**Su**15°13' **Ve**25°10' 11 Leo
3 Sag	2 Sco	A̲s̲11°32' R̲a̲6°43' 1 Libr	12 Virg

Joe Biden D10

Chart 4.4

Rāhu is at the second highest degree in the chart (counting in reverse). This is called the *Amātya-kāraka*, which represents professional assistance and powerful allies. Though Rāhu brought him success, there is always a price to pay with Rāhu. Whatever success he has achieved, it can show personal challenges he must overcome.

Rāhu is the last sub-daśā of his long Jupiter period. This is one of the more complex transitional phases in the planetary daśās. He has lived long enough to have experienced 18 years of Rāhu daśā, prior to Jupiter's current major daśā. He has been here before many times. This was a case of third time lucky for gaining the most powerful seat in U.S. politics, his last stab at it. Although he succeeded where he did not before, he knows it is ending. On some level, he is aware of Saturn's daśā, which began in September 2022. This is when he may need to step back from public life or slow down, although doing so would seem impossible in the current political climate (2023).

This is not only because he is in Saturn daśā, but because he is experiencing a Saturn stage of life. Now that he is 80 years of age, Saturn daśā is asking him to take a step back, as opposed to a young person with this configuration who may have to work even harder. When we add this to his Saturn looking at his rising sign from the opposite 7th house, it may mean he feels the pressure to work hard despite the need to slow down. Saturn in the 10th house from his 10th house (7th house) can show an obstruction to his career. Yet there are more planets assisting him professionally, with Sun and Venus in Scorpio, in the 4th from his 10th house (argalā). Without these planets' support, I doubt he would still be in office. Though Rāhu gave him the power he wanted, Saturn asks him to pay back, or pay it forward. He has declared as much in speeches where he has spoken about his role as a bridge to who is coming up behind him politically.

To see whether he would win the election in 2020, there were a few key ingredients to examine. First, the planetary daśā primes him for power, with Rāhu triggered alongside Jupiter. Counting from Jupiter to Rāhu and the same again, we arrive at his 11th house of gains. Jupiter was transiting Sagittarius at the time of the election, in a powerful position at the very end of the sign, in his 2nd house. The 2nd house relates to resources and his vision, as well as his speech. This expressed itself as him stating a case for healing and recovery for the U.S. We must place his chart in the context of what was going on at the time. His comforting words (Jupiter in 2nd) would have been sweet music to many voters' ears. Jupiter is the most comforting influence. This would have shown his ability to instil hope in voters' minds.

Jupiter's 5th, 7th, and 9th house aspects would have been triggered in Jupiter's daśā; thus, influencing his 1st and 3rd houses of self-promotion, and his 5th house of political power and increased followers.

He has the Moon in the 6th house, so we can view the planetary daśās from his 4th lunar mansion (kṣema). His Moon is in Aśvinī, so Rohiṇī is the 4th lunar mansion and associated with the Moon. Timelines 4.7 shows his planetary daśās starting with a major Moon daśā. He began a Mercury daśā in 2006 (see Timeline 4.8). This was a Mercury-Jupiter sub-daśā during the time of the election, before moving into the last phase of Mercury daśā, Mercury-Saturn, in March 2021, after he took office. It points to his gaining the presidency (Jupiter), but also the challenges he faced upon taking office (Saturn). This also points to Saturn playing a role in his need to withdraw from public life due to increased demands that impact his health. He begins Ketu in December 2023, by which time he is likely to wish to step back, whether or not he is able to.

Vimshottari (Ksh)

Start Date			Age	Dashas
3/	12/	1936	-6.0	Mo
4/	12/	1946	4.0	Ma
4/	12/	1953	11.0	Ra
4/	12/	1971	29.0	Jp
5/	12/	1987	45.0	Sa
4/	12/	2006 n	64.0	Me
5/	12/	2023	81.0	Ke
5/	12/	2030	88.0	Ve
5/	12/	2050	108.0	Su
4/	12/	2056	114.0	Mo
5/	12/	2066	124.0	Ma
5/	12/	2073	131.0	Ra

Timeline 4.7

Vimshottari (Ksh)

Start Date			Age	Dashas	
4/	**12/**	**2006**	**64.0**	**Me**	**Me**
2/	5/	2009	66.4	Me	Ke
29/	4/	2010	67.4	Me	Ve
27/	2/	2013	70.3	Me	Su
4/	1/	2014	71.1	Me	Mo
5/	6/	2015	72.5	Me	Ma
1/	6/	2016	73.5	Me	Ra
20/	12/	2018	76.1	Me	Jp
27/	3/	2021 n	78.3	Me	Sa
5/	**12/**	**2023**	**81.0**	**Ke**	**Ke**
2/	5/	2024	81.4	Ke	Ve
2/	7/	2025	82.6	Ke	Su

Timeline 4.8

Chara					
Start Date			**Age**	**Dashas**	
20/	**11/**	**2018**	**76.0**	**Sag**	**Sco**
21/	6/	2019	76.6	Sag	Libr
20/	1/	2020	77.2	Sag	Virg
21/	8/	2020	77.8	Sag	Leo
22/	3/	2021	78.3	Sag	Can
21/	10/	2021	78.9	Sag	Gem
22/	5/	2022 n	79.5	Sag	Tau
21/	12/	2022	80.1	Sag	Ari
22/	7/	2023	80.7	Sag	Pis
20/	2/	2024	81.2	Sag	Aqu
20/	9/	2024	81.8	Sag	Cap
21/	4/	2025	82.4	Sag	Sag

Timeline 4.9

The Chara daśā of Sagittarius is active from November 2018 to April 2025. The sub-daśās within the Sagittarius major daśā are shown in Timeline 4.9.

I have not added a year on for his natal exalted Jupiter, as it is retrograde, although this is the traditional Parāśara approach. Not including the added year, he would have been experiencing a Sagittarius-Leo daśā during the election. This points to coming into power, with Leo being his 10th, housing Rāhu. Sagittarius has its complications. Jupiter is exalted, yet retrograde, placed in the 8th house from Sagittarius, suggesting some downfall. This was the case when his son (Jupiter rules his 5th house) was involved in a scandal during the election.

Chart 4.5 is for the day of the election itself, and the third piece to consider, the transits on the day of the election. I cast the chart for the opening of the polls at 07.00 am on November 3rd, 2020 in Washington, DC.

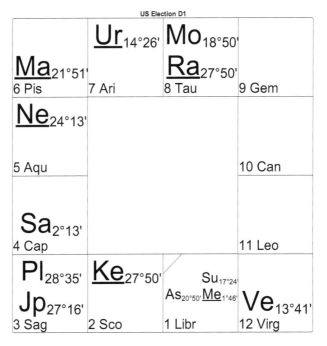

Chart 4.5

Ketu was transiting Scorpio, his 1st house, at the time of the election, where the Sun and Venus are in his natal chart. Scorpio is one sign that can experience Ketu powerfully, as it co-rules the sign along with Mars. When we add the fact that Rāhu is in Maghā, a lunar mansion associated with Ketu, we can see the theme of power more so. Rāhu exaggerates and distorts, of course. Ketu delivered the goods, yet whether he maintains his position remains to be seen. Losing something, whether power (Sun) or cognitive ability (Mercury), is suggested because of Ketu's transit to his 12th house of loss until the end of 2023. When we add this to his major Saturn daśā, this adds to the need to slow down.

Ketu highlights a strength that is not always seen in a person's chart. This is due to the lunar mansion it is placed in. Ketu is in a lunar mansion associated with Rāhu (Śatabhiṣāj), while Rāhu is in a lunar mansion associated with Ketu (Maghā). Thus, when he experiences Ketu, he also experiences Rāhu. When he experiences Rāhu, he experiences Ketu on some level, too. In other words, despite the losses Ketu inevitably brings, including his loss of cognitive function, Ketu is also powerful planet for him, activating Rāhu. But Rāhu itself is never straight forward. Once he entered Saturn dasa, it brought a steadier period for the U.S. Yet it also has shown his personal decline in such a prominent role. He may feel like stepping back from the heavy workload, even while Saturn piles it on.

Joe Biden's life is one of many losses and tragedies. He lost his first wife and a daughter in a car accident in December 1972, when he was experiencing a planetary daśā of Moon-Mars (see Timeline 4.10). The Moon is in his 6th house of accidents, in Aries, which Mars rules. Mars is in the 12th house of losses, in the sign Libra, ruled by Venus. Venus is in Scorpio, exchanging the 1st and 12th signs with Mars. This shows his experiences of losses, which would have been more acute when both Moon and Mars were active in his chart.

Vimshottari						
Start Date			Age	Dashas		
6/	9/	1942	-0.2	Ke	Jp	
12/	8/	1943	0.7	Ke	Sa	
20/	9/	1944	1.8	Ke	Me	
17/	**9/**	**1945**	**2.8**	**Ve**	**Ve**	
17/	1/	1949	6.2	Ve	Su	
17/	1/	1950	7.2	Ve	Mo	
18/	9/	1951	8.8	Ve	Ma	
17/	11/	1952	10.0	Ve	Ra	
18/	11/	1955	13.0	Ve	Jp	
19/	7/	1958	15.7	Ve	Sa	
18/	9/	1961	18.8	Ve	Me	
18/	7/	1964	21.7	Ve	Ke	
18/	**9/**	**1965**	**22.8**	**Su**	**Su**	
5/	1/	1966	23.1	Su	Mo	
7/	7/	1966	23.6	Su	Ma	
12/	11/	1966	24.0	Su	Ra	
6/	10/	1967	24.9	Su	Jp	
25/	7/	1968	25.7	Su	Sa	
7/	7/	1969	26.6	Su	Me	
13/	5/	1970	27.5	Su	Ke	
18/	9/	1970	27.8	Su	Ve	
18/	**9/**	**1971**	**28.8**	**Mo**	**Mo**	
19/	7/	1972	29.7	Mo	Ma	
17/	2/	1973	30.2	Mo	Ra	
18/	8/	1974	31.7	Mo	Jp	
18/	12/	1975	33.1	Mo	Sa	
19/	7/	1977	34.7	Mo	Me	

Timeline 4.10

The conditional planetary daśā Dvisaptatī samā applies to his birth chart (see Timeline 4.11). We can use this when the ascendant ruler is in the 7th house or the 7th house ruler is in the ascendant. Venus, his 7th house ruler, is in his 1st house, so can use this to see relationship matters for him. Dvisaptatī samā runs in the order of the weekday rulers, i.e., Sun, Moon, Mars, Mercury, Jupiter, Venus, Saturn, and Rāhu, but does not include Ketu, as Ketu is not about desire for relationships.

Dwisaptati sama

Start Date			Age	Dashas
9/	7/	1937	-5.4	Mo
10/	7/	1946	3.6	Ma
10/	7/	1955	12.6	Me
9/	7/	1964	21.6	Jp
9/	7/	1973	30.6	Ve
10/	7/	1982	39.6	Sa
10/	7/	1991	48.6	Ra
9/	7/	2000	57.6	Su
10/	7/	2009	66.6	Mo
10/	7/	2018 n	75.6	Ma
10/	7/	2027	84.6	Me
10/	7/	2036	93.6	Jp

Timeline 4.11

Jupiter's major daśā was active in these daśās, from 1964. His first marriage took place in 1966. This was within a Venus sub-daśā, i.e., Jupiter-Venus (see Timeline 4.12). Jupiter is the planet with the lowest degrees in his chart. This is called *Dara-kāraka*. The planet with the highest degree shows the individual's biggest life lessons and soul journey, the *Ātma-kāraka*, or 'soul planet', while the planet with the lowest degree shows the partner. Jupiter daśā would have shown a strong need for him to meet a partner.

Jupiter rules his 5th house of children and he did begin having children in its daśā. Yet this also confirms Jupiter's weakness when exalted, though retrograde, in Cancer, with the loss of his wife and daughter in a tragic accident in 1972 (see Timeline 4.12). This occurred in Jupiter-Mercury. Mercury is in his 12th house of loss.

Dwisaptati sama

Start Date			Age	Dashas	
9/	**7/**	**1964**	**21.6**	**Jp**	**Jp**
24/	8/	1965	22.8	Jp	Ve
9/	10/	1966	23.9	Jp	Sa
24/	11/	1967	25.0	Jp	Ra
8/	1/	1969	26.1	Jp	Su
23/	2/	1970	27.3	Jp	Mo
10/	4/	1971	28.4	Jp	Ma
25/	5/	1972	29.5	Jp	Me
9/	**7/**	**1973**	**30.6**	**Ve**	**Ve**
24/	8/	1974	31.8	Ve	Sa
9/	10/	1975	32.9	Ve	Ra
23/	11/	1976	34.0	Ve	Su

Timeline 4.12

Dwisaptati sama

Start Date			Age	Dashas	
9/	**7/**	**1973**	**30.6**	**Ve**	**Ve**
24/	8/	1974	31.8	Ve	Sa
9/	10/	1975	32.9	Ve	Ra
23/	11/	1976	34.0	Ve	Su
8/	1/	1978	35.1	Ve	Mo
23/	2/	1979	36.3	Ve	Ma
9/	4/	1980	37.4	Ve	Me
25/	5/	1981	38.5	Ve	Jp
10/	**7/**	**1982**	**39.6**	**Sa**	**Sa**
25/	8/	1983	40.8	Sa	Ra
9/	10/	1984	41.9	Sa	Su
23/	11/	1985	43.0	Sa	Mo

Timeline 4.13

He remarried within the daśā of Venus (see Timeline 4.13), in 1977, during a Venus-Sun daśā. This shows Venus' role as 7th house ruler, a straight-forward indicator for marriage. But without using this conditional planetary daśā based on the 7th house, it may be hard to spot the potential for marriage in the typical planetary daśā. The Sun is with Venus, of course. Thus, the Sun triggers Venus. In the Viṁśottarī daśā, the Sun was active from 1965. Both point to the potential of marriage.

He had finished his Venus viṁśottarī daśā by the age of 22, in 1965, but was too young to get married for most of it. Venus began when he was 2 years of age. Therefore, we must always use daśās in context. While it may not be obvious that the Sun daśā would show marriage, except because the Sun is with Venus, when we add this to the conditional daśā related to marriage, we can be assured of it.

There is another conditional daśā we can apply to his chart. Ṣaṣṭi-hāyanī repeats after 60 years and is applicable when the Sun is in the 1st house (see Timeline 4.14). This relates to power and position. This is especially the case for Joe Biden with the Sun ruling his 10th house of power and position. This is yet another sign of his coming into power after the election of November 2020.

He was coming to the end of his Sun daśā and began Mars on November 25th, 2020. While Mars hides in his 12th house in his chart, the Sun is in the most prominent 1st house. The last sub-daśā within the Sun daśā is Sun-Jupiter. This further suggests a position of power (Sun) and his good luck (Jupiter). Yet Mars' daśā, and its position in his 12th house, reflected his initial lack of visibility as a president during a global pandemic.

Mars is placed in the 3rd from his 10th house. Having a cruel planet in the 3rd house from any area of the chart is seen as helpful, as it shows someone's ability to fight for that thing. In this case, Mars in the 3rd from his 10th shows his willingness to fight for his position.

Shastihayani

Start Date			Age	Dashas	
25/	**11/**	**2020**	**78.0**	**Ma**	**Ma**
26/	7/	2022 n	79.7	Ma	Mo
27/	7/	2023	80.7	Ma	Me
26/	7/	2024	81.7	Ma	Ve
26/	7/	2025	82.7	Ma	Sa
26/	7/	2026	83.7	Ma	Ra
27/	7/	2027	84.7	Ma	Jp
26/	3/	2029	86.3	Ma	Su
25/	**11/**	**2030**	**88.0**	**Mo**	**Mo**
2/	7/	2031	88.6	Mo	Me
6/	2/	2032	89.2	Mo	Ve
13/	9/	2032	89.8	Mo	Sa

Timeline 4.14

ELIZABETH TAYLOR'S
MARRIAGES 1950 – 1991

Elizabeth Taylor was born at 02.30 a.m. on February 27th, 1932 in London, UK. Chart 4.6 shows her South Indian-style birth chart using sidereal calculations (Citrapakṣa Ayanāṁśa) and whole sign houses.

Elizabeth Taylor D1

Ra₄°₂₁' Ve₂₄°₁₆' Ur₂₄°₉' 5 Pis	6 Ari	7 Tau	Pl₂₇°₁₈' 8 Gem
Su₁₄°₂₃' Me₁₄°₃₄' Ma₈°₄₀' 4 Aqu			Jp₂₂°₁₆' 9 Can
Sa₇°₂₄' 3 Cap			Ne₁₃°₄₁' UL₂₀°₂₁' 10 Leo
2 Sag	As₂₀°₂₁' 1 Sco	Mo₂₂°₅₀' 12 Libr	Ke₄°₂₁' 11 Virg

Chart 4.6

Elizabeth Taylor is a good example to use for marriages, simply because she had so many. She married eight times, to seven different people, marrying Richard Burton on two occasions.

There are a couple of noteworthy configurations in her birth chart to suggest that multiple marriages could be a possibility. The first is that Venus, the ruler of the 7th house of relationships, is in the 5th house, with Rāhu, an indicator of excess. Venus exalts in Pisces, which shows a romantic at heart, but also most probably an idealism that would not suit staying married to any one person for very long. Rāhu shows where we obsess, even become addicted. For Elizabeth Taylor, this may show an addiction to the beginning phase of a relationship, i.e., the 5th house of romance.

Another reading of her chart from the Moon's perspective in Libra is that the Venus-Rāhu combination goes to the 6th house. Venus in the 6th can show an excessive longing for love and affection. Venus also has a death-like experience in the 6th house, which may be felt as a loss of love, or a sense that one is not getting enough. Its exalted position in Pisces may have exaggerated, even distorted, this feeling alongside Rāhu. Timeline 4.15 shows Elizabeth Taylor's planetary daśās.

She began her major Saturn daśā at 12 years of age in 1944 and had completed this period by the age of 31, in 1963, by which time she had already married on four occasions. In fact, she began receiving proposals from a young age, as soon as she began her Saturn daśā, even before she could marry legally in the UK. She first married in May 1950, during her Saturn-Mercury daśā. Why would Saturn show marriage? It may not be so obvious from a first glance that Saturn in the 3rd house would bring marriage, except that Saturn rules the 3rd and 4th houses for this Scorpio native.

Major Daśās:

Jupiter: 30 Sep 1928 - 30 Sep 1944

Saturn: 30 Sep 1944 - 30 Sep 1963

Mercury: 30 Sep 1963 – 30 Sep 1980

Ketu: 30 Sep 1980 - 01 Oct 1987

Venus: 01 Oct 1987 - 01 Oct 2007

Sun: 01 Oct 2007 - 30 Sep 2013

Moon: 30 Sep 2013 - 01 Oct 2023

Mars: 01 Oct 2023 - 01 Oct 2030

Rāhu: 01 Oct 2030 - 30 Sep 2048

Timeline 4.15

The 3rd house is the house of sex, while the 4th is the house of happiness. However, this alone wouldn't show marriage. For that, we must look at the planet with the lowest degree, the Dara-Kāraka, representing her partner. This planet is Saturn.

Rāhu and Ketu always move backwards, so we must subtract the degree at which they are from the total 30 degrees of the sign. They are at only 4 degrees and have actually moved all the way through backwards these signs, and are therefore at a high degree, the highest in fact. Rāhu, therefore, becomes the Ātma-Kāraka, the 'king of the chart'. Rāhu, as King, can show someone feeling cheated. When combined with Venus, as ruler of the 7th house, placed in the 5th house, she may have felt this in her relationships. Her 3rd husband, Michael Todd, died tragically, of whom she would later say she was her happiest with. This sense of feeling cheated out of something would have fuelled her need to quickly re-marry, which she did just over a year later, in May 1959.

Saturn-Mercury was active when she first married Conrad Hilton. We can see why Saturn would show partners, but what about Mercury? Mercury is associated with the lunar mansion Venus is in, i.e., Revatī, so it has a link to Venus and relationships. Any time a planet is active in a daśā, it will activate its lunar mansions and any planets placed therein. Here, Mercury has the potential to start marriage, especially when combined with Saturn. Saturn can often create challenges, which was certainly the case for her experience in her first marriage, which was an abusive relationship according to tabloid reports.

Another technique used in Indian astrology to see the partner, as opposed to the relationship dynamics, is to look at the 12th house. The 7th house merely shows her experience of relationships, not those with whom she would have a relationship. We calculate this from the 12th house of loss. The notion is that the marriage partner, or a meaningful relationship, is someone who you will give of yourself completely. This is actually a 12th house indication. The calculation that is used is called an *ārūḍha*, meaning 'attainment', showing the relationships she attains, based on the position of the 12th house ruler. Counting from the 12th house to the planet that rules this sign, and counting the same again, we arrive at what is called the *Upapada Lagna*, shown as UL in Leo in her chart (see Chart 4.6). Venus rules her 12th house, Libra, and is in Pisces. Counting inclusively from Libra to Pisces is a 6 count. Counting from Pisces with the same count shows the Upapada Lagna in Leo. *Upa* means 'closest to', representing the nearest and dearest, while *Lagna* is the Sanskrit word used for the ascendant, meaning 'marriage', referring to marriage between heaven and earth when she was born. In this context, marriage is fitting. This shows the first marriage partner specifically, although it shows relationships dynamics throughout life.

We can also take the Moon in her 12th whole sign house in Viśākhā and calculate her timeline beginning with the 4th lunar mansion (kṣema), which is Mūla. This means we can calculate her daśās, starting with Ketu (see Timelines 4.16 and 4.17).

She began Venus daśā when she first married. This is a clear sign of the need for marriage, as her 7th house ruler, placed in her 5th house. She was in a period of Venus-Jupiter when she first married in May 1950, with Venus in Pisces, Jupiter's sign. Jupiter in Cancer looks at Venus in Pisces as they are both in the same element.

Vimshottari (Ksh)

Start Date			Age	Dashas
30/	8/	1930	-1.5	Ke
30/	8/	1937	5.5	Ve
30/	8/	1957	25.5	Su
31/	8/	1963	31.5	Mo
30/	8/	1973	41.5	Ma
30/	8/	1980	48.5	Ra
31/	8/	1998	66.5	Jp
31/	8/	2014 n	82.5	Sa
31/	8/	2033	101.5	Me
31/	8/	2050	118.5	Ke
31/	8/	2057	125.5	Ve
31/	8/	2077	145.5	Su

Timeline 4.16

Vimshottari (Ksh)

Start Date			Age	Dashas	
30/	**8/**	**1937**	**5.5**	**Ve**	**Ve**
29/	12/	1940	8.8	Ve	Su
30/	12/	1941	9.8	Ve	Mo
31/	8/	1943	11.5	Ve	Ma
30/	10/	1944	12.7	Ve	Ra
30/	10/	1947	15.7	Ve	Jp
30/	6/	1950	18.3	Ve	Sa
30/	8/	1953	21.5	Ve	Me
30/	6/	1956	24.3	Ve	Ke
30/	**8/**	**1957**	**25.5**	**Su**	**Su**
18/	12/	1957	25.8	Su	Mo
18/	6/	1958	26.3	Su	Ma

Timeline 4.17

This would have showed her ease in getting into relationships and to marry at such a tender age. However, Venus-Saturn began the month after she married in May and would show the problems she had with her first marriage. Venus-Saturn daśās are problematic anyway, as the impulse to do what one wants (Venus) can conflict with what is one's commitments (Saturn). Her first marriage lasted only until January 1951, a few months after they wed.

Looking at her Chara sign-based daśās (see Timelines 4.18 and 4.19), we can see the correlation and timing for her first marriage to Conrad Hilton in May 1950, when Leo was active. In fact, Leo was active a couple of years prior to her first marriage, when she was only 16 and not legally allowed to marry, so we must also place her daśās in context. It's interesting to note that although this was the case, she actually received a marriage proposal as soon as she began the Leo daśā at 16, from a suitor who wished to marry her as soon as she turned 18. That Saturn was also active from an early age, considering Saturn's role, makes this more relevant.

In the Chara daśā (see Timeline 4.19), Leo-Pisces was active when she first married in May 1950. However, there is a controversy and discrepancy I should highlight once again. If you were to put in the rule given by Parāśara, that an exalted planet adds on one year, it would add two years; one for her exalted Venus, and one for her exalted Jupiter.

Chara

Start Date			Age	Dashas
27/	2/	1932	-0.0	Sco
26/	2/	1935	3.0	Libr
27/	2/	1940	8.0	Virg
26/	2/	1947	15.0	Leo
26/	2/	1953	21.0	Can
26/	2/	1962	30.0	Gem
26/	2/	1970	38.0	Tau
27/	2/	1980	48.0	Ari
26/	2/	1990	58.0	Pis
27/	2/	1998	66.0	Aqu
26/	2/	2009	77.0	Cap
26/	2/	2021 n	89.0	Sag

Timeline 4.18

Chara

Start Date			Age	Dashas	
26/	**2/**	**1947**	**15.0**	**Leo**	**Virg**
28/	8/	1947	15.5	Leo	Libr
27/	2/	1948	16.0	Leo	Sco
27/	8/	1948	16.5	Leo	Sag
26/	2/	1949	17.0	Leo	Cap
28/	8/	1949	17.5	Leo	Aqu
26/	2/	1950	18.0	Leo	Pis
28/	8/	1950	18.5	Leo	Ari
26/	2/	1951	19.0	Leo	Tau
28/	8/	1951	19.5	Leo	Gem
27/	2/	1952	20.0	Leo	Can
27/	8/	1952	20.5	Leo	Leo

Timeline 4.19

According to this rule, she would have been in a daśā of Leo-Libra in May 1950. Pisces, as we have seen earlier, is an obvious sign of marriage, considering that Venus, the 7th ruler, is there. Yet Venus also rules Libra, so we could make an argument for Libra as well. I only highlight this as an alternative approach, as many astrologers use the added year for exalted planets.

Elizabeth Taylor's birth chart has many marriage possibilities because of Venus' exaltation and conjunction with Rāhu in the 5th, but also because of the role of the UL in Leo, as well as Saturn's role as the planet with the lowest degree. The sign Cancer offers yet more opportunity for marriage, as it houses Jupiter, the 5th house ruler, the ruler of where Venus is in Pisces. She experienced her Cancer daśā throughout the 1950s (see Timeline 4.20), during which she was married on four occasions.

Her second marriage to Michael Wilding took place in February 1952, and a third marriage to Michael Todd, in February 1957. Michael Todd died tragically in a plane crash (note: Rāhu rules aviation) in March 1958, when she was concurrently experiencing her Saturn-Mars daśā. Mars could have been challenging for marriage, not least because it rules her 6th house of celibacy, but is in her 4th house, aspecting her 7th house. She married Eddie Fisher soon after her loss, in May 1959, in a Saturn-Rāhu daśā, which again highlights Rāhu's role.

Chara

Start Date			Age	Dashas	
26/	**2/**	**1953**	**21.0**	**Can**	**Gem**
27/	11/	1953	21.8	Can	Tau
28/	8/	1954	22.5	Can	Ari
29/	5/	1955	23.2	Can	Pis
27/	2/	1956	24.0	Can	Aqu
27/	11/	1956	24.8	Can	Cap
28/	8/	1957	25.5	Can	Sag
29/	5/	1958	26.2	Can	Sco
27/	2/	1959	27.0	Can	Libr
27/	11/	1959	27.8	Can	Virg
27/	8/	1960	28.5	Can	Leo
28/	5/	1961	29.2	Can	Can

Timeline 4.20

Chara

Start Date			Age	Dashas	
26/	**2/**	**1962**	**30.0**	**Gem**	**Tau**
28/	10/	1962	30.7	Gem	Ari
28/	6/	1963	31.3	Gem	Pis
27/	2/	1964	32.0	Gem	Aqu
27/	10/	1964	32.7	Gem	Cap
28/	6/	1965	33.3	Gem	Sag
26/	2/	1966	34.0	Gem	Sco
28/	10/	1966	34.7	Gem	Libr
28/	6/	1967	35.3	Gem	Virg
27/	2/	1968	36.0	Gem	Leo
27/	10/	1968	36.7	Gem	Can
28/	6/	1969	37.3	Gem	Gem

Timeline 4.21

			Chara		
Start Date			**Age**	**Dashas**	
26/	**2/**	**1970**	**38.0**	**Tau**	**Ari**
28/	12/	1970	38.8	Tau	Pis
28/	10/	1971	39.7	Tau	Aqu
28/	8/	1972	40.5	Tau	Cap
28/	6/	1973	41.3	Tau	Sag
28/	4/	1974	42.2	Tau	Sco
27/	2/	1975	43.0	Tau	Libr
28/	12/	1975	43.8	Tau	Virg
27/	10/	1976	44.7	Tau	Leo
28/	8/	1977	45.5	Tau	Can
28/	6/	1978	46.3	Tau	Gem
29/	4/	1979	47.2	Tau	Tau

Timeline 4.22

She married Richard Burton twice, first in 1964 and again in 1975. Gemini was active for the first wedding, while Taurus, her 7th house, was active for the second (see Timelines 4.21 and 4.22). Gemini would pose problems in her relationship with Burton, as the 8th house represents obstacles. Saturn-Mercury would have posed problems for the very beginning of her married life. This is not only because Mercury rules the 8th house, which challenges relationships, but because Mercury is in the 4th house. Mercury in the 4th is a maraṇa position, a 'death-like' experience for the planet, one which resulted in her suffering at the hands of an abusive first husband in Saturn-Mercury, as well as issues with addiction (8th house signification) when married to Richard Burton in her major Mercury period.

She was once quoted as saying, "My troubles all started because I have a woman's body and a child's emotions." This shows up as Mercury in the 4th house, while Mercury was active in the planetary daśās from 1963 to 1980, and Gemini was also active in the sign-based daśās from 1962 until 1970. Taurus would have been better for her relationships as the 7th house, active in her chart for most of the 1970s.

She married twice more after leaving Burton, first to John Warner in 1976, and one last time, to Larry Fortensky in 1991, when she was finishing her Aries daśā and beginning her Pisces daśā (see Timelines 4.23 and 4.24). Interestingly, the longest she stayed unmarried was during the 1980s, which was her Aries years. Aries for Scorpio rising is the 6th house of celibacy. This was also a Ketu major daśā, which often shows a need to renounce something.

Pisces was active in the 1990s (see Timeline 4.24), which shows another marriage, with Venus here in her birth chart. This was also her major Venus daśā. Venus began in 1987 but didn't show another marriage until 1991, when her Pisces daśā began. She was married for one last time in October 1991, and until October 1996.

Chara

Start Date			Age	Dashas	
27/	**2/**	**1980**	**48.0**	**Ari**	**Tau**
27/	12/	1980	48.8	Ari	Gem
28/	10/	1981	49.7	Ari	Can
28/	8/	1982	50.5	Ari	Leo
28/	6/	1983	51.3	Ari	Virg
28/	4/	1984	52.2	Ari	Libr
26/	2/	1985	53.0	Ari	Sco
28/	12/	1985	53.8	Ari	Sag
28/	10/	1986	54.7	Ari	Cap
28/	8/	1987	55.5	Ari	Aqu
28/	6/	1988	56.3	Ari	Pis
28/	4/	1989	57.2	Ari	Ari

Timeline 4.23

Chara

Start Date			Age	Dashas	
26/	**2/**	**1990**	**58.0**	**Pis**	**Ari**
28/	10/	1990	58.7	Pis	Tau
29/	6/	1991	59.3	Pis	Gem
27/	2/	1992	60.0	Pis	Can
27/	10/	1992	60.7	Pis	Leo
28/	6/	1993	61.3	Pis	Virg
26/	2/	1994	62.0	Pis	Libr
28/	10/	1994	62.7	Pis	Sco
29/	6/	1995	63.3	Pis	Sag
27/	2/	1996	64.0	Pis	Cap
28/	10/	1996	64.7	Pis	Aqu
28/	6/	1997	65.3	Pis	Pis

Timeline 4.24

Aum Tat Sat

SANSKRIT GLOSSARY

Abhijit, intercalary lunar mansion; 'great victory'; northern star Vega; used for auspicious timing

Ādhāna, 8th star; 8th in a sequence of daśās; 'accepting'; 'receiving'

Aditi, mother of the Adityas; 'infinite'; ruler of Punarvasu

Agni, god of fire; ruler of Kṛttikā

Ahirbudhnya, god of the deep sea; the cosmic ocean; ruler of Uttara Bhādrapada

Ajaikapada, a form of Śiva standing on one leg in penance; ruler of Pūrva Bhādrapada; 'one-footed goat'

Amātya-kāraka, planet with the second highest degree regardless of sign; 'advisor'; 'minister'

Anurādhā, lunar mansion between 3° 20' and 16° 40' sidereal Scorpio; 'under Radha'

Āpas, goddess of water; ruler of Pūrvāṣāḍha

Argalā, technique showing how planets, signs and houses influence each other; 'bolted down'

Ārdrā, lunar mansion between 6° 40' and 20° 00' sidereal Gemini; 'moist'

Artha, wealth creation; one of the four main aims of life.

Ārūḍha: tangible results of a sign based on the position of its ruling planet; 'attainment'

Aryaman, god of customs and agreements; ruler of Uttara Phālguṇī

Āśleṣa, lunar mansion between 16° 40' and 30° 00' sidereal Cancer; 'clinging'

Aṣṭakavarga, scoring system using 7 planets and ascendant to ascertain strength of planets and houses; '8 divisions'

Aṣṭottarī, conditional daśā used when Rāhu is in the 4th, 5th, 7th, 9th, or 10th house from ruler of ascendant, *and* Night birth during waxing Moon, or Day birth during waning Moon

Aśvinī, lunar mansion between 0° 00' and 13° 20' sidereal Aries; 'horse woman'

Aśvinī-Kumāra, the horse-headed twin physicians to the Vedic gods; rulers of Aśvinī

Ātma-kāraka, planet with highest degree regardless of sign; 'significator of self'; 'soul significator'

Atimitra, 9th star; 9th in a sequence of daśās; 'great friend'

Āyana, the four main aims in life: *dharma*, *artha*, *kāma*, and *mokṣa*; 'direction'

Ayanāṁśa, longitudinal difference between tropical and sidereal calculations

Bādhaka, a sign and planet that creates blocks; 'obstruction'

Bhaga, god of good fortune; ruler of Pūrva Phālguṇī

Bharaṇī, lunar mansion between 13° 20' and 26° 40' sidereal Aries; 'she who bears'

Bhāva, house; 'state'; 'condition'

Bhukti, planetary sub-daśās; 'ripened'; 'to eat'

Bṛhaspati, priest of the gods, ruler of Puṣya

Cakra, in reference to a horoscope; 'wheel'

Calit, movable house divisions based on location

Chara, progressed signs; 'movable'

Charakāraka, 7 and 8 planet scheme used to delineate certain people based on the planets' degrees; 'moving significators'

Chaturaśitī, conditional daśā used when 10th house ruler is in the 10th house

Citrā, lunar mansion between 23° 20' sidereal Virgo and 6° 40' sidereal Libra; 'brilliant'

Citrapakṣa, ayanāṁśa placing Spica at 0° Libra to calculate sidereal longitudes

Dara-kāraka, planet with the lowest degree regardless of sign; 'significator of spouse'

Daśā, planetary or sign-based period; 'circumstance'

Dhaniṣṭhā, lunar mansion between 23° 20' sidereal Capricorn and 6° 40' sidereal Aquarius; 'wealthy'

Dharma, one of the four main aims in life; 'purpose'

Dṛṣṭi, planetary or sign-based aspects; 'sight'

Dvisaptatī Samā, conditional daśā used when ascendant ruler is in 7th house or 7th house ruler is in ascendant

Gochāra, movement of planets through the division of the ecliptic

Grahas, the nine 'graspers': the five visible planets, Sun, Moon and two lunar nodes

Guṇas, three underlying 'impulses' or 'qualities' of Vedic thought

Hasta, lunar mansion between 10° 00' and 23° 20' sidereal Virgo; 'hand'

Indra, chief of the gods; ruler of Jyeṣṭhā
Indrāgni, god ruling Viśākhā; a combination of Indra and Agni

Janma, 1st star; 1st in a sequence of daśās; 'start'; referring to the Moon's position and first daśā
Jyeṣṭhā, lunar mansion between 16° 40' and 30° 00' sidereal Scorpio: 'eldest'

Kāma, one of the four main aims in life; 'pleasure'
Ketu, south node of the Moon; 'flag'
Kṛttikā, lunar mansion between 26° 40' sidereal Aries and 10° 00' sidereal Taurus; 'to cut'
Kṣema, 4th star; 4th in a sequence of daśās; 'safe'; 'secure'
Krūra, 'cruel'

Lagna, 1st whole sign house or ascendant; 'marriage'; referring to the marriage between heaven and earth on the horizon

Mahādaśā, major planetary or sign-based daśā; 'great period'
Mahāpuruṣa, yoga formed when visible planets are in an angle house within their own or exalted sign; 'great soul'
Maghā, lunar mansion between 00° 00' and 13° 20' sidereal Leo; 'mighty'
Mantra, sacred sounds to 'protect the mind'
Mitra, 8th star; 8th in a sequence of daśās; 'friend'
Mokṣa, one of the four main aims in life; 'liberation'

Mṛgaśirṣā, lunar mansion between 23° 20' sideral Taurus and 6° 40' sidereal Gemini; 'deer head'

Mūla, lunar mansion between 00° 00' and 13° 20' sidereal Sagittarius; 'root'

Nakṣatras, the 27 lunar mansions or constellations; 13° 20' divisions of the ecliptic; 'to arrive at'

Nārāyaṇa, sign-based daśā; life direction

Nirṛti, goddess of death; ruler of Mūla

Pada, 3° 20' minutes of arc; 'step'

Pitṛs, ruler of Maghā; 'forefathers'

Prajāpati, ruler of Rohiṇī; 'god of creation'

Pratyarī, 5th star; 5th in a sequence of daśās; 'well-matched opponent'

Praveśa, referring to daśā praveśa and the beginning of a new period; 'beginning'; 'entrance'

Punarvasu, lunar mansion between 20° 00' sidereal Gemini and 3° 20' sidereal Cancer; 'light again'

Pūrva Bhādrapada, lunar mansion between 20° 00' sidereal Aquarius and 3° 20' sidereal Pisces; 'former auspicious steps or feet'

Pūrva Phālguṇī, lunar mansion between 13° 20' and 26° 40' sidereal Leo; 'former fruitful'

Pūrvāṣāḍha, lunar mansion between 13° 20' and 26° 40' sidereal Sagittarius; 'former invincible'

Pūṣan, ruler of Revatī; 'nourisher'

Puṣya, lunar mansion between 3° 20' and 16° 40' sidereal Cancer; 'flowering'

Rāhu, north node of the Moon

Rajas, one of the three guṇas; 'agitation'

Rāśi, 30-degree divisions of the ecliptic; 'Sun signs'

Revatī, lunar mansion between 16° 40' and 30° 00' sidereal Pisces; 'abundant'

Rohiṇī, lunar mansion between 10° 00' and 23° 20' sidereal Taurus; 'red lady'

Rudra, ruler of Ārdrā; 'howler'

Sādhaka, 6th star; 6th in a sequence of daśās; 'skills'

Sampat, 2nd star; 2nd in a sequence of daśās; 'gain'

Sandhi, referring to a junction between two daśās; also junction between two signs; , 'junction'

Sannyasa, (sometimes spelled saṃnyāsa), 'renunciate'

Sarpas, rulers of Āśleṣa; 'serpents'

Ṣaṣṭi-hāyanī, conditional daśā, used when Sun is in ascendant

Śatabhiṣaj, lunar mansion between 6° 40' and 20° 00' sidereal Aquarius; '100 healers'

Sattva, one of the three guṇas; 'harmony'

Saumya, 'kind'

Savitṛ, Sun deity; ruler of Hasta

Siddi, 'power'; 'skill'

Śiva, 'god of destruction'

Śiva Lingam, Śiva's 'wand of light'

Soma, Moon god; ruler of Mṛgaśirṣā; 'elixir'

Śravaṇa, lunar mansion between 10° 00' and 23° 20' sidereal Capricorn; 'listening'

Svātī, lunar mansion between 6° 40' and 20° 00' sidereal Libra; 'individuality'

Tamas, one of the three guṇas; 'inertia'

Upapada, special ascendant to see spouse; 'close to'
Upasana, 'worship'
Utpanna, 5th star; 5th in a sequence of daśās; 'arisen'; 'produced'
Uttara Bhādrapada, lunar mansion between 3° 20' and 16° 40' sidereal Pisces; 'latter auspicious steps'
Uttara Phālguṇī, lunar mansion between 26° 40' sidereal Leo and 10° 00' sidereal Virgo; 'latter fruitful'
Uttarāṣāḍha, lunar mansion between 26° 40' sidereal Sagittarius and 10° 00' sidereal Capricorn; 'latter invincible'

Vadha, 7th star; 7th in a sequence of daśās; 'deadly'
Vajravadha: 'death by thunderbolt'
Varuṇa, god of the sea; ruler of Śatabhiṣāj
Vasus, rulers of Dhaniṣṭhā; 'eight elemental demigods'
Vāyu, ruler of Svātī; 'wind'
Vipaṭa: 3rd star; 3rd in a sequence of daśās; 'disagreement'
Viśākhā, lunar mansion between 20° 00' sidereal Libra and 3° 20' sidereal Scorpio; 'decisive'
Viṣṇu, ruler of Śravaṇa; 'god of sustenance'
Viśvadevas, gods of intellectual development; rulers of Uttarāṣāḍha
Viśvakarmā, ruler of Citrā; 'celestial architect'

Yama, god of death; god of dharma; ruler of Bharaṇī; 'discipline'
Vidyā, 'knowledge'; 'science'

Yoga, 'union'; 'combination', with reference to a combination of planets

Yogi, planet ruling auspicious point in the horoscope, calculated by combining the Sun's and Moon's degrees

Yoni, symbol of Bharaṇī lunar mansion; 'vulva'

APPENDIX

Ketu-Ketu Sub-Sub-Daśās (4 months, 27 days)
1) Ketu-Ketu-Ketu (8.575 days)
2) Ketu-Ketu-Venus (24.5 days)
3) Ketu-Ketu-Sun (7.35 days)
4) Ketu-Ketu-Moon (12.25 days)
5) Ketu-Ketu-Mars (8.575 days)
6) Ketu-Ketu-Rāhu (22.05 days)
7) Ketu-Ketu-Jupiter (19.6 days)
8) Ketu-Ketu-Saturn (23.275 days)
9) Ketu-Ketu-Mercury (20.825 days)

Ketu-Venus Sub-Sub-Daśās (1 year, 2 months)
1) Ketu-Venus-Venus (2 months, 10 days)
2) Ketu-Venus-Sun (21 days)
3) Ketu-Venus-Moon (I month, 5 days)
4) Ketu-Venus-Mars (24.5 days)
5) Ketu-Venus-Rāhu (2 months, 3 days)
6) Ketu-Venus-Jupiter (1 month, 26 days)
7) Ketu-Venus-Saturn (2 months, 6.5 days)
8) Ketu-Venus-Mercury (1 month, 29.5 days)
9) Ketu-Venus-Ketu (24.5 days)

Ketu-Sun Sub-Sub-Daśās (4 months, 6 days)
1) Ketu-Sun-Sun (6.3 days)
2) Ketu-Sun-Moon (10.5 days)
3) Ketu-Sun-Mars (7.35 days)
4) Ketu-Sun-Rāhu (18.9 days)
5) Ketu-Sun-Jupiter (16.8 days)
6) Ketu-Sun-Saturn (19.95 days)
7) Ketu-Sun-Mercury (17.85 days)
8) Ketu-Sun-Ketu (7.35 days)
9) Ketu-Sun-Venus (21 days)

Ketu-Moon Sub-Sub-Daśās (7 months)

1) Ketu-Moon-Moon (17.5 days)
2) Ketu-Moon-Mars (12.25 days)
3) Ketu-Moon-Rāhu (1 month, 1.5 days)
4) Ketu-Moon-Jupiter (28 days)
5) Ketu-Moon-Saturn (1 month, 3.25 days)
6) Ketu-Moon-Mercury (29.75 days)
7) Ketu-Moon-Ketu (12.25 days)
8) Ketu-Moon-Venus (1 month, 5 days)
9) Ketu-Moon-Sun (10.5 days)

Ketu-Mars Sub-Sub-Daśās (4 months, 27 days)

1) Ketu-Mars-Mars (8.575 days)
2) Ketu-Mars-Rāhu (22.05 days)
3) Ketu-Mars-Jupiter (19.6 days)
4) Ketu-Mars-Saturn (23.275 days)
5) Ketu-Mars-Mercury (20.825 days)
6) Ketu-Mars-Ketu (8.575 days)
7) Ketu-Mars-Venus (24.5 days)
8) Ketu-Mars-Sun (7.35 days)
9) Ketu-Mars-Moon (12.25 days)

Ketu-Rāhu Sub-Sub-Daśās (1 year, 18 days)

1) Ketu-Rāhu-Rāhu (1 month, 26.7 days)
2) Ketu-Rāhu-Jupiter (1 month, 20.4 days)
3) Ketu-Rāhu-Saturn (1 month, 29.85 days)
4) Ketu-Rāhu-Mercury (1 months, 23.55 days)
5) Ketu-Rāhu-Ketu (22.05 days)
6) Ketu-Rāhu-Venus (2 months, 3 days)
7) Ketu-Rāhu-Sun (18.9 days)
8) Ketu-Rāhu-Moon (1 month, 1.5 days)
9) Ketu-Rāhu-Mars (22.05 days)

Ketu-Jupiter Sub-Sub-Daśās (11 months, 6 days)

1) Ketu-Jupiter-Jupiter (1 month, 14.8 days)
2) Ketu-Jupiter-Saturn (1 month, 23.2 days)
3) Ketu-Jupiter-Mercury (1 month, 17.6 days)

4) Ketu-Jupiter-Ketu (19.6 days)
5) Ketu-Jupiter-Venus (1 month, 26 days)
6) Ketu-Jupiter-Sun (16.8 days)
7) Ketu-Jupiter-Moon (28 days)
8) Ketu-Jupiter-Mars (19.6 days)
9) Ketu-Jupiter-Rāhu (1 month, 20.4 days)

Ketu-Saturn Sub-Sub-Daśās (1 year, 1 month, 9 days)
1) Ketu-Saturn-Saturn (2 months, 3.175 days)
2) Ketu-Saturn-Mercury (1 month, 26.525 days)
3) Ketu-Saturn-Ketu (23.275 days)
4) Ketu-Saturn-Venus (2 months, 6.5 days)
5) Ketu-Saturn-Sun (19.95 days)
6) Ketu-Saturn-Moon (1 month, 3.25 days)
7) Ketu-Saturn-Mars (23.275 days)
8) Ketu-Saturn-Rāhu (1 month, 29.85 days)
9) Ketu-Saturn-Jupiter (1 month, 23.2 days)

Ketu-Mercury Sub-Sub-Daśās (11 months, 27 days)
1) Ketu-Mercury-Mercury (1 month, 20.575 days)
2) Ketu-Mercury-Ketu (20.825 days)
3) Ketu-Mercury-Venus (1 month, 29.5 days)
4) Ketu-Mercury-Sun (17.85 days)
5) Ketu-Mercury-Moon (29.75 days)
6) Ketu-Mercury-Mars (20.825 days)
7) Ketu-Mercury-Rāhu (1 month, 23.55 days)
8) Ketu-Mercury-Jupiter (1 month, 17.6 days)
9) Ketu-Mercury-Saturn (1 month, 26.525 days)

Venus-Venus Sub-Sub-Daśās (3 years, 4 months)
1) Venus-Venus-Venus (6 months, 20 days)
2) Venus-Venus-Sun (2 months)
3) Venus-Venus-Moon (3 months, 10 days)
4) Venus-Venus-Mars (2 months, 10 days)
5) Venus-Venus-Rāhu (6 months)
6) Venus-Venus-Jupiter (5 months, 10 days)
7) Venus-Venus-Saturn (6 months, 10 days)

8) Venus-Venus-Mercury (5 months, 20 days)
9) Venus-Venus-Ketu (2 months, 10 days)

Venus-Sun Sub-Sub-Daśās (1 year)
1) Venus-Sun-Sun (18 days)
2) Venus-Sun-Moon (1 months)
3) Venus-Sun-Mars (21 days)
4) Venus-Sun-Rāhu (1 months, 24 days)
5) Venus-Sun-Jupiter (1 month, 18 days)
6) Venus-Sun-Saturn (1 month, 27 days)
7) Venus-Sun-Mercury (1 month, 21 days)
8) Venus-Sun-Ketu (21 days)
9) Venus-Sun-Venus (2 months)

Venus-Moon Sub-Sub-Daśās (1 year, 8 months)
1) Venus-Moon-Moon (1 month, 20 days)
2) Venus-Moon-Mars (1 month, 5 days)
3) Venus-Moon-Rāhu (3 months)
4) Venus-Moon-Jupiter (2 months, 20 days)
5) Venus-Moon-Saturn (3 months, 5 days)
6) Venus-Moon-Mercury (2 months, 25 days)
7) Venus-Moon-Ketu (1 month, 5 days)
8) Venus-Moon-Venus (3 months, 10 days)
9) Venus-Moon-Sun (1 month)

Venus-Mars Sub-Sub-Daśās (1 year, 2 months)
1) Venus-Mars-Mars (24.5 days)
2) Venus-Mars-Rāhu (2 months, 3 days)
3) Venus-Mars-Jupiter (1 month, 26 days)
4) Venus-Mars-Saturn (2 months, 6.5 days)
5) Venus-Mars-Mercury (1 month, 29.5 days)
6) Venus-Mars-Ketu (24.5 days)
7) Venus-Mars-Venus (2 months, 10 days)
8) Venus-Mars-Sun (21 days)
9) Venus-Mars-Moon (1 month, 5 days)

Venus-Rāhu Sub-Sub-Daśās (3 years)
1) Venus-Rāhu-Rāhu (5 months, 12 days)
2) Venus-Rāhu-Jupiter (4 months, 24 days)
3) Venus-Rāhu-Saturn (5 months, 21 days)
4) Venus-Rāhu-Mercury (5 months, 3 days)
5) Venus-Rāhu-Ketu (2 months, 3 days)
6) Venus-Rāhu-Venus (6 months)
7) Venus-Rāhu-Sun (1 month, 24 days)
8) Venus-Rāhu-Moon (3 months)
9) Venus-Rāhu-Mars (2 months, 3 days)

Venus-Jupiter Sub-Sub-Daśās (2 years, 8 months)
1) Venus-Jupiter-Jupiter (4 months, 8 days)
2) Venus-Jupiter-Saturn (5 months, 2 days)
3) Venus-Jupiter-Mercury (4 months, 16 days)
4) Venus-Jupiter-Ketu (1 month, 26 days)
5) Venus-Jupiter-Venus (5 months, 10 days)
6) Venus-Jupiter-Sun (1 month, 18 days)
7) Venus-Jupiter-Moon (2 months, 20 days)
8) Venus-Jupiter-Mars (1 month, 26 days)
9) Venus-Jupiter-Rāhu (4 months, 24 days)

Venus-Saturn Sub-Sub-Daśās (3 years, 2 months)
1) Venus-Saturn-Saturn (6 months, 0.5 days)
2) Venus-Saturn-Mercury (5 months, 11.5 days)
3) Venus-Saturn-Ketu (2 months, 6.5 days)
4) Venus-Saturn-Venus (6 months, 10 days)
5) Venus-Saturn-Sun (1 month, 27 days)
6) Venus-Saturn-Moon (3 months, 5 days)
7) Venus-Saturn-Mars (2 months, 6.5 days)
8) Venus-Saturn-Rāhu (5 months, 21 days)
9) Venus-Saturn-Jupiter (5 months, 2 days)

Venus-Mercury Sub-Sub-Daśās (2 years, 10 months)
1) Venus-Mercury-Mercury (4 months, 24.5 days)
2) Venus-Mercury-Ketu (1 month, 29.5 days)
3) Venus-Mercury-Venus (5 months, 20 days)

4) Venus-Mercury-Sun (1 month, 21 days)
5) Venus-Mercury-Moon (2 months, 25 days)
6) Venus-Mercury-Mars (1 month, 29.5 days)
7) Venus-Mercury-Rāhu (5 months, 3 days)
8) Venus-Mercury-Jupiter (4 months, 16 days)
9) Venus-Mercury-Saturn (5 months, 11.5 days)

Venus-Ketu Sub-Sub-Daśās (1 year, 2 months)
1) Venus-Ketu-Ketu (24.5 days)
2) Venus-Ketu-Venus (2 months, 10 days)
3) Venus-Ketu-Sun (21 days)
4) Venus-Ketu-Moon (1 month, 5 days)
5) Venus-Ketu-Mars (24.5 days)
6) Venus-Ketu-Rāhu (2 months, 3 days)
7) Venus-Ketu-Jupiter (1 month, 26 days)
8) Venus-Ketu-Saturn (2 months, 6.5 days)
9) Venus-Ketu-Mercury (1 month, 29.5 days)

Sun-Sun Sub-Sub-Daśās (3 months, 18 days)
1) Sun-Sun-Sun (5.4 days)
2) Sun-Sun-Moon (9 days)
3) Sun-Sun-Mars (6.3 days)
4) Sun-Sun-Rāhu (16.2 days)
5) Sun-Sun-Jupiter (14.4 days)
6) Sun-Sun-Saturn (17.1 days)
7) Sun-Sun-Mercury (15.3 days)
8) Sun-Sun-Ketu (6.3 days)
9) Sun-Sun-Venus (18 days)

Sun-Moon Sub-Sub-Daśās (6 months)
1) Sun-Moon-Moon (15 days)
2) Sun-Moon-Mars (10.5 days)
3) Sun-Moon-Rāhu (27 days)
4) Sun-Moon-Jupiter (24 days)
5) Sun-Moon-Saturn (28.5 days)
6) Sun-Moon-Mercury (25.5 days)
7) Sun-Moon-Ketu (10.5 days)

8) Sun-Moon-Venus (1 month)
9) Sun-Moon-Sun (9 days)

Sun-Mars Sub-Sub-Daśās (4 months, 6 days)
1) Sun-Mars-Mars (7.35 days)
2) Sun-Mars-Rāhu (18.9 days)
3) Sun-Mars-Jupiter (16.8 days)
4) Sun-Mars-Saturn (19.95 days)
5) Sun-Mars-Mercury (17.85 days)
6) Sun-Mars-Ketu (7.35 days)
7) Sun-Mars-Venus (21 days)
8) Sun-Mars-Sun (6.3 days)
9) Sun-Mars-Moon (10.5 days)

Sun-Rāhu Sub-Sub-Daśās (10 months, 28 days)
1) Sun-Rāhu-Rāhu (1 month, 18.6 days)
2) Sun-Rāhu-Jupiter (1 month, 13.2 days)
3) Sun-Rāhu-Saturn (1 month, 21.3 days)
4) Sun-Rāhu-Mercury (1 month, 15.9 days)
5) Sun-Rāhu-Ketu (18.9 days)
6) Sun-Rāhu-Venus (1 month, 24 days)
7) Sun-Rāhu-Sun (16.2 days)
8) Sun-Rāhu-Moon (27 days)
9) Sun-Rāhu-Mars (18.9 days)

Sun-Jupiter Sub-Sub-Daśās (9 months, 18 days)
1) Sun-Jupiter-Jupiter (1 month, 8.4 days)
2) Sun-Jupiter-Saturn (1 month, 15.6 days)
3) Sun-Jupiter-Mercury (1 month, 10.8 days)
4) Sun-Jupiter-Ketu (16.8 days)
5) Sun-Jupiter-Venus (1 month, 18 days)
6) Sun-Jupiter-Sun (14.4 days)
7) Sun-Jupiter-Moon (24 days)
8) Sun-Jupiter-Mars (16.8 days)
9) Sun-Jupiter-Rāhu (1 month, 13.2 days)

Sun-Saturn Sub-Sub-Daśās (11 months, 12 days)
1) Sun-Saturn-Saturn (1 month, 24.15 days)
2) Sun-Saturn-Mercury (1 month, 18.45 days)
3) Sun-Saturn-Ketu (19.95 days)
4) Sun-Saturn-Venus (1 month, 27 days)
5) Sun-Saturn-Sun (17.1 days)
6) Sun-Saturn-Moon (28.5 days)
7) Sun-Saturn-Mars (19.95 days)
8) Sun-Saturn-Rāhu (1 month, 21.3 days)
9) Sun-Saturn-Jupiter (1 month, 15.6 days)

Sun-Mercury Sub-Sub-Daśās (10 months, 6 days)
1) Sun-Mercury-Mercury (1 month, 13.35 days)
2) Sun-Mercury-Ketu (17.85 days)
3) Sun-Mercury-Venus (1 month, 21 days)
4) Sun-Mercury-Sun (15.3 days)
5) Sun-Mercury-Moon (25.5 days)
6) Sun-Mercury-Mars (17.85 days)
7) Sun-Mercury-Rāhu (1 month, 15.9 days)
8) Sun-Mercury-Jupiter (1 month, 10.8 days)
9) Sun-Mercury-Saturn (1 month, 18.45 days)

Sun-Ketu Sub-Sub-Daśās (4 months, 6 days)
1) Sun-Ketu-Ketu (7.35 days)
2) Sun-Ketu-Venus (21 days)
3) Sun-Ketu-Sun (6.3 days)
4) Sun-Ketu-Moon (10.5 days)
5) Sun-Ketu-Mars (7.35 days)
6) Sun-Ketu-Rāhu (18.9 days)
7) Sun-Ketu-Jupiter (16.8 days)
8) Sun-Ketu-Saturn (19.95 days)
9) Sun-Ketu-Mercury (17.85 days)

Sun-Venus Sub-Sub-Daśās (1 year)
1) Sun-Venus-Venus (2 months)
2) Sun-Venus-Sun (18 days)
3) Sun-Venus-Moon (1 month)

4) Sun-Venus-Mars (21 days)
5) Sun-Venus-Rāhu (1 month, 24 days)
6) Sun-Venus-Jupiter (1 month, 18 days)
7) Sun-Venus-Saturn (1 month, 27 days)
8) Sun-Venus-Mercury (1 month, 21 days)
9) Sun-Venus-Ketu (21 days)

Moon-Moon Sub-Sub-Daśās (10 months)
1) Moon-Moon-Moon (25 days)
2) Moon-Moon-Mars (17.5 days)
3) Moon-Moon-Rāhu (1 month, 15 days)
4) Moon-Moon-Jupiter (1 month, 10 days)
5) Moon-Moon-Saturn (1 month, 17.5 days)
6) Moon-Moon-Mercury (1 month, 12.5 days)
7) Moon-Moon-Ketu (17.5 days)
8) Moon-Moon-Venus (1 month, 20 days)
9) Moon-Moon-Sun (15 days)

Moon-Mars Sub-Sub-Daśās (7 months)
1) Moon-Mars-Mars (12.25 days)
2) Moon-Mars-Rāhu (1 month, 1.5 days)
3) Moon-Mars-Jupiter (28 days)
4) Moon-Mars-Saturn (1 month, 3.25 days)
5) Moon-Mars-Mercury (29.75 days)
6) Moon-Mars-Ketu (12.25 days)
7) Moon-Mars-Venus (1 month, 5 days)
8) Moon-Mars-Sun (10.5 days)
9) Moon-Mars-Moon (17.5 days)

Moon-Rāhu Sub-Sub-Daśās (1 years, 6 months)
1) Moon-Rāhu-Rāhu (2 months, 21 days)
2) Moon-Rāhu-Jupiter (2 months, 12 days)
3) Moon-Rāhu-Saturn (2 months, 25.5 days)
4) Moon-Rāhu-Mercury (2 months, 16.5 days)
5) Moon-Rāhu-Ketu (1 month, 1.5 days)
6) Moon-Rāhu-Venus (3 months)
7) Moon-Rāhu-Sun (27 days)

8) Moon-Rāhu-Moon (1 month, 15 days)

9) Moon-Rāhu-Mars (1 month, 1.5 days)

Moon-Jupiter Sub-Sub-Daśās (1 year, 4 months)

1) Moon-Jupiter-Jupiter (2 months, 4 days)

2) Moon-Jupiter-Saturn (2 months, 16 days)

3) Moon-Jupiter-Mercury (2 months, 8 days)

4) Moon-Jupiter-Ketu (28 days)

5) Moon-Jupiter-Venus (2 months, 20 days)

6) Moon-Jupiter-Sun (24 days)

7) Moon-Jupiter-Moon (1 month, 10 days)

8) Moon-Jupiter-Mars (28 days)

9) Moon-Jupiter-Rāhu (2 months, 12 days)

Moon-Saturn Sub-Sub-Daśās (1 year, 7 months)

1) Moon-Saturn-Saturn (3 months, 0.25 days)

2) Moon-Saturn-Mercury (2 months, 20.75 days)

3) Moon-Saturn-Ketu (1 month, 3.25 days)

4) Moon-Saturn-Venus (3 months, 5 days)

5) Moon-Saturn-Sun (28.5 days)

6) Moon-Saturn-Moon (1 month, 17.5 days)

7) Moon-Saturn-Mars (1 month, 3.25 days)

8) Moon-Saturn-Rāhu (2 months, 25.5 days)

9) Moon-Saturn-Jupiter (2 months, 16 days)

Moon-Mercury Sub-Sub-Daśās (1 year, 5 months)

1) Moon-Mercury-Mercury (2 months, 12.25 days)

2) Moon-Mercury-Ketu (29.75 days)

3) Moon-Mercury-Venus (2 months, 25 days)

4) Moon-Mercury-Sun (25.5 days)

5) Moon-Mercury-Moon (1 month, 12.5 days)

6) Moon-Mercury-Mars (29.75 days)

7) Moon-Mercury-Rāhu (2 month, 16.5 days)

8) Moon-Mercury-Jupiter (2 months, 8 days)

9) Moon-Mercury-Saturn (2 months, 20.75 days)

Moon-Ketu Sub-Sub-Daśās (7 months)

1) Moon-Ketu-Ketu (12.25 days)
2) Moon-Ketu-Venus (1 month, 5 days)
3) Moon-Ketu-Sun (10.5 days)
4) Moon-Ketu-Moon (17.5 days)
5) Moon-Ketu-Mars (12.25 days)
6) Moon-Ketu-Rāhu (1 month, 1.5 days)
7) Moon-Ketu-Jupiter (28 days)
8) Moon-Ketu-Saturn (1 month, 3.25 days)
9) Moon-Ketu-Mercury (29.75 days)

Moon-Venus Sub-Sub-Daśās (1 year, 8 months)

1) Moon-Venus-Venus (3 months, 10 days)
2) Moon-Venus-Sun (1 month)
3) Moon-Venus-Moon (1 month, 20 days)
4) Moon-Venus-Mars (1 month, 5 days)
5) Moon-Venus-Rāhu (3 months)
6) Moon-Venus-Jupiter (2 months, 20 days)
7) Moon-Venus-Saturn (3 months, 5 days)
8) Moon-Venus-Mercury (2 months, 25 days)
9) Moon-Venus-Ketu (1 month, 5 days)

Moon-Sun Sub-Sub-Daśās (6 months)

1) Moon-Sun-Sun (9 days)
2) Moon-Sun-Moon (15 days)
3) Moon-Sun-Mars (10.5 days)
4) Moon-Sun-Rāhu (27 days)
5) Moon-Sun-Jupiter (24 days)
6) Moon-Sun-Saturn (28.5 days)
7) Moon-Sun-Mercury (25.5 days)
8) Moon-Sun-Ketu (10.5 days)
9) Moon-Sun-Venus (1 month)

Mars-Mars Sub-Sub-Daśās (4 months, 27 days)

1) Mars-Mars-Mars (8.575 days)
2) Mars-Mars-Rāhu (22.05 days)
3) Mars-Mars-Jupiter (19.6 days)

4) Mars-Mars-Saturn (23.275 days)
5) Mars-Mars-Mercury (20.825 days)
6) Mars-Mars-Ketu (8.575 days)
7) Mars-Mars-Venus (24.5 days)
8) Mars-Mars-Sun (7.35 days)
9) Mars-Mars-Moon (12.25 days)

Mars-Rāhu Sub-Sub-Daśās (1 year, 18 days)
1) Mars-Rāhu-Rāhu (1 month, 26.7 days)
2) Mars-Rāhu-Jupiter (1 month, 20.4 days)
3) Mars-Rāhu-Saturn (1 month, 29.85 days)
4) Mars-Rāhu-Mercury (1 month, 23.55 days)
5) Mars-Rāhu-Ketu (22.05 days)
6) Mars-Rāhu-Venus (2 months, 3 days)
7) Mars-Rāhu-Sun (18.9 days)
8) Mars-Rāhu-Moon (1 month, 1.5 days)
9) Mars-Rāhu-Mars (22.05 days)

Mars-Jupiter Sub-Sub-Daśās (11 months, 6 days)
1) Mars-Jupiter-Jupiter (1 month, 14.8 days)
2) Mars-Jupiter-Saturn (1 month, 23.2 days)
3) Mars-Jupiter-Mercury (1 month, 17.6 days)
4) Mars-Jupiter-Ketu (19.6 days)
5) Mars-Jupiter-Venus (1 month, 26 days)
6) Mars-Jupiter-Sun (16.8 days)
7) Mars-Jupiter-Moon (28 days)
8) Mars-Jupiter-Mars (19.6 days)
9) Mars-Jupiter-Rāhu (1 month, 20.4 days)

Mars-Saturn Sub-Sub-Daśās (1 year, 1 month, 9 days)
1) Mars-Saturn-Saturn (2 months, 3.175 days)
2) Mars-Saturn-Mercury (1 month, 26.525 days)
3) Mars-Saturn-Ketu (23.275 days)
4) Mars-Saturn-Venus (2 months, 6.5 days)
5) Mars-Saturn-Sun (19.95 days)
6) Mars-Saturn-Moon (1 month, 3.25 days)
7) Mars-Saturn-Mars (23.275 days)

8) Mars-Saturn-Rāhu(1 month, 29.85 days)
9) Mars-Saturn-Jupiter (1 month, 23.2 days)

Mars-Mercury Sub-Sub-Daśās (11 months, 27 days)
1) Mars-Mercury-Mercury (1 month, 20.575 days)
2) Mars-Mercury-Ketu (20.825 days)
3) Mars-Mercury-Venus (1 month, 29.5 days)
4) Mars-Mercury-Sun (17.85 days)
5) Mars-Mercury-Moon (29.75 days)
6) Mars-Mercury-Mars (20.825 days)
7) Mars-Mercury-Rāhu (1 month, 23.55 days)
8) Mars-Mercury-Jupiter (1 month, 17.6 days)
9) Mars-Mercury-Saturn (1 month, 26.525 days)

Mars-Ketu Sub-Sub-Daśās (4 months, 27 days)
1) Mars-Ketu-Ketu (8.575 days)
2) Mars-Ketu-Venus (24.5 days)
3) Mars-Ketu-Sun (7.35 days)
4) Mars-Ketu-Moon (12.25 days)
5) Mars-Ketu-Mars (8.575 days)
6) Mars-Ketu-Rāhu (22.05 days)
7) Mars-Ketu-Jupiter (19.6 days)
8) Mars-Ketu-Saturn (23.275 days)
9) Mars-Ketu-Mercury (20.825 days)

Mars-Venus Sub-Sub-Daśās (1 year, 2 months)
1) Mars-Venus-Venus (2 months, 10 days)
2) Mars-Venus-Sun (21 days)
3) Mars-Venus-Moon (1 month, 5 days)
4) Mars-Venus-Mars (24.5 days)
5) Mars-Venus-Rāhu (2 months, 3 days)
6) Mars-Venus-Jupiter (1 month, 26 days)
7) Mars-Venus-Saturn (2 months, 6.5 days)
8) Mars-Venus-Mercury (1 month, 29.5 days)
9) Mars-Venus-Ketu (24.5 days)

Mars-Sun Sub-Sub-Daśās (4 months, 6 days)
1) Mars-Sun-Sun (6.3 days)
2) Mars-Sun-Moon (10.5 days)
3) Mars-Sun-Mars (7.35 days)
4) Mars-Sun-Rāhu (18.9 days)
5) Mars-Sun-Jupiter (16.8 days)
6) Mars-Sun-Saturn (19.95 days)
7) Mars-Sun-Mercury (17.85 days)
8) Mars-Sun-Ketu (7.35 days)
9) Mars-Sun-Venus (21 days)

Mars-Moon Sub-Sub-Daśās (7 months)
1) Mars-Moon-Moon (17.5 days)
2) Mars-Moon-Mars (12.25 days)
3) Mars-Moon-Rāhu (1 month, 1.5 days)
4) Mars-Moon-Jupiter (28 days)
5) Mars-Moon-Saturn (1 month, 3.25 days)
6) Mars-Moon-Mercury (29.75 days)
7) Mars-Moon-Ketu (12.25 days)
8) Mars-Moon-Venus (1 month, 5 days)
9) Mars-Moon-Sun (10.5 days)

Rāhu-Rāhu Sub-Sub-Daśās (2 years, 8 months, 12 days)
1) Rāhu-Rāhu-Rāhu (4 months, 25.8 days)
2) Rāhu-Rāhu-Jupiter (4 months, 9.6 days)
3) Rāhu-Rāhu-Saturn (5 months, 3.9 days)
4) Rāhu-Rāhu-Mercury (4 months, 17.7 days)
5) Rāhu-Rāhu-Ketu (1 month, 26.7 days)
6) Rāhu-Rāhu-Venus (5 months, 12 days)
7) Rāhu-Rāhu Sun (1 month, 18.6 days)
8) Rāhu-Rāhu-Moon (2 months, 21 days)
9) Rāhu-Rāhu-Mars (1 month, 26.7 days)

Rāhu-Jupiter Sub-Sub-Daśās (2 years, 4 months, 24 days)
1) Rāhu-Jupiter-Jupiter (3 months, 25.2 days)
2) Rāhu-Jupiter-Saturn (4 months, 16.8 days)
3) Rāhu-Jupiter-Mercury (4 months, 2.4 days)

4) Rāhu-Jupiter-Ketu (1 month, 20.4 days)
5) Rāhu-Jupiter-Venus (4 months, 24 days)
6) Rāhu-Jupiter-Sun (1 month, 13.2 days)
7) Rāhu-Jupiter-Moon (2 months, 12 days)
8) Rāhu-Jupiter-Mars (1 month, 20.4 days)
9) Rāhu-Jupiter-Rāhu (4 months, 9.6 days)

Rāhu-Saturn Sub-Sub-Daśās (2 years, 10 months, 6 days)
1) Rāhu-Saturn-Saturn (5 months, 12.45 days)
2) Rāhu-Saturn-Mercury (4 months, 25.35 days)
3) Rāhu-Saturn-Ketu (1 month, 29.85 days)
4) Rāhu-Saturn-Venus (5 months, 21 days)
5) Rāhu-Saturn-Sun (1 month, 21.3 days)
6) Rāhu-Saturn-Moon (2 months, 25.5 days)
7) Rāhu-Saturn-Mars (1 month, 29.85 days)
8) Rāhu-Saturn-Rāhu (5 months, 3.9 days)
9) Rāhu-Saturn-Jupiter (4 months, 16.8 days)

Rāhu-Mercury Sub-Sub-Daśās (2 years, 6 months, 18 days)
1) Rāhu-Mercury-Mercury (4 months, 10.05 days)
2) Rāhu-Mercury-Ketu (1 month, 23.55 days)
3) Rāhu-Mercury-Venus (5 months, 3 days)
4) Rāhu-Mercury-Sun (1 month, 15.9 days)
5) Rāhu-Mercury-Moon (2 months, 16.5 days)
6) Rāhu-Mercury-Mars (1 month, 23.55 days)
7) Rāhu-Mercury-Rāhu (4 months, 17.7 days)
8) Rāhu-Mercury-Jupiter (4 months, 2.4 days)
9) Rāhu-Mercury-Saturn (4 months, 25.35 days)

Rāhu-Ketu Sub-Sub-Daśās (1 year, 18 days)
1) Rāhu-Ketu-Ketu (22.05 days)
2) Rāhu-Ketu-Venus (2 months, 3 days)
3) Rāhu-Ketu-Sun (18.9 days)
4) Rāhu-Ketu-Moon (1 month, 1.5 days)
5) Rāhu-Ketu-Mars (22.05 days)
6) Rāhu-Ketu-Rāhu (1 month, 26.7 days)
7) Rāhu-Ketu-Jupiter (1 month, 20.4 days)

8) Rāhu-Ketu-Saturn (1 month, 29.85 days)
9) Rāhu-Ketu-Mercury (1 month, 23.55 days)

Rāhu-Venus Sub-Sub-Daśās (3 years)
1) Rāhu-Venus-Venus (6 months)
2) Rāhu-Venus-Sun (1 month, 24 days)
3) Rāhu-Venus-Moon (3 months)
4) Rāhu-Venus-Mars (2 months, 3 days)
5) Rāhu-Venus-Rāhu (5 months, 12 days)
6) Rāhu-Venus-Jupiter (4 months, 24 days)
7) Rāhu-Venus-Saturn (5 months, 21 days)
8) Rāhu-Venus-Mercury (5 months, 3 days)
9) Rāhu-Venus-Ketu (2 months, 3 days)

Rāhu-Sun Sub-Sub-Daśās (10 months, 24 days)
1) Rāhu-Sun-Sun (16.2 days)
2) Rāhu-Sun-Moon (27 days)
3) Rāhu-Sun-Mars (18.9 days)
4) Rāhu-Sun-Rāhu (1 month, 18.6 days)
5) Rāhu-Sun-Jupiter (1 month, 13.2 days)
6) Rāhu-Sun-Saturn (1 month, 21.3 days)
7) Rāhu-Sun-Mercury (1 month, 15.9 days)
8) Rāhu-Sun-Ketu (18.9 days)
9) Rāhu-Sun-Venus (1 month, 24 days)

Rāhu-Moon Sub-Sub-Daśās (1 year, 6 months)
1) Rāhu-Moon-Moon (1 month, 15 days)
2) Rāhu-Moon-Mars (1 month, 1.5 days)
3) Rāhu-Moon-Rāhu (2 months, 21 days)
4) Rāhu-Moon-Jupiter (2 months, 12 days)
5) Rāhu-Moon-Saturn (2 month, 25.5 days)
6) Rāhu-Moon-Mercury (2 months, 16.5 days)
7) Rāhu-Moon-Ketu (1 month, 1.5 days)
8) Rāhu-Moon-Venus (3 months)
9) Rāhu-Moon-Sun (27 days)

Rāhu-Mars Sub-Sub-Daśās (1 year, 18 days)
1) Rāhu-Mars-Mars (22.05 days)
2) Rāhu-Mars-Rāhu (1 month, 26.7 days)
3) Rāhu-Mars-Jupiter (1 month, 20.4 days)
4) Rāhu-Mars-Saturn (1 month, 29.85 days)
5) Rāhu-Mars-Mercury (1 month, 23.55 days)
6) Rāhu-Mars-Ketu (22.05 days)
7) Rāhu-Mars-Venus (2 months, 3 days)
8) Rāhu-Mars-Sun (18.9 days)
9) Rāhu-Mars-Moon (1 month, 1.5 days)

Jupiter-Jupiter Sub-Sub-Daśās (2 years, 1 month, 18 days)
1) Jupiter-Jupiter-Jupiter (3 months, 12.4 days)
2) Jupiter-Jupiter-Saturn (4 months, 1.6 days)
3) Jupiter-Jupiter-Mercury (3 months, 18.8 days)
4) Jupiter-Jupiter-Ketu (1 month, 14.8 days)
5) Jupiter-Jupiter-Venus (4 months, 8 days)
6) Jupiter-Jupiter-Sun (1 month, 8.4 days)
7) Jupiter-Jupiter-Moon (2 months, 4 days)
8) Jupiter-Jupiter-Mars (1 month, 14.8 days)
9) Jupiter-Jupiter-Rāhu (3 months, 25.2 days)

Jupiter-Saturn Sub-Sub-Daśās (2 years, 6 months, 12 days)
1) Jupiter-Saturn-Saturn (4 months, 24.4 days)
2) Jupiter-Saturn-Mercury (4 months, 9.2 days)
3) Jupiter-Saturn-Ketu (1 month, 23.2 days)
4) Jupiter-Saturn-Venus (5 months, 2 days)
5) Jupiter-Saturn-Sun (1 month, 15.6 days)
6) Jupiter-Saturn-Moon (2 months, 16 days)
7) Jupiter-Saturn-Mars (1 month, 23.2 days)
8) Jupiter-Saturn-Rāhu (4 months, 16.8 days)
9) Jupiter-Saturn-Jupiter (4 months, 1.6 days)

Jupiter-Mercury Sub-Sub-Daśās (2 years, 3 months, 6 days)
1) Jupiter-Mercury-Mercury (3 months, 25.6 days)
2) Jupiter-Mercury-Ketu (1 month, 17.6 days)
3) Jupiter-Mercury-Venus (4 months, 16 days)

4) Jupiter-Mercury-Sun (1 month, 10.8 days)

5) Jupiter-Mercury-Moon (2 months, 8 days)

6) Jupiter-Mercury-Mars (1 month, 17.6 days)

7) Jupiter-Mercury-Rāhu (4 months, 2.4 days)

8) Jupiter-Mercury-Jupiter (3 months, 18.8 days)

9) Jupiter-Mercury-Saturn (4 months, 9.2 days)

Jupiter-Ketu Sub-Sub-Daśās (11 months, 6 days)

1) Jupiter-Ketu-Ketu (19.6 days)

2) Jupiter-Ketu-Venus (1 month, 26 days)

3) Jupiter-Ketu-Sun (16.8 days)

4) Jupiter-Ketu-Moon (28 days)

5) Jupiter-Ketu-Mars (19.6 days)

6) Jupiter-Ketu-Rāhu (1 month, 20.4 days)

7) Jupiter-Ketu-Jupiter (1 month, 14.8 days)

8) Jupiter-Ketu-Saturn (1 month, 23.2 days)

9) Jupiter-Ketu-Mercury (1 month, 17.6 days)

Jupiter-Venus Sub-Sub-Daśās (2 years, 8 months)

1) Jupiter-Venus-Venus (5 months, 10 days)

2) Jupiter-Venus-Sun (1 month, 18 days)

3) Jupiter-Venus-Moon (2 months, 20 days)

4) Jupiter-Venus-Mars (1 month, 26 days)

5) Jupiter-Venus-Rāhu (4 months, 24 days)

6) Jupiter-Venus-Jupiter (4 months, 8 days)

7) Jupiter-Venus-Saturn (5 months, 2 days)

8) Jupiter-Venus-Mercury (4 months, 16 days)

9) Jupiter-Venus-Ketu (1 month, 26 days)

Jupiter-Sun Sub-Sub-Daśās (9 months, 18 days)

1) Jupiter-Sun-Sun (14.4 days)

2) Jupiter-Sun-Moon (24 days)

3) Jupiter-Sun-Mars (16.8 days)

4) Jupiter-Sun-Rāhu (1 month, 13.2 days)

5) Jupiter-Sun-Jupiter (1 month, 8.4 days)

6) Jupiter-Sun-Saturn (1 month, 15.6 days)

7) Jupiter-Sun-Mercury (1 month, 10.8 days)

8) Jupiter-Sun-Ketu (16.8 days)
9) Jupiter-Sun-Venus (1 month, 18 days)

Jupiter-Moon Sub-Sub-Daśās (1 year, 4 months)
1) Jupiter-Moon-Moon (1 month, 10 days)
2) Jupiter-Moon-Mars (28 days)
3) Jupiter-Moon-Rāhu (2 months, 12 days)
4) Jupiter-Moon-Jupiter (2 months, 4 days)
5) Jupiter-Moon-Saturn (2 months, 16 days)
6) Jupiter-Moon-Mercury (2 months, 8 days)
7) Jupiter-Moon-Ketu (28 days)
8) Jupiter-Moon-Venus (2 months, 20 days)
9) Jupiter-Moon-Sun (24 days)

Jupiter-Mars Sub-Sub-Daśās (11 months, 6 days)
1) Jupiter-Mars-Mars (19.6 days)
2) Jupiter-Mars-Rāhu (1 month, 20.4 days)
3) Jupiter-Mars-Jupiter (1 month, 14.8 days)
4) Jupiter-Mars-Saturn (1 month, 23.2 days)
5) Jupiter-Mars-Mercury (1 month, 17.6 days)
6) Jupiter-Mars-Ketu (19.6 days)
7) Jupiter-Mars-Venus (1 month, 26 days)
8) Jupiter-Mars-Sun (16.8 days)
9) Jupiter-Mars-Moon (28 days)

Jupiter-Rāhu Sub-Sub-Daśās (2 years, 4 months, 24 days)
1) Jupiter-Rāhu-Rāhu (4 months, 9.6 days)
2) Jupiter-Rāhu-Jupiter (3 months, 25.2 days)
3) Jupiter-Rāhu-Saturn (4 months, 16.8 days)
4) Jupiter-Rāhu-Mercury (4 months, 2.4 days)
5) Jupiter-Rāhu-Ketu (1 month, 20.4 days)
6) Jupiter-Rāhu-Venus (4 months, 24 days)
7) Jupiter-Rāhu-Sun (1 month, 13.2 days)
8) Jupiter-Rāhu-Moon (2 months, 12 days)
9) Jupiter-Rāhu-Mars (1 month, 20.4 days)

Saturn-Saturn Sub-Sub-Daśās (3 years, 3 days)
1) Saturn-Saturn-Saturn (5 months, 21.475 days)
2) Saturn-Saturn-Mercury (5 months, 3.425 days)
3) Saturn-Saturn-Ketu (2 months, 3.175 days)
4) Saturn-Saturn-Venus (6 months, 0.5 days)
5) Saturn-Saturn-Sun (1 month, 24.15 days)
6) Saturn-Saturn-Moon (3 months, 0.25 days)
7) Saturn-Saturn-Mars (2 months, 3.175 days)
8) Saturn-Saturn-Rāhu (5 months, 12.45 days)
9) Saturn-Saturn-Jupiter (4 months, 24.4 days)

Saturn-Mercury Sub-Sub-Daśās (2 years, 8 months, 9 days)
1) Saturn-Mercury-Mercury (4 months, 17.275 days)
2) Saturn-Mercury-Ketu (1 month, 26.525 days)
3) Saturn-Mercury-Venus (5 months, 11.5 days)
4) Saturn-Mercury-Sun (1 month, 18.45 days)
5) Saturn-Mercury-Moon (2 months, 20.75 days)
6) Saturn-Mercury-Mars (1 month, 26.525 days)
7) Saturn-Mercury-Rāhu (4 months, 25.35 days)
8) Saturn-Mercury-Jupiter (4 months, 9.2 days)
9) Saturn-Mercury-Saturn (5 months, 3.425 days)

Saturn-Ketu Sub-Sub-Daśās (I year, I month, 9 days)
1) Saturn-Ketu-Ketu (23.275 days)
2) Saturn-Ketu-Venus (2 months, 6.5 days)
3) Saturn-Ketu-Sun (19.95 days)
4) Saturn-Ketu-Moon (1 month, 3.25 days)
5) Saturn-Ketu-Mars (23.275 days)
6) Saturn-Ketu-Rāhu (1 month, 29.85 days)
7) Saturn-Ketu-Jupiter (1 month, 23.2 days)
8) Saturn-Ketu-Saturn (2 months, 3.175 days)
9) Saturn-Ketu-Mercury (1 month, 26.525 days)

Saturn-Venus Sub-Sub-Daśās (3 years, 2 months)
1) Saturn-Venus-Venus (6 months, 10 days)
2) Saturn-Venus-Sun (1 month, 27 days)
3) Saturn-Venus-Moon (3 months, 5 days)

4) Saturn-Venus-Mars (2 months, 6.5 days)
5) Saturn-Venus-Rāhu (5 months, 21 days)
6) Saturn-Venus-Jupiter (5 months, 2 days)
7) Saturn-Venus-Saturn (6 months, 0.5 days)
8) Saturn-Venus-Mercury (5 months, 11.5 days)
9) Saturn-Venus-Ketu (2 months, 6.5 days)

Saturn-Sun Sub-Sub-Daśās (11 months, 12 days)
1) Saturn-Sun-Sun (17.1 days)
2) Saturn-Sun-Moon (28.5 days)
3) Saturn-Sun-Mars (19.95 days)
4) Saturn-Sun-Rāhu (1 month, 21.3 days)
5) Saturn-Sun-Jupiter (1 month, 15.6 days)
6) Saturn-Sun-Saturn (1 month, 24.15 days)
7) Saturn-Sun-Mercury (1 month, 18.45 days)
8) Saturn-Sun-Ketu (19.95 days)
9) Saturn-Sun-Venus (1 month, 27 days)

Saturn-Moon Sub-Sub-Daśās (1 year, 7 months)
1) Saturn-Moon-Moon (1 month, 17.5 days)
2) Saturn-Moon-Mars (1 month, 3.25 days)
3) Saturn-Moon-Rāhu (2 months, 25.5 days)
4) Saturn-Moon-Jupiter (2 months, 16 days)
5) Saturn-Moon-Saturn (3 months, 0.25 days)
6) Saturn-Moon-Mercury (2 months, 20.75 days)
7) Saturn-Moon-Ketu (1 month, 3.25 days)
8) Saturn-Moon-Venus (3 months, 5 days)
9) Saturn-Moon-Sun (28.5 days)

Saturn-Mars Sub-Sub-Daśās (1 year, 1 month, 9 days)
1) Saturn-Mars-Mars (23.275 days)
2) Saturn-Mars-Rāhu (1 month, 29.85 days)
3) Saturn-Mars-Jupiter (1 month, 23.2 days)
4) Saturn-Mars-Saturn (2 months, 3.175 days)
5) Saturn-Mars-Mercury (1 month, 26.525 days)
6) Saturn-Mars-Ketu (23.275 days)
7) Saturn-Mars-Venus (2 months, 6.5 days)

8) Saturn-Mars-Sun (19.95 days)
9) Saturn-Mars-Moon (1 month, 3.25 days)

Saturn-Rāhu Sub-Sub-Daśās (2 years, 10 months, 6 days)
1) Saturn-Rāhu-Rāhu (5 months, 3.9 days)
2) Saturn-Rāhu-Jupiter (4 months, 16.8 days)
3) Saturn-Rāhu-Saturn (5 months, 12.45 days)
4) Saturn-Rāhu-Mercury (4 months, 25.35 days)
5) Saturn-Rāhu-Ketu (1 month, 29.85 days)
6) Saturn-Rāhu-Venus (5 months, 21 days)
7) Saturn-Rāhu-Sun (1 month, 21.3 days)
8) Saturn-Rāhu-Moon (2 months, 25.5 days)
9) Saturn-Rāhu-Mars (1 month, 29.85 days)

Saturn-Jupiter Sub-Sub-Daśās (2 years, 6 months, 12 days)
1) Saturn-Jupiter-Jupiter (4 months, 1.6 days)
2) Saturn-Jupiter-Saturn (4 months, 24.4 days)
3) Saturn-Jupiter-Mercury (4 months, 9.2 days)
4) Saturn-Jupiter-Ketu (1 month, 23.2 days)
5) Saturn-Jupiter-Venus (5 months, 2 days)
6) Saturn-Jupiter-Sun (1 month, 15.6 days)
7) Saturn-Jupiter-Moon (2 months, 16 days)
8) Saturn-Jupiter-Mars (1 month, 23.2 days)
9) Saturn-Jupiter-Rāhu (4 months, 16.8 days)

Mercury-Mercury Sub-Sub-Daśās (2 years, 4 months, 27 days)
1) Mercury-Mercury-Mercury (4 months, 2.825 days)
2) Mercury-Mercury-Ketu (1 month, 20.575 days)
3) Mercury-Mercury-Venus (4 months, 24.5 days)
4) Mercury-Mercury-Sun (1 month, 13.35 days)
5) Mercury-Mercury-Moon (2 months, 12.25 days)
6) Mercury-Mercury-Mars (1 month, 20.575 days)
7) Mercury-Mercury-Rāhu (4 months, 10.05 days)
8) Mercury-Mercury-Jupiter (3 months, 25.6 days)
9) Mercury-Mercury-Saturn (4 months, 17.275 months)

Mercury-Ketu Sub-Sub-Daśās (11 months, 27 days)
1) Mercury-Ketu-Ketu (20.825 days)
2) Mercury-Ketu-Venus (1 month, 29.5 days)
3) Mercury-Ketu-Sun (17.85 days)
4) Mercury-Ketu-Moon (29.75 days)
5) Mercury-Ketu-Mars (20.825 days)
6) Mercury-Ketu-Rāhu (1 month, 23.55 days)
7) Mercury-Ketu-Jupiter (1 month, 17.6 days)
8) Mercury-Ketu-Saturn (1 month, 26.525 days)
9) Mercury-Ketu-Mercury (1 month, 20.575 days)

Mercury-Venus Sub-Sub-Daśās (2 years, 10 months)
1) Mercury-Venus-Venus (5 months, 20 days)
2) Mercury-Venus-Sun (1 month, 21 days)
3) Mercury-Venus-Moon (2 months, 25 days)
4) Mercury-Venus-Mars (1 month, 29.5 days)
5) Mercury-Venus-Rāhu (5 months, 3 days)
6) Mercury-Venus-Jupiter (4 months, 16 days)
7) Mercury-Venus-Saturn (5 months, 11.5 days)
8) Mercury-Venus-Mercury (4 months, 24.5 days)
9) Mercury-Venus-Ketu (1 month, 29.5 days)

Mercury-Sun Sub-Sub-Daśās (10 months, 6 days)
1) Mercury-Sun-Sun (15.3 days)
2) Mercury-Sun-Moon (25.5 days)
3) Mercury-Sun-Mars (17.85 days)
4) Mercury-Sun-Rāhu (1 month, 15.9 days)
5) Mercury-Sun-Jupiter (1 month, 10.8 days)
6) Mercury-Sun-Saturn (1 month, 18.45 days)
7) Mercury-Sun-Mercury (1 month, 13.35 days)
8) Mercury-Sun-Ketu (17.85 days)
9) Mercury-Sun-Venus (1 month, 21 days)

Mercury-Moon Sub-Sub-Daśās (1 year, 5 months)
1) Mercury-Moon-Moon (1 months, 12.5 days)
2) Mercury-Moon-Mars (29.75 days)
3) Mercury-Moon-Rāhu (2 months, 16.5 days)

4) Mercury-Moon-Jupiter (2 months, 8 days)
5) Mercury-Moon-Saturn (2 months, 20.75 days)
6) Mercury-Moon-Mercury (2 months, 12.25 days)
7) Mercury-Moon-Ketu (29.75 days)
8) Mercury-Moon-Venus (2 months, 25 days)
9) Mercury-Moon-Sun (25.5 days)

Mercury-Mars Sub-Sub-Daśās (11 months, 27 days)
1) Mercury-Mars-Mars (20.825 days)
2) Mercury-Mars-Rāhu (1 month, 23.55 days)
3) Mercury-Mars-Jupiter (1 month, 17.6 days)
4) Mercury-Mars-Saturn (1 month, 26.525 days)
5) Mercury-Mars-Mercury (1 month, 20.575 days)
6) Mercury-Mars-Ketu (20.825 days)
7) Mercury-Mars-Venus (1 month, 29.5 days)
8) Mercury-Mars-Sun (17.85 days)
9) Mercury-Mars-Moon (29.75 days)

Mercury-Rāhu Sub-Sub-Daśās (2 years, 6 months, 18 days)
1) Mercury-Rāhu-Rāhu (4 months, 17.7 days)
2) Mercury-Rāhu-Jupiter (4 months, 2.4 days)
3) Mercury-Rāhu-Saturn (4 months, 25.35 days)
4) Mercury-Rāhu-Mercury (4 months, 10.05 days)
5) Mercury-Rāhu-Ketu (1 month, 23.55 days)
6) Mercury-Rāhu-Venus (5 months, 3 days)
7) Mercury-Rāhu-Sun (1 month, 15.9 days)
8) Mercury-Rāhu-Moon (2 months, 16.5 days)
9) Mercury-Rāhu-Mars (1 month, 23.55 days)

Mercury-Jupiter Sub-Sub-Daśās (2 years, 3 months, 6 days)
1) Mercury-Jupiter-Jupiter (3 months, 18.8 days)
2) Mercury-Jupiter-Saturn (4 months, 9.2 days)
3) Mercury-Jupiter-Mercury (3 months, 25.6 days)
4) Mercury-Jupiter-Ketu (1 month, 17.6 days)
5) Mercury-Jupiter-Venus (4 months, 16 days)
6) Mercury Jupiter-Sun (1 month, 10.8 days)
7) Mercury-Jupiter-Moon (2 months, 8 days)

8) Mercury-Jupiter-Mars (1 month, 17.6 days)

9) Mercury-Jupiter-Rāhu (4 months, 2.4 days)

Mercury-Saturn Sub-Sub-Daśās (2 years, 8 months, 9 days)

1) Mercury-Saturn-Saturn (5 months, 3.425 days)

2) Mercury-Saturn-Mercury (4 months, 17.275 days)

3) Mercury-Saturn-Ketu (1 month, 26.525 days)

4) Mercury-Saturn-Venus (5 months, 11.5 days)

5) Mercury-Saturn-Sun (1 month, 18.45 days)

6) Mercury-Saturn-Moon (2 months, 20.75 days)

7) Mercury-Saturn-Mars (1 month, 26.525 days)

8) Mercury-Saturn-Rāhu (4 months, 25. 35 days)

9) Mercury-Saturn-Jupiter (4 months, 9.2 days)

RESOURCES

TIMELINE ASTROLOGY APP

Download the app to find out where the Moon was when you were born - and where it is each day. Input your birth data to calculate your planetary daśās. Use the app to plan daily activities.

VEDIC ASTROLOGY SOFTWARE

Jagannatha Hora is a free Jyotiṣa Vedic Astrology software at vedicastrologer.org. Download it to calculate many planetary and sign-based daśās, including viṁśottarī and chara.

The chart calculations and illustrations used in this book are from *Shri Jyotish Star*, available for purchase at shrijyotishstar.com.

Other Vedic astrology software packages available for purchase are at goravani.com, parasharaslight.com and vedic-astrology.net.

ONLINE CHART CALCULATORS

Astro-seek.com has a free *Vimshottari Dasha Periods* calculator. Select *Sidereal Astrology Calculator*, *Lahiri Ayanamsha*, and *Whole Sign* under *House System*, if using your chart alongside this book.

Deva.guru has both free and paid subscriptions to calculate your birth chart and daśās.

RECOMMENDED READING

Science of Light Vol. 1 by Freedom Cole
Jyotishionary and *The Spirit that Moves Us* by Pearl Finn
Jyotiṣa Fundamentals by Visti Larsen
Vimshottari Dasha, Udu Dasas, and *Narayana Dasa* by
Sanjay Rath
Komilla Sutton has a range of books available for the
beginner to the more advanced Vedic astrology student,
available at komilla.com.

BIBLIOGRAPHY

Cole, F., *Science of Light Vol. 1*, (Nevada City: Science of Light LLC. 2018), p. 105.

David G. Blanchflower, *Is Happiness U-shaped Everywhere? Age and Subjective Well-being in 132 Countries* (NBER Working Paper No. 26641, 2020), < https://www.nber.org/system/files/working_paper s/w26641/w26641.pdf, (accessed 14 June 2022).

Foss, A.., *Yoga of the Planets* (Virginia, USA: ShriSource Publications, 2016). pp. 500 – 517.

Gil Brand, R., "Decoding Vimshottari Dasha", British Association of Vedic Astrology online lecture, 16 September 2012.

Goswami, B. M., Vashisth L. K., *Lal Kitab*, (New Delhi, Motilal Banarsidass Publishers (Pvt. Limited), 2003).

Harness, D., "Pluto: A Neo-Vedic View", *Denis Harness*, [web blog], Date Unknown, https://dennisharness.com/articles/pluto-a-neo-vedic-view/, (accessed 14 June 2022).

Rath, S., *Bṛhat Nakṣatra*, (New Delhi: Sagittarius Publications, 2008).

Rath, S., "Nakshatra Mandala", (lecture handout presented to the British Association of Vedic Astrology, London, received on 7 March 2009).

Sastri, V. Subramanya, *Vaidyanatha Dikshita's Jataka Parijata*, Vol. III (New Delhi: Ranjan Publications, 2008).

Sharma, G. C., *Brihat Parasara Hora Sastra Vol. 2* (New Delhi: Sagar Publications, 1995), p. 162.

Wallis, C. "Near Enemy #11: You can choose how to respond", Hareesh [web blog], 30 August 2019, https://hareesh.org/blog/2019/8/30/near-enemy-11-you-can-choose-how-to-respond (accessed 14 June 2022).

CHART DATA & SOURCE

Tiger Woods, December 30, 1975; 10.50 p.m. PST; Long Beach, CA, USA; 118° W 11', 33° N 46'; (Source: astro.com; AA Rodden Rating).

Joe Biden, November 20, 1942; 08.30 a.m. EST; Scranton, PA, USA; 75° W 39', 41° N 24'; (Source: astro.com; A Rodden Rating).

Elizabeth Taylor, February 27, 1932; 02.30 a.m. GMT; London, England; 0° W 10', 51° N 30': (Source: astro.com; AA Rodden Rating).

INDEX